The Future Is Ours

Shaun Bowler
University of California, Riverside

Gary M. Segura
Stanford University

 |

Los Angeles | London | New Delhi
Singapore | Washington DC

Los Angeles | London | New Delhi
Singapore | Washington DC

FOR INFORMATION:

CQ Press

An Imprint of SAGE Publications, Inc.

2455 Teller Road

Thousand Oaks, California 91320

E-mail: order@sagepub.com

SAGE Publications Ltd.

1 Oliver's Yard

55 City Road

London, EC1Y 1SP

United Kingdom

SAGE Publications India Pvt. Ltd.

B 1/I 1 Mohan Cooperative Industrial Area

Mathura Road, New Delhi 110 044

India

SAGE Publications Asia-Pacific Pte. Ltd.

33 Pekin Street #02-01

Far East Square

Singapore 048763

Acquisitions Editor: Charisse Kiino

Production Editor: Belinda Josey

Copy Editor: Janine Stanley-Dunham

Typesetter: C&M Digitals (P) Ltd.

Proofreader: Barbara Johnson

Indexer: Indexing Partners

Cover Designer: Stefan Killen Design

Marketing Manager: Christopher O'Brien

Library of Congress Cataloging-in-Publication Data

Bowler, Shaun

The future is ours: minority politics, political behavior, and the multiracial era of American politics / Shaun Bowler and Gary M. Segura.

p. cm.
Includes bibliographical references and index.

ISBN 978-1-60426-727-3 (pbk.: alk. paper)

1. Minorities—Political activity—United States. 2. United States—Politics and government—21st century. 3. Political participation—United States. 4. Ethnicity—Political aspects—United States. 5. Race—Political aspects—United States. 6. Group identity—Political aspects—United States. I. Segura, Gary M. II. Title.

E184.A1B69 2012
320.973089—dc23   2011025068

This book is printed on acid-free paper.

11 12 13 14 15 10 9 8 7 6 5 4 3 2 1

To our families

To Jadie, Verity, and Jessica . . .

—SB

To Gary, Juan, Enrique, and Ana . . .

—GMS

"*Once social change begins, it cannot be reversed. You cannot uneducate the person who has learned to read. You cannot humiliate the person who feels pride. You cannot oppress the people who are not afraid anymore. We have seen the future, and the future is ours.*"

(Cesar Chavez
Address to the Commonwealth Club in
San Francisco, November 9, 1984)

Shaun Bowler is professor of political science at University of California, Riverside. Bowler is a member of the board of the American National Election Study and a member of the editorial board of *Electoral Studies* and *Journal of Politics*. In 2009–2010 he was president of the Western Political Science Association. He works on the relationship between voters and institutions in representative democracy. His previously coauthored books include *Demanding Choices* (2000), a study of direct democracy, and *Loser's Consent* (2007), a study of the impact of losing elections on political attitudes. He coedited, along with Gary M. Segura, *Diversity in Democracy* (2006), a study of minority political behavior in contemporary U.S. politics.

Gary M. Segura is professor of American politics and chair of Chicano/a studies at Stanford University. Segura is also a principal in the polling firm Latino Decisions. His work focuses on issues of political representation, and the politics to America's growing Latino minority. Among his most recent publications are the coauthored book *Latino Lives in America: Making It Home* (2010), and the articles "Su Casa Es Nuestra Casa: Latino Politics Research and the Development of American Political Science" (2007), "Race and the Recall: Racial Polarization in the California Recall Election" (2008), "Hope, Tropes, and Dopes: Hispanic and White Racial Animus in the 2008 Election" (2010), and "Assimilation, Incorporation, and Ethnic Identity in Understanding Latino Electoral and Non-Electoral Political Participation" (2011). His coauthored book *Latinos in the New Millennium: An Almanac of Opinion, Behavior, and Policy Preferences* will be published in 2012. Segura is one of three principal investigators of the 2012 American National Election Study and in 2009–2010 was the president of the Midwest Political Science Association. In 2010 he was elected a fellow of the American Academy of Arts and Sciences.

CONTENTS

TABLES, FIGURES, AND BOXES

Tables

Figures

Boxes

PREFACE

I n this book, we examine the political behavior of minority voters in U.S. politics. We pay particular attention to the significant demographic change now occurring in the United States and to the increasingly critical role that racial and ethnic minorities will play in reshaping the two-party system. A nation whose population and electorate were once overwhelmingly white is rapidly becoming a nation where racial and ethnic diversity no longer simply refers to the size of the African American population but, rather, to the size of the black, Latino, and Asian American populations. States and metropolitan areas whose politics were long structured on the black-white racial divide have to come to grips with a trilateral or even quadrilateral racial and ethnic politics. Minority groups differ meaningfully in their social and political experiences, and, not surprisingly, politics between and among minority groups is every bit as complex as between minorities and the white majority.

Of course, these minority groups do have some things in common. Chief among the commonalities is that unlike a majority of white voters in every national election since 1964, minority voters cast a majority—and often a supermajority—of their votes for Democratic candidates. Without these minority voters, Democrats would be uncompetitive on the national stage and in dozens of states.

What, then, do we know about the political beliefs and behaviors of these non-white racial and ethnic groups? A recent and rapid increase in both data and scholarship on these groups means we know quite a lot, and in this book we try to examine the central questions of political behavior research as they apply to communities of color in the United States. Specifically, the book examines political participation, both electoral and nonelectoral, and voting preferences, policy opinions, orientations toward government, and legislative representation of African Americans, Latinos, and Asian Americans, often in direct comparison with one another and with non-Hispanic whites. We show that minority Democratic partisanship—long a feature of African American and Latino politics and increasingly in Asian American politics as well—is not merely an affective attachment, a habit, or a relic of the Civil Rights era but, rather, is rooted in beliefs about the role of government. Minority voters, to varying degrees, believe in government and, more often than not, favor an energetic and active government over the more limited variety so often touted by conservatives. In short, a majority of minority Americans are liberals. And their share of the national population is growing rapidly with obvious consequences.

We pay particular attention to issues of identity, immigration, voting rights, and values as important forces that may challenge or reshape the existing partisan trajectory. The emergence of mixed-race identification and intermarriage complicates the relationship between demography and electoral outcomes. Likewise, immigration politics has historically crossed party lines while exacerbating intraparty cleavages, and it represents an important potential source of between-group political contention—a possibility we explore in greater detail in the book itself.

Drawing upon recent data sources and primary political science and sociological research, the book grounds the examination of these questions in the empirical traditions of American politics research. On each subject, we take the reader through the received knowledge of decades of political behavior research and then offer a data-based examination of whether (and exactly how) minority citizens differ from members of the white majority, on whose behavior most of the received knowledge is built. The data examinations are simple and presented in a nontechnical fashion, but throughout the book we attempt to engage questions of research design and analysis that expose the reader to the logics of social science inquiry, even as we present the topical material.

In this book, we make three main points.

First, many aspects of minority political behavior are accessible, within limits, by social science analysis. Second, that said, there are a number of places where both social science analysis and data are inadequate. Throughout the book we point out places where more work is needed—and we hope that some of our student readers will be people to take up that work. Part of the reason for saying that is because many standard approaches to political behavior are grounded in studies of non-Hispanic whites. There is nothing inherently wrong in that emphasis in and of itself, but studies of political behavior based on the majority of the population may not hold for nonmajority populations. Nor may they hold when the majority changes.

Third, while minority politics involves the study of minorities, it also involves the study of politics. We are mindful that we need to locate the study of minority politics in the broader context of American politics. We develop an argument in the book that begins by establishing the partisan "state of play" for minority voters—that minority voters' Democratic preference is considerable, broad based, and fully consistent with the issue preferences and core beliefs about government exhibited by large portions of minority group populations. We go on to suggest that demography will, in fact, be destiny, that shrinking white population shares will increasingly constrain GOP electoral chances, without significant change on three dimensions: first, substantial socioeconomic diversification among minorities, which may allow diversification of issue preferences and beliefs about government; second, a concomitant change of rhetoric on the part of the right that is perceived—correctly or not—as racially motivated and hostile; and, third, a willingness for minority voters to make individual, rather than group-based, evaluations of parties and candidates. Without all of those changes—each of which we think is unlikely for reasons we detail in this volume—the demographic changes under way in the United States may well usher in a long period of Democratic dominance.

Instructor's Resources. To use the many tables, figures, and maps in the book in your classroom, please go to http://college.cqpress.com/sites/parties andelectionsir/ to download all the book's graphics which are available in PDF and PowerPoint.

ACKNOWLEDGMENTS

Thanks are due to a long list of people. More than in many books, the bibliography in this one is a list of the many colleagues and dear friends whose work, creativity, and insight have helped shape the arguments presented here. We stand on the shoulders of other scholars in the Western Political Science Association; Midwest Political Science Association; the Race, Ethnicity and Politics section of the American Political Science Association; and the Politics of Race, Immigration, and Ethnicity Consortium—with whom we shared countless conversations, panels, roundtables, and late-night drinks that significantly helped form this work and our thoughts.

Special thanks to David Lublin of American University and Helena Rodrigues of the University of Arizona, who generously allowed us to draw on earlier collaborative work on some of the topics here.

The project benefitted from two waves of research assistance at Stanford, including Andy Parker and Andy Hiller (dubbed "the Andys"), who gathered much of the literature, representation, and demographic data, and Jessica Aylward and Nipun Kant (dubbed, to their chagrin, "the new Andys"), who tirelessly combed through the mountains of survey data that inform many of the chapters here.

The University of California, Riverside, and Stanford University provided resources that allowed us to do some of the research on which this book is based. We thank the proposal and manuscript reviewers for an unusually careful and thoughtful reading of the manuscript: Andrew Aoki, Augsburg College; Tony Affigne, Providence College; Kerry Haynie, Duke University; Sylvia Manzano, Texas A&M University; Valerie Martinez-Ebers, University of North Texas; Tom Schaller, University of Maryland-Baltimore County; Christina Suthammanont, Texas A&M University-San Antonio; and Cara Wong, University of Illinois at Urbana-Champaign. We thank Charisse Kiino at CQ Press—who worked with us from the very start of the project—for her patience in waiting (and waiting) for the manuscript to be complete, as well as Nancy Loh, editorial assistant, and Belinda Josey, production editor, both of whom helped prepare the manuscript for publication. We offer a special thanks to Janine Stanley-Dunham, who edited the final version for CQ Press and was invaluable in cleaning our language and catching our embarrassingly numerous errors.

Finally, we thank our families, who endured (and endure) our ongoing distraction.

Demography Is Destiny!
Or . . . You Just Never Know . . .

How will American political behavior look in ten years, or twenty? Normally, our answer to any conjecture about future political phenomena is to assume that the past is prologue and that changes, however inevitable, are generally more marginal than substantial, more incremental than revolutionary. But there are moments in the life of a polity when the social and political forces that drive our politics shift so significantly, and intersect, that change is more discontinuous, abrupt, and consequential.

We believe we are witnessing one such break. This book is our attempt to think through the contours of political behavior as they are evolving in this current, disruptive, moment. Our focus is on racial and ethnic minorities, who compose a growing share of our population and electorate, who are themselves becoming more diverse, about whom we know less with respect to traditional indicators of political belief and orientation, and who collectively represent decisive votes in American elections. Our claim is that the intersection of two historic processes has created a unique set of circumstances that have the potential to significantly reshape our politics through the behavior of these groups and the individual citizens who compose them.

The first force is that of demography. Somewhere in the latter part of the twenty-first century, Anglos (non-Hispanic whites) will no longer constitute a majority but only a plurality in a multiethnic America. This demographic reality, a "majority-minority" America in which non-Hispanic whites make up less than 50 percent of the population, has already come to pass in four states, including our two most populous, California and Texas, and others are not far behind. It is already the case that minority population shares exceed 25 percent of the population in a score of additional states.

Immigration and rapidly increasing Asian American and Latino populations are largely responsible for these trends, as African American populations are projected to remain relatively stable as a share of U.S. residents, hovering just above or below 13 percent. As a consequence, it is not simply the share of the population accounted for by non-Hispanic whites that is changing over time, but also the relative presence and electoral importance of other groups. We have a lot to say about the political demography of the United States in Chapter 2.

These shifting demographics—and most notably the growth in Asian and Latino populations—are very likely to produce an equally sizable shift in America's politics and political institutions. How America evolves as a society and a polity depends on whether and how these new Americans have access to existing institutions, and the degree to which these institutions, set out in the eighteenth century, are able and willing to accommodate the changing demographics of the twenty-first century. It is to these questions that this book was originally planned to address.

A FUNNY THING HAPPENED ON THE WAY TO THE PUBLISHER

In November 2008, a black man, an African American who was also an *African American*, the son of an immigrant and the product of a mixed-race marriage, was elected president of the United States. Even as we write these words, we are reminded—indeed, overwhelmed—by the improbable nature of the event. Before the primary season started, most political scientists would not have predicted this outcome (no matter what they might claim now, after the fact), and Barack Obama's election was inconsistent with our received knowledge on dozens of topics in political behavior, including racial threat and its effects, the likelihood of racially polarized bloc voting among whites, the specific salience of immigration in the period leading up to the election, America's discomfort with mixed-race identities, and decades of research on racial politics and messaging in American elections (for example, Sonenshein 1990; Terkildsen 1993; Valentino et al. 2002). In fact, we both remember Democratic activists, perfectly happy with then senator Obama's political identity but desperate to win the White House after eight years of George W. Bush, moaning loudly that only the Democrats—in a year when they just could not lose—would choose to nominate a black freshman senator with an unusual, vaguely Muslim-sounding name.

Nevertheless, Senator Obama became President Obama. His election and presidency—and, in addition, specifically *how* he was elected—is the second system shock we believe will substantially reshape our political future. Obama's election has two effects. First, having a person of color as president of the United States is almost certainly going to be a transformative moment for citizens of color, in general, and African Americans in particular. While the election of this president does not wipe away the structural barriers or resource constraints that have historically shaped minority orientations to the political system, having a person of color, someone intimately connected to the minority and immigrant experiences in the United States, may fully reorient how minority voters see the political system. Logically, the political aspirations of minority voters and their concomitant expectations regarding government performance will be revised as a consequence of the most profound form of descriptive representation possible, the presidency. These effects are possibly, even likely, visited on perceptions of the political system, trust, levels of civic engagement, political information levels and overall interest in politics, and even strength of partisanship.

On the other hand, unreasonably high expectations and lofty aspirations might give rise to even greater levels of alienation or disappointment as individuals come to terms with the likely observation that Obama's presidency alone does not change all of the social disadvantages that are suffered by citizens of color. As many African Americans were mired in poverty the day after the inauguration as the day before. As many undocumented aliens lived in fear of the authorities. Changed policies may alleviate some minority disadvantages, but it would be foolish to expect that generations of social inequality will fall in the face of efforts by a single administration, even if those issues were that administration's priority. Of course, minority expectations might be tempered with a necessary dose of realism, but while the effects are uncertain, our expectation of some effects seems a given. To this end, minority political behavior is changed by the Obama presidency.

Obama's path to the presidency is an even more remarkable aspect of how this event changes our understanding of minority political behavior. On the one hand, Obama won handily. Final results indicate that he received approximately 53 percent of the vote, the first Democrat to win an outright majority since Jimmy Carter, and the Electoral College victory was even more sweeping. Obama won states such as Virginia, Indiana, and North Carolina, redrawing the national electoral map in a manner more far reaching than most prognosticators would have expected. On the other, despite a severe economic downturn under an administration of the opposing party, an incumbent president with popularity ratings in the 20s; two overseas wars that were either unpopular, going poorly, or both, and a dramatic increase in Democratic registration nationwide in the months and years preceding the election, Obama lost among white voters, 55–43, according to national exit polls. What carried Obama to victory was a 95 percent share of the African American vote, a 67 percent share of the Latino vote, 62 percent among Asian Americans, and 66 percent among all others. While Obama's share of white voters, at 43 percent, was higher than all but two Democratic nominees since 1964, analysts have pointed to the results among African Americans and Latinos to pronounce 2008 the most racially polarized national election in American history (Ansolabehere and Stewart 2009).

Minority voters are a critical part of the Democratic coalition. Without minority voters reflecting these dramatic pro-Democratic distributions, Democrats do not win national elections. The pattern reflected in the 2008 presidential election is, frankly, frequently manifested at the congressional district and state levels as well; that is, Republicans usually win a majority of the white vote, and always do at the national level, suggesting that minority votes are essential to Democratic competitiveness.

This is not to say that white voters are not critical. Logically, of course, each voter is of equal importance and a significant reduction in Democratic share of white votes would be impossible to make up with minority votes, particularly African American votes, which are already so heavily skewed Democratic that there is virtually no room for improvement. But barring large and enduring shifts in white preferences, which are already divided, minority voters hold the key to Democratic competitiveness. If minority voters move even slightly in the direction of distributions that mirror those of whites, Democrats are sunk. We explore the Democratic coalition's reliance on minority voters in detail in Chapter 3.

Fortunately for Democrats, most of the research on partisan identification suggests that it is quite stable over time, both individually and in the aggregate (Green and Palmquist 1990, 1994; Green, Palmquist, and Schickler 2002). Unfortunately for Republicans, the notion that demography is destiny becomes more ominous. We have already indicated the degree to which minority voters are increasing as a share of the national electorate, a subject we will explore in greater detail. Absent significant shifts in party coalitions, that portion of the electorate that favors Republicans—non-Hispanic whites—is shrinking, while those portions favoring Democrats—nearly everyone else—is growing substantially.[1] Moreover, Obama's election, we have suggested, may hold special significance for minority populations that may enhance their identity with the Democratic Party.

Taken together, the two critical factors of demography and the Obama electoral coalition appeared in 2008 to imply a possible Democratic realignment, as large and enduring as that which accompanied the Great Depression and New Deal and which dominated American politics for a generation. Obviously, lots of assumptions underpin such a claim, chief among them the assumption of stability in the models of partisan attachment and identity that have driven voter preference until now. There were good reasons to question whether this enduring majority would come into existence, questions rooted in the very notions of minority identity and interests, which we explore further in Chapter 5.

2010 ELECTIONS IN CONTEXT

With the president riding high in the polls immediately after inauguration, GOP strategists were rightfully concerned. But the summer of 2009 represented the emergence of a reaction—a strong reaction—to the new president, his electoral coalition, and their agenda. Beginning with a town hall meeting on July 10, 2009, hosted by then Delaware congressman Mike Castle (R-DE), noisy, anti-Obama reactions emerged among GOP constituencies across the country. While the debate taking place at that moment was focused principally on the then developing health care reform bill, it was hard to escape the very real sense that it was the person of the president himself that had become the focus of all the attention.

At that Delaware town hall one particular constituent rose to ask the Congressman why he had not initiated an investigation of the legitimacy of Obama's native citizenship. This conspiracy theory—dubbed birtherism—entails the belief that the president was not born in Hawaii, has never produced a valid birth certificate, and is therefore not a legitimately elected president because he is not a "natural born" citizen of the United States. These claims began during the 2008 election. Readily available evidence refuting each of these claims leads only to greater beliefs in conspiracy, which of course is implicit in the nature of all conspiracy theories. In 2010 some polls showed as much as half of all Republicans believed that President Obama was not legitimately eligible for the office.[2] The constituent in question at the Castle town hall meeting got increasingly excited as she spoke and ended shouting, "I want my country back." Applause was resounding.

The pleading shout "I want my country back," and the belief that the president was somehow an illegitimate occupant of the office, reflect a fundamental discomfort with the existing political reality and the emerging political era. We, of course, cannot know what this citizen was thinking when she shouted that phrase, or to whom she believed she had "lost" her country, but polls suggest this episode reflected the views of a significant share of the population. It is our view that persistent questions of legitimacy, the metaphors of theft and "rightful ownership" of the country, are reflective of the deep-seated racial structures and historical hierarchies in American society and politics. These structures and hierarchies are, in turn, coupled with a recognition—perhaps not as clear as ours but there nonetheless—that America was changing, that the existing racial order would be short lived, and that the privileged position of non-Hispanic whites in the political order may not last forever.

The mobilization of dissatisfaction reflected in the comments and concerns of that town hall, coupled with ongoing economic problems and spectacularly weak messaging from the Democratic majority and the Obama administration, led to an electoral catastrophe for Democrats in the November 2010 elections. Republicans gained control of the House of Representatives with a record-setting turnaround, picked up hundreds of state legislative seats and governorships, and gained seven seats in the Senate. If the election of Obama, and the rapid growth of minority voters, signaled a coming Democratic era, it clearly has not gotten off to a great start.

In Chapter 3, we examine the 2010 elections a bit more. We think that those elections reinforce, rather than call into question, our views regarding the parties and their futures. While Republicans improved their standing across the electorate, they won a majority only of white voters, just as they had in every election for the preceding decade. Majorities in all other groups remained Democratic. In fact, as we will report in Table 3-4, 90 percent of all GOP votes came from non-Hispanic whites (and this number is likely an underestimate of the actual share, for reasons we explain in Chapter 3). There is little to find in the 2010 elections to suggest that the social and political dynamics will not continue to be a significant challenge for the GOP in coming years.

MINORITY BEHAVIOR IN A NEW ERA

Students of political behavior hoping to gain a fuller understanding of minority political attitudes and actions must do so fully cognizant of the strategic circumstances in which minority voters find themselves. Political attitudes and preferences do not form in a vacuum but, rather, are shaped by the historical forces that created current circumstances, by efforts on the part of other actors in the system to shape and reshape outcomes, and by the results of earlier actions on future interests. The strategic location of minority voters as the growing and pivotal share of the electorate will almost certainly affect the behavior of candidates, parties, and institutions and, in the long run, affect policy. Resulting policies, in turn, are highly likely to reconfigure minority interests in the future. Partisanship, vote choice, turnout, and political attitudes of African Americans, Latinos, Asian Americans, and, indeed, whites must be understood within this context.

In order to explore exactly how the polity and the institutions that serve it are likely to change in the coming century, we intend to examine the political behavior and political representation of the new non-white Americans. Our goal is to compare their patterns of behavior with the standard models of political behavior and representation that have been developed over the past fifty years of academic study, drawn from data sets dominated by white voters and, whenever minorities are considered at all, reflecting a black-white racial structure in the American polity rather than the multiracial democracy emerging today. We suspect that those models are partially or fully inapplicable to these new populations, possibly wholly inadequate to the task of understanding a racial and ethnic America that has heretofore never existed.

In Chapter 2, we detail our discussion of demographic change and identify demographic processes. The past generation has seen a tremendous change in the racial and ethnic composition of the U.S. population. What was once a society with a predominantly Anglo population has changed in a remarkably short span of time to become a much more diverse one. We detail both what those changes are and, just as important, where those changes have taken place. One of the points we make in this chapter is that we see differences in where America's minority populations live. As we show, which minority community is involved in minority politics varies quite substantially by region. While minority politics in the South still concerns relations between Anglos and African Americans, in the Southwest and West it is the Latino population that is the dominant minority population, and in some cities in the West—notably, San Francisco and Seattle—Asian Americans are the major political players. These demographic changes have altered the identity of who the minorities are who are involved in minority politics.

But politics is not—or at least not just—about numbers. One of our concerns throughout this book is to keep the politics in the phrase *minority politics* very much in mind at all times. In Chapter 3 we show the political consequence of these population shifts for the major parties. Using data from recent elections we show how—and where—minority voters matter to electoral politics, and in the future where minority voters will matter more. Our main argument is that minority voters will hold the keys to electoral success for any party in the coming century. Currently, the Democratic coalition can be a majority in American elections but only to the degree that racial and ethnic minorities identify with the party. Presently, the GOP is a predominantly Anglo party, even as Anglos make up a decreasing share of both the population and the electorate. If these patterns in racial and ethnic vote choice continue, then the coming century promises to be one of Democratic success (although perhaps with some bumps and reversals along the way, as in 2010). That pattern of success will hold only assuming that nothing will change.

One way in which we may see change is if voter loyalties to the parties change—for example if non-white voters do not stay supporters of the Democratic Party but switch to the Republican Party. The demographic patterns we outline in Chapter 2 are, effectively, irreversible, so for the GOP to change the dynamics, it must somehow find a way to change minority partisanship and bring that switch about. After all, and as the Republicans may point out, party loyalties can change. As the party of Lincoln, the GOP once attracted considerable African American support (to the extent that such support was allowed) prior to the New Deal. In Chapter 4 we take up the question of voter loyalty to the parties and examine how voters develop loyalty to parties and why it is that voters have the loyalties they do. We examine party allegiance by racial and ethnic group to see who supports whom and how stalwart they are. While African American loyalty to the Democratic Party is both well known and well entrenched, this pattern is not so true for either Latinos or Asian Americans. Republican Party strategists might find some grounds for optimism in seeing that Latino voters, in particular, seem less firmly rooted in the Democratic camp, but increasingly so as Republican rhetoric effectively thwarts political diversification of minorities. However, the growing leaning toward the Democratic Party among Asian Americans presents some counter to that optimism.

Related to this question of loyalty is a set of questions on the issues about which voters are concerned. People may develop loyalties to parties for several reasons, but people may also support political parties because of the policies the parties offer on issues that people care about. In Chapter 5, we explore the issues that are of concern to minority voters. In doing this we look at just how politically distinctive America's minority voters are. Minority politics, as an object of research or action, would be considerably less interesting if minority voters had views of politics undifferentiated from those of whites. But, of course, we know that this is not the case (Kinder and Winter 2001). Minorities do have different views from Anglos on a range of different political issues, often related to the provision of government services and goods (for example, education, security and public safety, infrastructure, a social safety net, facilities for public recreation). We show in Chapter 5 that minorities have views that are quite different from those of Anglo voters on these policy questions. Either as a consequence of social circumstances and perceived need or from a more collectivist or civic republican notion of common good, we will show that minority voters prefer higher levels of public good provision and have priorities that often differ from those of their Anglo fellow citizens. There are, then, issue-based reasons for minority voters to support the parties they do, and the issues that minorities care about make them politically distinct from white voters.

Through Chapter 5, one of the assumptions of our argument is that minorities will turn out and vote. In Chapter 6 we show just how big of an assumption that is to make. Turnout rates among African Americans are high, but this is not the case for either Latinos or Asian Americans. The electorate, in other words, does not look like the population, with obvious consequences for the political fortunes of the two major parties. In Chapter 6 we discuss why it is that turnout rates differ across individuals and across groups.

In Chapter 7 we also consider the ways in which minorities participate in politics other than by voting. In some respects patterns of minority political participation are distinctive from those of Anglos not just because, for some groups, turnout at election time is lower but also because some minorities have greater participation in what are thought of as the more burdensome and time-consuming acts of going on marches or demonstrations. In some instances, of course, this is because minorities were denied the right to vote and prevented from turning out and voting even if they wanted to. But it also seems to be the case that minority politics demonstrates that politics is about more than voting. Minority citizens are more willing to engage in more costly forms of political action than are white voters.

Voting, of course, is still important. So, too, is how those votes are translated into political power. We cover some of this in Chapter 3, but in Chapter 8 we look more closely at the workings of representation to see how the system of elections translates vote strength into political strength. As we show, the question of minority representation is one that has greatly concerned the court system. It is not simply a question of who is allowed to vote, but also how the districts in which people vote are composed, how the boundaries of those districts are drawn and, perhaps most importantly, who represents minority voters. One of the topics we take up in this chapter is that of "descriptive" representation and whether representatives reflect the makeup of their district.

After having looked at the question of how the political system—and in particular the system of elections—may represent or reflect minorities, we then turn to look at how minorities view that system. This we do in Chapter 9. The question of how citizens relate to their government is key in predicting whether they have the wherewithal, interest, and levels of empowerment to act effectively on their own behalf. In this chapter we examine several key behavioral concepts regarding core orientations to government. We find that minority voters are no more disaffected or alienated by their government than white voters, despite a history of ill treatment. On the other hand, the level of knowledge—the information resource—necessary to act effectively may be missing. We discuss the implications of both.

In Chapters 10 and 11 we consider the ways in which minority citizens interact with others. In Chapter 10 we examine how "American" minorities are. On the face of it this may seem an odd thing to do—by virtue of birth or naturalization, of course minorities are American. But there is sometimes a sense in which minority citizens are not seen as "really" American because minorities, and especially more recent immigrants, do not share a core set of values that make for being American. What we mean by "values" politics is, as you might expect, something that requires some definition. In Chapter 10 we define what is meant by the term *values* and look at the values held by minorities. We compare those values with those held by Anglos. What we find is that—just as in Chapter 5—when it comes to the role of government in society, minorities have views that are distinct from those held by Anglos. Generally speaking (and despite the concerns we explore in Chapter 9), minorities are more supportive of government having an active role than are Anglos. In other ways, however, and especially when it comes to the role of faith and personal responsibility, minority voters are very definitely "American," in many ways even more so than Anglo voters.

This theme of American-ness is taken up in our chapter on immigration and immigrants, Chapter 11. The United States is a society of immigrants, and each wave of immigration has generated a similar set of concerns and issues, whether we are discussing Irish immigrants in the nineteenth century or Mexican ones today. This longer-term perspective is important. The United States has generally had a large population of non-U.S.-born residents. It was only in the post–World War II period that the share of the foreign born shrank, and it is largely by using that period as the point of comparison that current numbers seem so high. That said, it is the case that the United States now contains very large numbers of non-U.S.-born citizens and residents. Immigration as an issue and immigrants as a population are both very politically consequential. As with the discussion of "values"—and in fact related to that discussion—concerns over immigration are often related to perceptions of whether immigrants want to be like us, or not. To use a term from social science, the concern is whether new immigrants will *assimilate* to the United States. We show in this chapter that immigrants do, indeed, want to be like us in the key ways people worry about—speaking English and being people of faith.

Finally, we consider how minority politics is shifting to become more complex. In the past, minority politics could be cast as one of a conflict between African Americans and Anglos. Changing demographics have changed that "dyadic" relationship (between black and white) into a more complex one in which Latinos and Asian Americans have entered as new players, possibly as partners but possibly, too, as rivals. In Chapter 12 we look at how intergroup relations work in practice. A particular topic of interest has been the possibility of a black-brown coalition between African Americans and Latinos; we examine examples of that coalition and the possibility of other, rival, coalitions. One thing is plain: the old view of minority politics as a contest between black and white has gone.

We conclude the book with some thoughts on what this all means for American politics and leaders of American political parties. The politics of the United States is, we argue, at a tipping point in terms of the balance between the two parties. This balance will be shifted according to whether and how minority Americans will engage in politics. Throughout the book our emphasis is on the politics of that minority political involvement and engagement. We set out some expectations of what we think may happen. Often those expectations will be phrased in terms of conditions that have to hold—party X will win *provided that* or *if. . . .* One of the reasons for advancing these kinds of conditions is that we are conscious there are limits to our knowledge of how minorities do engage in politics: minority politics remains a relatively understudied area and this does leave consequences for how precise predictions can be. A second reason for emphasizing the conditions is that outcomes do depend on how people engage. One of the clearest normative statements we make is that we believe that engagement is worthwhile and that Americans of all races and ethnicities are better off if they engage in their politics and their government.

Demography, Identity, and a Changing America: A Not-So-Simple Examination of Rapid Change*

Demographic trends often have political implications. Take, for example, rising life expectancy. This would seem to be a politically uncontroversial—and very welcome—trend. Life expectancy in the first half of the twenty-first century is a lot longer than it was in the first half of the twentieth century across all racial and ethnic groups and both sexes. According to the CDC, the average life expectancy of men and women in the year 1904 was just under fifty years of age, but by 2004 the average life expectancy was approaching eighty (Centers for Disease Control and Prevention 2009). Such a trend hardly seems very controversial. The "graying" of society is a tribute to healthy living and scientific advances in medicine, and it simply means we will all live longer into a healthier old age than in times past.

But there are politically relevant issues raised by this trend. With more retirees there will be a need to provide—and pay for—more retirement benefits. Health care costs, too, will rise. Who will pay for retirement benefits that may—now—need to stretch for nearly twenty years past retirement age? Who will pay for extended health care coverage? If we raise the retirement age to hold constant—or at least slow the growth of—the number of years of retirement benefits, how much faster must the American economy grow to provide employment opportunities for new workers?

Not all the issues associated with a graying population need involve money. There are also regulatory issues to consider. Some of the regulations may be fairly minor, for example, can someone be too old to have a driver's license? And if so, who decides that age—that is, who counts as "old" and who counts as "too old"? Some regulations brought into question by age-related illnesses are, however, much harder to answer: should we allow euthanasia, or not?

We can raise some more straightforward "political" questions, too: Will older citizens take part in politics? After all, if older voters form a larger share of the population, they will also form a larger share of the electorate—and we

---

*Portions of this chapter were adapted from Segura, Gary M., and Helena Alves Rodrigues. 2006. "Comparative Ethnic Politics in the United States: Beyond Black and White." *Annual Review of Political Science*, 9:375–395.

are all used to thinking of elections in terms of demographic blocs. If there are issues of pension costs and benefits and health care coverage, then, pretty obviously, older voters have something at stake. Some states—notably, Florida and, to a lesser extent, Arizona—have large numbers of retirees who may be able to decide elections. Do the retirees in such states vote as they did in their younger days—split between Democrat and Republican—or do they vote as a "gray" bloc around an issue or set of issues? It is certainly the case that organizations such as the AARP (formerly, the American Association of Retired Persons) try to mobilize a "gray" identity, which means retirees will indeed vote as a bloc.

Demographic patterns, then, can have many implications, some more obviously political than others. They may shift the electorate and also shift issues that a society may have to resolve. In this book the relevant demographic change is in the racial and ethnic composition of the United States. And just as new and important political issues accompany the "graying" of American society, so too are there implications of the diversification of America. Sadly, minority voters, and minority political action, are not always well understood. The models and theories we use to understand political action have their origins at a different time in which the racial and ethnic composition of American society was less complex.

An additional complication concerns the endurance or mutability of racial and ethnic identities. Racial identities are historically constructed, can vary over time, and are—at least in part—subjective (Omi and Winant 1986). While we can directly observe the graying of the American population, and have a clear understanding of what it means to be sixty-five years old, definitions of categories such as "Latino" and "Asian American" have boundaries that are far less distinct and more frequently changing. This makes prognostication on these dimensions more hazardous than on others, a theme we will return to throughout this chapter.

The mutability of ethnic and racial identity is more than an academic question. As we will detail in this chapter and in the chapters to come, ethnic and racial identity have long been identified as an important political resource on which groups and individuals can draw for assistance in forming preferences, discerning new information, motivating political action, and reshaping the political world. Dawson (1994) has offered the concept of a "utility heuristic" whereby the group—in his book, African Americans—makes judgments about candidates and issues with the group's interests in mind. Similarly, group identity can be an important motivator, helping groups raise voter turnout and overcoming collective action problems (Chong 1991). In-group attachments, that is, attachments to the group with which the person strongly identifies,[1] can shape views and change behavior. If, however, attachment to group identity is fleeting, or conditioned on a host of historical factors that may change quickly, its importance as a resource or heuristic will be short lived and the implications of demographic change less important. For example, if Hispanic Americans come to be viewed as white ethnics—as their Italian predecessors were—rather than a racially distinct group, the growth of the Latino population, rather than portending important political change, may in fact signal a resurgence of the white population as the nation's majority and white attitudinal and behavioral patterns as the norm (Skerry 1997). Similarly, the view that Asians would be afforded status as "honorary whites" (Bonilla-Silva 2003) would both undermine the uniqueness that we might attribute to Asian American politics and undercut our views regarding the importance of their population growth.

To start, however, we will assume for the moment that racial categories are meaningful to the members of each group and to the observing public. After we discuss the magnitude and implications of demographic change, we will return to this question of identity and its effects.

POPULATION TRENDS IN THE UNITED STATES

We begin our discussion of minority politics within the United States with a straightforward and well-known fact: the United States is becoming a less wholly Anglo society and much more racially and ethnically diverse. Table 2-1 displays the figures from that demographic change, and Figure 2-1 provides a visual representation.

At first glance Table 2-1 shows something quite straightforward. The racial and ethnic composition has changed, is changing, and will continue to change, making a more diverse America. The categorization into Asian, black, Latino, Native American, and white is a familiar and common one. It appears as a standard question on forms such as school applications that people are asked to complete every day.

TABLE 2-1	Percentage of the Population 2010 Census, and Projections to 2050				
	2010	2020	2030	2040	2050
Asian	4.7	5.4	6.1	6.9	7.5
African American	12.2	12.7	12.7	12.6	12.5
Latino or Hispanic	16.3	19.4	23.0	26.7	30.2
Non-Hispanic white	63.7	60.1	55.5	50.8	46.3

Sources: Numbers for the 2010 census come from U.S. Census Bureau. 2010. Karen R. Humes, Nicholas A. Jones, and Roberto R. Ramirez. "Overview of Race and Hispanic Origin: 2010: 2010 Census Briefs." March 2011. www.census.gov/prod/cen2010/briefs/c2010br-02.pdf (accessed June 1, 2011). Projection figures from Jennifer M. Ortman and Christine E. Guarneri. 2008. "United States Population Projections: 2000 to 2050." www.census.gov/population/www/projections/2009projections.html (accessed June 1, 2011).

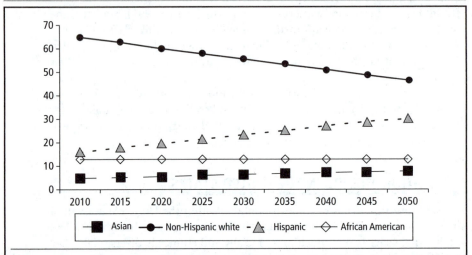

FIGURE 2-1 **Projected Racial and Ethnic Composition of the U.S., 2010–2050**

Sources: Projection figures from Jennifer M. Ortman and Christine E. Guarneri. 2008. "United States Population Projections: 2000 to 2050." www.census.gov/population/www/projections/analytical-document09.pdf and and www.census.gov/population/www/projections/2009projections.html (accessed June 1, 20011).

America is a very different place than it was just a generation ago. And a generation from now, it will again have changed considerably. Before the middle of this century, European Americans—whites, if you will—no longer will compose a majority of the American population. While the authors may or may not be around to witness this moment, our students and children will.

As we mentioned in Chapter 1, changes such as these have myriad implications. While we are explicitly interested in the political, we would be remiss if we did not at least offer a glimpse of the socioeconomic and cultural implications. For whites, their declining population share either results in a concomitant decline in their collective control of capital, political office, and culture or they will instead have to come to terms with the increasing and increasingly uncomfortable mismatch between population characteristics and their share of power and influence. More likely, both will be the case.

Rogers Smith (1997) has chronicled the uneven and occasionally jarring redefinitions of the national "us" that have been necessitated by history and characterized the long history of the expansion of our national community, citizenry, and electorate over the past 300 years or so. Importantly, that process has always been incremental, one that allowed for the expansion of "us" so long as there continued to be a "them" (our words, not Smith's), a set of groups and identities still firmly outside the boundaries of our national identity. It is the presence of the externalized other that makes possible the modest expansion of the groups defined as "in" the society.

But the demographic trends in Table 2-1 and Figure 2-1 are anything but incremental. A brief window into the change in white population illustrates two key points. First, the white population as a share of the national population has declined precipitously, after a long period of stability. Second, the definition of *white* has become narrower with the emergence of an identified Hispanic subcategory beginning in 1970 and, in 2000, the identification of mixed-race persons.

From the founding through the turn of the last century, white population share actually increased, driven largely by significant European immigration with very little immigration from other parts of the world. From 1900 to 1970, there was an unprecedented stability in white population share, this despite the eventual inclusion of Native American populations in the count (they were, for much of our history, excluded), as well as the reopening of immigration in the 1960s and the removal of some of the race-based restrictions in the 1950s. This level of long-term stability, accompanied by the unprecedented population growth in the wake of World War II, means that many Americans—in fact, most Americans over age thirty or so, have recollections of a society that was between 80 percent and 90 percent white. For those over forty, the America of their (our) youth was over 85 percent white.

The second key change, illustrated by Table 2-1a, is the incremental modification of what it means to be "white" in American society. While race theorists have often spoken of the expansion of whiteness in the nineteenth century to include Irish, Italians, Slavs, and eventually Jewish immigrants, we are now observing the self-redefinition of a number of groups "out" of whiteness. The table illustrates the two most significant: the trend of both whites and Hispanics themselves to see Latinos as non-white and the emergence of the mixed-race identity, best reflected in the modification of the census race question to allow respondents to check one "or more." The census asks Hispanic ancestry as a question distinct from race. Among self-identified Hispanics, 47.9 percent identified themselves as white in 2000, while 42.2 percent chose "some other race" as their racial identity, the vast portion of which wrote in some version of Hispanic or a Latin American national origin as their racial identity.[2] In 2010, the share choosing "some other race" declined to 36.7 percent, while the "white" share increased to 53 percent, perhaps as a consequence of the charged political environment over immigration and Latino population growth.[3]

The option, then, of selecting more than one racial categorization has been available to those Hispanics who see Hispanicity as a race since 1970. In 2000, all Americans had the opportunity to check more than one racial identity, allowing a formal count of Americans whose racial identity is no longer solely in one of the racial categories. But as more Americans identify as mixed-race or as Hispanic, a group with a clear social identity distinct from that of

TABLE 2-1A   Historical Trends in White Identification in the U.S. Census

Year	White	Non-Hispanic white	Hispanic (any race)	Non-Hispanic and not in combination	Non-Hispanic two or more races
1800*	81.1%	—	—	—	—
1850	84.3%	—	—	—	—
1900	87.9%	—	—	—	—
1950	89.5%	—	—	—	—
1960	88.8%	—	—	—	—
1970	87.5%	83.2%	4.7%	—	—
1980	83.1%	79.6%	6.4%	—	—
1990	80.3%	75.6%	9.0%	—	—
2000	77.1%	70.9%	12.5%	70.4%	1.6%
2010	74.8%	65.3%	16.4%	63.7%	1.9%

Sources: U.S. Census Bureau. "United States—Race and Hispanic Origin: 1790 to 1990," table 1. September 13, 2002. www.census.gov/population/www/documentation/twps0056/tab01.pdf.

*www.census.gov/population/www/documentation/twps0056/tab01.pdf

"whites," the share of the American population who are viewed—by themselves or others—as truly "white," as members of the historical and established "majority," has declined.

The shaded boxes of Table 2-1a capture the demographic dynamics as they are lived and understood in the United States. After seventy years of stability above 85 percent of the national population, the social majority we see, and who see themselves, as "white" has declined by 20 percentage points in the span of a single generation.

Such dramatic changes in the composition of the national population will create significant moments of cultural change, expansion, and evolution. These will be (and have been) greeted with, at best, uneven levels of enthusiasm and, at worst, spasms of nativism and xenophobia that have so often characterized the history of American politics (Hofstadter 1964). Linguistic traditions and language fluency, cultural practices and social norms, religious observance, and differences in values or priorities will—indeed already do—raise challenges in the workplace, the classroom, the church, and the courtroom, to say nothing of the ballot box. And emerging population groups and their members are themselves the source of significant political contestation that will shape the partisan distribution in the electorate and the range of citizen views on a variety of issues of public concern.

HOLD EVERYTHING! SIX CAVEATS REGARDING THE EXTRAPOLATION OF RACE CATEGORIES AND THEIR EFFECTS INTO THE FUTURE

This recent change in the "definition" of *white,* however, illustrates several key assumptions that bear considerable examination. Specifically, our argument regarding the importance of demography in shaping the next era in American politics presupposes at least some level of stability in these racial categories, our willingness and ability as a society to continue partitioning Americans—indeed, all people—according to these troublesome proper names, the continued association of these categories with divisions in American politics and society, and political meaningfulness attached to them in the minds of group members.

In this section we make six points in relation to Table 2-1 suggesting that while race is very likely to remain an enduring and influential social construct for understanding politics and social change, we should be cautious in how we use those categories and the confidence with which we extrapolate trends and associations into the future. We will then turn our attention to the political importance of racial identity and the pitfalls of extending the logics of identity across different racial and ethnic minority groups in the United States.

1) Is race a set of transhistoric and mutually exclusive categorizations?

The numbers reported in Table 2-1 and illustrated in Figure 2-1 understate the degree of diversity in the United States, since they are based on figures in which people are assigned to one, and only one, category. That counting rule clearly is at odds with reality: large and growing numbers of Americans have multiple heritages. The 2000 census questionnaire was the first to allow respondents to select more than one race. Nationwide, approximately 2 percent of the population, nearly 7 million Americans, marked identification with two or more races (CensusScope).

Still, the main categories are there, on the forms you complete, in the press stories you read, and in this book. They are comfortingly familiar. One downside to the familiarity of these categories is that they can be said to imply that racial and ethnic categories are fixed and permanent. But are they—is someone's race permanent? That might seem an odd question to ask, but recall the discussion of "graying" above. When are you old? When the government tells you that you are "old"? Or is it the first time someone in a restaurant calls you "sir" or "madam"? Or is it when someone does not bother to ask for your ID? Or is it when you yourself feel old?

All those kinds of ways of defining *old* are ways in which *race* may defined. The government, for example, may well assign people or deny people a particular racial and ethnic category. These kinds of categorizations can have meaningful consequences for individuals: for example, being seen as legitimately Native American can have implications for an individual's access to federal benefits or revenue from gaming operations. Portuguese are European, not a separate ethnic identity. In U.S. history, a series of categorizations (that is, who counts as a member of which racial and ethnic group) have had stark consequences. One consequence, for example, has been to define some people as citizens and some as not. As Haney López (1997, 2004) notes, one of the early acts of Congress was to restrict naturalization of citizenship to whites in 1790. But: "Whether one was 'white' . . . was often no easy question" (Haney López 1997, 1). It was one that required successive legal cases to resolve: were people from China, or of Turkish or Arab ancestry, "white" or not? The category of "Hispanic," for example, was an American government creation for statistical purposes whose meaning is subject to contestation and, in some environments, may have no meaning at all. In Europe, for example, being Spanish or Portuguese might be a national category involving a real noun on a passport, but people from Spain and Portugal are European and not seen, by other Europeans, as a distinctive racial category. To take another non-U.S. example, in the interwar period between World Wars I and II, people from Greece and Malta were considered "semi-colored" by Australian immigration policy, and restrictions were placed on people from those countries moving to Australia. Closer to home, in California, one question in the early twentieth century was whether Armenians should be categorized as Asian or European. That is, governments may define the categories into which people are assigned. Or, perhaps more subtly, by *not* having a category on a census form that allows you to check "multiple identities," this simply—and arbitrarily—stops that identity.

Another way of defining categories means having one's race defined for you by other people. Sometimes they may be government officials—police officers, for example (as Haney López recounts)—but sometimes it could just be someone you interact with at school or the mall treating you in a particular way, or not treating you in a particular way.

Race is, in other words, "socially constructed"; that is, a racial or ethnic category is not fixed but malleable, and it is rooted in social practice, convention, law, stereotype, and prejudice rather than only in our genes. Clearly, if categories can be defined by laws or government regulations, then racial categories are not transhistoric—they can change significantly over time. In most instances individual identities are fixed, since race constructions are neither formed nor reformed overnight. But the categories can and do change, and it is quite possible that someone's race at birth can change by the time of his or her death. If that can happen—and we gave examples of it happening in the past—then clearly the categorizations and classification of people by race and ethnicity have to be treated with some caution. Sometimes one's categorization simply depends on the categories listed on the form to be counted, and who is doing the counting.

But there are other ways, too, in which race may be socially constructed. One way is based on how people respond to you. It may be difficult to see this change over time but perhaps easier to see as you move across a country. For example, in their respective coverage the East Coast *New York Times* has tended to refer to "Hispanic" voters and "Black" voters at election times, while the West Coast *Los Angeles Times* has tended to write about "Latino" voters and "African American" voters. Now, many people may not see a whole lot of difference between those terms, but they do illustrate that different regions may talk about race in different ways. It may not just be talk. For a long time in the U.S. South, African Americans were constantly reminded of being "black" by a whole range of formal and informal reminders. Some reminders were very explicit with written rules—separate drinking fountains or entrances, where someone sat on the bus. These kinds of expectations were fairly rigid in the South but not so rigid in the West. Omi and Winant (1986, 1994) are sociologists who especially stress the importance of these kinds of interactions in the formation of racial identities and, even, the idea of races themselves. A dramatic example might be seen before and after the September 11, 2001, attacks. On September 10, being Arab American or Iranian American in an airport was not something that brought about too much comment or reaction from other passengers or airport staff. It would be surprising indeed, however, if Arab Americans were not made to feel differently about themselves, and their community, since September 11.

Communities themselves may also make efforts to maintain distinct identities. These efforts may be somewhat formal and institutionalized. For example, a community may encourage language or religious school on the weekend or make an effort to celebrate certain festivals in public. In addition to encouraging certain kinds of behavior, communities may discourage other kinds of behavior by imposing informal sanctions on people who do not conform. A controversial example is the degree to which "acting white" is open to sanctions within the African American and, to some extent, Latino communities (where the absence of Spanish fluency can be a source of discredit). Some evidence suggests that there are indeed some penalties to "acting white" that have obvious negative consequences for educational advancement (see, in particular, the work of Roland Fryer),[4] though we are hesitant to generalize from the limited exploration of this topic.

Race is not simply a matter of physical appearance (assuming for the moment that we have an actual way of defining that) but also of how one is treated. There is as well room for another way in which identities may be formed: by the individuals themselves. Now, there may be limits to how one can define one's own identity, especially if everyone else—the law, businesses, and even other people—is defining it for you. It may even be that people have some scope to craft their own identity and choose ethnic identifiers because they like them and have positive feelings about those attachments and modify the American to, for example, Irish American or Mexican American as a matter of pride. Even those free to choose, however, may face some constraints. Haney López, for example, has written of his own experiences of having an Anglo father and a Latina mother: up to a point he could decide for himself whether he is Anglo or Latino, or both. The new census categories give him that last option—but only from 2000 onward. At some point, and as he makes clear in some biographical notes in the preface to his work, he changed his identity: changing his name from Ian Haney to Ian Haney López. It is also clear that how much freedom he had to define himself in the way that he himself chose depended not just on others but also his own social standing—as he stopped being a scruffily dressed undergraduate and began to be a better-dressed law student. Other social markers, and in particular social class, may allow some people more leeway than others in defining themselves.

Here, too, we would not want to overstate this point. The centrality of appearance and the historical fetishism with skin tone and other physical manifestations of ancestry certainly constrain the ability of many individuals to define their racial selves. At some level, changes in dress, socioeconomic status, and forms of public expression can only go so far if the "audience," those perceiving the individual or group, police the boundaries of identity with firm categories, strong stereotypes, and a predisposition to discriminate between in- and out-group members. And, of course, people without status, money, and power probably have a lot less ability to modify dress, occupation, and public presentation even if they would be accepted by the "majority."

We also want to make it clear that understanding race as contingent—that is, as determined in part by other cultural factors and circumstances—socially constructed does *not* mean that race is not real. It is not real in a scientific sense, but as a lived experience and a historic fracturing line that shaped national histories and individual lives, it is an undeniably important phenomenon in understanding the history of the United States and the globe, one that is distinct from class, language, and sect. We merely want to reinforce the observation that race and racial constructs are constantly shifting and evolving and are inherently endogenous to other aspects of human behavior, not the least of which is politics.

2) If people of different characteristics are born into a society and no one counts them, do those races really exist?

What this brief discussion shows is that the standard and familiar categories need to be taken with a pinch of salt—even as we use them throughout this book. Simply deciding to count minority populations can have a political dimension in and of itself. France, for example, does not collect (at least not officially) figures on racial breakdown: if you are French you are French regardless of ethnicity or race (at least officially). Given that the categories of Table 2-1 are more than a little arbitrary, you might be thinking that maybe the French are on to something in not collecting data on these categories.

Perhaps if we abandoned those categories, we would abandon the existence of "hyphenated-Americans," that is, everyone would just be American. After all, if race can be socially constructed as we talk about it—and as government agencies define it—then having important government agencies not "see" race anymore might help stop divisions.

California's Proposition 54 in 2003, in fact, attempted to do just that. It intended to change the state constitution to "prohibit state and local governments from using race, ethnicity, color, or national origin to classify current or prospective students, contractors, or employees in public education, contracting, or employment operations." It did not prohibit classification by sex (although one might ask why not, given the stated goals of the proposal). Part of the argument in support of the proposal was a version of a social construction argument: government-imposed racial classification has in the past been used to divide people. As supporters put it in their message appearing in the official ballot pamphlet:

> The unrelenting, daily racial categorization of people by the government is one of the most divisive forces in American society. It is constantly emphasizing our minor differences, in opposition to our better instincts that tell us to seek our common interests and common values.
>
> (California Secretary of State 2003)

Part of the difficulty with this argument is that, as with many social construction arguments, it understands racial categories as extremely malleable—that is, too malleable in light of the racial history in the United States and other parts of the developed world. But just because racial categories may be socially constructed does not mean they are easy to change. In fact, it may be that because society as a whole constructs them, this fact makes them especially resilient. Simply because the government stops collecting data does not make enduring issues of discrimination or underrepresentation go away. For example, Japan saw a series of efforts to do away with discrimination toward a supposedly lower-caste, "burakumin" group, including passing a law that made it very hard for people to look up the family origins of nonfamily members. Recently, however, Google Maps published maps of feudal Japan that allowed the identification of areas settled by the lower caste at that time, allowing easier identification of caste heritage (through where people or their ancestors lived). The maps were of residential patterns from centuries ago, and yet the concern was that modern-day citizens would use them to help express ancient prejudices (Lewis 2009). In the face of such a deeply held social construction, formal and governmental rules seem quite weak. Attitudes toward "burakumin" have persisted for a very long period of time, despite formal rules that outlaw discrimination and the formal abandonment of castes.

Racial and ethnic categories—and their social and economic effects—are as hard to change as they are arbitrary.

But, perhaps more importantly, the absence of data gathered in terms of nation or ethnicity of origin, sectarian identity, and other key distinctions in California, in France—or indeed anywhere that demographic characteristics are associated with distributions on disadvantage, social pathologies, or simple needs—makes it far more difficult to identify and diagnose, let alone remediate, inequalities of opportunity and treatment.

As the French are finding out, it can be important to learn about problems that may be group specific: without information on the group, then it is hard to find a solution and sometimes identify the problem. To return again to our example of age, we can divide the U.S. population into those eleven years and younger and those sixty-five years and older with everyone else in the middle category (which we will put to one side for the moment). So taking the two groups—the very young and the elderly—it is the case that poverty is a condition affecting more than twice as many of one of those groups as the other. The official poverty rate in 2000 for one of those groups was 3 percent and for the other just over 1 percent. These proportions imply that for one group, 3 million people live in poverty—a large number. But for the other group 8 million people live in poverty. Now, depending on our own political beliefs and ideologies, we may or may not believe that these issues of poverty are of much concern, so it may not matter too much which group has more poverty. But assuming for the moment that an antipoverty program is something we might want to at least discuss, then, if we did not collect data by age, we simply could not think about such a program, because there was no way—except by chance—that we could identify those who needed help. We could not craft sensible programs, because the needs of the elderly in poverty differ from the needs of small children in poverty. Perhaps, too, antipoverty programs cost a lot more for one group than another. Without knowing which group was most affected by poverty, we could not begin to assess those things. We may still decide not to do anything about the issue—perhaps it is too difficult or too costly to resolve—but without being able to identify the target group, we would, at the very least, be wasting a lot of time, effort, and money on government actions that missed that target. Indeed we would not be able to identify that a problem existed specific to any age group in the first place.[5]

For France the social issues primarily relate to immigrants and descendants of immigrants from North Africa. But without much information on how many people are involved, where they live, and what the nature and size of the problems may be, there is little sense of how to address those social issues. In the case of the United States, for example, as opponents of Proposition 54 noted in their message appearing in the official ballot pamphlet, health care issues differ across the groups noted in Table 2-1:

> White women are diagnosed with breast cancer at a higher rate. Asian Americans are at higher risk for Hepatitis-B. Latinos are more likely to die from complications of diabetes. African Americans die from heart disease.

Unless we have data by these groups it becomes hard to both identify the problems and tailor solutions.

All of which is to say that measured or not, race and ethnic cleavages so structure social and economic phenomena in this country and others that their importance persists without regard to whether we examine them or not. Those advocating for the abolition of race and ethnicity as official data-gathering categories for government may well be motivated by a desire to move toward a post-racial future. Alternatively, and perhaps more plausibly, advocates of that view may be taking a "kill the data gatherer" approach, preferring not to know how income, education, life chances, and other measures of social well-being vary across groups because they recognize that racial and ethnic disparities never acknowledged are almost certainly never solved.

3) Is "immigrant" a racial and ethnic category?

A third point in relation to Table 2-1 concerns immigration. Much of the growth in minority population among Asian and Latino communities has come from immigration. In 2000, roughly 11 percent of the U.S. population was born outside the United States. Of the 31 million foreign-born population, for example, roughly 16 million (52 percent) were from Latin America and around 8 million (26 percent) from Asia. Immigration over the past generation has contributed to this diversity, and—at least so far as Asian/Pacific Islander and Latino populations are concerned—race, ethnicity, and immigration status overlap.

There is a tendency to see this wave of foreign-born Americans as a new trend, to see the groups (Latino and Asian) as internally homogenous categories, and to see immigrant and minority as synonymous terms. None of these views are especially true.

Take, for example, the size of the foreign-born population. While it is the case that this figure was up from 8 percent in 1990, it is still lower than figures found in each census from 1870 to 1930. In 1910, for example, just under 15 percent of the U.S. population was foreign born (U.S. Census Bureau 1999). In that year 30 percent of New York state's population was foreign born. The current figures thus do not seem unduly high in that historical perspective. Furthermore, one reason the United States does not face as many pressures from a "graying" population (funding retirement benefits and so on) as do Japan and Western Europe is that immigration means the average age of the U.S. population is younger than those of other regions.

It is, however, true that one of the big differences between today and 100 years ago is that the sources of immigration are different. But this does not mean that immigrant groups are homogenous within each racial and ethnic group. Table 2-2 shows the heritage (but not immigration status) of Asians and Latinos in the United States. It lists the top five countries/regions of origin for those populations.

As can be seen, by contrast to the Latino population, which is dominated by immigrants from Mexico, Asian Americans make up a very diverse group in terms of national heritage and, hence, language, cultures, and traditions. But even Latino immigrants embrace a range of different national origins. The last group listed in the table is not immigrants at all. This group is composed of Native Americans and Alaska Natives. Together these populations account for almost 3 million people in 2010, but less than 1 percent of the total U.S. population. We know, perhaps, least of all about this group. One thing we do know, however, is that this grouping too embraces a great deal of diversity between native nations. What Table 2-2 helps to underscore, then, is that broad

TABLE 2-2 National/Tribal Origin of Asians, Latinos, and Native Americans, 2010 Census

	Asian		Latino		American Indian Alaska Native
China	22.8%	Mexico	63%	Cherokee	16%[1]
India	19.4	Puerto Rico	9.2	Navajo	15
Philippines	17.4	Central America	7.9	Sioux	6
Vietnam	10.6	South America	5.5	Chippewa	6
Korea	9.7	Cuba	3.5	Choctaw	4
Japan	5.2	Dominican Rep.	2.8		
		Spain	1.3		
Number	14,674,252		50,477,594		2,932,248[2]
Percentage of total population	4.7		16.4		< 1%

Sources: Total population: U.S. Census Bureau. Karen R. Humes, Nicholas A. Jones, and Roberto R. Ramires. "Overview of Race and Hispanic Origin: 2010: 2010 Census Briefs." March 2011. www.census.gov/prod/cen2010/briefs/c2010-br-02.pdf. (accessed June 1, 2011). Asian population: U.S. Census Bureau. 2000. Demographic Profile of the United States, table DP-1. Hispanic population: "The Hispanic Population: 2010." www.census.gov/prod/cen2010/briefs/c2020br-04.pdf. Native population: "The American Indian and Alaska Native Population: 2000; Census 2000 Brief." February 2002. C2KBR/01-15. www.census.gov/prod/2002pubs/c2kbr01-15.pdf.

[1] Tribal percentages from the 2000 census. Figures from 2010 not yet available by time of publication.

[2] Native population from the 2010 census.

categorizations such as those displayed and used in Table 2-1 are often useful shorthand descriptions, but they often imply a far greater degree of homogeneity within categories than may actually exist.

What about the overlap between being *immigrant* and being *minority*? Sometimes the temptation is to use the terms synonymously, but while there is overlap between being an immigrant and being a member of a minority group, there are also distinctions, too: not all Latinos and Asians are immigrants, and not all immigrants are Latino or Asian. This distinction makes for an important difference. Immigrants who were children in their native country and arrive later in life are likely to have very different interactions with U.S. society from the very outset, even if they share the same nominal racial or ethnic category as someone native born. There may be language barriers, different expectations, and certainly experiences they do not share with anyone who went to elementary and middle school in the United States (they did not, for example, learn basic facts about each state or build a volcano). More importantly, depending on the age in which they immigrated, first-generation immigrants of all races and ethnicities are likely to have identities formed in relation to quite different social settings. It is easy to see this in relation to attitudes toward politics formed by historical circumstances: Cubans immigrating after Castro's revolution, Irish immigration after the famine, Jews fleeing Hitler's Germany, Cambodians and Vietnamese arriving after U.S. wars in that region. All these immigrants are likely to bring with them formative experiences. The formative experience need not be caused by something as dramatic as the examples we just gave. Generally speaking, if your early childhood experiences take place in a one-party Communist state or other non-democracy, you are quite likely to have very different attitudes toward politics than if you were brought up in a country where elections were regular features of politics.

If we think about how race may be socially constructed in different ways across different contexts, we can easily see how, for first-generation immigrants who come to the United States as adults or in their late teens, the categories of Table 2-1 may make little sense. Older immigrants are quite likely to bring with them a preestablished "identity." Even within the categories of Table 2-1, then, depending on the period we choose, we might reasonably expect to see differences in attitude and outlook between immigrants from Costa Rica and Nicaragua, Jamaica and Haiti, or China and Taiwan. That is, even if we choose people who are not only immigrants and not only placed in the same Table 2-1 categories but also are from the same region, we are still likely to have quite different attitudes and opinions simply based on their formative experiences. Subsequent generations, however, that is, those brought up in the United States, will have their identity formed by U.S. experiences. In a very crude sense what we may see is that the "immigrant" identity becomes relatively less important and the "race and ethnic" identity becomes relatively more important, down the different generations of immigrants (first-, second-, third-, and so on). Therefore, while immigration status and ethnicity do overlap and intersect, it is not always in straightforward ways. Self-consciousness about race may simply not matter so much to first-generation immigrants as to successive generations.

One other complication is likely to be that of class. There are class differences, on average, between the different groups listed in Table 2-1, but there are also class differences between immigrants even within the same group. A Mexican immigrant coming to the United States in order to work on a tech visa in Silicon Valley will have very different social status and life chances than someone who came across the border to work as agricultural labor in the neighboring Central Valley. While the standard story of immigration and immigrant success has someone arriving in the United States with two suitcases and $50, it is worth remembering that some immigrants arrive with far, far more, others with far less. It seems likely, as we noted earlier, that differences in wealth, status, and power allow more leeway in self-identification. This would also seem to hold for immigrants, too.

4) How might race politics vary within the United States?

Our fourth point in relation to Table 2-1 is that, in part owing to immigrations patterns, the geographical distribution of minority populations is not equal across the United States. Table 2-3 lists states by their population growth between the two census years of 2000 and 2010. Again, the general pattern should come as little surprise: generally speaking, the states in the South and West are growing in population faster than the ones in the North and East. These fast-growing states are also ones with large minority populations, and the data in this table make it clear that population growth across America is overwhelmingly driven by minority population growth. For many states, especially those growing more slowly, absent minority growth there would be shrinkage in state populations. In fact, Table 2-4 shows some of these trends in the shrinking of the majority or plurality of non-Hispanic whites.

Figures 2-2, 2-3 and, 2-4 show the distributions across the states of African American, Latino, and Asian American populations, respectively.

As can be seen, while the United States is becoming more diverse nationally, the content of that diversity varies depending on the state in which one lives: there is a spatial distribution to minority populations. African Americans are, relatively speaking, concentrated in the South, Latinos in the South and Southwest, and Asian Americans in California and a few major metro areas (for example, Seattle, Houston, and New York/New Jersey). One consequence of the various combinations of settlement is that some states have very large minority populations. California, Hawaii, New Mexico, and Texas are states with "majority-minority" populations, that is, states where over 50 percent of the population are minority. Maryland, Mississippi, Georgia, New York, and Arizona are states where roughly 40 percent of the population is minority.

Concentrations in population are also seen below the state level in patterns of residential segregation in cities—if we take a map of a city, we are likely to see regions of the city with heavier concentrations of population provided by one of the groups in Table 2-1. The racial and ethnic makeup of most neighborhoods in the United States is quite different than we might expect if, say, the mixing of people was purely random. For example, if the population is composed 50–50 of group Reds and Blues and people interacted more or less at random, we might expect to see diverse social networks: half of one's friends and neighbors might be from the other group; 50 percent of a Red's neighbors would be Blue and vice versa. But life in the United States is not like that: people often live in ethnically distinct neighborhoods.

Almost all the official means of segregating neighborhoods have now been removed. It is nevertheless possible to see some residues of those laws. For example, old housing deeds might still have restrictions as to whom a house may be sold. Those restrictions are no longer legal or constitutional, but you may still find those earlier provisions written in the document. Despite the ending of overt forms of legal discrimination in housing, unofficial residential segregation persists at the local (city) level that is quite pronounced. By some estimates, in a typical U.S. city perhaps as many as two-thirds of African

TABLE 2-3 Top 10 and Bottom 10 States Ranked by Population Growth, 2000–2010

Rank	State	Growth percentage	Minority growth percentage	Rank	State	Growth percentage	Minority growth percentage
1.	Nevada	35.1	78.1	41.	Pennsylvania	3.4	33.1
2.	Arizona	24.5	45.2	42.	Illinois	3.4	16.7
3.	Utah	23.7	64.8	43.	Massachusetts	3.1	35.8
4.	Idaho	21.1	62.5	44.	Vermont	2.7	51.8
5.	Texas	20.5	38.6	45.	West Virginia	2.4	28.8
6.	North Carolina	18.4	37.9	46.	New York	2.1	11.9
7.	Georgia	18.3	39.8	47.	Ohio	1.6	20.0
8.	Florida	17.6	43.3	48.	Louisiana	1.0	7.4
9.	Colorado	16.9	37.3	49.	Rhode Island	0	31.1
10.	South Carolina	15.2	22.3	50.	Michigan	0	8.5
	Average	21.1	46.9		Average	1.9	24.5

Source: U.S. Census Bureau. Karen R. Humes, Nicholas A. Jones, and Roberto R. Ramirez. "Overview of Race and Hispanic Origin: 2010: 2010 Census Briefs." March 2011. www.census.gov/prod/cen2010/briefs/c2010br-02.pdf (accessed June 1, 2011).

TABLE 2-4 States with Largest Change in Racial and Ethnic Composition, 2000–2010

	Non-Hispanic whites as % total population 2000	Non-Hispanic whites as % total population 2010	Difference
Nevada	65	54	−11
Florida	65	58	−7
Maryland	62	55	−7
Delaware	72	65	−7
Texas	52	45	−7
Georgia	63	56	−7
New Jersey	66	59	−7
California	47	40	−7
Washington	79	73	−6
Connecticut	77	71	−6
Arizona	63	58	−5
Massachusetts	82	79	−3
Rhode Island	82	79	−3

Source: U.S. Census Bureau. 2010. Karen R. Humes, Nicholas A. Jones, and Roberto R. Ramirez. "Overview of Race and Hispanic Origin: 2010: 2010 Census Briefs." March 2011. www.census.gov/prod/cen2010/briefs/c2010 br-02.pdf (accessed June 1, 2011).

FIGURE 2-2   **Density of African American Population as a Share of Total, 2000 Census**

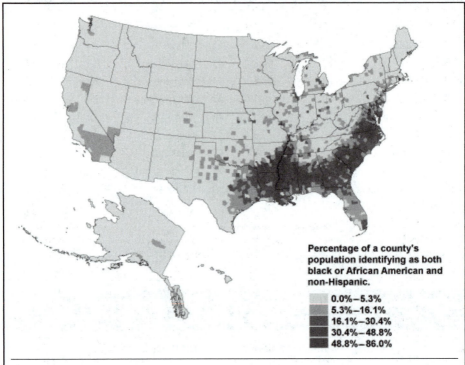

Percentage of a county's population identifying as both black or African American and non-Hispanic.

- 0.0%–5.3%
- 5.3%–16.1%
- 16.1%–30.4%
- 30.4%–48.8%
- 48.8%–86.0%

Source: "African American Population," www.censusscope.org/us/map_nhblack.html. Censusscope.org at the University of Michigan.

Americans would have to change neighborhoods to produce an even distribution of blacks across the city (Cutler, Glaeser, and Vigdor 1999).[6]

It is hard to know how to interpret (and measure) such segregation that does exist. The impulse to separate need not be discriminatory against another group. Some of the incentive to want to live together might simply be that it is easier to maintain linguistic or religious traditions if people from the same group live in the same neighborhood. Work by Janet Landa (1995), for example, shows how shared ethnic ties can help promote trade and business, so there may be an economic incentive to keep community ties close. Of course, despite these kinds of motivations, residential segregation below the level of the state may reflect the fact that people really want to live in neighborhoods composed of other people "just like them."

Work by Thomas Schelling (1978), however, implies that segregation may not require deeply entrenched racism to exist before it occurs. It can happen even if people on average have a fairly slight preference to be with other people like themselves. Schelling showed this at work using a simple physical model:

FIGURE 2-3   **Density of Latino Population as a Share of Total, 2000 Census**

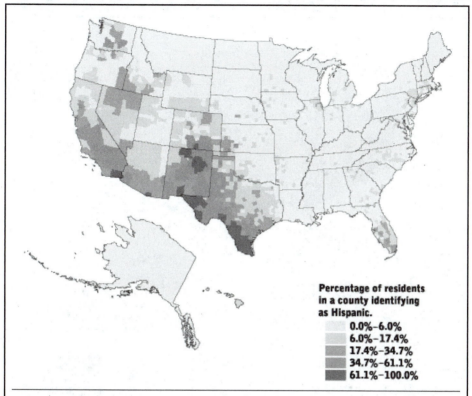

Percentage of residents
in a county identifying
as Hispanic.

- 0.0%–6.0%
- 6.0%–17.4%
- 17.4%–34.7%
- 34.7%–61.1%
- 61.1%–100.0%

Source: "Hispanic Population," www.censusscope.org/us/map_hispanicpop.html. Censusscope.org at the University of Michigan.

He took a checkerboard and two types of coins—say nickels and pennies. He placed the coins at random on the board (leaving a few empty spaces) and then made a rule that a coin—representing a person—would stay put if at least half of its neighbors (that is, the coins in the surrounding squares) were the same as itself, but would prefer to move otherwise. Ideally it would move to a square with neighbors more to its liking. As coins begin to move away from squares they do not like, two things happen. First, they begin to disturb the patterns of other coins. If a penny like me moves away, then that disturbs the proportion of pennies in the neighborhood of my next-door penny. If that penny moves, it unsettles the proportion for its neighbor too. Second, the consequence of this sequence of being disturbed and moving can produce quite segregated neighborhoods of pennies and nickels. It is possible to see this for yourself with a checkerboard and some coins, although a quick web search will find lots of animations of the process at work and even agent-based games where you can see the process unfold and play with it yourself.

FIGURE 2-4   **Density of Asian American Population as a Share of Total, 2000 Census**

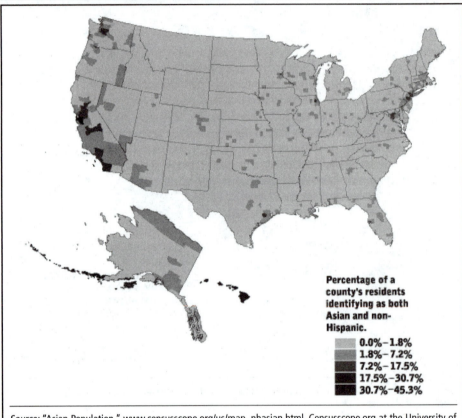

Percentage of a
county's residents
identifying as both
Asian and non-
Hispanic.

- 0.0%–1.8%
- 1.8%–7.2%
- 7.2%–17.5%
- 17.5%–30.7%
- 30.7%–45.3%

Source: "Asian Population," www.censusscope.org/us/map_nhasian.html. Censusscope.org at the University of Michigan.

The depth of this in-group preference, and by extension the degree of out-group bias, is really captured, then, by the strength of this like-type preference in neighbors. Obviously if pennies exclusively wanted to be with pennies and nickel with nickels (that is, entrenched discrimination or racism), we would see segregation happen very quickly. But Schelling's point was that it is possible to see "segregation" of coins come about even with quite mild preferences for one's own kind; for example, if the actors just would like to have between 30–40 percent of their neighbors like them (rather than 100 percent), particularly if there is a wide variety of preferred levels of likeness. Or, put another way, many people would be fine if more than half their neighbors were different from them. But since some people want a more homogenous group of neighbors, they leave, and their departure changes the distribution by group among the remaining neighbors, crossing the preferred line of more original inhabitants who also leave, and so on, until we see the unraveling process and pronounced segregation in some models.

The Schelling model can seem quite artificial. It is nevertheless instructive because it shows that even small moves away from randomness can result in quite separate residential areas. As some of Fryer's work (2005) shows, even that very small move away from randomness can produce persistent separate patterns of hiring.[7]

You might be thinking at this point, "That's all very interesting, but so what?" Simple, abstract models—such as the kind used by Schelling and Fryer—can help simplify the real world and make us be clear about the kinds of social processes taking place. These models may not be "real" in the sense that, say, someone using opinion poll data from real people might be said to have that connection, but they are instructive and thought provoking. That said, when we do look at real data, then actual preferences for living in mixed neighborhoods shows no group expressing a preference for minority status.[8] Real-world people of all races and ethnicities definitely prefer to live in neighborhoods of people who are are quite a lot like themselves.

What we see, then, is an important spatial component to minority populations. Trends such as those seen in Figure 2-1 do not unfold across the United States in the same way. We see an uneven geographical distribution of minority populations across states, and, further, we see other distributions at the sub-state—city and local—levels. We can even see this in reference to those who identify themselves as multiracial. Figure 2-5 shows the distribution of those who identify themselves in this way.

The distribution is skewed toward the West and Southwest. The combinations also differ by state: in Hawaii the most common combination is Asian and Hawaiian; in Oklahoma it is White and American Indian (CensusScope). As CensusScope notes, multiracial America is not simply a reflection of urban melting pots.

5) Does all racial contestation involve non-Hispanic whites?

A fifth point in relation to Table 2-1 is that it hides changing balances between minority populations relative to one another. Demographic projections such as those in Table 2-1 are usually framed in terms of a discussion where the balance between two groups—Anglos and "others"—is changing. The focus, in other words, is on Anglos versus everyone else. In some ways it makes sense to frame the discussion that way. For a (very) long time Anglos were the dominant group against whom claims of rights were made by minorities within the context of a largely conflictual relationship. The history of race relations in the United States, indeed much of its history, can be understood as a process in which minority groups—and in particular African Americans—laid claims to their rights as Americans against white opposition. But the changing patterns of Table 2-1 imply changes in that relationship from one of conflict between non-Hispanic whites and everyone else to one that is not necessarily conflictual and one that is lived between minority groups as well.

FIGURE 2-5   **Density of Multiracial Population as a Share of Total, 2000 Census**

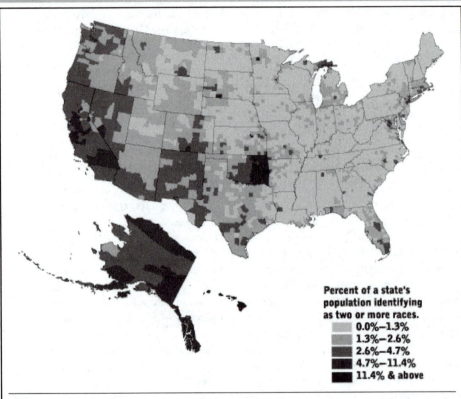

Source: "Multiracial Population," www.censusscope.org/us/map_multiracial.html. Censusscope.org at the University of Michigan.

As cities and states become majority-minority, then politics—even minority politics—may not simply be those of one group against another but are more likely to require coalition building across groups. For example, in two cities in which whites have become a minority—Memphis and New Orleans—Anglos have become a central vote bloc in helping to determine electoral success or failure of (minority) mayoral candidates (Liu 2006). Black candidates in a predominantly black city thus have a better chance of winning if they can also appeal to (at least a few) white voters and build alliances and coalitions with that group.

Second, the framing need not be seen as one that pits only Anglos against a minority group; rather, we could see competition between minority groups, too. Taking a closer look at Table 2-1 gives us Figure 2-6.

What we see are changes among minority groups. At the end of the twentieth century Latinos replaced African Americans as the largest of the minority

FIGURE 2-6   **Changing Relative Share of Minority Groups within the U.S. Population**

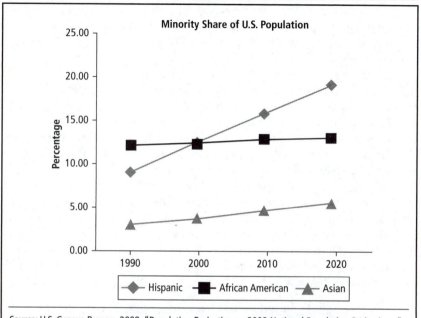

Minority Share of U.S. Population

Source: U.S. Census Bureau. 2008. "Population Projections—2008 National Population Projections," www.census.gov/population/www/projections/summarytables.html (accessed April 25, 2010).

groups. This can have important consequences in terms of minority political power. Take, for example, one of the nation's largest cities—Los Angeles. Some recent electoral history brings together some of the threads we have talked about so far. In the 1970s a biracial combination of black voters and Jewish liberals—who lived in quite different parts of the city—allied to give the mayoralty to (African American) Tom Bradley. By the early part of this century, however, in-migration (immigration) meant that roughly 40 percent of the residents of the city were foreign born, 90 percent of whom were Latino or Asian, with Mexicans forming the single largest group. Overall, Latinos made up about 46 percent of the city's population by 2000 and, in large part, were concentrated in the eastern part of the city (U.S. Census Bureau 2008, American FactFinder).

The inability of the (white) incumbent to keep together the black-white coalition meant that the 2005 mayoral primary was a contest between a Latino candidate, two Anglos, and an African American. The black-white coalition was split, and the Latino candidate—Antonio Villaraigosa—won largely with Latino and some white liberal support that can be tracked across different areas of the city.[9]

The story of the LA mayor's race combines a number of elements of the discussion in this chapter so far: spatially segregated communities in a majority-minority city form cross-race coalitions to achieve political power. The Villaraigosa victory shifted power from a coalition in which African Americans were an important part, indeed leaders, to a Latino-led coalition. Political contest, then, is not so much between a minority group and Anglos as between minority groups.

There are two ways of looking at these trends. On the one hand, it might be seen as a relief from the framing of minority politics in the way often implied by Table 2-1: a minority group always and everywhere engaged in conflict with Anglos. The electoral stories from Memphis, New Orleans, and Los Angeles show that minority candidates can, in some circumstances, win support from Anglos (and, most recently in New Orleans, a white candidate might find considerable support from minority voters). Surely this is a welcome sign of a move away from entrenched racial bloc voting.

On the other hand, and as the authors of the study on Los Angeles note, the news for African Americans in LA may not be so good. Having accomplished political power only after a long struggle, now that position is seen as "fragile" and subject to being challenged, not by whites but by other, newer, minorities. Although, as we discuss in Chapter 12, there may be hope for African American political success in "black-brown" or other multiracial coalitions.

6) Does race inhere in individual experiences, or is race better understood as a social or collective phenomenon that interacts with other forms of social institution?

Some of these trends and differences focus on ethnicity or race and imply an individual rather than a social perspective. Take, for example, marriage. Above we talked about spatial segregation, but social segregation also occurs and does so within the institution of marriage. While the numbers of Americans identifying with multiple racial identities have increased, marrying across racial lines remains a rare event, accounting for approximately 1 percent of white marriages, 5 percent of black marriages, and 14 percent of Asian marriages with differences in patterns by ethnicity. Asians, for example, intermarry almost exclusively with whites.[10]

Another example of individual behavior within these broader demographic categories is that of religion. Most Americans are devout, and religion has figured prominently in American political development. The role of various churches in abolitionist movements and, later, the Civil Rights Movement shows the centrality of churches in important social movements in U.S. history. Even away from large historical events such as abolition or civil rights, church membership is an important part of social and political life. At a minimum a church can be seen as an important means by which identities are structured and reinforced: Being a member of group X involves regular attendance at a place of worship. Many places of worship—whether it is a church, mosque, synagogue, or temple—also offer a range of additional programs and services that further bolster identity. Summer camps, language instruction, and social events are examples of services that help to support the mission of the faith while at the same time extending the sense of community and supporting the identity of that community. Through the building and extension of social capital, religious faiths also build and extend identity.

Many of these political consequences are implicit. A church may run a day camp during summer simply to help children or, possibly, raise some revenue. The fact that it helps build identities is often something of an afterthought. But sometimes churches are quite explicitly political. Squaring explicit political action with the constitutional demands of separation between church and state can be a challenge, but faiths can, and do, express political involvement. This might be support in large numbers of candidates (for example, the Christian Coalition and the Republican Party in the 1990s), or it may be of specific issues. For example, both the Catholic and Mormon Churches gave explicit support to campaigns to limit gay marriage in California's Proposition 8 in 2008. Churches, then, have important political consequences in both implicit and explicit ways.

When we note that most Americans are devout, we mean that Americans regardless of race and ethnicity are devout. It is worth underscoring both how important religious identities are and, also, how they relate to the patterns of Table 2-1. The type of faith adhered to by Americans varies by ethnicity. Table 2-5 shows patterns of faith by ethnicity, and there are clear, and quite

TABLE 2-5   Religious Affiliation of Race and Ethnic Groups (in percentages)

	Total	Non-Hispanic White	Black	Asian	Latino
Protestant	51	53	78	27	23
Catholic	24	22	5	17	58
Mormon	2	2	< 0.5	1	1
Jehovah's Witness	1	< 0.5	1	< 0.5	1
Jewish	2	2	< 0.5	< 0.5	< 0.5
Muslim	1	< 0.5	1	4	< 0.5
Buddhist	1	1	< 0.5	9	< 0.5
Hindu	< 0.5	< 0.5	< 0.5	14	< 0.5
Unaffiliated	16	16	12	23	14
	100%	100%	100%	100%	100%

Source: Pew Forum on Religion & Public Life. 2008. "U.S. Religious Landscape Survey." http://religions.pew forum.org/pdf/report-religious-landscape-study-full.pdf (accessed April 25, 2010).

straightforward, variations: Latinos are heavily Catholic, African Americans predominantly Protestant.

Martin Luther King once observed—at least so far as blacks and whites are concerned—"The 11 o'clock hour on Sunday is the most segregated hour in American life." This seems to be less true for some faiths and churches than others. For example, roughly 30 percent of U.S. Catholics and a 25 percent of U.S. Jehovah's Witnesses are now Latino. But still, denominational divisions mean that to some extent churchgoing remains a socially segregated activity.[11]

POLITICAL CONSEQUENCE OF THE SPATIAL DISTRIBUTION: AN EXAMPLE

The patterns and processes examined in this chapter have political consequences. Take, for example, a very simple consequence: the composition of the electorate. As Figure 2-7 shows, the electorate—or at least the number of eligible voters (a distinction we make clearer in a following chapter)—is growing more racially and ethnically diverse. Given population growth from immigration and births, this trend will continue.

The change in the composition of the electorate is a fairly straightforward political consequence of the change in composition of the population. But, as

FIGURE 2-7 **Racial and Ethnic Composition of the Electorate**

Racial and Ethnic Composition of Eligible Voters 1988–2008

	1988	1992	1996	2000	2004	2008
(top)	1	1.5	2.1	2.5	3.3	3.4
Asian	4.7	4.9	6.2	7.1	8.2	9.5
Latino	11.1	11.3	11.7	11.2	11.6	11.8
White	82.1	81.6	79.2	77.7	75.2	73.4

Legend: Asian □ Latino ■ African American ■ White

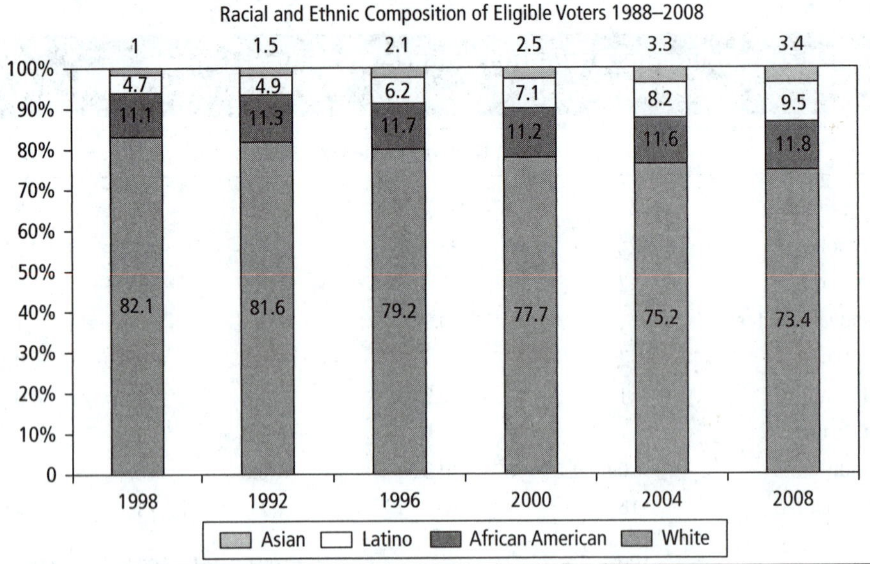

Source: Mark Hugo Lopez. Pew Hispanic Center," Dissecting the 2008 Electorate: Most Diverse in U.S. History." Figure 2, April 30, 2009. http://pewresearch.org/pubs/1209/racial-ethnic-voters-presidential-election (accessed April 25, 2010).

in the example of a "graying" population with which we began this discussion, some of these consequences may not be immediately obvious. We can illustrate how far reaching these consequences may be by taking the Schelling model of "tipping," which we described earlier. Schelling's interest in that model lay in trying to understand "white flight" from U.S. cities. In the decades following World War II, whites began leaving cities—especially in the Northeast—and moving into the suburbs. As the Schelling model illustrates, this shift of whites need not have reflected widespread and deeply entrenched bigotry in order to take place. All that was required was for people to have, on average, a preference for living with more people like themselves. On the other hand, the presence of entrenched bigotry would only exacerbate the process in terms of pace and depth. Whatever the case, Schelling shows us that once people began to act on that preference, it had a self-sustaining momentum. If one person moved to the suburbs, meaning there were fewer whites in a neighborhood, this would prompt another person to move, and when that person moved, that would mean there would be even fewer white families in the neighborhood, prompting someone else to move, and so on until the neighborhood was emptied of Anglos.

But, you might think, so what? So some people sort themselves out to be with people they like. That is not too different from what happens at tables in school cafeterias—it simply reflects what some people want—where is the politics? Once we have segregated areas, then other events follow on that are political. First, we may see attempts to keep neighborhoods relatively homogenous through political channels. This is easiest to see in condos and housing associations, where rules often regulate what residents can and cannot do in some detail. But other laws and rules—on zoning, on mortgages and mortgage lending—can be used to maintain segregation at least on the basis of income. What may have begun as a preference ended up as something much more institutionalized in laws and rules and housing codes, all of which can and do involve political fights and disputes at the local level.

Second, what we saw during the period of white flight was a downward spiral for many American cities. As people left the cities, so did business and tax revenue, and lower tax revenues mean declining services, which prompted more people to leave. Even if people did not particularly care about the racial and ethnic composition of the street they lived on, they may have cared about the schools their kids went to or the crime rate; such people would leave for the suburbs, further depressing tax revenue. That downward spiral meant more inequality in public services between minority and Anglo areas.

One public service that became especially contentious was that of education. In the 1971 decision of *Swann v. Charlotte-Mecklenburg Board of Education*[12] the U.S. Supreme Court mandated busing as a means of redressing inequalities in education, a policy that generated a long series of protests and displays of public opposition. The introduction of busing in turn helped to promote the spread of private education as wealthier white families fled the public school system to move their children into private schools, but it still might have had the overall desired effect were it not for the follow-up case of *Milliken v. Bradley* (1974).[13] This decision restricted busing to within school district boundaries, which had the effect of actually incentivizing white flight by redefining district lines as impenetrable walls behind which suburban parents could "shield" their children from desegregation efforts. In short, while the underlying process of white flight might be represented by a few pennies and nickels on a chess board, the political, economic, and social consequences of residential segregation have rippled throughout the postwar period in cities across the United States in disagreements over education, housing, and city services.

The historical experience has varied greatly, since the levels of demographic diversity vary cross-sectionally, as do the attitudes held by non-Hispanic whites. Some states have large black populations, while others have almost no African Americans. Some cities are multiethnic with no clear majority, while others have large white or black majorities that shape city politics. While the "traditional" pattern of racial competition has been white/black, immigration has created newer environments at the city, metropolitan, and state levels where three, four, or even five racial and ethnic identities contend for power and policy outcomes. Demographic patterns, in short, have political consequences.

THE COMPARABILITY AND EFFECTS OF RACIAL AND ETHNIC IDENTIFICATION ACROSS GROUPS

By now you should be sold on two central claims. First, we have attempted to persuade the reader that recent demographic changes in the United States with regard to the racial and ethnic composition of the population are historic in size, scope, and composition. Second, we have examined the many nuances of racial and ethnic identification that would suggest caution regarding conclusions about future categories and distributions.

But to what end? That is, why do racial and ethnic identities matter to politics? Earlier in Chapter 1 and the early pages of this chapter, we alluded to the considerable variation between the political preferences of whites and nonwhites in the United States and to the historic role of race as a central feature of American politics.

Here we turn our attention to the claim that racial identity is a key feature of understanding American politics. We focus first on why identity has been shown to matter, as a political resource and a method of mobilization and information processing that is pivotal in helping racial and ethnic minority groups effectively engage the political process and secure desired outcomes. Second, we will focus on whether the earliest findings on identity, rooted in the historical and political experience of African Americans, can be reasonably extended to groups such as Asian Americans and Latinos, whose cultural and historic roots reflect less the common historic experiences that so bind African Americans together.

Political Effect of Identity: A Foundational Example

In the early 1980s the sociologist William Julius Wilson published the now canonical study *The Declining Significance of Race* (1980). In it he contended that the central struggle for black America was disadvantage, that African American movement into the middle class was well under way, and that beyond race (which was by no means gone as a social predictor), we needed to look to class segmentation and subordination to understand African American life. Part of his observations included the socioeconomic diversification of African Americans, which would inevitably lead to a diversity of policy preferences and, ultimately, party allegiances and voting behavior.

Challenging this view is Michael Dawson's *Behind the Mule* (1994). For starters, Dawson challenges Wilson's estimation of black mobility, illustrating that African American income earners in the middle class were often in the lower reaches of that range, frequently worked in the public sector, and therefore continued to rely on the discretion of others as to how long they remained in that class. They usually had far less wealth—net assets as opposed to income—than other Americans deemed middle class. As a consequence, economic diversification was fragile, and it has yet to be associated with any meaningful political diversification. Most African Americans hold policy positions that they believe serve the interests of the entire group (and especially the common economic conditions within the group), and partisan identity is so skewed as to approach virtual unanimity.

Dawson concluded that class remained firmly subordinate to race in the political calculi of African American citizens. African Americans of all classes remain distinctly aware of the economic and social vulnerability of the black majority. For many African Americans, the salience of their racial identity, the emotional and social importance of their "blackness," and the sense that the entire group faces collective obstacles to economic and political power form the basis of a sense of "linked fate," that what happens to the group will have a great deal to do with the life's chances and prospects of the individual.

Linked fate serves as a resource for mobilization; it can be activated by elites, advocacy groups, and candidates for public office for the purpose of mobilizing the group in the pursuit of collective ends (Bobo and Gilliam 1990; Uhlaner 1989). Disadvantaged by their relative lack of resources, African Americans may be brought to the polls in surprisingly high numbers on the basis of strong in-group affinity and sense of group purpose.

Moreover, African Americans, Dawson (1994) suggests, use this collective identity as an important information shortcut, one able to simplify and organize the political world. When faced with a new issue or policy proposal, African Americans can make sense of it through the use of the "black utility heuristic," that is, evaluating alternatives on the basis of how they might affect the collective interests of black citizens (Bobo, Dawson, and Johnson 2001). Racial identity, then, serves as a proto-ideology to impose what Phil Converse (1964) might understand as "constraint" on African American policy attitudes.

This coherence in policy attitudes further serves the goal of mobilization, in that internal divisions on matters of policy are seldom—though clearly not never, see Cohen (1999)—able to derail efforts at mobilization and electoral impact.

As a consequence, levels of political participation among African Americans far exceed what we might expect based on a socioeconomic model of participation (Uhlaner et al. 1989). Apart from the usual resources of education and income, black voters and candidates can draw on the resource of group consciousness and solidarity to mobilize turnout and accumulate votes behind a single preference or candidate.

The Importance of Linked Fate

Few books on race politics have had the impact of *Behind the Mule*. Dawson provided a plausible explanation for the profound partisan skew in the black community, one that persisted stubbornly even as some African Americans found their way into the American economic fast track. Race provided a way for group members to both organize the political world and make sense of new issues, and the in-group ties could be used to great effect to help the group have greater electoral impact, even in the absence of the money and education that usually characterize systematic repeat voters.

This notion of collective identity and its implications may well, however, be a point of distinction between African Americans and other minority groups. The experience of slavery gives to African Americans a shared—and brutal—history. The different national origins of other minority groups imply less sharing and commonality. Sometimes, indeed, historical experiences in originating countries have been ones of conflict within minority groups now in the United States. Twentieth-century history, for example, contains examples of bitter and violent conflict between Japan and Korea and between Japan and China that must surely limit the claim of common historical memory for descendants of these national groups. While there have clearly been efforts at group-based appeals for political participation, usually emanating from advocacy organizations or elected officials, it is fair to say that neither Asian Americans nor Latinos enjoy anywhere near this level of group-based solidarity from which to build a political movement (Junn and Masuoka 2008a; Junn and Masuoka 2008b; Masuoka 2008). In fact, the very "group-ness" of Latinos and Asian Americans (Espiritu 1992; Tam 1995) is a notion that is still the subject of considerable contestation.

The principal obstacle for both groups, to different degrees, is the fundamental mismatch between the pan-ethnic identifier as a political concept and a social reality that, in fact, is primarily driven by ethnic identity and national origin. Most work on pan-ethnic identity among Latinos, for example, has found that while Latinos strongly identify with their national origin group (that is, Mexicans), or something along these lines, their attachment to the pan-ethnic identity "Latino" is far less strong, often secondary or missing altogether (Jones-Correa and Leal 1996). This is, in part, due to the considerable heterogeneity across Latino national origin groups, both political and experiential (Garcia 1982; Stokes 2003). In addition, until fairly recently the Latino social experience has been one that has been segmented geographically as well as along national origin lines. Puerto Ricans were a predominantly northeastern population, Cubans in South Florida, and Mexican Americans in Texas, California, and the American Southwest. Pan-ethnicity as a concept is not particularly meaningful when the totality of an individual's social connections to other Latinos is confined to a single national origin group.

Not surprisingly, it is in cases in which enclaves of residents from multiple national origin groups live in close proximity where pan-ethnicity, as an identity or political resource, becomes more relevant. Padilla (1985) identified just such a process in metropolitan Chicago, where the proximity of Mexican and Puerto Rican populations and shared histories of political and economic exclusion made the conditions particularly favorable for the emergence of a Latino pan-ethnic identity that had political meaning.

In 1985, however, Padilla's Chicago was comparatively unique. By contrast, population increase and geographic dispersion throughout the past two decades have, together, substantially increased the likelihood that Latinos of multiple national origin groups live and work in close proximity. Cubans, for example, now represent only about one-third of Florida's Latinos, having been joined by substantial Puerto Rican, Dominican, Colombian, Venezuelan, and even Mexican populations. Both Mexicans and Dominicans have joined New York City's preexisting Puerto Rican population in large and politically significant numbers. Central Americans, primarily Salvadoran, Guatemalan, and Nicaraguan, are present in large numbers in Southern California, where they must coexist and possibly cooperate with Mexican Americans, and in the Washington, D.C., area, where the local community includes substantial South American (especially Colombian) populations. There are many more places in this society today, then, where Latino populations are sufficiently diverse to make pan-ethnic identification and cooperation a relevant issue. Pan-ethnicity is more likely to matter as an aspect of group identity when national origin identity is no longer sufficient to capture the locally relevant population.

In such environments a pan-ethnic identity and an accompanying political consciousness simultaneously improve both the likelihood that disparate national origin groups of Latinos will identify shared political and social circumstances and interests and, importantly for political purposes, enlarge the group making the claim. Candidates with Hispanic surnames can seek and receive support across communities in a pan-ethnic paradigm that they could not if the relevant and dominant political identities were ethnic-specific. Similarly, voting rights claims under the standard handed down in *Thornburg v. Gingles* (1986) require groups of sufficient size and political unity, a threshold more easily reached when pan-ethnic Latino unity is a political reality.

Can a pan-ethnic identity serve as a political resource for Latinos to the same degree that racial identity and solidarity does for African Americans? For now, we suspect that the answer is no. Among the most recent explorations of this question is Stokes's (2003), in which she finds that while there is some evidence of a connection between identity and political participation, it is modest and varies considerably in form and process across the different Latino national origin groups.

It is important to note, however, that pan-ethnic sentiments are not necessarily a *sine qua non* of mobilization and representation when subgroup members are present in sufficient numbers. For example, Puerto Rican activism in New York City politics, Cuban dominance of Miami, and Mexican American influence in Los Angeles did not historically depend on pan-ethnic identity, since each group was sufficiently strong in the specific local context to flex political muscles on its own (Hero 1992). In these contexts, strong national origin identities are sufficient to serve as a resource for political action. But for Latinos to exert power on a national stage in a manner similar to that of African Americans, such an effort would no doubt be easier if Cubans, Puerto Ricans, Mexican Americans, and other Latino subgroups saw themselves as part of a larger identity with shared interests.

Pan-ethnicity as a politically useful identity is even more problematic for Asians (Tam 1995; Aoki and Nakanishi 2001). Though ethnically and even racially diverse, Latinos have a common language and, in large measure, common religious identity. The globalization and integration of Spanish-language media serve to provide common cultural mileposts. The terms *Latino* and *Hispanic* convey both cultural and geographic proximity.

By contrast, the group "Asian Americans" contains numerous languages, traditions, religious identities, and even histories of national conflict. What Asians primarily share in common is signified by the pan-ethnic terminology used—geography. As a consequence, pan-ethnic identity has historically not been politically relevant. Models of political participation, preferences, and partisanship all demonstrate substantial between-group differences across Asian national origin groups (Lien 2001). Moreover, the significantly smaller population size, when compared with Latinos or African Americans, makes this an even greater problem for Asians than Latinos in that there are seldom sufficient subgroup populations to allow for national identity to substitute for a racialized one in making claims on the political system. While locales have emerged with sufficient Asian population to exert local political power, at the national level the problem of numbers will continue to be vexing for Asian Americans, as national origin groups or a pan-ethnic identity, for some time to come.

While linked fate and the black utility heuristic provided Dawson with the answer to the questions raised by the mismatch between Wilson's expectations and political reality, it is less clear that these two critical concepts can move very easily into a discussion of Latinos or Asian Americans. Nevertheless, it is certainly worth exploration. As we will show in our discussions of two-party competition and public opinion on policy, both Latinos and Asian Americans do have a collective identity, at least insofar as manifestations of preferences and behaviors exhibit collective characteristics and clear segmentation from whites. If this is a manifestation of in-group identification and solidarity, then we might reasonably expect the skew in party and policy preferences to continue, with significant political effect.

SUMMARY

While the patterns of Table 2-1 tell a particular story, that story is, as we have argued, subject to some important qualifications. In the following chapters we will still use terms such as *Latino* or *Asian American* as a convenient shorthand. That said, the various qualifications and caveats that we have mentioned in the six points of nuance, as well as our uncertainty regarding the equivalence of identity as a political force and resource across racial and ethnic minority groups in the United States, suggest we should use those terms with some caution. They are simplifications that may be convenient, but sometimes they simplify away too many things, and so we should treat the labels with some caution.

For the most part our discussion of some simple demographic trends has shown what we know from personal experience: the everyday lives of Americans are often separated by race and ethnicity. People live, marry, and worship within communities of people like them. There are, as we have seen, some points of contact: more marriages across communities, resulting in more children who have multiple identities. There are also more churches that have more diverse congregations. The patterns of Table 2-1 and Figure 2-1 illustrate quite a lot of diversity in aggregate but not necessarily so much in the individual level everyday lives of many people.

Of course, we might want to distinguish between ordinary people (masses) and the leaders of political or social organizations (elites). While masses may not come in contact with people from members of other groups all that often, except, perhaps, at work, this is less true of elites. Take the simple example of city politics used above—New Orleans, Los Angeles, and Memphis. In those cities the racial and ethnic balance means that political leaders and candidates from one group will have to meet and do business with political leaders, leaders of organizations, and church leaders from racial and ethnic groups different from their own. Changing racial balances means that political leaders have to make more of an effort to engage across racial group boundaries in meaningful ways, especially perhaps in city politics.[14]

At the mass level, however, separate institutions catering to non-Hispanic whites might have a few more empty seats than they used to. The trends we examined in the composition of the American public show that after a long period of stability in white population share, that number has dropped precipitously while the collective share of Americans who are African American, Asian American, Native American, Latino, or of mixed race has climbed to almost 35 percent.

The previous point does bring us to more obviously political kinds of questions in relation to Table 2-1. The changing population implies a changing citizenry that is comparable to changing the franchise. At the beginning of the twentieth century, extending the vote to women meant that the political system had to accommodate millions of different voices, as did allowing African Americans to exercise their rights as Americans. Similarly, previous waves of immigration meant that the political system had to accommodate millions of different voices then, as well. The political system accommodated those new voices. From our perspective looking back on the century where those changes took place, the accommodations seem inevitable and natural . . . of course women should be allowed to vote, of course African Americans should be allowed to vote, and so on. But those changes did not seem so natural at the time.

Now we have some new changes—new voices, accented voices added to the system—younger, more blue-collar, more immigrant than at any time in 100 years. How they respond to the political system—and how the political system responds to them—poses an obvious set of questions: How will these different groups turn out and vote? And for whom? If the patterns of Tables 2-3 and 2-4 are anything to go by, then we are seeing substantial changes in electorates in a number of states with clear potential to influence the kinds of candidates who win and the kinds of policies they propose. These changes challenge our conventional wisdom regarding political behavior and party competition, and we suggest they will significantly shape the political system in the coming era.

chapter 3

Electoral Competition and the Democratic Reliance on Minority Vote

I n this chapter we pay closer attention to the role American minorities play in determining electoral outcomes. Specifically, we will focus on the degree to which Democratic politicians are dependent on minority votes to get elected. Our central claim is that the electoral coalition underpinning Democratic victories in national and most statewide races is critically reliant on the minority vote. Non-white voters therefore already play a key role in determining election outcomes for the Democratic Party as the Republican Party becomes, in effect, a white political party.

On the one hand these demographic trends look set to enlarge and cement Democratic political dominance, if not in the near term, then in the long. But that is the case only if we are willing to assume that party preferences within each racial and ethnic group remain relatively constant. As we argue below, if economic mobility and social change trigger substantial diversification of partisan and candidate preferences among non-white voters, and/or if the Republican Party changes strategy, the Democrats could be sunk.

RACIAL IDENTITY AND CANDIDATE VIABILITY

When we evaluate the degree to which race might impact an electoral contest, there are two avenues worthy of consideration. First, and most obviously, candidates from racial and ethnic minority groups may face old-fashioned discrimination; that is, some percentage of the electorate, for reasons rooted in the array of attitudes we generally associate with "racism," in its purest form, refuse to vote for candidates from other racial and ethnic groups (Hurlbert 1989; Segura and Fraga 2008). Citizens who hold stereotypical and negative beliefs about candidates from other racial and ethnic groups would be hard pressed to vote for such a candidate, even if the candidate was very similar to the voter on many, most, or even all issues.

The election of Barack Obama was something of a surprise, then, to political science, since it violated well-established findings in the discipline regarding the willingness of whites to vote for a candidate of color. Non-white candidates by and large do not win in majority-white constituencies (Lublin 1999; Epstein and O'Halloran 1999a and b; Canon et al. 1996). While there is some modest dissent in the research community by scholars focused on moments of electoral success (Thernstrom 2009; Swain 1993), the evidence is overwhelming that Latino and African American politicians *who are preferred by minority voters* struggle in constituencies where whites are a majority (Lublin 1999; Segura and Fraga 2008).

Over the past decade, a huge portion of African American and Latino members of Congress were initially elected from majority-minority districts, and the exceptions were indeed exceptional. A majority of the African American members to emerge from solidly white constituencies in recent memory were Republicans. Former members include Gary Franks of Connecticut and J. C. Watts of Oklahoma, the former a very liberal Republican elected in a Democratic-leaning district and the latter a former football standout at the University of Oklahoma (Watson 1998). Today Allen West (R-FL) and Tim Scott (R-SC) serve, both very conservative Republicans with very white constituencies (in the case of West, virtually an all-white constituency).

These two new Republican African American members of Congress illustrate issues of authenticity and representation implicit in a focus on minority elected officials, which we will discuss in greater length in Chapter 8. While polling at the district level is hard to come by, it is unlikely in the extreme that either Scott or West is the preferred candidate of most African American voters.

Evidence of racial polarization abounds at every level of government (Shaw 1997; Segura and Fraga 2008). One way of seeing this is to look at the number of elected officials by ethnicity. Table 3-1 reports the Latino or Hispanic membership in the House of Representatives in the 112th Congress. There are twenty-four members of the House who are of Latin American ancestral origin; seventeen are Democrats and seven Republicans. Only six of those twenty-four members were elected from districts in which Latinos are not an outright majority, three Democrats and three Republicans.

For the three Democrats, their electoral success is somewhat easy to explain. In two of those three cases, Latinos and African Americans together constitute a majority. The remaining case includes Ben Ray Luján from New Mexico. Though Luján's district is only about 38 percent Hispanic, the Third Congressional District of New Mexico is also around 19 percent Native American (and Luján himself lives in Nambé Pueblo), meaning the total minority population approaches 60 percent, no doubt contributing to his 27-point victory in the 2008 congressional election. The last Latino elected from a majority-white congressional district was John Salazar from Colorado, defeated for reelection in 2010. In short, no Latino Democrat is elected from a district without a majority-minority population.

The three Republicans representing majority-white districts—Jaime Herrera Beutler (R-WA-3), Bill Flores (R-TX-17), and Raul Labrador (R-ID-1)—were elected from districts in which Latino voters are irrelevant to the outcomes and largely Democratic in identity. That is, these Latinos were elected in a district where minority preferences have no political effect. We offer a detailed assessment of their election in 2010 in Chapter 8.

TABLE 3-1   Hispanic Members of the 112th Congress (House), with District Demographics

Name		State	District number	% Latino	% Black+ % Latino
Joe Baca	D	CA	43	65.8	
Xavier Becerra	D	CA	31	69.8	
Jaime Herrera Beutler	R	WA	3	4.6	
Francisco Canseco	R	TX	23	65.6	
Henry Cuellar	D	TX	28	79.1	
Mario Diaz-Balart	R	FL	25	68.9	
Bill Flores	R	TX	17	15.4	
Charlie Gonzalez	D	TX	20	69.6	
Raul M. Grijalva	D	AZ	7	55.1	
Luis V. Gutierrez	D	IL	4	73.0	
Ruben Hinojosa	D	TX	15	79.8	
Raul Labrador	R	ID	1	6.8	
Ben Ray Luján[1]	D	NM	3	38.3	40.0
Grace F. Napolitano	D	CA	38	74.8	
Ed Pastor	D	AZ	4	67.1	
Silvestre Reyes	D	TX	16	81.2	
David Rivera	R	FL	25	68.9	
Ileana Ros-Lehtinen	R	FL	18	63.9	
Lucille Roybal-Allard	D	CA	34	80.8	
Linda T. Sanchez	D	CA	39	65.8	
Loretta Sanchez	D	CA	47	70.2	
Jose E. Serrano	D	NY	16	66.1	
Albio Sires	D	NJ	13	48.4	60.5
Nydia M. Velazquez	D	NY	12	46.0	54.1

Note: Shaded cells represent four Latino Republicans elected in 2010.

[1]Luján's district is also 19.6 percent Native American.

In 2011 there are forty-two African American members of the House of Representatives and all but two are Democrats (see Table 3-2). Only five of the forty Democrats represent districts without a black or "black + Latino" majority, and two of those—Barbara Lee (D-CA, Ninth) and Gwen Moore (D-WI, Fourth)—represent districts in Oakland, California and Milwaukee, Wisconsin, in which the total minority population is well over 40 percent,

TABLE 3-2 African American Members of the 112th Congress (House), with District Demographics

Name	Party	State	District number	% Black	% Black + % Latino
Karen Bass	D	CA	33	26.8	63.2
Sanford D. Bishop Jr.	D	GA	2	48.3	51.2
Corrine Brown	D	FL	3	52.3	
G. K. Butterfield	D	NC	1	49.9	53.8
Andre Carson	D	IN	7	30.8	38.4
Hansen Clarke	D	MI	13	58.7	
Yvette D. Clarke	D	NY	11	55.7	
William Lacy Clay	D	MO	1	54.4	
Emanuel Cleaver II	D	MO	5	24.2	32.2
James E. Clyburn	D	SC	6	55.4	
John Conyers Jr.	D	MI	14	61.3	
Elijah E. Cummings	D	MD	7	58.1	
Danny K. Davis	D	IL	7	53.5	
Donna Edwards	D	MD	4	55.3	
Keith Ellison	D	MN	5	13.4	22.3
Chaka Fattah	D	PA	2	59.5	
Marcia L. Fudge	D	OH	11	58.8	
Al Green	D	TX	9	37.7	76.6
Alcee L. Hastings	D	FL	23	53.6	
Jesse L. Jackson Jr.	D	IL	2	66.9	
Sheila Jackson Lee	D	TX	18	38.3	80.2
Eddie Bernice Johnson	D	TX	30	38.6	81.5
Hank Johnson	D	GA	4	55.9	
Barbara Lee	D	CA	9	21.8	43.2
John Lewis	D	GA	5	50.1	
Gregory W. Meeks	D	NY	6	51.1	
Gwen Moore	D	WI	4	34.3	49.7
Donald M. Payne	D	NJ	10	55.9	
Charles B. Rangel	D	NY	15	27.7	72.5
Laura Richardson	D	CA	37	23.1	70.6
Cedric Richmond	D	LA	2	64.1	
Bobby L. Rush	D	IL	1	64.7	
David Scott	D	GA	13	54.5	
Robert C. Scott	D	VA	3	54.3	
Tim Scott	R	SC	1	21.1	
Terri Sewell	D	AL	7	63.5	
Bennie Thompson	D	MS	2	66.4	
Edolphus Towns	D	NY	10	60.6	
Maxine Waters	D	CA	35	30.6	82.9
Melvin Watt	D	NC	12	44.1	54.1
Allen West	R	FL	22	3.8	
Frederica Wilson	D	FL	17	56.3	

Note: Shaded cells represent two African American Republicans elected in 2010.

and with strong Democratic majorities, thereby classifying both districts as "minority influence." The remaining three are Andre Carson's district in metropolitan Indianapolis, Emanuel Cleaver's in Kansas City, Missouri, and surrounding areas, and Keith Ellison's in Minneapolis. Each district has a clear white majority whose support is critical to the election of these three members. In the case of Cleaver and Ellison, the partisan complexion of the districts is heavily Democratic; Carson's is the most competitive. In summary, 92.3 percent of all African American Democrats serving in the House are elected from majority-black, majority-minority, or minority-influence districts. Nevertheless, the election of three African Americans from majority-white constituencies represents an important break from the historical pattern and a significant improvement in black electoral fortunes. The two newly elected African American Republicans, who we profile in Chapter 8, were elected in overwhelmingly white districts and without meaningful black support.

This pattern is repeated at others levels of government. In general, elected officials share the race or ethnicity of the majority population in the jurisdiction they represent, and an overwhelming share of minority candidates tend to be Democrats. As in the case of the House of Representatives, exceptions to this pattern are so rare as to be able to be identified by name. Among the best known, Douglas Wilder (VA), Deval Patrick (MA), Bill Richardson (NM), Susana Martinez (NM), and Brian Sandoval (NV) were elected governors of their respective states, and Edward Brooke (MA), Carol Moseley-Braun (IL), Mel Martinez (FL), Robert Menendez (NJ), Ken Salazar (CO), Barack Obama (IL), and Marco Rubio (FL) were elected to the U.S. Senate from majority-white states.

Even in these successful minority candidacies, however, some important caveats bear noting. First, minority Republicans can be uniquely advantaged. As GOP nominees, they can count on substantial white support from a nearly-all-white party while still attracting substantial crossover voting from communities of color on the Democratic side (Barreto 2007, 2010). Brooke, Mel Martinez, Susana Martinez, Sandoval, and Rubio were Republicans and therefore benefited in this way, and both Martinez and Rubio represent the best-known majority-GOP community of color in the country, south Florida Cubans. Additionally, Mosley-Braun was defeated for reelection, Menendez was originally appointed before facing the voters, Richardson's state is approximately 45 percent Latino, and Obama faced only token opposition in the wake of a scandal that drove the elected GOP nominee from the race.

Nevertheless, it is fair to say that black and Latino candidates have occasionally broken through. But placed in the context of all gubernatorial and senatorial elections, and recognizing that African Americans and Latinos together compose over a quarter of the nation's population, these breakthroughs are best understood as exceptional. Minority election to public office in majority-white constituencies remains extremely uncommon, particularly at higher levels of government.

It is worth noting that Asian Americans do not fit this pattern precisely. Outside of the state of Hawaii, where 41.65 percent of residents in the 2000 census reported being Asian American (and fully 58 percent reported being either fully Asian or of mixed ancestry including an Asian identity), there are few places in America where Asians are sufficiently populous to secure electoral dominance in a geographic constituency (U.S. Census Bureau 2002). As a consequence, outside of Hawaii, Asian representatives generally do *not* represent majority-Asian constituencies. And lacking Asian-majority constituencies, there are very few places where Asian Americans have broken through. In fact, outside of Hawaii, only three governors (Gary Locke, D-WA; Bobby Jindal, R-LA; and Nikki Haley R-SC) have been elected, and only S. I. Hayakawa (R-CA) was elected to the Senate. Today there are two Asian American members of the Senate, Japanese American Daniel Inouye and mixed Chinese American and native Hawaiian Islander Daniel Akaka, both representing Hawaii.[1] In addition, a handful of Asian Americans serve in the House of Representatives, including Judy Chu, Doris Matsui, and Mike Honda (all D-CA), Steve Austria (R-OH), Bobby Scott (D-VA), Mazie Hirono (D-HI), Colleen Hanabusa (D-HI), Hansen Clarke (D-MI), and David Wu (D-OR) (see Table 3-3). In the cases of Chu, Hanabusa, Hirono, Honda, and Matsui, the districts did have significant Asian populations, but only Hanabusa's is majority-Asian and, excluding Hirono's, none of the rest could even be broadly considered an Asian-"influence" district. Chu, elected in a special election, actually represents a majority-Latino district (62.3 percent) but defeated a Latino primary opponent to go on to represent the Democrats in the general election in this heavily Democratic district. Both Clarke and Scott are of mixed ancestry that includes

TABLE 3-3   Asian American Members of the 112th Congress (House), with District Demographics

Name	Self-identification	Party	State	District number	% Asian in congressional district
Steve Austria	Filipino	R	OH	7	0.9
Judy Chu	Chinese	D	CA	32	18.4
Hansen Clarke	African American/Bangladeshi	D	MI	13	1.2
Colleen Hanabusa	Japanese	D	HI	1	54.3
Mazie Hirono	Japanese	D	HI	2	31.1
Mike Honda	Japanese	D	CA	15	17.6
Doris Matsui	Japanese	D	CA	5	15.5
Robert C. Scott	African American/Filipino	D	VA	3	1.4
David Wu	Chinese	D	OR	1	5.0

both Asian and African American forbears and were elected from majority-black districts.

The point, of course, is that it is tough sledding for non-white candidates outside of constituencies where their racial/ethnic group holds at least a plurality of votes. We have more to say about representation in Chapter 8, but this pattern of electability is fairly well established at every level of government. There are many possible explanations for why this pattern of exclusion exists. Consequently there is hot debate regarding the mechanisms at work. It could be due to racial polarization in voting (whites will not vote for minority candidates) or it could be due to patterns within the parties themselves. Patterns of candidate recruitment and campaign funding may disadvantage minority candidates (Highton 2004). Part of the difficulty in sorting through these explanations is that they tend to reinforce each other in a self-fulfilling prophecy: a candidate who has a slim chance of winning will not attract many donors, further depressing the candidate's chances and turning off more donors.

Some of these patterns are seen less severely at the local level. There are many more minority elected officials at the local level elected with the help of white votes. This is especially the case *after* a minority has been elected to office (Hajnal 2001). That is, once voters (and donors) have seen a minority candidate perform well in office, then they are much more willing to support that candidate in subsequent elections. Of course, the problem for minority candidates remains winning in that first election, and in any case this trend has not emerged in higher levels of office.

RACE AND PARTY COALITIONS

Debates about the race of the candidate, while important in helping us to understand something about how elections work (for example, the role of self-fulfilling prophecies) and about descriptive representation, do tend to shift focus away from a deeper point: Race is deeply embedded in the coalitional structure and policy platform of the American party system. It is probably an overstatement to say that American politics is really a story about race, but it is the case that race and racial issues have formed a central part of American political debate and American elections in the post–World War II period, at least so far as domestic politics is concerned.

Specifically, racial attitudes of white voters, coupled with the long-standing issue concerns of the political parties with respect to the interests of minority Americans, inject the effects of racial and ethnic animus into partisan elections, even when both candidates are white. To the extent that one political party is more closely associated with the interests of African Americans and Latinos, voters harboring resentment, prejudice, or other negative emotions for those groups are less likely to vote for candidates from that party. But more than voting alone, the issue basis of parties has also been shaped by the politics of race.

Since the 1960s the association of the Democratic Party with the interests of non-white Americans has served simultaneously to closely connect minority voters with Democratic candidates and to signal to a sizable number of white voters that the Democratic Party is not their natural home. In the last presidential election, in 2008, the Democratic Party received approximately 95 percent of the African American vote, 67 percent of the Latino vote, 62 percent of the Asian American vote, and 66 percent of all "others" (including a significant number of indigenous and mixed-race voters) in the national exit polls, compared with a mere 43 percent of white votes. Such a substantial gap is both a good indicator of the racial element of the party coalitions as well as a visible reminder to all voters of the degree to which political parties can be associated with group interests.

While 2008's was obviously an unusual election, the racial basis of party coalitions is not specific to that election. We can, for example, examine the racial and ethnic presidential vote on Sen. John Kerry in 2004, and in the congressional elections of 2006, as points of comparison. According to the exit polls,[2] John Kerry also received a minority of the white vote and majorities from all other groups. Kerry's share of the national popular vote was 48 percent overall, but exit polls place his share of the white vote at a mere 41 percent, while his share of the African American vote was 88 percent, his share of the Latino vote at least 53 percent,[3] his share of the Asian American vote was 56 percent, and his share of all "others" 54 percent (see Table 3-4). Though his overall minority voter percentages were not as high as Obama's, Kerry's white vote share was worse, and there was significant polarization between whites and non-whites. Voting in the 2006 congressional elections (we report the vote in House races here) was generally more Democratic in overall distributions, with the share of the national House ballots going to Democrats climbing to 53 percent, a healthy improvement on Kerry's 48 percent. Nevertheless, the polarization in vote by race and ethnicity remains strong. While the GOP's majority among whites was unusually modest at 51 percent, perhaps not surprising in a catastrophic election for them in which they lost control of both chambers of Congress, their share of the non-white constituencies' votes ranged from a high of 42 percent ("other race") to a low of 10 percent (African Americans). Finally, in the dramatic comeback of the GOP in the 2010 election, GOP white voter share appears to have climbed to 60 percent, according to the exit polls. But the pattern of polarization remains the same—a majority of every other racial and ethnic identity in the society cast their votes for Democrats. From the Democrats' surge to power in 2006 and 2008 to the GOP triumphs in 2004 and 2010, the pattern of preferences across all four elections is more alike than different.

These voting patterns are not just apparent to scholars and journalists—they are also widely known to voters and, hence, help shape party images in the minds of the voters (Mendelberg 2001; Baumer and Gold 1995). Whether motivated by anti-black or anti-Latino animus (Kinder and Sanders 1996; Segura and Valenzuela 2010) or simply a more race-neutral form of self

TABLE 3-4 National Popular Vote Share by Race and Ethnicity, 2004, 2006, 2008, and 2010

	2004 Presidential elections			2006 House elections			2008 Presidential elections			2010 House elections		
	Electorate share	Bush	Kerry	Electorate share	GOP	Dems	Electorate share	McCain	Obama	Electorate share	GOP	Dems
Whites (non-Hispanics)	77	58	41	79	51	47	74	55	43	78	60	37
African Americans	11	11	88	10	10	89	13	4	95	10	9	90
Asian Americans	2	44	56	2	37	62	2	35	62	1	40	56
Latinos or Hispanics	8	44	53	8	30	69	9	31	67	8	34	64
Others	2	40	54	2	42	55	3	31	66	2	43	53
Total		51	48		45	53		46	53		52	45

Source: National exit polls as tabulated by CNN, 2004 and 2008.

Notes: Cell entries are percentages and do not report vote for third parties; hence they may total less than 100. Electorate columns may not add to 100 owing to rounding.

interest, the association of Democrats with the interests of minorities has helped to cement white majorities behind GOP candidates, majorities that often include working-class and poor whites in southern states.[4] Of course, it was not always so. The parties have engaged in a long and historic inversion on the issues of race since the end of the Civil War, when the GOP was iden- tified as the party of the Union, Emancipation, and Reconstruction, until today, when the party is overwhelmingly white in both the electorate and in office and most successful in southern states, where race relations have been at the heart of a series of turning points in U.S. political development.

As we reported in Tables 3-1 to 3-3, the share of minority elected officials who are Democrats is exceedingly high. This may, in fact, be a product of the first dynamic we described—that is, the generally low willingness of whites to vote for candidates of color; but it serves mightily to reinforce the second dynamic—that is, if most minority elected officials are Democrats, it is easier for subtle and not-so-subtle campaign messages (Mendelberg 2001) to connect the interests of minorities with the Democrats in the minds of the white voters.

There is some evidence that there may be short-term political benefits from heightening that apparent connection. Take, for example, the Texas redis- tricting controversy in the mid-2000s. As part of a strategy to enlarge the GOP majority in the House of Representatives, then majority leader Tom DeLay persuaded a newly elected Texas GOP legislative majority to redraw congres- sional district lines in the middle of the decade, a practice usually reserved for the year following the decennial census on which seats are apportioned and redistricted. As with any gerrymander attempt, the new districts advantaged the party drawing the map, in this instance the Republicans. We would, there- fore, expect to see more Republican legislators and fewer Democrats after any such gerrymander.

Less visible, however, was the compositional effect on the Texas congres- sional delegation in terms of party and race. Prior to the redistricting, the results of the 2002 congressional elections produced 17 Democrats (of 32 seats in the House), which included 10 Anglos and 7 persons of color (2 African Americans and 5 Latinos). After the redistricting, the 12 remaining Democrats included 9 persons of color (6 Latinos and 3 African Americans, an increase of one each over the pre-DeLay districts), or 75 percent non-white, whereas every GOP member of the House from Texas was a non-Hispanic white. As for the 3 remaining white Democrats, 2 (Gene Green, Nineteenth Congressional Dis- trict [CD], and Lloyd Doggett, Twenty-Fifth CD) represent districts that are both almost two-thirds Hispanic. Both of those districts are exceedingly likely to elect Latino candidates upon the retirement of these very popular non- Hispanic incumbents. Only Chet Edwards, in the Seventeenth CD, represented an area with a solid white majority, and though he won the 2008 race for reelection with only 51.7 percent of the vote, he did not survive the 2010 elec- tion, losing, ironically, to a Latino, Bill Flores.

As it stands now, the Democratic delegation of nine seats includes seven racial and ethnic minorities, or 78 percent minority. Should Green's seat and

Doggett's seat be taken over by Hispanics upon their retirement, as we expect, the Texas Democratic delegation to the House would be 100 percent persons of color. The Republican delegation of twenty-three has two Latinos and twenty-one non-Hispanic whites, or 91 percent white. That is racial polarization.

In very general terms, the Democrats are the party of minority voters and the Republican Party is not. We can see this pattern repeated throughout the political system, from the White House, through Congress, to the states.

RACE AND PRESIDENTIAL ELECTIONS

When Barack Obama was elected to the presidency, his campaign was aided by substantial political winds at his back. The economic collapse in the fall of 2008, coupled with the deep personal unpopularity of the incumbent George W. Bush and persistent opposition to the war in Iraq meant that any Democratic candidate would have had a strong chance of winning that year. The Obama campaign built on these structural advantages by running a remarkably disciplined and effective campaign that included innovative get-out-the-vote strategies on top of any advantages from the candidate himself. This effort yielded a 53 percent majority in the popular vote and an even stronger performance in the Electoral College.

All of these advantages should be set against the backdrop of historic difficulties faced by candidates of color in majority-white constituencies. Obama's election represents a remarkable exception. Since the United States remains a majority-white electorate, Obama's win is another instance of that rare occurrence of a non-white candidate elected in a majority-white constituency. Lest we get too swayed by the importance of this outcome, we need to examine the nature of the electoral coalitions that underpin his success, and how and why that successful outcome was different from the previous election, when fellow Democrat John Kerry (D-MA) went down in defeat.

Neither Kerry nor Obama won a majority of the white vote. In fact, no Democrat has won a majority of the white vote since Lyndon Johnson did in 1964. John Kerry's performance of 41 percent among whites is actually quite consistent with the recent past. Gore was estimated to receive about 42 percent of the white vote in 2000. Bill Clinton got about 44 percent in 1996.[5] In fact, the high watermark for Democratic share of non-Hispanic white votes, since 1964, has been Jimmy Carter's 47 percent in 1976 (Noah 2008).

This brief account illustrates just how critical minority voters are to any prospects for Democratic victory. Summarizing the numbers we present in the last paragraph in simpler terms, if only whites had voted, Democrats would not have won any presidential election since 1964.

Just how big is this effect? Remember that presidential elections are really fifty state elections plus the District of Columbia. Figure 3-1 (A) represents the Electoral College map that resulted from the 2004 presidential election. In this fairly close contest, President Bush bested Senator Kerry 286–252, and as the

FIGURE 3-1 **Comparing the Electoral College Outcomes for the 2004 Presidential Election (states won by Kerry shaded)**

A. All voters, Bush 286 electoral votes, Kerry 252 electoral votes

B. Whites only, Bush 476 electoral votes, Kerry 62 electoral votes

Note: Exit polls in Oregon show a fifty-fifty breakdown of white vote.

election night dramatics made clear, a small shift of the vote in Ohio could have changed the outcome entirely. By contrast, Figure 3-1 (B) is an illustration of the Electoral College vote had only white Americans cast ballots. States shaded as "Democratic" are the only states in which a majority of non-Hispanic whites voted Democrat. The change is dramatic. Under this scenario, the race would have been a landslide, with President Bush receiving 476 electoral votes to Kerry's 62. Senator Kerry carried the white vote in his home state of Massachusetts and only seven other states. The exit polls suggest the Anglo vote in Oregon was too close to call.

At first blush this claim may not be convincing. After all, isn't assuming the loss of all minority votes an exaggerated and unreasonable scenario? Actually, it is a simple thought experiment but a telling one. It is essentially the same as assuming that minorities split their vote more or less evenly between the two parties. Our thought experiment, then, essentially asks: what if minorities found the GOP as appealing a party as the Democrats and distributed their votes more evenly than they do at present? If this were so, Kerry's loss would have been catastrophic.

How about 2008? Figure 3-2 (A) represents the Electoral College results of the 2008 election. Then senator Obama racked up a sizable victory over Sen. John McCain, receiving about 53 percent of the overall vote to McCain's 46 percent, and an impressive Electoral College total of 365 votes to McCain's 173. Though victory is surely preferred to defeat, and Obama clearly improved on Kerry's performance four years earlier, it is important to note that Obama still won only 43 percent of the non-Hispanic white vote, as we reported in Table 3-4. His strong majorities in the other racial and ethnic groups—95 percent of African Americans, 67 percent of Latinos, 62 percent of Asian Americans, and 66 percent of "others"—carried him to victory in many of the states he won. Figure 3-2 (B) illustrates the Electoral College map in the absence of minority voters. Although his performance is better than Kerry's, Obama's victory would have turned to substantial defeat, 315–223.

The map in Figure 3-2b is startling in comparison to the actual outcomes; however, fairness dictates that we note how improved it looks vis-à-vis Figure 3-1 (B). Obama outperformed Kerry among whites in many states and would still have managed to win sixteen states in the absence of minority support. It would not have been enough to secure a victory, but neither would it have been a landslide.

Obama's share of the non-Hispanic white vote varied quite widely, of course. In the sixteen states shaded in Figure 3-2b, he won a majority, but in others he did not do so well. Table 3-5 lists the eight states in which Obama's share of the non-Hispanic white vote was the smallest. In these states his share of the Anglo vote ranged from a high of 30 percent in Arkansas to a low of just 11 percent in Mississippi and 10 percent in Alabama. To place this in perspective, this means that while McCain received 55 percent of the white vote nationwide, in these states he won the votes of nine of every ten white voters.

FIGURE 3-2 **Comparing the Electoral College Outcomes for the 2008 Presidential Election (states won by Obama shaded)**

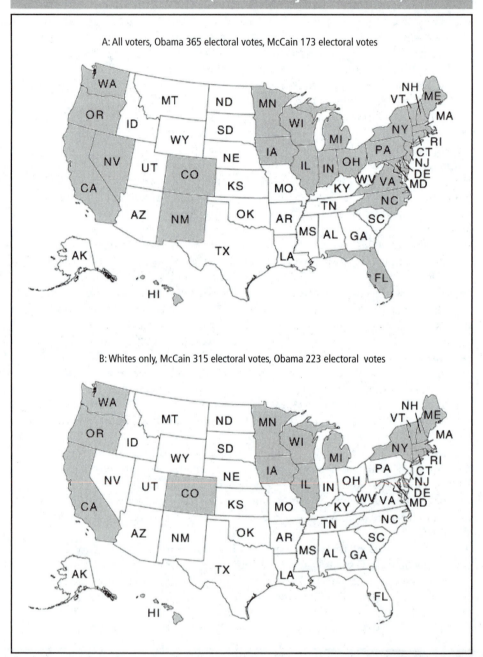

A: All voters, Obama 365 electoral votes, McCain 173 electoral votes

B: Whites only, McCain 315 electoral votes, Obama 223 electoral votes

TABLE 3-5   Selected States: Obama and Kerry Shares of Non-Hispanic White Vote, 2004–2008 (in percentages)

	Obama	Kerry	Change 2004–2008
Arkansas	30	36	−6
Oklahoma	29	29	—
South Carolina	26	22	4
Texas	26	34	−8
Georgia	23	23	—
Louisiana	14	24	−10
Mississippi	11	14	−3
Alabama	10	19	−9

Source: Edison Mitofsky exit polls, as reported by cnn.com.

Moreover, as Table 3-5 also reports, in all but one of these states, Obama either earned the same share of white votes that Kerry did or in fact saw the white voter share decline, in some instances sharply. Figure 3-3 illustrates the comparison of Obama and Kerry white vote shares. In unshaded states, Obama outperformed Kerry. In all of the rest, his white vote share was equal to or less than that of Kerry, despite having run a more effective campaign, with better funding, against an opponent facing difficult political winds. While some of those states were in New England, Senator Kerry's home region, it is difficult to ignore the regional concentration of the rest in the states of the Old South. In states such as Louisiana, Mississippi, Arkansas, and Alabama, the decline is substantial.[6]

It is worth noting that we might have presented these Electoral College maps in reverse, examining GOP electoral vote in the absence of white voters. It would not have been a particularly interesting presentation, in that every state would be shaded identically. In 2004 and 2008, indeed in elections spanning the last several generations, the GOP has polled a majority of minority voters in exactly zero states.

The comparison of the elections in 2004 and 2008 illustrates each of the dynamics we identified in the early parts of this chapter. First, Democratic electoral fortunes at the presidential level are closely intertwined with minority group preferences, and Democrats are generally not the preferred party for a majority of non-Hispanic white voters. Second, this is true when the nominee is white and therefore is not entirely a consequence of white unwillingness to vote for candidates of color. However, the comparison of the two elections also allows us to identify places where the generally improving fortunes of Democrats nationally were not matched locally. These places, which swam against the

FIGURE 3-3 **Comparison of Anglo Vote Shares for Kerry and Obama**

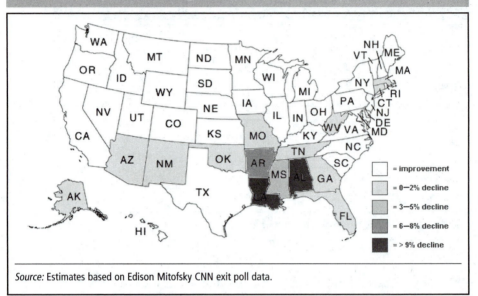

Source: Estimates based on Edison Mitofsky CNN exit poll data.

national tide, are concentrated in states with long histories of racial conflict and African American exclusion, and it is difficult to dismiss the notion that the Democratic nominee's race might have something to do with this.

There is one more item worth noting with respect to the presidential preferences of white and non-white voters. Turning back to Table 3-4, exit poll and other estimates for the 2000 turned-out electorate find it about 80.7 percent white, the 2004 electorate as 77 percent white, and the 2008 electorate as 74 percent white. Minorities make up a smaller share of midterm election voters, but even their share in the 2010 GOP landslide was smaller than in the 2006 Democratic takeover. The trend is unmistakable. As we illustrated in the last chapter, the demographic trends estimated by the Census Bureau suggest that this pattern will continue and, if anything, the pace of the change may actually quicken. Assuming that current voting patterns persist and assuming no change in GOP strategy, in the long run the average Democratic share of the two-party vote can be expected to climb in future elections. In the next chapter, we attempt to estimate that trajectory.

RACE AND CONTROL OF CONGRESS

The presidency is a special office, to which Americans attach greater significance and emotional importance than any other. The uniqueness and high salience of that office might be thought to imply that presidential elections would see high levels of racial polarization that are not matched at lower levels of elected office. However, such is not the case. When we look to the Senate and

House, much of the patterns we observe in presidential elections are repeated. Democratic strength in both bodies is substantially buoyed by minority votes.

United States Senate

Take, for example, the U.S. Senate. In the 112th Congress, the Senate has 53 members elected as Democrats or Democratically identified independents.[7] Excluding Joe Lieberman, as mentioned in the note, of those 52, elected or reelected collectively across the 2006, 2008, and 2010 federal elections, 16 would have lost were it not for disproportionate support of non-white voters.[8] That is, the Democrats would have won only 36 of those 52 seats and the Democratic share of the Senate in the 112th Senate would have been a mere 37, rather than the 53 seats it ultimately collected. In most instances, the African American and Latino votes made the difference. It is worth noting, however, that in Alaska Sen. Mark Begich's election in 2008, it was Native Alaskans who carried him over the finish line.

This number of senators elected with only a minority of the non-Hispanic white vote, however, actually understates the effect of minority voters on the composition of the Senate. First, two members—Jon Tester of Montana and Jeff Merkley of Oregon—were elected with pluralities of the white vote, 49 percent and 48 percent, respectively, more than their opponents but less than a majority. Second, many of the remaining seats held by Democrats with a majority of white support were, in fact, incumbents reelected. And more than a few of those incumbents, whose vote share was enhanced by that incumbency and the political advantages it affords, actually did rely on minority voters when first elected to the Senate.

Which senators with apparent white majorities might owe their job to non-white voters? Let us start with those still struggling to attract whites to their fold. Even as long-term incumbents, several Democratic senators get only a modest majority of white voters.[9] Sen. Debbie Stabenow (D-MI) is a good case in point. When she was originally elected in 2000, her share of the white vote was 45 percent, meaning that minority voters where critical to her first victory, even if their importance has faded as a consequence of her incumbency. For Dianne Feinstein, her white vote share was just 50 percent in 2000, actually a decline from her first election, when she received 52 percent of the white vote in 1992 in a special election. For Maria Cantwell of Washington, her 57 percent of the white vote in 2006 would appear to suggest solid support among non-Hispanic whites, but in 2000, when she was first elected against Slade Gorton, she polled just 47 percent of the white vote and was reliant on minority voters to reach her one-point victory.

So while thirty-six of the Democratic senators in the 112th Congress were reelected as incumbents with majority-white support, there is good evidence to suggest that a fair number of them would not have been elected in the first instance in the absence of minority support. And as the Feinstein case illustrates, where a generally uncontroversial incumbent sees her non-Hispanic white vote share decline long after her first race, Democratic claims to white majorities can remain contingent or threatened, even long into well-established political careers.

It would be hard to overstate the significance of minority support to Senate Democrats. Eight of those receiving majority-white support got white vote shares below 54 percent. Of those winning in spite of losing among whites, the depth of that disadvantage is sometimes breathtaking. Four senators (Harry Reid-NV, Barbara Boxer-CA, Claire McCaskill-MO, and Jim Webb-VA) received just 42 percent of the white vote in their most recent election. Al Franken (MN) got just 40 percent of the white vote, while Kay Hagan (NC) received just 39 percent of the white vote. Mary Landrieu (LA) received only 33 percent of the vote among non-Hispanic whites.

In the absence of reliable minority support, Democratic prospects for controlling the Senate are nil. At no point in the past thirty years has the

---

BOX 3-1 **Native Americans in Office**

We have spent considerable time discussing the African American, Latino, and Asian American populations of elected officials, but have devoted little attention to Native Americans. This has a great deal to do with the relative population size. Table 3-6 reports the states with the largest share of their population being from Native American, Native Alaskan, or Hawaiian indigenous groups.

Alaska has, by far, the largest population share. New Mexico, Hawaii, South Dakota, Oklahoma, and Montana fill out the top six. Three states—California, Arizona, and Texas—have indigenous populations in excess of 200,000 persons, placing them among the most populous indigenous communities, but in the context of much larger overall populations, the population share represented by the indigenous is small.

The number of elected officials from Native American and other indigenous nationality groups is sizable in some instances. Table 3-7 reports the legislative representation of each of these states.

Oklahoma, Alaska, and Hawaii have elected the largest number and largest share of state legislators. The Oklahoma House is almost 18 percent native, a consequence of the state's history as designated "Indian" territory. The Alaska Senate (15 percent) and Hawaii Senate (20 percent) are also among the chambers with the strongest native group. Two states with large native populations, Texas and California, have no indigenous representation at all in their legislatures.

TABLE 3-6 States with the Highest Native/Indigenous Population (in percentages)	
Alaska	15.23
New Mexico	9.72
Hawaii	9.17
South Dakota	8.49
Oklahoma	8.03
Montana	6.45

Source: National Caucus of Native American State Legislators.

Democratic majority been large enough to weather the loss of members for whom minority voters are critical and still retain the fifty-one votes necessary to have controlled the body.

It is also worth noting that the Senate remains an unusually white body, regardless of party. After the elections of 2010, only four sitting senators were from racial and ethnic minority groups. Latino Robert Menendez was elected to represent New Jersey but, importantly, initially gained the office through appointment. Marco Rubio (R-FL) is the newly elected Latino senator from Florida. The remaining two are the aforementioned Inouye (Asian American) and Akaka (Asian and Native Hawaiian), both from Hawaii. Three others had recently served and left on their own terms. Ken Salazar of Colorado resigned

TABLE 3-7   Native American/Indigenous Representation in States with Largest Populations and Population Shares

State	Chamber	Number	% of Chamber	Partisanship
Alaska	House	4	10	3 D, 1 R
	Senate	3	15	3 D
Arizona	House	2	3.30	2 D
	Senate	1	3.30	1 D
California	Assembly	0		
	Senate	0		
Hawaii	House	6	11.76	6 D
	Senate	5	20.00	5 D
Montana	House	3	3.00	3 D
	Senate	3	6.00	3 D
New Mexico	House	4	5.71	4 D
	Senate	2	4.76	2 D
Oklahoma	House	18	17.82	8 D, 10 R
	Senate	5	10.42	4D, 1R
South Dakota	House	2	2.86	2 D
	Senate	1	2.86	1 D
Texas	House	0		
	Senate	0		

Source: National Caucus of Native American State Legislators.

to become secretary of the interior, Roland Burris was appointed to fill Obama's unexpired term and did not seek election, and Mel Martinez of Florida resigned for personal reasons and held the seat to which Rubio was elected.

Importantly, all but two of these individuals were Democrats. Martinez and his successor were the lone Republicans in the 111th and 112th Senates. In fact, since the end of Reconstruction, only six non-whites have ever been elected to the Senate as Republicans. Ben Nighthorse Campbell, a Native American from Colorado, originally elected in 1992 as a Democrat but who switched parties in 1995, was reelected as a Republican in 1998. Prior to Campbell, you have to go back to Hiram Fong (HI), Edward Brooke (MA), and S. I. Hayakawa (CA), who left office in 1977, 1979, and 1983, respectively. The Democrats have done only slightly better, with around ten total non-white members.[10]

United States House of Representatives

There are 73 self-identified persons of color serving in the 112th House of Representatives. Of these, 10 are in the Republican majority, and 63 are in the Democratic minority.

Assessing the effect of minority voters on control of the House of Representatives is, on the one hand, a simpler matter than for the Senate and, on the other, a bit more complex. In the 112th Congress, Republicans hold the majority of 242 to 193. Since only 10 members of the GOP majority are racial and ethnic minorities (and, as we have mentioned, many of those were elected without minority voters' support), minority votes did not shape the current majority. On the other hand, in the 111th Congress the Democrats held an 81-seat majority in the chamber, with 64 minority members (most elected in majority-minority or minority-influence districts). It might be tempting to conclude that neither Democratic nor Republican control depends on minority representatives. This would be an error.

First, in the absence of minority legislators overwhelmingly elected by minority voters, the Democrats are not in the game. Drop all minority legislators (or, rather, imagine minority legislators were as likely to come from either party), and the GOP majority is overwhelming, 232 to 130. This majority would be creeping up toward the two-thirds vote necessary to override vetoes and amend the Constitution.

Second, we cannot look at minority members as the sole measure of minority voter influence. Many minority voters live in majority-white districts, and, just as in the Senate, many white Democrats in the House still represent significant minority populations without which they could not win their seats. We earlier noted the example of the two surviving white Democrats in the Texas delegation, who represent heavily Latino districts. This is the case for every white Democrat from the South and many from the Southwest and California. If we examine the results of the 2006 exit polls reported in Table 3-4, racial and ethnic minorities accounted for almost a third of all Democratic votes, representing over 16 percent of the Democrats' 53 percent majority. In

2010, minority voters cast 35 percent of all Democratic votes, or 15.7 percent of the 45 percent share they received.

RACE AND STATE LEGISLATIVE REPRESENTATION

Relatively few individuals serve in Congress. With only 435 House seats and 100 Senators, the opportunities for minority voters to make a difference are constrained by the large constituency sizes and the limits this places on the likelihood that minority voters are electorally significant. This limitation might actually cause us to underestimate minority electoral effect, though the evidence from Congress alone suggests that the effect is sizable.

Perhaps a better place to look for minority representation would be the state legislatures. Excluding Nebraska's non-partisan, unicameral chamber, the forty-nine remaining states elect over 7,200 individual legislators and state senators, and the ninety-eight chambers provide a greater laboratory for examining the effect of minority votes on Democratic fortunes than merely recounting the effects in the U.S. Congress.

Looking at the 2007–2008 state legislatures,[11] the partisan complexion of minority legislators is overwhelmingly Democratic. Table 3-8 reports the partisan distribution of legislators by groups.

In terms of the parties, it is important to remember that the majorities of elected officials in both parties are made up of non-Hispanic whites. Nevertheless,

TABLE 3-8   Partisan Distribution of State Legislators and State Senators by Race and Ethnicity, 2007–2008

	State lower chambers			State senates		
	Total	Democratic	Republican	Total	Democratic	Republican
Whites	4,649	2,300	2,349	1,671	785	886
		49.5%	50.5%		47.0%	53.0%
African Americans	464	457	7	158	155	3
		98.5%	1.5%		98.1%	1.9%
Asian Americans	61	50	11	24	23	1
		82.0%	18.0%		95.8%	4.2%
Latinos or Hispanics	189	157	32	60	52	8
		83.1%	16.9%		86.7%	13.3%
	5,363	2,964	2,399	1,913	1,015	898

Sources: National Conference of State Legislators, National Association of Latino Elected and Appointed Officials, National Asian Pacific American Political Almanac, and the Joint Center for Political and Economic Studies. More recent data not yet available at the time of publication.

the composition of the two parties is quite telling. Of all 2,964 Democrats serving in state lower chambers,[12] 77.6 percent of them are non-Hispanic whites, while the remaining 22.4 percent identify as a racial or ethnic minority. Of the 2,399 Republicans serving in state lower chambers, 97.9 percent of them are white, while persons of color compose only 2.1 percent of GOP state legislators. State senates are more or less the same. Of the 1,015 Democratic members serving in the forty-nine upper chambers, 77.3 percent of them are white. The comparable share among the 898 Republicans is 98.7 percent. In fact, the total number of non-white GOP state senators going into the 2008 elections, nationwide, was twelve (one Asian, three African Americans, and eight Latinos, three of which were from South Florida), and non-white state legislators totaled fifty.

Since the preponderance of non-white state legislators is Democratic, it follows that their impact on the partisan control of legislative chambers is meaningful. In the 2007–2008 legislative years, the Democrats controlled 30 of the 49 lower chambers, and 29 of the 49 senates. Recall that the vast majority of non-white legislators—specifically African Americans and Latinos—represent constituencies that are dominated by those groups. We can begin by assuming that these are the only seats where minority voters have made a difference for the Democrats, an assumption that means we underestimate, rather than overestimate, their effect on Democratic competitiveness. If, instead of the observed outcome, we assumed that minority legislators were evenly distributed between the parties (or that only the white legislators were in the body, which is functionally equivalent), we would observe 12 of the 30 state houses (40 percent) and 8 of the 29 senates (28 percent) controlled by Democrats switch to GOP control or become tied.

It is important to note that this is not merely a regional phenomenon. That minority legislators are critical to Democratic prospects in the South is not surprising, and among the state houses whose control in 2008 would have switched are Alabama, Louisiana, Mississippi, North Carolina, and Tennessee. Both New Mexico and California are in that number as well, largely owing to Latino legislators. But minorities were also pivotal to Democratic majorities in Illinois, Indiana, Michigan, New Jersey, and Pennsylvania. In the state senates, minorities were key to southern senates in Louisiana, Oklahoma, Tennessee, and Virginia but also in such far-flung places as California, Hawaii, New Jersey, and New Mexico.[13] And in states such as New York, which had a GOP majority in 2008 and subsequently shifted Democrat in 2009, the GOP's narrow majority (31–29) would have been a huge margin (31–15) were it not for minority state senators.

Again, looking only at the minority legislators as a measure of minority voter influence likely underestimates the effect of those voters. Of the almost 7,300 state legislators, 55 percent of whom are Democrats, there are doubtless countless cases where white Democratic state legislators are elected with only a minority of non-Hispanic white votes. This is particularly likely to be true in

states with high levels of racial polarization, where white votes for Demo
are comparatively hard to come by. Recall that in Louisiana, Mississippi, a
Alabama, Barack Obama received 14 percent, 11 percent, and 10 percent of tl
white vote, respectively. It is difficult to conceive of a scenario, then, whereby
many of the 103 white Democrats in those states' lower chambers would man-
age to get elected on the basis of white votes alone.

SUMMARY

While it is common knowledge that minority voters form a core part of the
Democratic coalition, the analysis here—from the president through Congress to the state house—illustrates just how thoroughgoing the dependence
of the Democratic Party on minority votes is. Without the substantial skew
of minorities to the Democratic Party, not only would it not hold the White
House or the Senate, as well as twenty of the fifty-nine state legislative
chambers it held in 2008, in many cases the Democratic Party would not
even come close enough to have a realistic chance of competing. The evidence of changing demography suggests that non-white Americans will
become a more important voting bloc in American politics. The evidence of
this chapter suggests minorities already are pivotal to Democratic electoral
success.

This importance as a vote bloc has not, however, translated into large
numbers of minorities elected to office. To be sure, the trend is upward, but
levels of representation do not seem commensurate with electoral importance.
This is, of course, more an issue for the Democratic Party than the Republicans. Republicans have used a decades-long strategy of reaching out to and
mobilizing white voters—particularly in the South—to remain electorally
competitive, and they are often successful. Again the trends may well reinforce
each other: the incentive to encourage minority candidates is lower if minorities will not vote Republican, and minorities may be less willing to vote Republican if there are no minority candidates. That said, this argument cannot apply
to the Democratic Party.

In terms of political futures, the GOP needs to engage in some rethinking
of strategy. Absent a substantial shift of minority voters away from current patterns, that whites-only strategy will become electorally unviable over time as
demography takes its toll. The white share of the electorate has been declining
even as the strength of minority preference for Democrats increases. The
Democrats, too, will need to rethink whether they are willing to encourage and
accommodate more candidates of color.

In the chapters that follow, we explore what effect, if any, the pivotal nature
of minority votes will have on minority policy preferences, political views, and
orientations to government. To some extent, we doubt that minority voters
fully understand the powerful position they hold in the Democratic coalition.
We see evidence that at least some in the GOP recognize the demographic

disadvantage for what it is and urge message change and outreach, but it is clear so far that this recognition has not appreciably driven policy, strategy, or rhetoric. Nevertheless, we believe that this position is sure to reshape how minorities perceive government and how the Democrats deliver policy outcomes.

chapter 4

Party Identification and Two-Party Vote among Minority Citizens

The concept of party identification is a central one within political behavior. It is an explanation for how citizens and parties may be tied together that is grounded in a psychological approach to understanding politics. The textbook idea of party identification is a familiar one. Early in their lives, voters acquire a series of politically relevant opinions and attitudes, some of which orient them toward political parties. Just how early voters acquire these kinds of orientations can be found in any elementary and middle school around election time: many children, years away from being able to vote themselves, will have opinions on candidates for presidential elections. These opinions will not be deeply held or very carefully argued but are likely to be echoes of opinions they have heard expressed by parents or of opinions heard on TV shows watched in the home. The point is not so much that the opinions of children reflect coherent ideologies of politically minded prodigies but that these opinions exist at such a very early age and are often shaped in large part by family. Among those attitudes and opinions that develop early on are attachments to, or identifications with, political parties: voters will see themselves and define themselves as Democrats or Republicans almost as if it were a part of their identity, as people say, "I am a Christian," or "I am a Texan," or any number of other sources of identity located in culture, religion, or demography. This attachment is as much affective (emotional) as cognitive (information-driven).

These party attachments have two major consequences that are politically relevant. First, they help shape vote choice. Voters with party identifications will look to the party label as a major signpost indicating how to vote. People may stray every now and then and find a specific candidate appealing but will generally come home to "their" party and that party's candidates. The connection between expressed party identification and actual voting behavior is so strong that political scientists have developed the concept "normal vote," which is to assume that the baseline distribution of votes will be identical to the distribution of party identification.

Second, they help reinforce the use of information. The most obvious way to see this is in choice of information. These days heavily politicized cable TV, websites, and talk radio offer the electronic equivalent of the nineteenth-century politicized press. It is easy to see how people will tend to choose information sources most in tune with their own outlook. Perhaps a less obvious way in which partisanship interacts with information is through the interpretation of political events. Take a "hard" piece of politically relevant information such as the national unemployment rate. Let us say that it is 9 percent. But is that a "good" performance given the circumstances or a "bad" performance given the circumstances? The number alone may not tell us very much, but if we know the president and Congress are Democrats, then we can begin to form an opinion on whether the number is good or bad (depending in part on whether we are Democrats or not).

Partisanship, then, helps voters interpret political events and will do so in a way that helps reinforce one's existing party preference over time. Partisanship is very stable over time at the individual level, and generally speaking, identification with a party strengthens over time (Green and Palmquist 1994). Sometimes party identifications do change, but often these changes seem to require a change in someone's life circumstances. Upward social mobility, for example, will make people better off and so more likely to vote Republican as they begin to vote their self-interest in support of lower taxes and lower provision of public goods (that the better-off are less likely to use). Another way in which we can see changes in identification is through realignment, a process in which, loosely speaking, the identity of a party or parties changes and shakes up the kinds of social constituencies or social coalitions that form a party's vote bloc. Race has been one of the most important social constituencies in shaping, and being shaped by, relationships to American political parties.

While the importance of party in people's lives may have changed (and declined) a lot in recent decades, there is still enough talk of "red" and "blue" to imply that there are identities that are bound up with politics. Still, the idea that something such as politics can help shape part of someone's identity might seem a bit strange. After all, most people do not care that much about politics to begin with, and so the idea of someone being a fan of politics to the point that it almost becomes part of one's identity will seem implausible to someone not so interested in politics. But fandoms of other kinds exist and seem to operate in similar ways, and they do not always seem so strange. We all know that sports fandom can be more than a matter of watching a game on TV, because we all know people who go on road trips to see the team, pay attention to websites and "fantasy" team contests, or tune in to sports programming/call-in shows even in the off-season. Some even pay to buy and wear "official" branded clothing or merchandise carrying a team or player name. These fans, too, will tend to have quite detailed opinions on the decisions of refs/umpires in the last game and on the latest trades. Often, but not always, the sports team that generates this kind of identity is a team that has family associations from a hometown or early trips to see the team as a child. Being a sports fan, then, may have some similarities to being a fan of politics.

We can stretch the analogy of sports fandom a little further by noting two features of sports fandom that may apply to party identification. First, fans who watch a game tend to get very involved in the sport itself. It means they become connected to the wider sport, follow it and feel attached to it. Games that have lots of keen fans are often exciting ones, even for nonfans. Take, for example, the Super Bowl, World Series, or World Cup. Political fandom, or partisanship, operates in a similar way because it helps connect citizens to the democratic process; partisans who follow politics will become engaged by it and informed. Second, just as sports teams like having a large and loyal fan base because it means high attendance at sports events and more merchandising revenue, so, too, in politics, then, having loyalists (party identifiers) is good news for the political parties, which can rely on support and supporters at election time. This is especially true when we consider the intensity of attachment. A standard survey question sequence not only asks voters whether they feel an attachment to a party—and which one—but also how strongly they feel that sense of attachment. "Strong" partisans are ones who are the most hard-core loyal of fans. If fans are not so loyal, the team may have problems. Here is one place where the analogy between sports and politics begins to break down. While a sports team in a city where people are uninterested may try gimmicks (promotions and giveaways) or move the team to another city entirely, political parties cannot engage in either of these things when they are faced with an unenthusiastic vote base. What we might see is that a party has to change some issue positions in order to appeal to voters, but the problem of fickle voters willing to cast a ballot for any candidate who says something appealing will remain. Having voters who are not keen supporters will clearly affect turnout patterns and election results.

Just as there are limits to the analogy between sports fandom and party identification so, too, are there limits to the idea of party identification itself. There has, for example, been a long-term decline in the numbers of voters who have attachment to one of the two main parties and a rise in the number of people who have no connection to political parties or declare themselves "independents" (American National Election Studies 2005). While such trends may seem neither surprising nor worrying, these trends do worry some scholars because if party identification really is a means of connecting citizens to the wider political system, then declining identification means that fewer and fewer voters feel that connection. Those trends worry the parties, too. If voters are less attached to political parties and/or have weaker attachments (a case of de-alignment rather than re-alignment), then the parties have to try harder to woo voters who may also have become more fickle. For example, since strong partisans are more likely to vote a straight party ticket reliably, the growth of independents means candidates have to work harder to reach out to voters.

The changes in recent years, and the possibility of both de-alignment and re-alignment, have generated a series of discussions within the political science literature on the nature of party identification. These discussions to one side, it is still the case that a large share of the electorate expresses some kind of attachment to political parties and this attachment structures their vote choice.

POLITICAL PARTIES AND MINORITY VOTERS

So far this discussion has been about party identification as it applies in general to U.S. politics. We have not mentioned how this understanding of voting and political attitudes relates to minority politics, but party identification is relevant to minority politics in a number of ways.

First and foremost are some straightforward questions concerning which parties appeal to which minority groups. Given our brief outline of the relevance of party identification to politics, even these simple descriptive patterns can have wider political consequences. For example, we are used to the idea of political parties piecing together demographic groups in order to build electoral coalitions: the Jewish vote, the black vote, the "soccer mom" vote, the Catholic vote, and so on.

In terms of the nominal partisan patterns of minorities, this can be answered quite easily by Figure 4-1. Minority voters tend to lean Democrat.

Figure 4-1 records the self-reported partisan identification, from the 2004 National Politics Study (NPS) as well as the 2008 American National Election Study (ANES) and the 2008 General Social Survey (GSS). Comparing across surveys often produces some differences for a range of reasons.[1] What most characterizes Figure 4-1, however, is the consistency of the patterns regardless of source. By and large, minority voters of all groups are less likely to be Republican than are whites. Non-Hispanic whites are almost evenly distributed between Democrat and Republican (at least as far as the self-reported party is concerned). By contrast, Asian American and Latinos both are substantially more Democratic than whites and significantly less Republican. The party tilt among Latinos ranges from 20 to 30 percentage points, and for Asians from 10 to 20 points. African Americans remain an overwhelmingly Democratic population.

A couple of other items are worth noting in Figure 4-1. First, Latinos and Asian Americans are both more likely to decline to choose a party and are more likely to claim an independent than a GOP identity. Second, throughout this book we will caution against building strong interpretations of Asian American political behavior on the basis of the ANES and the GSS, given their very small sample sizes. Nevertheless, the results for Asians from these two studies are not meaningfully different from those drawn from the NPS, which had a sizable and more reliable Asian subsample.

Party identification will show us some ways in which electoral coalitions may be built and also how stable they may be—at least for the time being. If voters have strong attachments to parties, this means they are more likely to stay loyal to the party and turn out and vote for that party.

These abstract statements of partisanship cover quite complex processes in reality. Take, for example, the well-known pattern that as a group African

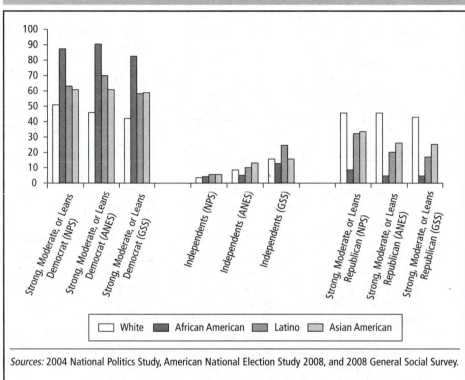

FIGURE 4-1   **Partisanship by Race (in percentages)**

Sources: 2004 National Politics Study, American National Election Study 2008, and 2008 General Social Survey.

Americans have shown strong loyalty to the Democratic Party since the 1960s. African Americans are overwhelmingly loyal to the Democratic Party. Moreover, they turn out and vote at high levels, higher indeed than might be expected based on simple socioeconomic factors (more on this later). Even such a simple and uncontroversial statement really reflects a more complicated set of relationships between party and race in U.S. history.

RACE AND PARTISANSHIP IN U.S. POLITICAL HISTORY

The relationship between parties and race in the United States is a long one. In the nineteenth century it was the Republican Party that was organized—and indeed partly founded—around opposition to slavery, and it was Lincoln, the first Republican president, who issued the Emancipation Proclamation. The association of Lincoln with emancipation and the Democrats with the Confederate South shaped the emerging partisanship of newly freed and enfranchised former slaves, and their children, as solidly Republican.

Things have changed since this early history, and it is the Democrats who are now more often publicly associated with support of minority interests and of minority voters. That changeover was the product of two long-term processes. First, northern Democrats moved to be at the vanguard of political action, especially on behalf of black Americans. This shift by the northern Democratic Party was the result of its ideological association with working-class, immigrant, and poor Americans in the rapidly industrializing North, coupled with the Great Migration of African Americans out of the Jim Crow South (Grossman 1991; Marks 1989). Seeking a more welcoming social climate and greater economic opportunity, blacks left a predominantly agricultural existence in the South for automobile, steel, meat-packing, manufacturing, and other heavy industrial jobs in the North, thereby joining the ranks of workers whose interests were the focus of much Democratic politics. The movement was sizable and accelerated by World War I. Marks (1989) estimates the total at over 1 million persons, with more than 400,000 moving just in the 1916–1918 period.

What is remarkable, in light of our perceptions of black partisanship today, is that this newly enfranchised northern electorate was solidly Republican in both partisan identity and in vote choice. Pinderhughes (1987) reports that as much as 70 percent of the African American vote in Chicago was consistently Republican and that Democrats managed a majority of black voters in only one mayoral election in that pre-1932 era—that of 1923.

The association of African Americans with the GOP had its roots in the history of the party, the contestation of the Civil War, and the emergence of Reconstruction regimes in the southern states (Weiss 1983). By the end of Reconstruction, however, black interests appeared at the heart of neither party, and the continued association of African Americans with the GOP is better described as inertial, rather than owed to any policy efforts on the part of Republican administrations to hold them. Weiss (1983) and Walton (1972a) chronicle the history of poor treatment of African American interests by GOP leaders. In fact, Woodrow Wilson was able to appeal to a sliver of the black vote, disgruntled with GOP indifference, by promising to do better, only to disappoint severely (Sitkoff 1978). Throughout the 1920s, African American dissatisfaction with the GOP grew. Herbert Hoover's leadership of the party was particularly hostile to meaningful black participation and inclusion, to say nothing of policies helpful to African American economic and social issues.

The textbook example of the process of realignment—that is, a change in patterns of party loyalty—is the New Deal coalition of 1932. In the wake of the Depression, President Franklin Delano Roosevelt (FDR) built a coalition around labor and white southerners as well as Jews and Catholics, ushering in the New Deal. The actions of the Roosevelt administration with respect to African Americans—in terms of appointments, outreach, and race neutrality of several New Deal programs—signaled the most "friendly" administration to black interests since the Civil War and Reconstruction. By 1936 black voters no longer saw the two parties as equivalent, and the grip of the GOP on African American partisan sentiment—and electoral choice—was fully and finally broken. FDR was rewarded with significant growth in black vote share. As is evident in Figure 4-2, this shift jump-started by the Depression continued over the next four decades and, by the 1970s, the current overwhelming Democratic tilt in black partisanship we observe today was fully in place.

Of course, not all Democrats were equally excited about their new electoral allies. Southern Democrats, in particular, were hostile to the inclusion of African Americans, typically pursuing discriminatory policies and maintaining racial boundaries at the state and local levels. Katznelson (2005) has documented the lengths to which southern Democrats went, in the legislative arena, to maintain that monopoly control even as they negotiated with their northern Democratic counterparts. Although many New Deal programs were specifically and intentionally nondiscriminatory, implementation was administered by the states rather than federal agencies, at the insistence of the southerners, thereby allowing state officials to maintain practices of maldistribution of government benefits and the white socioeconomic hegemony. The passage of the "Wagner Act," or National Labor Relations Act of 1935—a New Deal–era law governing labor and industrial relations and facilitating the formation of labor unions—was a triumph for organized labor and a key commitment of northern Democrats. To secure a majority for the act, however, meant that northern Democrats in Congress had to make concessions to southern Democrats, who were less enamored of organized labor, to secure their votes. Northerners exempted both agricultural labor and domestic labor from the provisions making union organization easier, both sectors of the southern economy in which African Americans were the overwhelming majority of the workforce. This deal was replicated shortly thereafter in the Fair Labor Standards Act of 1938, again exempting employment in fields largely filled by black labor in the South (Katznelson 2005).

The deal was short lived, of course, as those southern Democrats did eventually join the new GOP majority in passing the Taft Hartley Act in 1947, over the veto of President Harry Truman, severely undermining the cause of organized labor. The change of heart among southern Democrats was driven by the growing recognition that national labor standards and statutory support for labor organization would inevitably come to conflict with—and undermine— the Jim Crow regime (Katznelson 2005, 67). Indeed, the nationalization of any form of social legislation had at least the potential of "intruding" on existing patterns of race relations in the South.

Truman's decision to desegregate the military in 1948, coupled with a mild, but at the time, significant, civil rights plank in the Democratic platform, prompted a southern walkout from the 1948 Democratic National Convention, the splintering of the party, and the nomination of Strom Thurmond of South Carolina—who later went on to serve as a GOP senator from that state—as the presidential nominee of the "Dixiecrat" party. Thurmond won thirty-nine electoral votes, all from southern states. He won Alabama,

Louisiana, Mississippi, and South Carolina outright and picked up an additional vote from a "faithless elector"[2] in Tennessee.

The Republicans, meanwhile, had endured an extended exile from political power in the wake of the New Deal. Losses in five consecutive presidential elections were sufficiently jarring that the expansion of their electoral coalition had become an urgent necessity. The fracturing of the Democratic coalition along regional lines, over the issue of race, had not gone unnoticed, but liberalism on racial issues remained an accurate description of the attitudes of a significant share of GOP rank and file and officeholders well into midcentury. Carmines and Stimson (1989), who offer the most comprehensive political exploration of the great party inversion on the issue of race, point out that the Democratic burst of Civil Rights energy in 1948 was more the exception than the rule, and by several measures, Republicans—who, we should recall, were almost unknown in the South and, when present, were often more liberal than local Democrats—were more supportive in platform and action than the average Democrat (Carmines and Stimson 1989, 105, 111, 163).

The change in the Republican Party's attitude toward Civil Rights was precipitated by two events. First, the midterm elections of 1958 were uniquely disastrous for GOP moderates in both chambers of Congress, many of whom were replaced by more liberal Democrats. This change served simultaneously to make the GOP conference more conservative and the Democratic caucus more liberal, racially as well as in other ways. The second event was the nomination of Barry Goldwater as the GOP presidential nominee in 1964. Goldwater represented the first instance of what we have come to know as "movement conservatism" taking control of the GOP. Goldwater was an outspoken opponent of the 1964 Civil Rights Act and campaigned openly for its repeal as part of his presidential effort. Goldwater's opposition to the Civil Rights Act stemmed from his philosophical commitments to circumscribed government power, particularly the national government in Washington vis-à-vis the states. He saw the Civil Rights Act as extending central government power, in itself a bad thing. His opposition served to substantially increase his popularity among those opposing the civil rights process. Goldwater went down to spectacular defeat; in so doing he managed to win only five states beyond his home state of Arizona: Alabama, Georgia, Louisiana, Mississippi, and South Carolina. The message of the election was as clear as the result: GOP candidates could prevail in the South if they held a position on the "race question" that was demonstrably more conservative than that of their Democratic opponents.

In 1968, Richard Nixon's attempt to capitalize on a "southern strategy" was compromised by the candidacy of then governor of Alabama, George Wallace, running on a segregationist platform. In 1972, however, no such candidate was present, and Nixon's southern strategy, which included both implicit nods to the segregationist cause in the form of two controversial and unsuccessful nominations to the high court and explicit promises to reduce federal pressure on southern states to implement desegregation policy (Carmines and Stimson, 54, 104), could be fully implemented. Nixon swept the South in 1972 (and most of the nation, in fact).

This substantial shift in both Republican rhetoric and policy came against a backdrop of a dramatically changing Democratic electorate. Perhaps nowhere was this clearer than in the South, where the passage of the Voting Rights Act of 1965 enfranchised millions of potential African American voters, whose votes became more meaningful and influential in southern primaries. Newly enfranchised African Americans in the South chose a Democratic identity, despite their long suffering at the hands of southern Democrats, in part because of the appeal of Kennedy-Johnson policies but in part, too, as a recognition of the Democrats' monopoly on electoral power. Given Democratic dominance, the election that decided who was going to win was not so much the general election but the Democratic primary. If voters wanted a say they needed to register as Democrats.[3]

With the northern Democratic Party moving left, the movement of southern Democratic (white) politicians into the GOP camp accelerated. Ronald Reagan's successful candidacy in 1980—which included a postconvention kickoff speech affirming states' rights in Philadelphia, Mississippi, site of a horrific triple murder of Civil Rights advocates in 1963—cemented the electoral advantage Republicans had in pursuing southern white voters and set off an additional wave of party-switching from Democrat to Republican among elected officials. Between 1968 and 1988, the entire segregationist wing of the Democratic Party switched sides just as effectively, in part a consequence of the earlier switch of African Americans from Republican to Democrat.

Figure 4-2 displays the consequence of this history for the party loyalties of African Americans over time.

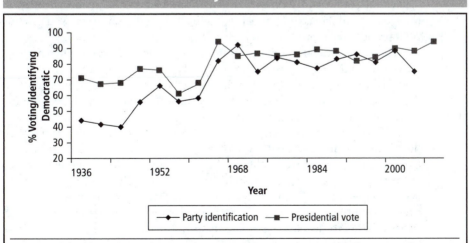

FIGURE 4-2   **African American Party Identification and Vote, 1936–2008**

Source: Michael Fauntroy, *Republicans and the Black Vote* (Boulder, Colo.: Lynne Rienner Publishers Inc., 2006). Used with permission by Lynne Rienner Publishers, Inc.

The story of staunch African American loyalty to, and identification with, the Democratic Party is thus a long one that developed over the course of the twentieth century. But the story does show that even deeply held party identifications can change over time.

The account of African American partisanship is necessarily tied to America's difficult history of slavery. The association of the Democratic Party with the interests of Hispanics is somewhat less complex. Although there have been significant Latin American–origin populations in the United States since at least the end of the Mexican-American War in 1848, Hispanics were neither counted effectively nor sufficiently populous to estimate vote share at a national level. Beginning with the candidacy of John Kennedy in 1960, a substantial share of Latino voters, principally Mexican Americans, registered and voted Democrat. DeSipio (1996) observes that there has clearly been a decline in overall vote share going to Democrats. This change might have been driven by the diversification of the Latino population in terms of national origin groups. South Florida Cubans, emphasizing a commitment to anticommunism grounded in their émigré experiences, have long identified with Republicans, and their numbers became politically significant in the 1970s and 1980s. Figure 4-3 covers the self-reported vote distributions for African Americans, Asian Americans, and Latinos together, for purposes of comparison, along with those of non-Hispanic whites.

Across multiple survey platforms and across multiple elections, it is apparent that the partisanship skew we observed in Figure 4-1 is a description of not just about how people think but also how they vote. Latinos, Asians, and especially African Americans exhibit stable, sizable preferences for Democratic candidates across branches of government, across survey platforms, and across time. African Americans remain the most uniformly Democratic, but the behavioral patterns of Latinos and Asians also are stable, giving Democrats between 60 and 75 percent of their votes in all elections, save John Kerry in the 2004 presidential election.

Figure 4-4 puts those numbers into an historical perspective by charting the change in these vote patterns over time. Two observations about Figure 4-4 are worth noting. The first is that the pattern of decline in Hispanic vote for the Democratic Party is driven heavily by shifts taking place in the late 1970s. Since then, the trend line is remarkably flat.

The second point about the trend line for Latinos is the "noisiness" of the trend in comparison with that of African Americans. Latino support for Democratic presidential candidates has been consistently a majority share, but it has varied up and down with a far wider interelection swing than we ever observe with African Americans. Latino partisanship has a much less sure pattern than African American partisanship. In part this reflects some issues relating to the lack of sufficient study (and undersampling) of Latino respondents for several decades. As with Asian American populations,

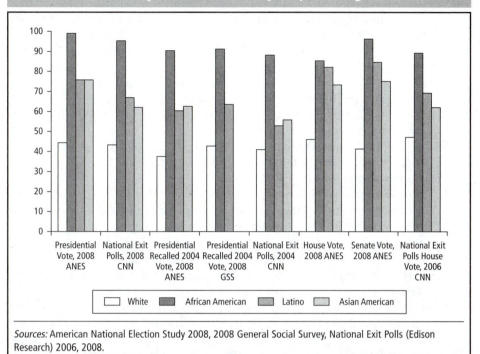

FIGURE 4-3 **Estimated Democratic Vote Share Across Sources and Elections, by Race and Ethnicity (in percentages)**

Sources: American National Election Study 2008, 2008 General Social Survey, National Exit Polls (Edison Research) 2006, 2008.

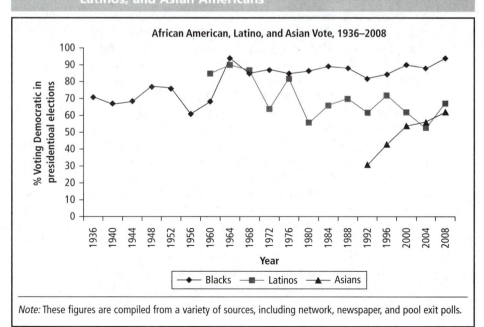

FIGURE 4-4 **Estimated Two-Party Presidential Vote for African Americans, Latinos, and Asian Americans**

Note: These figures are compiled from a variety of sources, including network, newspaper, and pool exit polls.

there tends to be relatively little hard and systematic information on Latino populations for much of the twentieth century. In large part the reason for this lack of information is related to the technology of survey sampling. For long periods of time Asian Americans and Hispanics composed fairly small percentages of the U.S. population, and so there were few respondents from these groups in most surveys. Just in the same way we see few respondents from North Dakota in national survey samples, but many more from California.[4]

For now, Latinos are a majority Democratic demographic group and have been for a long time, though with greater variation and lower overall mean support than among African Americans.

We know even less about Asian American politics than we do about either African American or Latino politics. In part, this is a function of group size. Even in 2010, Asian Americans had grown to about 4.9 percent of the national population[5] but only 2.5 percent of the electorate (Paral et al. 2008).[6] Lien et al. (2004a) note a fairly high degree of independence or "decline to state" party preferences among Asian Americans and suggest that this results from the long and well-documented (Frymer 1999) lack of interest on the part of national party organizations to do for non-white immigrants what they did for white ethnics in the latter part of the nineteenth and the early twentieth century—namely, to use political machines to incorporate new immigrant populations. Frymer (1999) suggests that the potential backlash among white voters made outreach to newly emerging non-white communities a losing political strategy, since these new communities were both very small and politically isolated.

In part as a consequence of lack of party outreach, non-partisanship is high. Data from the Pilot National Asian American Political Survey (PNAAPS) (Lien 2001), reported in Table 4-1, illustrate the very large percentages of respondents who identify as independents, are unsure, or refuse to take any partisan identity at all. These totals range from a low of 26 percent for South Asians to a high of 70 percent for Vietnamese.

Asian populations that do adopt partisan identities do so with some significant variation by national origin group as well. Lien et al. (2004a) suggest that a substantial share of Asian immigrants who came from nations with communist regimes were more likely to identify as Republican, following a pattern quite similar to Cuban Americans. For example, in the PNAAPS, only 12 percent of Vietnamese Americans identified as Democratic at any level, and Vietnamese was the only national origin group where Democratic identity was outstripped by Republican identity. By contrast, Democratic identity for the other groups was consistently greater than that of the GOP, with differences ranging from a 20-point Democratic advantage among Filipino Americans to a 34-point advantage among Japanese Americans.

This Democratic preponderance appears to be a fairly recent phenomenon. Lien (2001) examined a variety of local, state, and national polls and

Group	Democrat (strong, weak or lean)	Republican (strong, weak or lean)	True Independent or no party ID, or unsure
Chinese	33	10	57
Filipino	46	26	28
Japanese	49	15	37
Korean	46	23	31
South Asian	49	25	26
Vietnamese	12	17	70

Table 4-1   Asian American National Origin Groups and Partisan Identification, 2001

Source: Pilot National Asian American Political Survey, 2000–2001. Adapted from Lien, Conway, and Wong 2004.

Note: Percentages may not add up to 100 because of rounding.

suggested that Asian Americans became a majority Democratic voting bloc in about 1998. For this to be so, and for the PNAAPS to report the dramatic Democratic advantages we see in Table 4-1, the change would have been precipitous and startling. Figure 4-4 appears to suggest precisely that. It shows a rapid growth of Democratic vote choice among Asians in the last several elections. And it appears that Barack Obama received strong support from Asian Americans as well. Exit polls suggest that Asian Americans represented about 2 percent of the national electorate in 2008 and voted 62 percent for Obama (compared with 53 percent overall and 43 percent among non-Hispanic whites).[7]

Patterns of party identification—when coupled with demographic trends identified in earlier chapters—give us some idea of the kinds of party coalitions that exist in U.S. politics and which states will be "blue" or "red." The development of party identifications (or the lack of their development) has enormous consequences for the future of U.S. politics. Generally speaking, the demographic trends coupled with these current patterns of party loyalty suggest that the near term at least favors the Democrats. Figure 4-5 illustrates the limits of opportunity for the GOP given the current composition of its coalition.

In Figure 4-5, we project Democratic vote share in presidential elections based on some assumptions regarding turnout and vote choice and on projections of the change in the demographic compositions of the country. Obviously, we cannot say for sure what the future holds. In part,

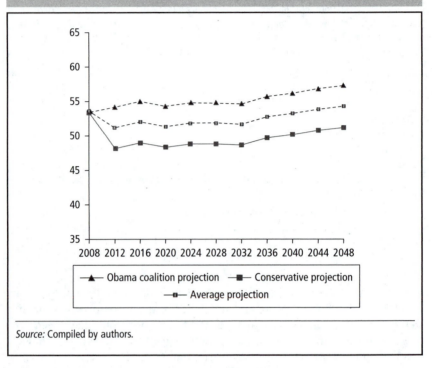

FIGURE 4-5 **Projected Democratic Vote Share under Varying Assumptions Regarding Vote by Racial/Ethnic Group (in percentages)**

Source: Compiled by authors.

this is because our projection is based on several different factors, including the population sizes, vote preferences, and turnout rates of each of the groups, and any of these factors could change. That said, the range of outcomes presented here should be understood as the realm of the likely. To generate our conservative projection, we use an estimate for white support for Democrats of 38 percent, close to their historical low nationally and well below the Democratic share in the last several elections, with the exception of 2010. We also peg other groups at or near historic lows, including African Americans at 85 percent Democratic, Latinos and others at 60 percent, and Asian Americans at 57 percent.[8] To generate a liberal projection, we assume the Obama coalition is holding. That is, we project two-party vote shares to be identical to those in the 2008 national exit polls. This may or may not be the highest possibility—while it is hard to imagine a higher vote share for Obama in the non-white racial groups, it is possible that white vote could exceed the 43 percent he received. So this line is not a wildly pro-Democratic projection. The average line is simply the mean of the two projections.

What do we see in Figure 4-5? Each line begins at the observed 2008 outcome. In no instance does the average of the projections drop below 50 percent. And the trend line is up for the Democrats. This is not to say that the GOP can never win. The conservative trend line is below 50 percent for the next seven presidential elections, and the GOP would be more than thrilled with seven wins in a row. But such an event is highly unlikely and would occur only under the most conservative scenario. Of all the likely outcomes between the conservative and Obama-coalition trend lines, the vast majority are above 50 percent.

Of course, twenty-eight years (or seven presidential elections) is a long time in American politics, and the historical lesson of African American partisanship is that patterns of partisanship are not fixed over the long term. But a significant departure from these patterns would require three conditions to be met, none of which we think is very likely in the short run. First, significant numbers of minorities would need to experience significant socioeconomic mobility to remove the economic bases of Democratic partisanship for at least parts of these populations. Second, after upward social mobility, individuals within these minority groups would have to prioritize economic voting over other factors shaping partisan sentiments and vote choice. As we described in detail in Chapter 2, the literature on identity, and especially the well-known work of Michael Dawson (1994), suggests that this is not likely. In-group solidarity and continued economic uncertainty cause minority voters to retain ethnic and working-class political preferences even as personal status changes. Finally, the GOP would have to significantly alter its message with respect to race and racial policies. Part of this strategy would be to shift attention to other matters. Indeed, McDaniel and Ellison (2008) discuss GOP attempts to recruit black and Latino Evangelicals into the GOP fold. But consistent with Frymer's (1999) observations, and as we outlined in detail in Chapter 3 and elaborated on in this chapter, the GOP coalition relies, at least in part, on its racial image. Significant alteration of this image could lose more votes than it gains. Outreach to Asian Americans might be less costly to the GOP, but there are fewer votes to be won there.

Of course, a fourth possibility exists but is not very likely—parties may change their policy platforms significantly and begin to appeal to voters in radically different ways. We think it unlikely, however, that the ideological complexion and policy positions of either party will change in any meaningful way in the near future. In Chapter 5 we explore the issue preferences of America's minority citizens to examine whether there is a genuine issue basis for partisan preference, which will tell us a great deal about the likelihood of significant political diversification among minority voters in the immediate future.

As we have seen, party loyalties are often established at a very early age. But political parties cannot simply throw up their hands and assume voters are out of reach. In fact, as citizens, we should want parties to try to woo voters and create new allegiances. Democracy is ill served if large shares of the electorate are ignored by one of two political parties.

In this chapter, we make some projections of vote share, but these projections depend in part on the parties not having terribly successful appeals to certain groups—on an assumption that the party coalitions more or less look the same over time. We have good reason to make that assumption.

But while some analysts see the "capture" of the African American vote by the Democratic Party—meaning that the GOP may not make many inroads there—it used to seem likely that the GOP could rely on the anticommunist sentiment of many Asian Americans to build support in that group. The struggle for Latinos, we are told, is over whether the group members vote their economic circumstances or their social values (though we will have a lot to say about this in Chapter 5).

Both Asian Americans and Latinos have less stable patterns of party loyalty, meaning that both groups are, in a sense, "in play." While we have raised some scepticism regarding exit poll findings, it is the case that these two groups show the most instability in their vote shares over the past several elections.

With this in mind, various leaders and strategists within each party are working hard to reach out to these two groups. For example, a website called The Americano is a conscious attempt by conservative and former GOP leader Newt Gingrich to appeal to Hispanic voters.[1] It includes a number of articles in Spanish. It is also possible to subscribe to Gringrich's tweets in English or Spanish.[2] Similarly, Democratic Asian Americans and Pacific Islanders are reaching out to grow their involvement in the party, in 2010 using both print and electronic campaign ads in English, Cantonese, Mandarin, Vietnamese, and Tagalog.

IMMIGRATION AND PARTISANSHIP

The partisanship of immigrants is an interesting topic for several reasons. As we have seen, the population of the United States contains, as it often has, a large number of immigrants. But immigrants are also interesting in terms of their partisanship. Partisanship is the product of a socialization process that often involves the transfer of identity from one generation (parents) to another (their children). The party loyalties of minorities who are immigrants have more complex patterns and roots than do native-born citizens because they are often socialized into the politics of different nations.

So far we have implicitly included immigrants within the broad racial and ethnic categorizations. But immigrants are especially interesting to our theoretical understanding of how party identification works in practice. This is so because, especially for immigrants who arrive later in life, their early childhood socialization will have had very little to do with "red" and "blue" states or the New Deal or any other alignment in U.S. politics. The political parties of their

Two points are worth noting about these kinds of websites and outreach efforts. First, they cater to the linguistic diversity within the different minority groups. Web-based campaign literature makes linguistically diverse outreach efforts cheaper for the parties to conduct—and hence more likely to be conducted. We can expect to see more efforts by both parties to engage in these (not so) new media efforts to reach out to minority communities.

Second, part of the difficulty with such efforts is that they may not be very effective in helping to change people's minds. This is true in large measure because they are too passive—expecting minority voters to "come to them," to stumble on the website, to seek out information about politics. One of the difficulties students and scholars of political science often face is that we care considerably more about politics than do most Americans. As a consequence, we significantly overestimate the amount of information that individual citizens have and the amount of energy they are willing to expend to get it.

Of course, sometimes even the effort of creating the website is intended as a symbolic gesture at outreach, which is far better than no gesture at all. But the examples above are ones where a party attempts to reach out to communities that, in some sense, need to be wooed, that have historic and valid reasons for alienation from the political system. We will show, in Chapter 6, that parties are comparatively disinterested in minority vote and that they contact minority voters far less frequently than they contact non-Hispanic white voters. As we noted, partisanship can lead people to be selective in the kinds of information they seek out, while nonpartisans may simply not seek out political information at all, and so these efforts may be more successful at strengthening or keeping support (among conservative Latinos or liberal Asian and Pacific Islanders) than in making converts.

---

[1] http://theamericano.com/2010/12/06/reviews-americanos-annual-hispanic-forum (accessed March 1, 2011).

[2] http://twitter.com/GingrichEspanol.

homeland are not present in U.S. elections, and the policy platforms and issues of U.S. parties are often very different from the ones they grew up with. Childhood and adolescence are key stages in socialization processes. Early in life children become exposed to their parents' political beliefs and opinions and often take those opinions on as their own—at least initially. An individual may experience social mobility or experience a realigning election, and these factors can, as we have noted, lead to someone changing those early opinions. But absent such change the theory of party identification suggests that ideas formed in childhood remain with voters throughout their lives.

How immigrants connect to the political system is thus an interesting question from the point of view of the theory of party identification, because a central component of that theory—childhood learning—is missing or, at least, not relevant. The few studies conducted on this topic show that as more time is spent in the United States, immigrants gradually become oriented toward the political system and do begin to acquire a political identity that is relevant to their new home (Wong 2000). For many this does seem to be shaped by experiences in their native country. One early study (Cain et al. 1991), for example, noted that Asian American immigrants, many of whom were refugees from brutal Communist regimes, leaned Republican. Experiences such as these are really important. As the work of Tam Cho (1999) shows, while the traditional emphasis of socioeconomic theories has emphasized factors such as education in explaining, for example, people's levels of participation, the study of immigrants shows that these factors have limited effects. Over and above demographic characteristics, experiences and socialization do have a great effect. Some of those experiences could be ones felt early on in their new home (Ramakrishnan and Espenshade 2001), but others could relate to experiences as children in native countries.

We will have more to say on reactions to immigrants in a later chapter. For now, we will reference a bit of our own work (Bowler et al. 2006). Anti-immigrant sentiments, expressed politically, may well shape the partisanship of the new citizens. There is good evidence taken from California in the mid-1990s that anti-immigrant rhetoric and the passage of a statewide ballot initiative targeting undocumented immigrants (and more) had significant impact on the political behavior of Latinos and others. Specifically, the passage of Proposition 187 halted a long-term drift of Latinos away from the Democrats and toward the Republicans and sent them rushing back into Democratic identification and voting behavior. That reversal also appeared in some of the younger cohorts of non-Hispanic whites.

SUMMARY

Partisanship is a core concept in political behavior, and its importance among minority citizens is, if anything, enhanced by the skew in their preferences. We have contended in this effort that minorities are a critical component of the Democratic coalition and that the future of minority voters with respect to party and vote preference may well determine the future of American politics.

The evidence suggests three things. First, the polarization of party and race is significant. Whites lean to the Republicans in identity and more heavily in two-party vote. By contrast, Latinos, Asians, and those marking "other" are heavily Democratic in identity and vote, more heavily Democratic than whites are Republican. And African Americans remain the most skewed in terms of party, with a huge preference for Democrats.

Second, there has been an interesting pattern of change and stability. Asian Americans have become dramatically more Democratic in the past fifteen years or so, marking one of the most significant shifts in minority partisan attachment we have ever witnessed. By contrast, Latinos fluctuate in their partisan attachments and vote choice but around a fairly stable mean. African American partisanship and vote have been remarkably stable for decades, since black Democratic identity solidified in the 1960s. This represented a historic shift away from the party of Lincoln to the party of the Civil Rights Act, one that forever altered the coalitional politics of both parties. The attachment of

African Americans to the Democrats is among the origins of Republican identity among southern whites. That strategy of mobilizing whites has kept Republicans competitive in national elections but dramatically narrowed their potential coalition.

Which brings us to our third implication. The interaction between partisan skew by race and the demographic change taking place in the United States has the potential to consign the GOP to long-term minority status as it lifts Democrats. This is only a potential, and naturally it relies on several assumptions and extrapolating a number of trends into the future. As such, the future remains unwritten. The demography is effectively irreversible, so for the GOP to change the dynamics, it must somehow find a way to change minority partisanship and trends.

If partisan attachment for minorities is purely affective, a matter of tradition more than cognition, there might be a significant opportunity for GOP inroads. Change the rhetoric and embrace the issues on language policy, immigration, and the like, and maybe there are votes to be had without significant costs among white constituencies. But if partisan attachment among minorities has an issue basis that extends beyond minority-specific concerns, if racial and ethnic minorities hold policy opinions that are genuinely to the left of non-Hispanic whites and the GOP, then the Republicans must hope for a change of heart among minority voters.

We turn our attention to this last issue, what minority citizens want from government, in the next chapter.

chapter 5

The Political Distinctiveness of American Minorities

Is there an issue basis for the partisan polarization by race we observed in Chapter 4? That is, are minority voter attachments to Democratic identity and candidates a product of tradition, a social convention without real policy content, or do minority voters generally agree more with Democratic policy preferences?

If everyone wanted the same things from government, it would not really matter very much whether patterns of political behavior varied across groups. It would not matter very much whether one group voted or stayed at home on Election Day and whether one group provided all the legislators and the other group provided none. If every group had similar tastes and preferences, then the policy outcomes—and presumably the collective happiness (or unhappiness) of each group of voters with that outcome—would not vary. Of course, a world where everyone agrees is not a very realistic picture of political life. Even if we just introduce two political parties into that picture, then straightaway we have two groups whose opinions and preferences on policies differ, and so straightaway it will matter if one of those groups got into power and the other did not. Once we introduce the possibility that there are other differences across groups, too, then the picture is complicated still further. The set of questions we examine in this chapter concerns just how different opinions are across racial and ethnic groups.

In many ways this is one of the central points in studying minority politics. It is differences of preferences—over what problems exist, what solutions should be adopted, which policies should be introduced or halted—that gives us the disagreement that politicians and political institutions help to resolve. If there were no real differences between minorities and Anglos, then the politics of minorities would be straightforward. Other differences—partisan ones, say, or class ones—may exist, but if there were no other differences across racial and ethnic groups, then minority politics would be simpler. In fact it might even be possible to say that minority politics would not really exist if minorities and non-Hispanic whites held shared views on most every political issue.

The reality, however, is that differences in policy preferences do exist across racial and ethnic groups. On many issues across a variety of dimensions, these groups differ substantially from the white majority, in terms of which issues are most important to shaping political preferences, as well as preferred policy outcomes. Not only that but African Americans, Latinos, and Asian Americans differ between and among themselves on what the important issues are and what the appropriate policy responses are to those issues.

We can examine just how distinctive minority voters may be by examining opinions across a range of issues. In this chapter we do so across four—very general—policy areas: minority issues, redistributive issues, public services, and social and moral issues. We discuss each of these policy areas in turn.

It would be natural for us to expect minority citizens to hold distinct preferences on what, for lack of a better term, we will call "minority issues." These are policy matters with specific relevance to one or more of the non-white racial and ethnic groups on which we are focusing our attention. Examples of this kind of policy area include language policy, broadly, and bilingual education, specifically; immigration policy and policies directed at immigrants themselves; hate crimes statutes; policies regarding affirmative action, civil rights protections, and equal opportunity enforcement; and voting rights. All of these matters are often contentious and are frequently constructed as a contest between the interests of the specific minority group in question and those of the broader population. All are issues with meaningful immediacy to many of the individuals in each group (and frequently to members of more than one of these groups), and it is no surprise that the distribution of preferences among minority citizens on these matters is very distinct from the opinions of many non-Hispanic whites.

We would also expect that the minority specificity of each issue is likely to raise its salience among the minority citizens: proposals on immigration and language, for example, will be more readily noticed by Latinos and Asian Americans than by African Americans, just as changes in farm price supports will be noticed more by farmers than steelworkers. Policy changes in these areas will increase the salience of racial and ethnic identity and prompt opinion formation on the policy proposals. We are also likely to see increases in in-group solidarity within the group as a consequence of policy proposals. For example, we might expect Latinos and Asian Americans—groups with very large foreign-born and second-generation populations—to hold very skewed and very similar views on matters of immigration, but have less in common on this issue with African Americans.

A second type of issue on which we might expect important differences includes matters of social welfare. These are class-specific policies that, while not explicitly racial, clearly have disproportionate impact among communities of color given socioeconomic stratification. Such issues are likely to include relief for the poor and antipoverty programs, more generally, unemployment insurance, public housing, and Medicare, indeed any program designed to alleviate the difficult circumstances of the poor and working class, in which minority populations sadly continue to find themselves overrepresented. They might also include broader redistributive policies such as college grants and student loans, health care reform, and school choice programs.

Obviously how big a gap we see both between minority groups and Anglos and among minority groups can vary quite a lot. The first policy area is likely to see bigger and more consistent differences between minorities and non-Hispanic whites than this area of social welfare policy. That said, Kinder and Winter (2001) do find some consistent and important differences between minorities and Anglos here, though both they and others (Bobo and Kluegel 1993; Kinder and Sanders 1996) have documented that the racial divide in opinion between whites and non-whites is considerably diminished when issues are framed in class rather than racial terms. That is, at least some social welfare policies can be discussed in ways that highlight the importance of race—sometimes in very subtle ways. For example, Winter (2006) argues that discussions of Social Security can and do imply a link between the policy and an elderly population that is disproportionately white. Consequently, Social Security policies are more warmly thought of by racially conservative voters than one might expect. On the other hand, policies aimed at helping the unemployed are sometimes seen as benefiting minorities—and especially African Americans. When policies are seen in this way, then support for the policy drops. When and how policies are seen in racial terms is, in part, an issue for political parties and their campaigns and rhetoric. For example, if a party would like to build support for—or opposition to—a particular social policy, then one way to do so might be to try to emphasize which racial group benefits from that policy. Research by Ismail White (2007) demonstrates that not all attempts at racially framing a policy work. And when they do work—when there is an effect—these attempts may not work in the same way across all voters. Still, the point remains that cueing or prompting a racial dimension to policy can help shape attitudes to policies themselves.

Our second group of policies, social welfare policies, is thus a little more complicated than the first group of minority policies. Social welfare policies need not be seen as "minority issues"—in which case we might not see as many differences between minorities and others as we would in the case of, say, immigration policy. But social welfare policies can, sometimes, be seen in racial terms. Sometimes, in fact, party campaigns may help emphasize the racial aspect to social welfare politics, and when that happens, we sometimes see shifts in public opinion on the policy itself.

The third group of policy in which we are interested, largely left unexplored in the literature, concerns policies without clear focus on minorities or class. On many of these matters—for example, environmental cleanup; police and fire protection; support for public schools, parks and recreation, and so on—minority opinion may still well be distinct from that of Anglos, but there may also be grounds for similarities in opinion. We call these policy areas "public services."

It is important here to come back to the idea of how social class may shape public opinion. It is straightforward to see that social class can shape opinion toward social welfare policies, since these are often redistributive policies associated with a social safety net. Some people may be wealthy enough to live in a private community that has lots of amenities and so, perhaps, do not really see the need for a public park for their children to play, they perhaps can hire full-time private security to supplement police protection, and they can afford to send their children to tuition-based schools. In short, these people and their families need not rely on public services. We would not be surprised if these individuals would prefer that government provide a lower level of social welfare policies and outputs and—hence—pay lower taxes. By contrast, others are so profoundly lacking in resources that they are entirely reliant on public services in education, recreation, and safety. We would expect these citizens to generally support higher levels of government action and public services provision. All of which is to say that general public service provision by government will still have a significant class component in the level and distribution of public support.

One important question is whether these second and third groups of issues—social welfare policies and public services provision—will produce less minority consensus than we see on minority-specific issues. Will we, in other words, see class divisions within minority groups as well as between minorities and Anglos? We would expect to see class divisions within minority groups come to the fore when explicit racial or ethnic stimuli are more muted. Importantly, if we do see such divisions, then socioeconomic mobility is more likely to lead ultimately to political diversification, since these issues are often at the heart of partisan competition. On the other hand, it is possible that the level of unity on explicitly racial policy items is more or less replicated on these more class-driven topics, raising two important possibilities. The first possibility is that strong racial identification and the concept of linked fate (Dawson 1994) led to the creation of what Dawson calls a "black utility heuristic." Extending this to other groups, we might understand this as there being a "lens" (appropriate to each group) that shades citizens' judgments about what is "in their interest." The second possibility relates to what Kinder and Winter (2001) think of as political philosophy or "principles" and what, in other circumstances, is understood as ideology. It may be that racial and ethnic minority groups exhibit more "collectivist" orientations—principles or orientations that create a preference for redistributive and collective benefits. Instead of preferring a laissez-faire or individualistic approach to policy, citizens may instead want a more active government involvement in guiding social outcomes. Of course, these two possibilities are not mutually exclusive. In both of these cases, either in-group identity and solidarity or ideological distinctiveness, minority political beliefs trump socioeconomic status and suggest that erosion of minority political unity—even on issues not clearly racial or ethnic on their face—and its partisan effects will be a much longer time coming.

In the following sections, we will illustrate the policy opinion dynamics we have just described at work among the American electorate. First, we will illustrate the degree of within-group and across-group minority consensus on explicitly racial and ethnic policy issues, on issues related to social welfare, and on general public service provision by government, and we will contrast those distributions with responses by non-Hispanic whites to the same policy dimensions. Once we can assess the degree to which race and ethnicity explain differences in opinion, we will be better positioned to speculate on a key question, namely, the effect economic success may have on partisan diversification and a de-racialization of two-party competition. Finally, we examine those social issues long seen as venues where minority opinion is distinctly conservative.

Our argument is simple. There is a strong issue basis for minority voters to hold a Democratic identity. Even when we consider social issues, there is little to suggest that Republicans have an easy hook on which to attract minority voters.

CONSIDERATION OF AGENDAS AND STABILITY

One word of caution is appropriate as we undertake this examination of issue preferences. We do not assume, and would not suggest, that minority issue positions are in any way permanent and incapable of change. Nor is it the case that we assume that the agenda, the issues that voters—including minority voters—care most about, is static. Issues come and go in the political system in ways both predictable and surprising (Kingdon 1984; Baumgartner and Jones 1996). Issues of concern to minority voters are no exception. For example, it is difficult for us today to conceive of a political arena where no one mentions immigration, but for much of the past century, immigration policy was relatively static. In the 1980s, sanctions against the apartheid regime in South Africa were of critical importance to many African American activists but today, almost 20 years after political change in South Africa, are obviously not a concern. The use of busing to integrate schools was a highly contentious issue for minorities and whites alike in the 1960s and early 1970s but, in the wake of adverse court decisions and the obsolescence of many consent decrees, no longer on the agenda (even as segregation in education remains a concern). Which issues are of concern to minority voters will vary over time, and which policies have a reasonable chance of enactment will vary considerably across political circumstances.

For our purposes, we focus on issues in the current political environment. Many of these—support for the poor, equal opportunity and civil rights, environment—are longstanding matters of public concern. Others may pass from the scene, as a consequence of agenda change, court decisions, or outside events that we cannot foretell. Nevertheless, we offer this view of minority issue opinion as a snapshot that is generally representative of agendas and views in today's political environment.

POLICY OPINION ON MINORITY-SPECIFIC ISSUES

As we suggested, it would not be surprising to find that minority opinion differs considerably from the opinion of whites on matters of policy related specifically to minorities themselves, whether this has to do with civil liberties, economic conditions, or even the contested nature of their membership in this society. It is also clear that there may be considerable disagreement between and among minority groups on these issues when the focus is more group specific.

Affirmative Action and Minority Living Standards

A clear illustration of this dynamic is provided by Tables 5-1 and 5-2, recounting popular support for affirmative action policies.

Table 5-1 reports attitudes on affirmative action from the 2004 National Politics Study. The question wording used in this study queries support for affirmative action as applied to "some groups." Two patterns are clear. The first is that all three minority groups are to the left of white Americans, reporting significantly greater support for affirmative action policies than whites. Blacks are, by far, the most liberal of the three groups and the only one of the three to register majority support for the policy, but both Asian Americans and Latinos are significantly more supportive than whites.

TABLE 5-1   Policy Opinions on Affirmative Action, General (in percentages)

Response category	Weighted pooled national sample	Unweighted responses by race and ethnicity			
		White (non-Hispanic)	African American	Hispanic or Latino	Asian American
Oppose strongly (1)	43.5	49.7	20.9	37.6	32.2
Oppose, not strongly (2)	27.8	26.4	28.0	25.6	34.7
Support, not strongly (3)	22.2	19.0	34.5	25.7	28.7
Support strongly (4)	6.5	4.9	16.6	11.1	4.4
Total N	2,838	901	728	728	481

Chi-square probability = 0.000

F-test probability from ANOVA = 0.0000

Source: 2004 National Politics Study.

Question wording: Some people say that because of past discrimination, some groups in society should be given preference in hiring and promotion. Others say that such preference in hiring and promotion is wrong because it gives some groups advantages they have not earned. How strongly do you favor or oppose preferential hiring and promotion? Are you strongly in favor, somewhat in favor, somewhat opposed, or strongly opposed to it?

		Unweighted responses by race and ethnicity			
TABLE 5-2	**Policy Opinions on Affirmative Action, Black Specific (in percentages)**				

Response category	Weighted pooled national sample	White (non-Hispanic)	African American	Hispanic or Latino	Asian American
Oppose strongly (1)	61.4	69.4	25.0	51.5	43.3
Oppose, not strongly (2)	21.5	20.0	21.3	22.4	43.3
Support, not strongly (3)	6.8	5.7	10.8	9.1	6.7
Support strongly (4)	10.3	5.0	42.9	17.1	6.7
Total N	1,873	1,002	464	340	30

Chi-square probability = 0.000

F-test probability from ANOVA = 0.0000

Source: American National Election Study 2008.

Question wording: Some people say that because of past discrimination, blacks should be given preference in hiring and promotion. Others say that such preference in hiring and promotion of blacks is wrong because it gives blacks advantages they have not earned. What about your opinion—are you FOR or AGAINST preferential hiring and promotion of blacks?

Table 5-2 reports attitudes on a nearly identical question, this time from the 2008 American National Election Study. This time, instead of leaving the beneficiary group ill defined, the question specifically references African Americans as the intended focus of the policy. As we noted above, tying racial groups to a policy area can produce differences in public opinions. This table provides some support for that argument. While it remains the case that all three minority groups[1] have opinions that are more liberal than those of whites, support for affirmative action among Latinos and Asians drops precipitously, with almost 87 percent of Asian Americans and 74 percent of Latinos opposing or strongly opposing the policy. By contrast, support among African Americans is somewhat stronger than it was in the more generic question wording.

The results on these two affirmative action questions illustrate both the advantages and the pitfalls of minority opinion on a clearly minority focused issue. Minority groups often have considerable agreement on issues of concern, holding mean opinions that are uniformly more pro-minority than do white Americans. On the other hand, between-group differences are present and, when the issue is identified with a single group, exacerbated into significant disagreement. Minority coalition is neither automatic nor unproblematic.

Affirmative action, of course, is a polarizing issue and one in which questions of gender are conflated with those of race. Affirmative action can also

BOX 5-1   Will Affirmative Action Go the Way of Busing?

Affirmative action was a major government policy aimed at redressing racial inequality. In recent years this approach has come under attack. Affirmative action has been banned in governmental behavior by state ballot initiatives such as Proposition 209 in California, and it has come under considerable scrutiny in the judicial branch. Most recently still, two cases from the state of Michigan raised the constitutionality of state affirmative action policies, with mixed results. In *Grutter v. Bollinger* (2003), the Supreme Court upheld an affirmative action policy for law school admissions that considered race and other characteristics as part of the school's emphasis on diversifying its student body and the legal profession, and the claims of diversity's impact on the quality of education. At the same time, in *Gratz v. Bollinger* (2003), the Supreme Court struck down the undergraduate affirmative action policy as too concretely advantaging one group of applicants vis-à-vis another, that is, as establishing virtual quotas.

Though the mixed nature of these two decisions left open the question of how long affirmative action is likely to survive, changes in the composition of the Supreme Court suggest that its future as an effective governmental policy could be limited. This issue, then, may in fact roll off the issue agenda of African Americans and others who support the policy—not by choice, but by the shocks of the political system. To foresee how this might occur, we look to the example of a previous effort at integration and racial redress, the policy of busing students.

In the wake of *Brown v. Board of Education* (1954) and *Brown II* (1955), desegregation of southern public accommodations—and particularly schools—proceeded at a frustratingly slow pace in the eyes of Civil Rights Movement activists. Encouraged by the phrase "all deliberate speed," officials resistant to integration fell back on dubious claims of careful planning, caution, and a danger of civil unrest to drag their feet in implementing integration. They were aided in this effort by federal judges in the South, many of whom offered narrow interpretations of statute and precedent designed to minimize the actual effects of new policies and higher court decisions. In one example, a federal judge ruled that integration practices were not required to desegregate schools that were "naturally" segregated by neighborhood, rather than as a consequence of de jure school district policies. The effect of such a claim would have been to kill meaningful desegregation, since neighborhoods then, and to a significant extent today, were extremely segregated by race.

After the U.S. Supreme Court ruled that school choice was not sufficient alone to achieve integration,[1] the case was refiled. In the landmark case of *Swann v. Charlotte-Mecklenburg Board of Education* (1971), the Court unanimously upheld a lower court decision requiring busing and redistricting to overcome the effect of neighborhood segregation on school enrollments. This decision served as the precedent on which many federal school desegregation cases rested.

Resistance to busing was fierce and not confined to the South. Since "naturally" segregated schools, as a consequence of neighborhood segregation, had been held to be just as impermissible as intentionally segregated schools, school districts across the country found themselves having to reconsider attendance areas and busing policies to achieve racial balance. Popular opposition was widespread and, occasionally, violent.

In a critical case, *Milliken v. Bradley* (1974), the Supreme Court placed a major limitation on the busing solution by ruling that busing orders could not cross school district lines unless there was evidence of de jure segregation being practiced by the two jurisdictions in question. In order to escape school desegregation, all white parents had to do was move across district boundaries to escape the reach of integration orders and the busses. Busing, as a solution to school segregation, was effectively dead. It would be hard today to speculate on minority attitudes—or, for that matter, non-Hispanic white attitudes—on busing. Indeed, most polling organizations stopped asking public opinion questions on this topic decades ago.

---

[1] In *Green v. County School Board* (1968).

		Unweighted responses by race and ethnicity			
Response category	Weighted pooled national sample	White (non-Hispanic)	African American	Hispanic or Latino	Asian American
Government should help (1)	9.1	3.7	33.5	15.1	6.5
(2)	8.0	6.4	13.9	9.2	16.1
Agree with both (3)	33.8	31.7	40.5	37.5	38.7
(4)	19.5	23.5	5.2	14.5	6.5
No special treatment (5)	29.6	34.7	6.9	23.7	32.3
Total N	1,280	924	173	152	31

TABLE 5-3   Policy Opinions on Standard of Living of Blacks (in percentages)

Chi-square probability = 0.000

F-test probability from ANOVA = 0.0000

Source: 2008 General Social Survey.

Question wording: Some people think that (Blacks/African Americans) have been discriminated against for so long that the government has a special obligation to help improve their living standards. Others believe that the government should not be giving special treatment to (Blacks/African Americans).

been seen as zero-sum. There may be winners and losers in affirmative action, and that perspective can also lead to changes in opinion. Better indicators of preferences with respect to minority-focused policy are therefore questions on support for minority living standards. The 2008 General Social Survey asks this question with respect to blacks, specifically, and the results are presented in Table 5-3.

Table 5-3 again illustrates the complexity of between-group relations and minority policy preferences. Like the black-specific affirmative action wording, this question again makes specific reference to African Americans. Again, all three minority groups are to the left of whites in their responses. For all racial groups except whites, the modal response is the "middle position," that is, to agree with both statements—that government has a special obligation to African Americans to improve their living standards and that no special treatment should be offered. The modal response for whites was to fully agree with only the "no special treatment" phrase.

Among whites, 58.2 percent of respondents selected responses on the side of "no special treatment," while only 17.1 percent selected options on the side of "special obligation." While Asian Americans and Latinos are less extreme than whites in their views, the comparable distributions still lean considerably in the direction of "no special treatment." For Latinos, 38.2 percent chose one of the two options on this side, compared with 24.3 percent on the side of "special obligation," while among Asian Americans (again, with a very small sample), the comparable figures are 38.8 percent to 22.6 percent. Not surprisingly, among African American respondents, only 12.1 percent articulated a "no special treatment" response, compared with 47.4 percent holding a belief that government has a "special obligation" to improve black living standards. While both Asian Americans and Latinos hold more generous views than whites, it would be wrong to conclude that minority opinion on this matter was consensual across groups or that African Americans enjoy strong policy support among Latinos or Asian Americans.

Immigration and Its Effects

Affirmative action and views on government commitment to minority living standards illustrate two key dynamics in minority opinion about minority-specific issues. First, minority citizens are consistently more liberal than non-Hispanic whites on such issues as affirmative action and aid to minorities, but between-group differences are meaningful, especially when African Americans are specifically identified as the policy beneficiary.

Immigration policy and the effects of immigration in American society are minority-focused issues but ones where African Americans are not generally seen as the group at issue. On this topic we may well see differences between and among minority groups. Table 5-4 reports results on a question regarding the pace of immigration to the United States. When asked whether the number of immigrants should be increased, decreased, or remain the same, the modal response is "the same" for all groups except whites, but again we

TABLE 5-4 Policy Attitudes on Immigrant Admissions Policy (in percentages)

Response category	Weighted pooled national sample	Unweighted responses by race and ethnicity			
		White (non-Hispanic)	African American	Hispanic or Latino	Asian American
Increased a lot (1)	3.7	2.3	6.4	8.8	5.3
Increased a little (2)	7.9	6.9	9.3	12.9	5.3
Remain the same (3)	34.4	31.0	32.6	53.1	68.4
Reduced a little (4)	23.7	25.1	24.4	16.3	10.5
Reduced a lot (5)	30.3	34.7	27.3	8.8	10.5
Total N	1,260	922	172	147	19
		Chi-square probability = 0.000			
		F-test probability from ANOVA = 0.0000			

Source: 2008 General Social Survey.

Question wording: Do you think the number of immigrants to America nowadays should be.

must point out considerable across-group variation. For whites, 59.8 percent want to see immigration reduced. For Latinos and Asians, the comparable figures are 25.1 percent and 21.0 percent, respectively, not surprising given their average proximity to the immigration experience. Importantly, the comparable figure for African Americans is 51.7 percent, less conservative than for non-Hispanic whites but still a majority in favor of slowing the rate of immigration.

The reason for this position is best illustrated in Table 5-5. This table reports respondents' beliefs regarding the effect of immigration on job availability for natural-born Americans. While 23.7 percent of both Asian American and Latino respondents somewhat or strongly agreed with the claim that immigrants take away jobs from born Americans, the comparable number is 30.4 percent among non-Hispanic whites. But, most importantly, 52.0 percent of African American respondents reported somewhat or strongly agreeing with this claim. This difference in responses could represent attitudinal distinctions between African Americans and other Americans on the net impact of immigration, or it might more directly reflect the economic position of African Americans and the likelihood that they, more than others, are forced to compete with new immigrants in the labor market. Whatever the cause, African American beliefs about the effects of immigration on jobs are consistent with the more general preference expressed by African Americans as a group for reducing the pace of immigration to the United States and likely a continued point of disagreement between them and other minority groups in the society.

TABLE 5-5   Policy Opinions on Immigration and Jobs (in percentages)

Response category	Weighted pooled national sample	Unweighted responses by race and ethnicity			
		White (non-Hispanic)	African American	Hispanic or Latino	Asian American
Strongly agree (1)	10.4	8.6	26.3	10.9	4.1
Somewhat agree (2)	19.8	21.8	25.7	12.8	19.6
Somewhat disagree (3)	25.4	27.2	20.0	19.2	29.2
Strongly disagree (4)	44.5	42.4	28.0	57.1	47.2
Total N	3,184	900	739	744	494
		Chi-square probability = 0.000			
		F-test probability from ANOVA = 0.0000			

Source: 2004 National Politics Study.

Question wording: Immigrants take jobs away from people who were born in America.

Attitudes about the pace of immigration and its effect on jobs are similarly reflected in preferences regarding border enforcement policy. When asked whether spending on border enforcement should increase, decrease, or stay the same, 56.6 percent of African Americans (along with 56.9 percent of non-Hispanic whites) favor beefing up border security expenditure, compared with 47.3 percent of Asian Americans and only 38.5 percent of Latinos. (See Table 5-6.) On this issue, African Americans again have more in common with white Americans than with other minorities.

Death Penalty

Finally, we look at the question of the death penalty. Although there is nothing inherently racial about the death penalty, per se, the racial justice or injustice of its application in the United States has long been subject to question (Peffley and Hurwitz 2007). Scholars have suggested that the application is endogenous to both the race of the alleged perpetrator and the race of the victim, where crimes involving non-white perpetrators and white victims receive harsher penalties, including death, than crimes with non-white victims and/or white perpetrators. As a consequence, we have for some time conceived of the death penalty as an issue of racial concern, and the evidence here seems to bear this out (Soss et al. 2003).

Table 5-7 reports the distribution of opinion by racial and ethnic identity on the use of the death penalty. Just over 60 percent of Americans favor or strongly favor death for those convicted of murder, 64.3 percent among *both*

TABLE 5-6   Policy Opinions on Immigration Enforcement Spending (in percentages)

Response category	Weighted pooled national sample	White (non-Hispanic)	African American	Hispanic or Latino	Asian American
		Unweighted responses by race and ethnicity			
Increase border spending (1)	51.1	56.9	56.6	38.5	47.3
Keep constant (2)	38.7	35.7	31.3	41.5	40.7
Decrease border spending (3)	10.3	7.5	12.1	20.0	12.0
Total N	3,139	897	737	730	484

Chi-square probability = 0.000

F-test probability from ANOVA = 0.0000

Source: 2004 National Politics Study.

Question wording: Now I would like to ask about various types of government programs. As I read each one, tell me if you would like to see spending for it increased, decreased, or if you would leave it the same. How about patrolling the border against illegal immigrants?

TABLE 5-7   Opposition or Support for Capital Punishment (in percentages)

Response category	Weighted pooled national sample	Unweighted responses by race and ethnicity			
		White (non-Hispanic)	African American	Hispanic or Latino	Asian American
Strongly favor (1)	32.1	35.4	20.1	31.4	28.7
Somewhat favor (2)	28.3	28.9	26.5	22.7	35.6
Somewhat oppose (3)	17.3	15.0	21.6	18.2	21.0
Strongly oppose (4)	22.3	20.7	31.9	27.7	14.7
Total N	3,177	900	728	740	491

Chi-square probability = 0.000

F-test probability from ANOVA = 0.0000

Source: 2004 National Politics Study.

Question wording: How strongly do you favor or oppose the death penalty for persons convicted of murder? Are you strongly in favor, somewhat in favor, somewhat opposed, or strongly opposed to it?

---

white and Asian Americans (though Asians seem somewhat less strong in their support). By contrast, the level of support is lower among Latinos, at 54.1 percent, still a majority but significantly lower than for whites and Asians. African American support comes in at 46.6 percent, still strong but significantly lower than any other group and decidedly lower than that among whites and Asians.

The uneven application of the death penalty, coupled with the overrepresentation of Latinos and especially African Americans in the criminal justice system, has made this issue racialized in a way that separates blacks and Latinos from whites and Asians. It is possible, too, that the prevalence of Roman Catholicism among Latinos and the church's opposition to capital punishment also plays a role. Skepticism about the death penalty should not, however, be understood as a lack of concern about crime, a subject we will return to shortly.

Summary

Our review of attitudes toward affirmative action, government's obligations to African Americans, and immigration policy illustrate two important dynamics that may shape, and also undermine, Democratic Party coalition building in the coming era. On the one hand, not surprisingly, minority groups in the United States consistently hold positions more favorable to minority interests than do whites, thereby creating an avenue of policy agreement with the party articulating those views, the Democrats.

On the other hand, while it is often the case that minority groups not directly affected by a policy hold more generous positions than whites do, this generosity is not across the board. Latinos and Asian Americans are far less supportive than blacks of the view that African Americans, historically disadvantaged, should receive government intervention and preferential treatment. Meanwhile, African Americans are every bit as conservative—sometimes even more so—as whites when it comes to immigration policy and border enforcement, a view that clearly stems from their perception that immigrants take native-born Americans' job opportunities.

On these minority-specific policies, then, there is evidence for both the claim that Democratic identification is consistent with issue preferences on matters of importance to particular minority groups and the notion that the Democratic coalition is vulnerable to disruption over disagreement between minority groups on some core preferences.

SOCIAL WELFARE AND PUBLIC SERVICES

Following Kinder and Winter (2001), we have suggested that issues involving inherently redistributive policies are likely to reflect significant racial polarization, if for no other reason than the clustering of racial and ethnic minorities at the lower end of the socioeconomic spectrum. We can take this logic a step further and suggest that even seemingly nonredistributive policies—normal governmental public service provision—have redistributive elements and so may well reflect the same racial polarization found in policies that more clearly reallocate resources between racial and ethnic groups.

As we noted earlier, minority opinions on these questions of public services are especially interesting in terms of party voting and party fortunes in future chapters. If minority support for the Democratic Party is attributable to the party's positions on civil rights and similar issues, then one could say that minority partisanship was unrelated to key elements of minority interests on a string of policy concerns. Yes, it may be that the Democratic Party reflected the views of minority voters on, say, affirmative action. As White argues, for example, not all issues are seen by African Americans through a racial lens (White 2007). After all, minority voters are not just "minorities"; they are also parents and commuters, homeowners and drivers, and a whole range of other "identities." And if their views on other issues—parks and schools, toll roads and rail links, crime and health care—were at odds with the Democratic platform, then this would provide fertile ground for the other party, should it temper its rhetoric with respect to racial issues. By contrast, if minority views on these nonracial policies were consistent with their majority partisan leanings, then minority voters could fairly be judged as self-interested and rational. It would also mean significantly less opportunity for the GOP to recruit additional minority voters merely by adjusting their views on the narrow range of explicitly racial issues.

In other words, looking at the policy preferences of minority voters on nonracial issues tells us something about not only just how distinctive minorities are in the political sense of having different preferences and tastes but also

TABLE 5-8   Government Improve the Poor's Standard of Living (in percentages)

Response category	Weighted pooled national sample	Unweighted responses by race and ethnicity			
		White (non-Hispanic)	African American	Hispanic or Latino	Asian American
Government in Washington (1)	19.9	13.8	40.7	32.7	25.0
(2)	12.2	11.4	15.3	13.7	12.5
Agree with both (3)	42.7	44.9	36.7	36.6	40.6
(4)	14.2	17.5	4.0	5.9	12.5
People help selves (5)	11.0	12.4	3.4	11.1	9.4
Total N	1,304	942	177	153	32

Chi-square probability = 0.000

F-test probability from ANOVA = 0.0000

Source: 2008 General Social Survey.

Question wording: Please look at the hand card. Some people think that the government in Washington should do everything possible to improve the standard of living of all poor Americans; they are at Point 1 on this card. Other people think it is not the government's responsibility, and that each person should take care of himself; they are at Point 5. Where would you place yourself on this scale, or haven't you made up your mind on this?

the possible range of options open to the political parties and their future electoral fortunes.

In order to explore these themes, what we need to do is to examine public opinion across racial and ethnic groups across a range of different policies.

Redistributive Policy

We examine three different questions regarding government attempts to improve the standard of living for all Americans, for the poor specifically, and to reduce inequality. The results are generally consistent but display important distinctions, and they are reported in Tables 5-8 through 5-10.

All three minority groups hold views more supportive than whites of government assistance to the poor. Looking at Table 5-8, while only 25.2 percent of whites report feeling that the government in Washington should "do everything possible," the comparable figure for Asian Americans was 37.5 percent, for Latinos was 46.4 percent, and for African Americans was 56 percent.

Turning to the question of government provision of a job and good standard of living for everyone, reported in Table 5-9, only 24.7 percent of whites lean in this direction, compared with 54.1 percent preferring to "let each person

TABLE 5-9   Government Ensures Everyone Has a Job and Good Standard of Living (in percentages)

Response category	Weighted pooled national sample	Unweighted responses by race and ethnicity			
		White (non-Hispanic)	African American	Hispanic or Latino	Asian American
Government should see to jobs/standard (1)	10.4	6.1	34.1	22.3	25.0
(2)	8.9	7.1	13.5	13.1	6.3
(3)	11.4	11.5	10.9	12.0	18.8
(4)	19.7	21.2	17.2	19.4	12.5
(5)	19.4	18.7	12.4	17.1	37.5
(6)	16.7	17.8	6.4	9.7	0.0
Let each person get ahead on their own (7)	13.6	17.6	5.6	6.3	0.0
Total N	997	523	267	175	16

Chi-square probability = 0.000

F-test probability from ANOVA = 0.0000

Source: American National Election Study 2008.

Question wording: Some people feel the government in Washington should see to it that every person has a job and a good standard of living. Suppose these people are at one end of a scale, at point 1. Others think the government should just let each person get ahead on their own. Suppose these people are at the other end, at point 7. And, of course, some other people have opinions somewhere in between, at points 2, 3, 4, 5, or 6. Where would you place YOURSELF on this scale, or haven't you thought much about this?

Note: Only half the sample was asked this question; Assignment Random.

get ahead on their own." Asian American responses (from a very small sample) were more generous, with 50.1 percent answering on the side of government guarantees, while 37.5 percent preferred the alternative (and not strongly). For Latinos, 47.4 percent preferred government intervention, while 33.1 percent preferred the alternative. Finally, for African Americans, 58.5 percent preferred government involvement, while only 24.4 percent offered a preference for more individual responsibility.

Finally, on the question of reducing social inequality, we find 44.5 percent of whites in Table 5-10 offering responses below the midpoint, that is, favoring to some degree government efforts to reduce inequality. For the minority groups, we find actually less support (though not statistically significantly less) among the very small Asian American sample, with only 37.6 percent favoring government intervention. For Latinos and African Americans, however, our earlier pattern holds true. A hefty 60.3 percent of Latinos favored government action to reduce inequality, and 67.3 percent of African Americans did so.

TABLE 5-10   Government Takes Steps to Reduce Inequality (in percentages)

Response category	Weighted pooled national sample	Unweighted responses by race and ethnicity			
		White (non-Hispanic)	African American	Hispanic or Latino	Asian American
Gov't reduce difference (1)	23.5	18.9	41.4	31.8	18.8
(2)	8.7	8.1	9.9	11.0	6.3
(3)	17.2	17.5	16.0	17.5	12.5
(4)	17.9	17.6	18.2	18.2	25.0
(5)	13.3	14.4	6.6	11.7	25.0
(6)	6.8	7.9	2.2	5.8	3.1
No government action (7)	12.8	15.7	5.5	3.9	9.4
Total N	1,318	951	181	154	32

Chi-square probability = 0.000

F-test probability from ANOVA = 0.0000

Source: 2008 General Social Survey.

Question wording: Some people think that the government in Washington ought to reduce the income differences between the rich and the poor, perhaps by raising the taxes of wealthy families or by giving income assistance to the poor. Others think that the government should not concern itself with reducing this income difference between the rich and the poor. Here is a card with a scale from 1 to 7. Think of a score of 1 as meaning that the government ought to reduce the income differences between rich and poor and a score of 7 meaning that the government should not concern itself with reducing income differences. What score between 1 and 7 comes closest to the way you feel?

While our analysis of Asian Americans is hampered by small sample sizes, we can make some general observations about redistributive policy. Overall, racial and ethnic minorities are to the left of whites. Of these groups, Asians hold views that appear to be the least distinct from whites, whereas Latinos and African Americans are significantly more liberal than non-Hispanic whites on these questions. African Americans consistently hold the most liberal positions on redistributive policy.

Public Service Provision

Earlier in this chapter we suggested that a third group of issues, beyond the explicitly racial and the clearly redistributive, may well show opinion distributions that reflect racial polarization. Even public service provision that is not *explicitly* redistributive—such as public education, environmental regulation, and the like—may be *inherently* so and therefore attract opinion distributions that are reflective of the broad socioeconomic inequalities in the society, many of which are closely associated with race.

To illustrate this, we look at opinion distributions across three broad areas of government concern. The first is public education. Public education is available to all and was intended to be so and is not obviously and pointedly redistributive. Nevertheless, it is very clear that those with the least resources are most in need of publicly provided education for their children. Is this difference in dependence reflected in preferences?

Table 5-11 reports the distribution on the very simple question of whether public education should receive increased funding, the same, or decreased funding. On a seven-point scale, where four (4) indicates a preference for no change, that option is the modal response overall and for every individual group except African Americans (whose modal response is the highest amount of increase). Nevertheless, a majority of respondents in all groups favor *some* level of increase. Even with this apparent level of consensus between the minorities and the majority, the differences between groups, however, are important. While 51.7 percent of non-Hispanic whites favor some increase, the comparable number is 60.1 percent for Asian Americans, 63.1 percent for African Americans, and 54.4 percent for Latinos. Moreover, 44.0 percent of African Americans preferred the "increase a lot" option (almost doubling that of Asian Americans and whites), while 29.4 percent of Latinos chose this strongest

TABLE 5-11 Preferences on Public Education Expenditure (in percentages)

Response category	Weighted pooled national sample	Unweighted responses by race and ethnicity			
		White (non-Hispanic)	African American	Hispanic or Latino	Asian American
Increase a lot (1)	25.3	23.3	44.0	29.4	22.9
(2)	21.9	23.0	15.5	19.2	22.9
(3)	5.9	5.4	3.6	5.8	14.3
Keep same (4)	32.8	33.7	26.0	31.8	28.6
(5)	3.4	3.2	2.3	2.6	0.0
(6)	5.2	5.6	3.4	6.3	5.7
Decrease a lot (7)	5.5	5.9	5.2	4.9	5.7
Total N	2,208	1,168	555	428	35

Chi-square probability = 0.000

F-test probability from ANOVA = 0.0003

Source: American National Election Study 2008.

Question wording: (What about) PUBLIC SCHOOLS (Should federal spending on public schools be INCREASED, DECREASED, or kept ABOUT THE SAME?) Should it be increased A GREAT DEAL, A MODERATE AMOUNT, or A LITTLE? Should it be decreased A GREAT DEAL, A MODERATE AMOUNT, or A LITTLE?

option. Whether we look at strength or extremity of opinion or merely the size of the majority for any level of increase, it is hard not to conclude that on the question of education spending, minorities are to the left of whites—perhaps not wildly so, but still more liberal.

A second public service issue is environmental protection. Again, water and air consumption are universal and are not readily thought of as redistributive. Nevertheless, as with education, those with fewer resources face more difficult obstacles to protecting themselves from environmental degradation. Without resources, one is less able to move to escape neighborhood toxicity, resist the placement of environmentally undesirable industry and public works in one's area, consume privately bottled water, or even own or rent housing with sufficient yard to obviate the need for park space. As with education, we contend, environmental spending is still subtly redistributive and could conceivably be reflected in public opinion.

When we look at preferences over spending on environmental issues, our findings show that African Americans, Latinos, and Asian Americans are all significantly more supportive of increased environmental spending when compared with non-Hispanic whites. (See Table 5-12.) Whether these preferences are a consequence of community vulnerability to the impacts of

TABLE 5-12   Preferences on Environment Expenditure (in percentages)

Response category	Weighted pooled national sample	Unweighted responses by race and ethnicity			
		White (non-Hispanic)	African American	Hispanic or Latino	Asian American
Increase a lot (1)	27.7	24.5	47.3	33.5	35.3
(2)	20.5	21.6	17.3	21.2	20.6
(3)	5.0	4.8	4.3	5.6	2.9
Keep same (4)	34.5	36.0	23.2	29.3	26.5
(5)	2.5	2.4	1.6	1.4	5.9
(6)	3.8	4.6	1.8	4.4	5.9
Decrease a lot (7)	6.0	6.1	4.5	4.7	2.9
Total N	2,190	1,156	560	430	34

Chi-square probability = 0.000

F-test probability from ANOVA = 0.0000

Source: American National Election Study 2008.

Question wording: (What about) PROTECTING THE ENVIRONMENT (Should federal spending on protecting the environment be INCREASED, DECREASED, or kept ABOUT THE SAME?) Should it be increased A GREAT DEAL, A MODERATE AMOUNT, or A LITTLE? Should it be decreased A GREAT DEAL, A MODERATE AMOUNT, or A LITTLE?

pollution or simply a reflection of more liberal attitudes on government expenditure, minorities in the United States appear significantly to the left of whites on this issue as well.

Finally, we examine expenditure on crime. No one desires to be a victim of crime, and efforts to reduce crime conceivably benefit all citizens. Minority attitudes on crime fighting represent a bit of a special case, however, because of the often difficult relationship between law enforcement officers and communities of color, on the one hand, and their significantly greater probability of being a crime victim, on the other (Ogawa 1998). Though much attention is paid to racial profiling, accusations of brutality and excessive force, and the obviously disproportionate rate of incarceration for minority males, there is also evidence that minorities favor greater crime-fighting efforts in part because of the vulnerability low-income communities have to criminal activity.

Here we focus on the issue of spending, in part because it avoids the entangling complexities just mentioned and in part because it again specifically focuses our attention on the part of criminal justice policy that could be interpreted as subtly redistributive. We report opinions on expenditures for fighting crime in Table 5-13. As in education, crime fighting is popular and the level of consensus across groups is quite high. For all groups a majority favors greater spending on fighting crime. Nevertheless, all three minority groups offer significantly greater support for increased expenditure on crime fighting.

Applying a straightforward partisan interpretation of this finding is a bit harder than for the cases of education and environmental spending. On the one hand, support for greater government expenditure on any issue could be interpreted as "liberal"; however, it is more difficult to apply that interpretation when

TABLE 5-13 Preferences on Crime-Fighting Expenditure (in percentages)

		Unweighted responses by race and ethnicity			
Response category	Weighted pooled national sample	White (non-Hispanic)	African American	Hispanic or Latino	Asian American
Spend more (1)	54.2	51.7	66.3	59.4	64.7
Keep same (2)	31.6	33.7	23.7	29.7	23.5
Spend less (3)	14.2	14.7	10.1	10.9	11.8
Total N	2,175	1,150	554	424	34

Chi-square probability = 0.000
F-test probability from ANOVA = 0.0000

Source: American National Election Study 2008.

Question wording: (What about) DEALING WITH CRIME (Should federal spending on dealing with crime be INCREASED, DECREASED, or kept ABOUT THE SAME?)

the expenditure is on crime fighting. So while we cannot necessarily conclude that these data illustrate a more liberal minority population, once again they clearly indicate the segmentation of preferences by race and ethnicity.

Summary

In summary, in examining the broad rubric of public service provision, on issues that are not explicitly racial nor clearly redistributive, we can see that there is an underlying class dynamic that, when coupled with the specific needs of communities of color for a variety of government services, makes even general public service provision subtly redistributive and suggests that minority preferences have a distinct distribution compared with whites.

The data presented here clearly illustrate that on issues of public education, protecting the environment, and fighting crime, minority respondents were consistently and significantly more likely than whites to favor greater government expenditure in each of these areas—that is, greater public service provision. While the issue of crime fighting is a bit more sociologically complex, it is fair to say, we believe, that these results reflect a broader "liberalism" of minority communities, a willingness and enthusiasm for the use of government action to address social issues and to enhance the use of public funds to pay for these endeavors. By any measure these opinion distributions are consistent with the Democratic dominance reflected in the two-party vote of these communities and suggest, at least on these issues, that this partisan identity and behavior, rather than being a purely affective identity, is reflective of an issue content. That is, on these issues as on those regarding specific minority concerns and redistributive social welfare policy, partisanship is consonant with group interests.

SOCIAL ISSUES AND MINORITY ATTITUDES: THE ACHILLES' HEEL OF DEMOCRATIC PARTY DOMINANCE?

One issue area in which minority voter loyalty to the Democratic Party may be threatened is in the area of social issues. This group of issues has often been identified as an important exception to the issue basis of minority support for the Democratic Party and, hence, a place where some minority voters could break away from the Democrats. The argument, buttressed by exit poll data on gay marriage bans, is that religious observance among African Americans and Latino Roman Catholicism makes these natural "values" voters, that is, voters willing to decide two-party votes on the basis of these issues and the candidates' and parties' stands. A similar pattern may hold with respect to attitudes toward abortion. There is already good evidence that these issues are not salient among Latinos, and the extreme partisan distribution among African Americans toward the Democrats is clearly inconsistent with such a claim (Nicholson and Segura 2005). Nevertheless, we examined minority group views on these two issues.

Attitudes toward Abortion

The results on abortion are not particularly informative, in large measure because the values gap, which could conceivably underpin a pro-GOP shift, appears to be absent. When asked in the American National Election Study in 2008 if abortion should be banned; allowed only in the case of rape, incest, or to protect the life of the mother; or always permitted, there is little meaningful difference across racial and ethnic groups. In Table 5-14, about one-third of Asians and Latinos favored "always" permitting abortion, compared with 39.5 percent of non-Hispanic whites. For all three groups, the modal (or most common) response was middle response (between 44.0 and 46.7 percent across the three), that is "in the case of rape, incest or to protect the life and health of the mother." So while non-Hispanic whites were slightly more permissive on this issue, they do not begin to compare with African Americans. Over 44.0 percent of African American respondents favored "always" permitting abortion. A strategy focused on abortion might make small inroads among Hispanics and Asians for the GOP but would seem counterproductive among African Americans.

Attitudes toward Gay and Lesbian Rights

Minority attitudes on gay and lesbian rights illustrate interesting patterns as well. While again these issues are of comparatively low salience to many minority communities, the GOP has long felt that socially conservative church-going minorities provide fertile ground for that party's message on

TABLE 5-14   Abortion Views (in percentages)

Response category	Weighted pooled national sample	Unweighted responses by race and ethnicity			
		White (non-Hispanic)	African American	Hispanic or Latino	Asian American
Never (1)	14.9	13.9	14.4	22.9	20.0
Rape/incest/protect mother (2)	45.8	46.6	41.3	44.0	46.7
Always (3)	39.3	39.5	44.3	33.1	33.3
Total N	1,014	532	271	175	15
		Chi-square probability = 0.064			
		F-test probability from ANOVA = 0.1433			

Source: American National Election Study 2008.

Question wording: There has been some discussion about abortion during recent years. Which one of the opinions on this page best agrees with your view? You can just tell me the number of the opinion you choose.

TABLE 5-15   Opinion on Gay Employment Antidiscrimination Protections (in percentages)

Response category	Weighted pooled national sample	Unweighted responses by race and ethnicity			
		White (non-Hispanic)	African American	Hispanic or Latino	Asian American
Favor strongly (1)	52.5	53.5	49.1	54.1	42.4
Favor not strongly (2)	20.9	22.0	16.7	17.2	27.3
Oppose not strongly (3)	11.5	10.5	13.4	13.0	6.1
Oppose strongly (4)	15.1	14.0	20.9	15.7	24.2
Total N	2,161	1,142	546	414	33

Chi-square probability = 0.002

F-test probability from ANOVA = 0.0780

Source: American National Election Study 2008.

Question wording: Do you FAVOR or OPPOSE laws to protect homosexuals against job discrimination? Do you favor such laws STRONGLY or NOT STRONGLY? Do you oppose such laws STRONGLY or NOT STRONGLY?

social issues and a potential opportunity to peel minority votes away from the Democrats.

National opinion surveys would seem to cast doubt on how successful this strategy may be. In Tables 5-15, 5-16, and 5-17, we report attitudes on gay and lesbian employment discrimination protection, adoption rights, and same-sex marriage policy. In Table 5-15 it is immediately apparent that a plurality of all four groups strongly favors extension of employment discrimination protection to gays and lesbians. Of the four, African Americans offer the weakest support, with 65.8 percent favoring or strongly favoring adoption of antidiscrimination laws, while the comparable numbers for Asians, Latinos, and non-Hispanic whites are 69.7 percent, 71.3 percent, and 75.5 percent, respectively. Still, it is hard to describe an almost two-thirds majority support among blacks as "weak," and we are particularly persuaded by the level of support among Latinos. Opposition to antidiscrimination legislation—even as applied to gays and lesbians—does not appear to be a big winner for the GOP among communities of color.

Support for gay and lesbian adoption rights is considerably lower than support for gay rights in other arenas among all groups, reflecting an inherent conservatism regarding the welfare of children and long-held stereotypes and fears associated with gays and lesbians (Lax and Phillips 2009; Ryan et al. 2004; Ross et al. 2008). The results, however, add further complexity to our story and are not a clear indication that minorities' social conservatism is a risk to their Democratic skew. Latinos hold views of gay adoption that are indistinguishable

TABLE 5-16   Attitudes on Adoption by Gay Men and Lesbians (in percentages)

Response category	Weighted pooled national sample	Unweighted responses by race and ethnicity			
		White (non-Hispanic)	African American	Hispanic or Latino	Asian American
Yes (1)	52.0	52.2	40.6	53.3	76.5
No (5)	48.0	47.8	59.4	46.8	23.5
Total N	2,177	1,151	549	415	34

Chi-square probability = 0.000

F-test probability from ANOVA = 0.0002

Source: American National Election Study 2008.

Question wording: Do you think gay or lesbian couples, in other words, homosexual couples, should be legally permitted to adopt children?

from non-Hispanic whites, as reported in Table 5-16, and the very small Asian sample appears dramatically more permissive on this question. Only among African Americans does gay and lesbian adoption rights face majority opposition. So while it is the case that African Americans appear more conservative on this issue, it is not the case that a substantial policy push against gay adoption is a clearly winning strategy for the GOP among all minority voters.

TABLE 5-17   Preferred Policy on Government Recognition of Same-Sex Relationships (in percentages)

Response category	Weighted pooled national sample	Unweighted responses by race and ethnicity			
		White (non-Hispanic)	African American	Hispanic or Latino	Asian American
No support (1)	31.2	27.0	50.3	49.5	22.2
Civil unions only (2)	35.2	39.4	27.5	27.8	43.3
Marriage (3)	33.6	33.6	22.2	22.7	34.5
Total N	3,112	884	690	705	478

Chi-square probability = 0.000

F-test probability from ANOVA = 0.0000

Source: 2004 National Politics Study.

Question wording: I am going to read you three statements. Which of the following statements comes closest to your view concerning same-sex couples? Should they (READ CHOICES).

Finally, we turn our attention to the deeply contentious issue of same-sex marriage. On this issue alone, conventional wisdom does appear to be supported by the data. Both African Americans and Latinos appear significantly less supportive of marriage equality and even civil unions than whites or Asians (this time, with a sizable sample). Approximately half of all black and Hispanic respondents in Table 5-17 favored no legal recognition, compared with only 22 percent of Asians and 27 percent of non-Hispanic whites. This is a significant difference on a visible policy issue and one that places blacks and Latinos at odds with gay and lesbian coalition partners in the Democratic coalition.

Summary

Abortion and gay rights are sometimes seen as the issues that distinguish minorities from other Democrats and conceivably a key to cracking that party's coalition. The opinion data presented here and elsewhere are far less convincing on this point. Specifically, on abortion Asians and Latinos were almost indistinguishable from whites, while African Americans were far more liberal. On gay rights there was considerable consensus across racial and ethnic groups supporting nondiscrimination protections, and little meaningful difference between Latinos and whites on adoption. African Americans were more conservative on adoption, and both African Americans and Latinos were less supportive of government recognition of same-sex relationships. So there are considerable inconsistencies within groups across issues and across groups on a single issue, hardly the basis for an unambiguous appeal and opening for the GOP.

RACE, CLASS, AND DISADVANTAGE: CAUSES AND CONSEQUENCES OF POLITICAL DISTINCTIVENESS—SOME CONCLUDING THOUGHTS

Across a range of public policy issues and issue dimensions, minority respondents to opinion polls express political views significantly to the left of white Americans. It is not simply the case that minorities are "single-issue" or even "single bundle of issues" voters for the Democrats. Minority policy preferences are aligned with the political left across a range of issues, not just those relating to race (for example, affirmative action). African Americans, Latinos, and Asian Americans are often more supportive, not only of minority-focused issue positions but also of explicitly redistributive policies with implicit minority beneficiaries, and greater public service provision, which we have also argued has an implicit minority benefit (Chong and Kim 2006).

Our exploration of policy preferences did reveal some potential cracks in the foundation of the Democratic coalition, cracks that could conceivably undermine minority contributions to Democratic dominance. First, Asians and Latinos expressed greater skepticism over minority policy initiatives when African Americans were the specified beneficiaries and, conversely, African

Americans expressed considerably more concern about immigration—particularly as it related to job competition. Interminority disagreement complicates coalitional politics and appears to reveal important tensions in between-group relations, ones documented at length elsewhere (Kim 2000; Vaca 2004; McClain et al. 2006).

Second, the issues of gay marriage and abortion provided some evidence for a social conservatism that could splinter minorities from the Democratic coalition. But we are aware of no evidence that any of these issues have ever figured prominently in the voting calculations of most minority voters, and the record is by no means homogenous with respect to issue preferences. African Americans appeared significantly more liberal on abortion and more conservative on gay marriage, while Latinos—who were also more conservative on gay marriage—appeared similar to whites on issues of adoption and antidiscrimination protection. In short, there is little evidence of a monolithic socially conservative minority viewpoint.

Finally, the distributions of issue opinion illustrated the greatest agreement across minority groups, and the most significant distancing from non-Hispanic whites, on explicitly redistributive and public service issues, positions that would appear to be associated with minority interests primarily because of the unfortunate concentration of minority group members in lower-income and lower-education cohorts. This raises the central concern of whether class and race operate distinctively among minority populations (Wilson 1980) or whether attachment to working-class issue positions transcends social mobility as a consequence of strong, in-group, racial identification (Dawson 1994). If greater socioeconomic mobility and diversification erode the distinctly liberal policy preferences of minority group voters, the consonance of Democratic identification and vote with minority interests would likewise erode, and with it potential Democratic dominance.

Any meaningful erosion of minority loyalty to, and identification with, the Democratic Party would seem to require the confluence of three factors and not simply social mobility. True enough, social mobility would seem to be one of the foundations of changing party loyalty, but, in addition, movement of important numbers of minority voters into the GOP column would require at least two other changes. First, there would need to be some observable GOP moderation on race-specific issues, a change that would appear to be important—based on the issue positions expressed on affirmative action and immigration—and unlikely, given the GOP's long-standing southern strategy.

Second, movement from "D" to "R" would also seem to require a willingness on the part of minorities themselves to let individualized self-interest rather than a group-based heuristic determine political preferences. If, as Dawson suggests, in-group identification transcends individual mobility, if the evaluative criteria were group based, then we could expect Democratic policy positions and the expressed preferences of minority voters to remain consistent over the longer term. In short, it will be some time before the GOP's voter base includes substantial minority votes.

Taking Part in Politics:
The Essence of Democracy

> Freedom of expression—in particular, freedom of the
> press—guarantees popular participation in the decisions and
> actions of government, and popular participation is the essence
> of our democracy.
>
> (Corazon Aquino)

We have argued that the future of the American political system will be shaped by the manner and degree to which minority citizens engage the political system. In particular, minorities will form a key group when it comes to the competition between political parties for the allegiances of voters and control of political institutions. Using demographic change as the foundation on which we raise the question, we have illustrated that the votes of minority citizens are crucial to the competitiveness of one of the two parties and almost wholly irrelevant to the other. It is also clear that on an entire range of issues (and classes of issues), minority voters' partisan skew reflects the skew in their preferences. That is, African Americans, Latinos, and increasingly Asian Americans hold policy preferences largely—indeed, overwhelmingly—consistent with their partisan identities and vote choice (Segura et al. 2006).[1]

Much of what we have discussed so far concerns attitudes and preferences. But the political future depends not just on the attitudes of minorities but also on whether or not minorities act on those preferences and vote or engage in other kinds of political action that will help to translate those preferences into policy (Browning et al. 1986; Hero 1992).

In this chapter and the next, we therefore turn our attention from attitudes to actual behavior. There are many different ways of participating in politics. Someone could display campaign stickers or signs, sign a petition, donate time and money to a political campaign, or join a protest march. The most obvious, and most studied, form of political participation is the decision to turn out and vote. For minorities the decision to vote is somewhat distinctive given historical and legal practices that have often made it harder—and in many instances impossible—to vote even though they are U.S. citizens.

Studies of the political behavior of citizens sometimes talk of participation in terms of how costly it is. Some forms of participation—voting, for example—take relatively little effort and so are seen as less costly. Other forms of participation—such as taking time to participate in a street march—are seen as more costly. Generally speaking, if someone engages in costly or time-consuming action—letter writing or protest marching—he or she is usually also engaged in less costly action, such as voting. Sometimes these acts of participation are seen as a ladder with a progression from the least to the most costly (Dalton 2006, chap. 3).

The metaphor of the ladder with one step following another does not always work as well where minorities are concerned. For starters, recent and undocumented immigrants cannot vote[2] and, if they were so inclined, would *have* to express their views in a more costly manner, such as engaging in marches or demonstrations. Sometimes, however, even minority citizens have had to engage in the more costly forms of participation because the historically easier options, notably voting, have been closed off to them through intimidation or other discriminatory practices. But the metaphor of a ladder is a reasonably useful image, since we can think of some of these acts as being less costly than others; signing a petition, for example, involves less investment of time and effort than joining a protest march. We can also see how this kind of progression of participation is built up and linked: generally speaking, those who engage in the more costly kinds of actions also engage in the less costly, and participation at one point in time is a good predictor of future participation, *ceteris paribus*.

VOTING

As we noted, turning out to vote is one of the least costly and more obvious acts of political participation. It is also highly consequential for minority politics. We saw in Chapter 3 that minority populations in growing numbers of jurisdictions around the country are pivotal to deciding the results of elections, provided they turn out and vote. If minority voters do not turn out and vote, then their voices will not be heard: a silent majority is a losing majority in pretty much every political process. An individual's decision to turn out and vote is thus an important one.

Political scientists have taken seriously the idea of the costliness of political participation, extending the idea to include the benefits from political participation to apply this cost-benefit calculation to the decision to turn out and vote. As economists might phrase it, individuals will choose to participate if, as a consequence of their participation, the benefit of participating outweighs the cost:

(1) Citizens will participate where p (Benefit) > Cost,

where B is the benefit, C is the cost, and p represents the important rider in the sentence above "as a consequence of their participation."[3] This "calculus" can be applied to any act of participation and, as we will see later in this chapter, is critical to collective forms of political action. But the classical application of this logic is to the decision to turn out and vote, and it is on that question that we will focus for the moment.

Costs. The costs of voting can be seen in terms of how difficult it is to vote. Some of these hurdles face all voters. All voters have to take the time to learn about the election and the candidates and go to the polls and possibly stand in line on Election Day or request and mail an absentee ballot. Likewise, onerous registration laws can make it more costly for people to vote and, hence, make it less likely they will vote. For example, having a lengthy residency period or only fewer opportunities to complete registration forms and having limited mail-in or absentee ballot opportunities all impose costs on everyone regardless of ethnicity.

Sometimes, however, minority voters have faced additional hurdles, for example, Jim Crow laws. Especially in the South, African Americans often faced a series of obstacles to exercising the vote, such as being asked to pass "literacy tests," which were often quite detailed examinations of knowledge of American government and history, examinations white voters were never asked to take. It is important to note that this phenomenon was not limited to the South or to African Americans. States and counties from every party of the country, including parts of California and Washington and boroughs of New York City, have faced additional scrutiny, federal intervention, and other measures as a consequence of exclusionary tactics surrounding the right to vote. The Voting Rights Act of 1965 (amended and/or extended in 1975, 1982, and 2006) was specifically written to overcome the use of legal and extralegal practices to exclude minorities from the voting booth and minimize minority political voice and power.

Other laws may impose differential costs but in less obviously drastic ways. For example, if forms were printed only in English, this would have a differential impact between different ethnic groups. While the 1975 inclusion of language minorities in the terms of the Voting Rights Act (VRA) redressed this language barrier for many such voters, its reach does not include all non–English speaking Americans. However, new provisions regarding voter identification cards—put in place to combat the largely illusory problem of voter fraud (Rosenfeld 2007)—have been shown to disproportionately disqualify minority, poor, and elderly voters, all qualified to vote but disqualified for failing to meet this newly imposed burden. The Supreme Court has thus far been unwilling to find this new burden undue, and so this process can be reasonably expected to continue and grow. While the requirement is applied to all, the adverse effect is centered on politically vulnerable populations.

Even with the VRA as law, tactics aimed at minority disenfranchisement continue today. Irregularities in purging felons from voter lists, unequal facilities and scarcer voting machines at polling places, intimidation by law enforcement officials and those posing as law enforcement officials, misleading voter "information" letters, and an endless array of improvised tactics have been

BOX 6-1   Felon Disenfranchisement

Denying citizens the right to vote simply on the basis of their race is an obvious example of discrimination that has implications for both who wins and who gets represented. There are other examples of ballot restrictions, too. States vary with respect to the kinds of restrictions they may have. While individuals are not banned from voting because they are too old or too poor, state rules on the use of a valid driver's license as an ID can affect whether the elderly and the poor can vote. If, for example, someone becomes too infirm to drive or rents rather than owns and so moves around a lot, he may not have a driver's license to prove he is able to vote (see, for example, www.brennancenter.org/page/-/d/download_file_50902.pdf). A seemingly simple and technical rule can, then, have consequences for who is allowed to vote and so have consequences for the composition of the electorate and, hence, elections.

Similarly, states often ban felons from voting. This website from a lobby group, www.sentencingproject.org/template/page.cfm?id=133, shows the range of different kinds of laws that are in place. See also the Brennan Center for Justice report at www.brennancenter.org/content/resource/de_facto_disenfranchisement.

Most states ban those in jail or on parole from voting. Roughly fourteen states ban ex-offenders who have served their time from voting, for extended periods or for life. On the face of it this may seem reasonable. Committing serious crimes may be a basis for denying someone the privilege of voting. Given the demographics of those convicted, however, a very large share of minority voters are disqualified from voting in this way. Manza and Uggen (2006) suggest that in some states as many as 1 in 4 black men cannot vote owing to a felony conviction. In 2004 approximately 5.3 million Americans were affected, 2 million of whom were African American. Felon disenfranchisement, then, has consequences for the racial composition of the electorate.

used in recent elections and come to national attention largely because of the closeness of the 2000 and 2004 presidential elections and the unique roles played by Florida and Ohio in those two races, respectively (Rosenfeld 2007). When voters in minority precincts must stand in line for hours because there were fewer voting booths per capita than in white precincts, some of those voters lose their right to vote—because they must go to work, care for children, or any of the other commitments of life that preclude waiting forever. In one instance, qualified black voters received letters suggesting that they may face prosecution for voting illegally, something they would not be doing but, nevertheless, these letters may cause uncertainty, fear, and abstention among those who receive them. These tactics are rarely investigated to the point of prosecution, and even when they are, the damage is done with respect to turnout and outcome in very close elections.

The costs of voting may not be high, but they are not zero. For racial and ethnic minorities, the costs are often higher and have historically been occasionally insurmountable. The right to vote is taken for granted by most citizens but should be understood as insecure or threatened for a substantial segment of our citizenry.

Benefits. Under the cost-benefit framework we identified above, the benefits of voting are usually cast in terms of the difference in what the voter gets from each candidate. If, for example, the two candidates (or parties) standing for election are far apart on the issues, then who wins matters quite a lot and a voter with viewpoints consistent with one of the two candidates will attach greater value to the preferred option winning. If, on the other hand, the candidates share many policy views or are ideologically very close, then it matters much less who wins with regard to what a voter might get in terms of policy. Voters will be more motivated to turn out when candidates differ on the issues and will be not quite so motivated when the candidates are close together. In addition, voting will cost less when the candidates are further apart, as information useful to making a choice is more available—that is, a greater ability to "tell the difference."

Issues vary in importance, of course, and voters often have to tolerate occasional points of disagreement on lesser issues with preferred candidates, so that they might still elect a candidate with whom they agree on the more salient issues. This is particularly likely to be so for racial and ethnic minority voters. It is very likely that there are specific issue stances that impact minority voters more than others. For example, anti-immigrant positions by one party or candidate may prompt immigrant-rich minority groups to register and turn out at higher levels, notwithstanding the costs (Pantoja et al. 2001). Similarly, candidates and parties deemed to have antipathy for racial minorities, engage in racially laden campaign messaging, or espousing educational, labor, or social policy positions adverse to their interests will attract the attention, and subsequent turnout, of African American and other minority voters (Barreto et al. 2005a and 2005b). The benefits of voting for all citizens, then, are enhanced when candidates and parties are seen in the eyes of the voters as different on important issues.

But even if voting is easy (that is, very low cost, or low C), and even if the voter sees large differences between one candidate winning over another (a large B from the election outcome), this still leaves open the question of what the chance is of one vote making a difference (p). That is, and thinking like an economist, even if the election is important, what difference do *you* and *your individual* actions make to determining the outcome?

Sometimes elections are close, and so the chance of someone making a difference might be, or seem to be, quite large. We know that voters are more likely to turn out when elections are close than if the election results are pretty much known ahead of time. We also know that in elections that are not expected to be close, those voters who expect to win will turn out and vote more often than those voters who expect to lose. Low turnout in U.S. elections may, for example, be a consequence of the fact that safe districts mean most legislative elections are a foregone conclusion.

One extension of this argument, so far as minority voters are concerned, is that turnout among minority voters is affected by the chances of a minority candidate winning a seat. Majority-minority seats should see higher levels of turnout and participation by minority voters. Some evidence suggests this is, in fact, the case for both Latinos and African Americans (Barreto et al. 2004; Bobo and Gilliam 1990; but see Gay 2001) but that the underlying social situation of minority voters may well work against there being too big of an effect (Harris et al. 2005).

But the question raised by equation (1) is that the participation by one individual hardly ever makes a difference to the outcome. Many find this a worrying, even disturbing point because it means that it is usually individually rational for each citizen to conclude that he or she is better off staying at home and not engaging in political participation. If everyone is rational in the sense that economists use the term, then everyone stays at home and no one votes or takes part.

Of course, not everyone does stay at home on Election Day and so there is a sense in which, right from the outset, expression (1) is limited in what it can tell us. Before discussing some ways in which it might make sense for people to participate, we should pause for a moment to note that oftentimes commentators and academics assume that the natural state of things is for people to participate in politics. But equation (1) poses the uncomfortable possibility that when it comes down to it, nonparticipation might be the more likely expectation, particularly when, as it is in most cases, there is uncertainty regarding what the payoff will be and near certainty that the participation of one individual will not affect the outcome.

This is an especially important question to ask when we consider more direct forms of political action, for example, demonstrations or protests such as those of the Civil Rights Movement. In these cases the costs of involvement can be huge, not simply in terms of the time commitment but also in terms of the chances of arrest or being subjected to violence. In these instances, the strong temptation for individually rational and instrumental citizens is to "free ride"—and to let others bear the burden of participation. In many ways this happens in voting, too. If the "right" candidate is going to win regardless of whether you vote, or even if the "wrong" candidate is going to win regardless of whether you vote, the question is not why wouldn't you turn out to vote but, rather, why should you?

Political scientists have wrestled with this paradox for some time. One answer to the question of why people should vote is that it is the right thing to do. This is the equivalent of adding a term—such as "civic duty" to equation (1):

(2) Citizens will participate where p (Benefit) + Duty > Cost,

where p (the probability of your vote making a difference), B (the benefit of "your" candidate winning as opposed to a rival candidate) and C (the costs of voting) are the same as in equation (1) but the new term, D, represents this sense of civic duty or obligation. Different authors use different terms to describe this D term; here we talk about it as duty or a sense that one should vote. Some (Downs 1957) have identified it as a commitment to the affirmation of democracy. Others see D as an expressive benefit, the emotional payoff one receives from performing one's civic duty, registering one's vote preference (even if it does not determine the outcome), having one's say.

The problem is that including D does not help us understand participation as much as we might think. First of all, the notion that a vote is an affirmation of democracy should also be subject to the discount represented by p; that is, what is the chance your vote "saves" democracy? Second, thinking about the emotional payoff of expressing a view or doing your duty is not thinking very much like an economist, since it implies that people may not be behaving in a narrowly instrumental way after all. Affective or emotional payoffs are generally understood as extrarational, though as we will discuss momentarily, others have come to disagree. Finally, it is especially difficult to talk about the "duty" to vote if voters believe that the system is stacked against them. In those cases activists may organize a boycott of elections to protest against the illegitimacy of the process. In other words, in some circumstances it could even be a duty not to vote.

So in some ways the inclusion of a D term hides more about the problem than it illuminates. But one way in which a version of this term may help comes in reference to minority politics and the sense of a shared or linked fate. If minority voters—in part as a consequence of their status as social and political opinion minorities and not only as ethnic minorities—see themselves as part of a wider African American or Latino or Asian American community, then we are likely to see a drive for political participation. That is, including a D term may make a great deal of sense when we consider minority political engagement, provided such an identity either exists or can be created.

As we noted when we discussed the evolution of identities, the idea of a shared or linked fate is an important one in understanding minority political engagement, particularly for African Americans (Tate 1993; Gay 2001, 2002, and 2004; and especially Dawson 1994), but possibly too for Asian Americans (Kim and Lee 2001; Masuoka 2006) and Latinos (Stokes 2003; Sanchez 2006), though as we indicated, that is less clear. A strong sense of community and of linked fate can discourage free riding and encourage or facilitate participation. Chong's work (1991) on the Civil Rights Movement, for example, shows the ways in which building a sense of community was important in creating a sense of obligation and helping persuade people to take part. Church groups were especially helpful in overcoming the problem of free riding in that movement, though Chong suggests that they might have been a bit late to the game before ultimately taking the leadership role. McKenzie's work (2004) confirms that informal ties in groups are important in building a sense of community that can help to overcome "free riding," especially when it comes to the more direct (and more costly) form of engagement in protests, demonstrations, or strikes.

With all this discussion as preface, let us look at actual patterns of participation among minority voters.

MINORITY ELECTORAL PARTICIPATION

Figure 6-1 displays the self-reported propensity of non-Hispanic whites, African Americans, Latinos, and Asian Americans to engage in the most fundamental forms of political participation—registration and voting. By contrast, Figure 6-2 estimates actual turnout by groups across electoral cycles. First, and most obviously, respondents overreport their participation on surveys, and those reflected in Figure 6-1 are no exception. Nevertheless, the distributions of self-reported activities clearly reflect the between-group differences in voting. Non-Hispanic whites systematically report the highest levels of participation—with the notable exception of self-reported registration in 2008—while only African Americans can claim to turn out voters at rates comparable to whites. By contrast, both Latinos and Asian Americans appear to have participation rates that systematically lag behind those of whites and blacks. The only exception to this in Figure 6-1 is the "recall" of the 2004 election in the General Social Survey by Asian Americans, and this self-report is based on a very small sample size and is clearly at odds with all of the other results in the figure.

It is also worth noting that the level of self-report of "knows where to vote" in the 2008 American National Election Study (ANES) survey lags considerably behind self-reported turnout and, not coincidentally, comes far closer to

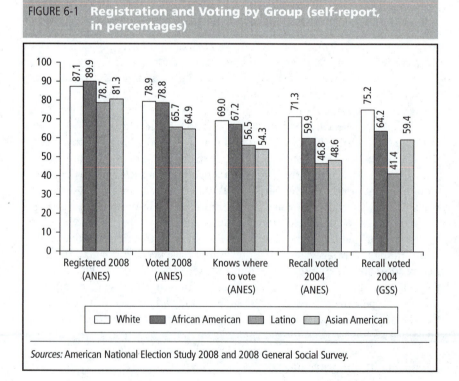

FIGURE 6-1 Registration and Voting by Group (self-report, in percentages)

Sources: American National Election Study 2008 and 2008 General Social Survey.

the actual turnout reported in Figure 6-2, substantially diminishing the over-reporting bias.

The results in Figure 6-2 are highly consistent with the self-reports in Figure 6-1. White and African American participation exceed that of Latinos and Asian Americans. The gap between whites and African Americans is diminishing over time, while both Asian Americans and Latinos appear to be improving across recent elections but still are turning out at rates fifteen to seventeen percentage points lower than the other groups.

How might political science provide insights into the differences reflected in Figures 6-1 and 6-2? Expressions we introduced earlier, specifically equations (1) and (2), are extremely useful in helping us to think through what is involved in participation and in offering ways of thinking about and categorizing what happens even in such a simple act as voting. For real-world citizens, the costs could be a decision over whether they can afford to take the hour off from work to go vote or how hard someone without a high school diploma will find it to figure out what the candidates are talking about. Such expressions as (1) and (2) are very useful indeed, but we

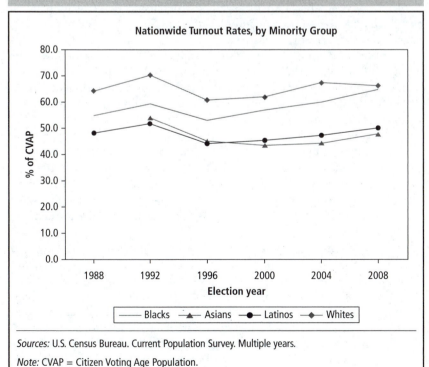

FIGURE 6-2   **Actual Turnout Estimate from the Current Population Survey**

Nationwide Turnout Rates, by Minority Group

Sources: U.S. Census Bureau. Current Population Survey. Multiple years.

Note: CVAP = Citizen Voting Age Population.

could use some greater sense of actual processes at work. The work of Verba, Schlozmann, and Brady (1995; "VSB" in what follows) provides a way to understand how people participate in different ways, especially if it involves people overcoming barriers to participation to engage in political activity and their work identifies the factors that help reduce or remove these barriers to participation.

Roots of Minority Difference

A necessary qualification when discussing minority participation in general is that any discussion really applies only to the modern era, which we date from 1965. Prior to the Voting Rights Act of that year many minority voters, in particular, African Americans, were simply prevented from voting. While, from the nineteenth century onward, African Americans were, in principle, U.S. citizens and guaranteed the vote by the Fifteenth Amendment, discriminatory laws and practices at the state level meant very few, if any, African Americans voted in elections through most of the twentieth century. Grofman et al. (1992) and others, for example, illustrate the disadvantage imposed by Jim Crow and vote suppression practices. In March 1965, before the passage of the VRA, only 19.3 percent of eligible African Americans in Alabama and 6.7 percent in Mississippi were registered to vote, and across the seven Deep South states, the regional average was 29.3 percent (Grofman et al. 1992, 23). Two years later (September 1967), after VRA passage and federal intervention, the regional average climbed to 52.1 percent and Alabama and Mississippi had rates of 51.6 percent and 59.8 percent, respectively.

For non-white non-African Americans, including Native Americans, the question of citizenship raised an additional barrier. Similarly, Latino voters often faced hurdles to participation that included suppression, language barriers, and outright exclusion, hurdles that were overcome only by concerted political action, as in the case of the Crystal City protests in 1963 and 1969 in which Mexican Americans mobilized and engaged in direct action simply in order to be allowed to vote. For Native Americans, the question of voter registration came only after the question of citizenship was settled in 1924. In general, the ladder of political participation for minorities often had rungs taken away. What that meant was that direct action—essentially skipping some rungs on the ladder of participation—was often needed in order to claim the right to vote.

As was the case for women prior to the twentieth century, the question of voter participation for minorities was moot, since minorities simply could not participate. Either the law did not allow participation even in principle or, even when the law allowed it, voting was denied in practice. More than most fields of study in political science, then, scholarship on minority political participation needs to be qualified by noting that we are referring to the current period. That history of discrimination is, of course, not forgotten and understandably colors attitudes toward the political system to this day. We take up those issues in a subsequent chapter.

The work of Verba and his colleagues offers three factors as explanations for how people either overcome these barriers and/or are driven to participate. These factors are that people have resources to participate, are recruited into politics, or have some psychological engagement with politics. In cruder terms, people participate in politics because they can, because they are asked to, or because they want to (VSB 1995, 15).

Contact and Mobilization

The first factor—being asked to participate in politics—operates in straight-forward ways. People are frequently asked to participate by being contacted directly by the political parties or by candidates and asked for their vote and/or their money.

In addition to this, a range of groups and organizations—not just political parties and candidates but also clubs, societies, and, especially, churches—provide channels for both recruiting people into politics and providing citizens with skills and resources to be able to participate. In that sense, this category of factors overlaps a little with the resource category if resources can be thought of as a skill set that can be acquired and practiced in a "nonpolitical" setting such as a church fund-raiser. It is in this way that the VSB argument can be seen to overlap with another broad set of arguments concerning "social capital" that has been given a great deal of prominence in the work of Robert Putnam, and before him, of course, de Tocqueville noted the importance of voluntary associations and civic groups in America's young democracy.

Part of Putnam's (2000) argument emphasizes the role that informal or private social groups can play in building social capital and hence both the basis and the skill sets of democratic citizens. At first blush this line of argument may seem somewhat odd. After all what link is there between organizing a church fish fry or Little League or American Youth Soccer Organization (AYSO) pizza party and political participation? The answer is that many of the skills are transferable. Organizing people involves having helpers show up on time and do their job, figuring out advertising and payments, and, not least, engaging in networking and "people skills," all skills that are useful in political campaigns and participation. Simply possessing these skills will not make someone interested in politics, but having these skills does make it easier for someone who is interested in politics to make a go of it. If you are interested in lobbying the local city hall or campaigning on a particular issue, then having previous experience in organizing mailing lists, printing flyers, arranging meetings, or twisting the arms of volunteers—even if was for a church group or sports team—makes it easier for you to do those things this time around.

VSB argue that some groups may be better than others in promoting participation. They highlight persistent differences across denominations in the effects of belonging to a church.[4] Like other kinds of social groups such as sports teams, churches are schools for civic engagement and some churches are better than others at encouraging participation. In particular, VSB see the Catholic Church as less encouraging of participation than many Protestant churches, and so the effect of church engagement on activity is especially likely to be seen among Protestants. The VSB argument also seems to help explain intergroup differences. In particular, the Catholicism of many Latino citizens in contrast to the Protestantism of African Americans would seem to imply that we should see lower than expected levels of participation by the former and higher than expected levels of participation from the latter, regardless of race. That is, it is possibly the case that some of the differences in rates of participation between racial and ethnic groups may be tied to differences in faith and not tied to race or ethnicity directly.

We can look at these two ways of "being asked to" participate—the mobilization efforts by parties or candidates and the effect of social groups such as churches—separately. In general, having parties and candidates contact voters to ask them to vote does make people more likely to turn out and vote. In fact, an earlier study, that by Rosenstone and Hansen (2003), placed a great deal of emphasis on the role of parties and other campaign organizations as vehicles helping to mobilize votes and argued that a lot of the failure of Americans to participate in politics could be laid at the doorstep of political parties that simply failed to try to mobilize voters (Rosenstone and Hansen 2003, 227). Such campaign contact can increase turnout by several percentage points, especially if the contact is personal in some way and does not appear to be part of a mass mailing. Door-to-door canvassing is seen to be especially effective as a direct way of asking people to vote in a personal way. On the other hand, mass e-mail lies at the other end of the effectiveness scale. While voters may respond to being asked directly for a vote, almost no one responds to a mass e-mail. These patterns also hold true for minority voters.

For a long period of time minorities were simply not asked to vote. Paul Frymer's work shows that the two main parties spent a great deal of time courting white swing voters. In doing so they distanced themselves from minority, especially African American, voters and their concerns. In this way minority voters may not always have their vote undermined by active discrimination—literacy tests or gerrymanders—but might have it passively undermined by simply not being asked to participate (Frymer 1999). Moreover, with race so central to the party structure, there are some disincentives for parties to even consider mobilizing minority voters, even if such a strategy would be effective for them. If some portion of the party's coalition holds salient racial sentiments in its political orientations, outreach by the party to minority voters may well cost it among other coalition constituencies.

When minority voters are asked to participate, what patterns do we see? Recent work on voter engagement has begun to use an "experimental" approach. This approach has a history, dating back to Harold Gosnell of the University of Chicago in the 1920s. In those early studies a random selection of voters received a postcard reminding them to vote, while another selection of voters were not sent such a card. Those who received the postcard (that is, those who were asked to participate) were more likely to turn out and vote than were those who did not receive it. This general technique has been updated and applied to turnout in the modern period and found similar results. It has also been applied specifically to the question of minority turnout. Ramirez (2005), for example, examines different kinds of contacting of Latinos by political parties. Nowadays, parties can ask voters to participate—to get out the vote (GOTV)—through a variety of different ways. Parties can contact voters via direct mail, through phone calls from real people, or via "robocalls"— recorded messages, often from famous names. Ramirez finds that phone calls from real people have a significant impact in increasing turnout on the order of 5 percent (see also Michelson 2006; Michelson et al. 2008). Wong (2004, 2005) finds similar effects for Asian Americans for both mail and phone contact when the contact is made "in-language."[5] That is, contacting minority voters in their own language does have a positive impact.[6] The resulting body of work has produced some very specific recommendations on how to increase turnout. This work suggests that we should not be disappointed in voters for not participating in politics—sometimes candidates and parties have not asked voters insistently enough to participate.

Figure 6-3 reports the frequency of party contact by racial and ethnic group in the 2008 presidential election. The pattern is very consistent with previous findings on contact and on Rosenstone and Hansen's (2003) caveat that we should be chastising parties for failing to engage minority voters. Almost 47 percent of non-Hispanic white citizens surveyed in the 2008

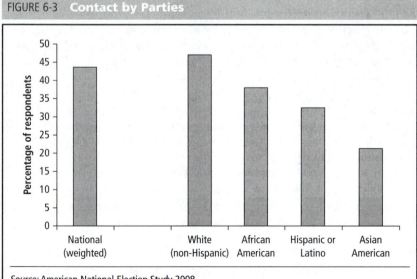

FIGURE 6-3   **Contact by Parties**

Source: American National Election Study 2008.

Question wording: As you know, the political parties try to talk to as many people as they can to get them to vote for their candidate. Did anyone from one of the POLITICAL PARTIES call you up or come around and talk to you about the campaign this year?

ANES study reported having been telephoned or visited by the parties. The comparable numbers are 38 percent for African Americans, 32.3 percent for Latinos, and 21.2 percent for Asian Americans. This decline is statistically significant and obviously important. It should be noted as well that 2008 is likely the high-water mark for mobilization of minority voters, with an African American Democratic nominee and generally increasing rates of minority electoral involvement. In earlier years we would expect the difference to be even greater. Moreover, contact is positively correlated with turnout among all groups ($r = .22$)[7] and is actually stronger among Asian Americans ($r = .30$) and Latinos ($r = .25$) than among non-Hispanic whites ($r = .21$). African American turnout is also connected to party contact but at a somewhat more modest level, perhaps as a consequence of their very strong mobilization efforts, overall and particularly in 2008 ($r = .17$). In short, racial and ethnic minorities are contacted significantly less frequently by political parties, party contact is uniformly related to turnout, and this effect is actually greater among Asians and Latinos.

But blaming the parties is, in some ways, too easy an answer. Campaigning by parties is very expensive and costs soon mount, but voters do not like the role money plays in politics. Expression (1) can be applied to how candidates decide to campaign and not just how voters decide to vote. Political campaigns nationwide and for all offices are increasingly expensive to run.[8] The issue is a serious problem, especially when we consider outreach efforts to minority voters in light of the findings from the literature on the effects of outreach efforts. While it is relatively easy and inexpensive to translate, print, and mail out a flyer or send an e-mail in several different languages, we know that these are the least effective forms of campaign mobilization efforts, often tossed immediately into the trash. As inexpensive as they are, there may be relatively little point in sending e-mails in Mandarin or Tagalog except, perhaps, for symbolic reasons. There is perhaps even less point in sending them only in English if the goal is to get people to turn out and vote. On the other hand, hiring bilingual campaign workers to go door to door to ask for the vote is much more effective (Michelson et al. 2008) but is also much more expensive. Simple economics alone will prevent many campaigns from doing intensive "in-language" campaigns in person except perhaps in areas with very large immigrant populations. Part of the problem here, of course, is that if voters do not turn out and vote, in part because they are not asked, then political campaigns might have a hard time justifying spending money and resources on groups that do not seem to turn out and vote—and so the group is not asked again.

The Role of Churches

If the patterns on asking people to vote help show that minority turnout is in line with VSB, the authors' argument on the role of social groups in promoting participation finds more mixed support when it comes to minority participation. On the one hand, the experience of African American communities, especially in inner-city communities, seems to bear out the prominent role of churches for political and social engagement (Tate 1993; Alex-Assensoh and Assensoh 2001; Harris 1994).[9] If anything, then, VSB's argument about the impact of church membership is even truer so far as some minority communities are concerned.

Recent work, however, challenges whether the more specific argument about the link between Catholicism and low participation holds for Latinos. Work by Jones-Correa and Leal (2001) shows that it is not Catholicism per se so much as church attendance that has an impact on political action. That is, they compare Protestant and Catholic Latinos. If VSB are right, then Protestant Latinos should see higher rates of participation. But we do not see such a pattern. Instead we see that those voters who attend church regularly are more likely to participate in politics than those who do not—regardless of denomination. In a sense we see evidence in support of Putnam's argument.

There are lots of good reasons for why VSB's arguments concerning Catholicism do not hold of late. For example, arguments about Catholicism may be time bound to the 1980s and 1990s (the period of their study). Since then the issues of gay marriage, abortion, and stem cell research have all come to the political agenda, and these issues may well result in high levels of political mobilization because they are important ("hot-button") issues for the Catholic Church, in particular. In addition, the impact of church membership may differ across racial and ethnic groups in ways not picked up by the predominantly Anglo sample in the VSB study. Jones-Correa and Leal argue, for example, that church attendance may be unusually important for Latinos because Latinos in particular have fewer avenues of social participation than Anglos. If richer Anglos participate in a range of church, charitable, and civic arenas while Latinos and other minorities participate in fewer, then the impact of church, the major form of engagement, is likely to be bigger.

Whatever the reasoning, however, it does not seem that the argument that there is something different about Catholic churches as schools for social capital helps us to understand why Latino rates of voting participation are lower than those of other groups. Furthermore, while differences between Protestants and Catholic are, given the predominance of the Christian faith among white and non-white Americans alike, important ones to understand, there are other faiths—Islam and Buddhism, in particular—that have growing numbers of faithful within the United States. We simply do not know how adherence to these faiths will shape participation.

To be clear, it may not be so much that the priest or parson is orchestrating explicitly political events such as voter registration campaigns or an amnesty movement—although those things can take place and of late churches of nearly all denominations have become much more involved in the specific issue of gay marriage. Rather, the effects of these organizations are through the surrounding events and occasions that help individuals practice people skills and, crucially, through the informal contacts and interactions with other parishioners that may help communicate and reinforce civic norms of participation (McKenzie 2004; Tate 1993) and may also help build a sense of identity

(Reese and Brown 1995). The opportunities exist in social contexts for people to build up relationships among one another over a long period of time. This time dimension is important because trust and reputation are properties built up over time. The social context of churches, then, is the motor that drives the effect in which we see social engagement producing political engagement.

While many arguments about informal or "nonpolitical" groups often talk about a series of groups or associations "like churches," there may be very few groups or associations that are, in fact, like churches. With the exception of churches, social organizations may well be short lived, temporary, or short of funds. In this case the effects of the social interaction may well also be short lived or temporary and not allow friendships and reputations to be built. In the case of churches, however, some of these problems do not exist, and, in consequence, churches are likely to have larger and more persistent effects than other forms of social organizations because they are longer lived and do tend to be somewhat better funded. For these reasons churches are more likely than many if not most other forms of social organization to provide the basis for the kinds of repeated social interaction that help social organizations promote political engagement. Hence discussions of effects on political participation that refer to social organizations "like churches" may really be just about churches.

There is good evidence, however, to suspect that churches and other social groups are playing a role in minority voter mobilization. Recall our findings in Figure 6-3 that political parties are less likely to contact minority voters than non-Hispanic whites, a systematic finding consistent with earlier work and with potentially dire consequences, given the consistently strong effect of contact in boosting turnout. In Figure 6-4, we examine contact by nonparty groups, contact that presumably could have come from churches, neighborhood groups, ethnic advocacy organizations, and others. What is most striking about the results in Figure 6-4 is that while the overall frequency of political contact is lower (as we would expect), there are no patterns of ethnic differentiation that we found in the partisan behavior. With the clear exception of Asian Americans (and we again remind the reader of the perils of small sample sizes), there is no distinction in the frequency of political contact by nonparty actors across whites, African Americans, and Latinos. In fact, the numbers are strikingly similar.

On the whole, then, VSB's arguments about being able to and being asked to participate help us understand who participates, but Verber et al. has relatively little to say about which voters want (or do not want) to participate, just as expression (2) really depended on individual level variation in a sense of civic duty. In part this is simply because it is hard, in fact it is extremely hard, to explain why some people are inherently more interested in politics than others—just as it is hard to explain why some people like ketchup and others do not. For example, it is not obvious why we should expect to see Latinos wanting to participate more than Asians (or vice versa) simply as a consequence of their ethnicity or race. Yet there are persistent differences across ethnic and racial groups even after we control for the "usual suspects" of

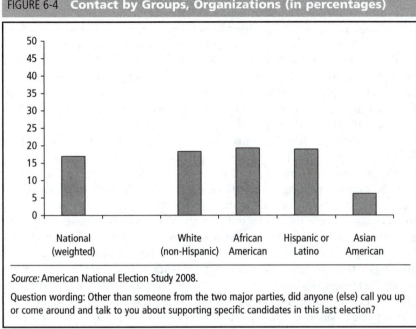

FIGURE 6-4   **Contact by Groups, Organizations (in percentages)**

Source: American National Election Study 2008.

Question wording: Other than someone from the two major parties, did anyone (else) call you up or come around and talk to you about supporting specific candidates in this last election?

income and education that do correlate with participation. We even see these persistent differences after we account for experiences due to immigration. It is quite likely, for example, that citizens who emigrated from a repressive society have an aversion to political activity and drawing attention to themselves. This would apply to Anglos who emigrated from Communist societies during the Cold War, just as it should apply to Latinos and Southeast Asians emigrating from the brutal dictatorships of their home regions. Immigrants from these societies may well regard contact with the political system with suspicion or even fear and shy away from participating. By contrast, one might expect non-white immigrants from India, Japan, or Costa Rica to regard democratic participation as a normal feature of society and, consequently, engage in politics more readily. Certainly Tam Cho (1999) finds that differences in immigration experience moderate even effects of income and education on participation, effects we think of as bedrock in explaining what drives political participation.

Generally speaking, however, and leaving to one side differences across groups and immigration status, then what we do see is that minority voters want to participate in politics at levels similar to—and for African Americans, greater than—that of Anglos. That is, a simple resource explanation of political participation would suggest that younger people, poorer people, and people with lower levels of education are less likely to participate in politics. Since minority populations tend to be younger, poorer, and less well educated, we would expect to see lower levels of participation among minorities. That said, once we account for these differences in socioeconomic status (SES), then at least some minority groups participate at levels similar to that of Anglos.

Of course, the root explanation of political participation and the one best established in the literature is the resource model—in VSB's term's, those who "can" participate (Campbell et al. 1960; Wolfinger and Rosenstone 1980). Examples of resources that reduce or remove barriers to participation are such things as time, money, education, and age, each of which can be associated with decreasing the costs of participation, making the costs more readily absorbable, increasing the benefits, and providing the opportunity to act if one chose.

Minority voters have been disadvantaged on these, and this has much to do with the generally lower rates of participation. These factors work in straightforward ways: people with less money and less time are less able to (that is, cannot) participate in politics; hence people with more time and money are likely to participate more. Those with surplus economic resources are also more likely to devote some of those to politics, providing them a greater voice and, by consequence, a greater sense of efficacy within the political system and a decreased likelihood of feeling cut off or excluded from its workings. Alas, economic resources, and even time to burn, are in short supply for most (though obviously not all) minority citizens. As a consequence, we would expect lower turnout of all minority groups. We would also expect less trusting and positive orientations to the political system, a question to which we will return in a later chapter.

Education is an important resource as well; it makes the political world more readily understandable, facilitates cause-and-effect reasoning between the party or views of the elected officials in charge and resulting policy outcomes, and increases the sheer amount of political information with which one comes in contact on a daily basis, even in the absence of effort (Gordon and Segura 1997). There are also life cycle effects that associate age with action. Besides the obvious effect that age is associated with income and, to a lesser extent, education, older voters tend to participate more in part because they may have more time on their hands (the kids are older and can look after themselves for an hour while the parent goes to vote). Finally, the social programs for the elderly, Social Security and Medicare, make older voters more closely beholden to government expenditure and the policy decisions affecting it.

In short, age, education, and income are critically important determinants of all forms of political participation. In light of our lengthy discussions of history, group identification, mobilization efforts, and other predictors, we are left to ask how well these resource arguments apply to non-white Americans. Are the resource arguments the underlying cause of minority difference, are they replaced by minority and group-specific effects, or are the two arguments complementary?

Testing Models of Minority Turnout

Returning to Figure 6-2, we observed substantially different turnout rates (and histories of turnout rates) by different groups in a baseline rate. Of course, we know that the baseline may mean very little because factors other than race affect someone's chance of turning out and voting. Specifically, we know that other factors—such "resources" as education—also affect turnout, and we therefore need to take them into account. Statistical models such as multiple regression[10] allow us to take account of these other factors. What we can do is run the statistical model including just the racial categories as a factor, then rerun the model including the other factors that we know have an effect, and then compare the results. We report the results from doing this in Figure 6-5 (full results of the statistical models that produce them are reported in Table 6-A-1). The "zero" line is the turnout estimate for non-Hispanic whites. The figure displays two bars for each group. One bar represents the baseline turnout (just including measures for ethnicity) compared with that of non-Hispanic whites, while the second bar represents the relationship between ethnicity and turnout after bringing in other factors, including age, education, and income.

FIGURE 6-5   **Minority Turnout Probability Relative to Non-Hispanic Whites, Observed and Estimated, Controlling for Other Factors**

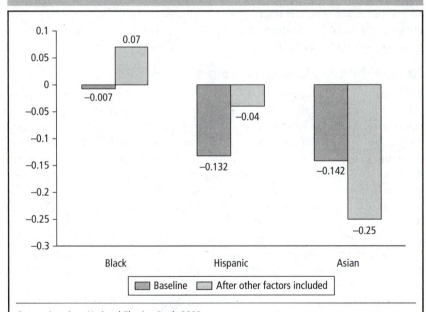

Source: American National Election Study 2008.

Note: Estimates are changes in predicted probabilities obtained from statistical models of self-reported vote, in the first instance accounting solely for race and ethnicity and in the second, controlling for income, education, age, contact, religious identity, religious observance, and the interactive identification of Latino Catholics and African American churchgoers. Statistical results are presented in Appendix Table 6-A-1 and Appendix Table 6-A-2. The statistical models are logit models—essentially a version of a multiple regression approach.

There are two "surprises" in these figures, one of which we have already mentioned. First, turnout by African Americans is very close to that of Anglos. When we remember that turnout is often associated with "resources" such as education and income and that, typically, levels of both resources are lower among African Americans than Anglos, then these figures become quite striking: African Americans turn out at much higher rates than they "should" according to standard political science models.

Once we take into account mobilization, age, religiosity, income, and education—accounting for those disadvantages among minorities and, instead, comparing minority citizens with white citizens of approximately similar demographic traits—African Americans vote *more* than whites (about 8 percent), and Latinos are much closer to whites in their behavior. That is, African Americans overperform their resource status, while Latinos are every bit as likely to vote as similarly situated non-Hispanic whites.

The second surprise is almost a mirror image of the first. Based on levels of education and income, Asian Americans vote far less often than they actually should, presenting something of a puzzle for the standard political science resource model.[11] Specifically, the fourteen-percentage-point disadvantage becomes a whopping 25 percent disadvantage when controlling for income, education, and the other effects. While the sample sizes in the ANES again indicate the need for caution, this finding of low Asian participation—even after controlling for SES—is consistent with the literature.

Electoral Participation beyond Voting

Elections involve voting, of course, but there are a variety of other behaviors that are directly related to elections and on which we have some good data. Apart from voting on Election Day (or, increasingly, by mail in the week or two prior), there are rallies, dinners, fund-raisers, and campaigns themselves, involving phone banks, precinct walking, and sign waving. While we have considerable evidence on the turnout differences among groups, we have comparatively less work on these other electoral activities.

Figure 6-6 uses data from both the National Politics Survey (NPS) and the American National Election Study to estimate participation in these other electoral activities by group. One interesting pattern is that respondents to the NPS systematically report more activity than ANES respondents. The reasons for this are not clear but may have something to do with sample frame, question order, and the like.

Three types of activities are explored in Figure 6-6: attendance at meetings, dinners, or rallies for a candidate; donations to candidate or party; and campaign volunteerism. Not surprisingly, and consistent with every other finding on American political behavior, the frequency of these activities is far lower than those of registration and voting. Two things should be immediately apparent as you examine Figure 6-6, particularly in light of Figures 6-1 and 6-2. First, whites are not systematically outperforming minorities in all areas. African Americans are out-rallying whites in both data sources, and Latinos out-rally whites in the ANES data. Blacks also out-campaign whites (and Latinos come

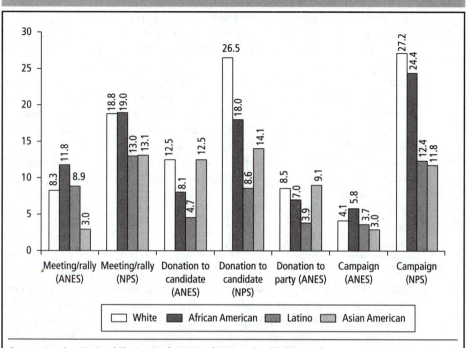

FIGURE 6-6   **Electioneering and Campaign Participation by Race and Ethnicity (in percentages)**

Sources: American National Election Study 2008 and 2004 National Politics Study.

Note: ANES estimate of meeting/rally attendance marginally significant (χ^2 test) at p =.08. ANES estimate of campaign activity (χ^2 test) insignificant at p =.37. All other between-group differences have p-values ≤.05 (χ^2 test).

close to matching non-Hispanic whites) in the ANES data (and the numbers for African Americans are close in the NPS).

One way in which Asian Americans excel, though, and in ways that are consistent with VSB, is through campaign donations. While the NPS data suggest whites are the big givers, the two ANES measures capturing giving to candidates and parties show Asians either indistinguishable from whites (giving to candidates) or even slightly outperforming them (giving to parties). This finding is consistent with some earlier work (Lai et al. 2001).

One question is whether donations lean toward one party. Lai et al. show Chinese and Japanese partisan donations are split, while Koreans and Vietnamese lean Republican, although one consistent finding was that "Asian donors respond foremost to Asian-American candidates" (Lai et al. 2001, 605).[12] One important component to contributions, at least for Asian Americans, is the contextual effect of place. Above we noted the effects of social interaction in a fairly structured setting, notably churches. But there are other ways in which contextual effects can be seen; there are other ways in which the interactions between people can have an effect on the political participation of an individual. Neighborhood effects are one prominent example of this kind of effect. People living and working close to each other may influence each other's opinions—even after taking account of individual factors that lead some people to donate to candidates. Tam Cho finds that donations are geographically clustered. Asian voters, for example, are more likely to donate to a party as the percentage of Asians in their area increases. Part, but not all, of this is due to residential segregation among and between ethnic groups (Tam Cho 2003). Tam Cho argues that these and similar patterns show the contextual effects of people influencing people through the processes of diffusion and contagion.

Still, Figure 6-6 highlights the difficulty for current political science theories in that there are persistent differences across ethnic and racial groups in the modes of participation that cannot be fully explained by the standard models. And, in fact, the patterns vary across different kinds of participation (voting, working on campaigns, donating on campaigns, and so on), suggesting that a one-size-fits-all model will not work well across groups or activities.

SUMMARY

The changes between the two models offered in Figure 6-5 illustrate both the similarities and differences between non-Hispanic whites and minority citizens, on the one hand, and among minority groups on the other. Variables capturing socioeconomic status largely erase the distinctions between Latino and white voters, suggesting that the Latino disadvantage is one of resources and further undermining claims of cultural deficiency, disinterest, and other factors (Hero 1992). By contrast, the control of socioeconomic status (SES) factors reintroduces distinctions between blacks and whites but in a more surprising way. Comparing individuals of like circumstances, African American citizens are actually more likely to vote than their similarly situated white fellow citizens, an effect that is sustained even in the presence for controls on contact and church attendance. Finally, to the extent that these limited data allow, Asian Americans are undermobilized, and correcting for education and income, dramatically so.

What, then, have we learned regarding our underlying questions on the future of American politics? Democratic candidates rely heavily on the black vote and are therefore advantaged by the overachievement of African Americans vis-à-vis their economic circumstances when it comes to turning out and voting. On the downside, however, should the black overperformance attenuate, the effect on Democratic candidacies could be huge.

With respect to Latinos, it would appear that the sky is the limit. Latinos are undermobilized by the parties, and their deficit in turnout can be significantly accounted for by their economic circumstances. Significant socioeconomic mobility could yield significant increased turnout, particularly if accompanied by a bigger investment in the parties in increasing their attendance at the polls. Such an event would pay significant dividends for

Democrats, so long as the economic mobility did not significantly undermine the Democratic skew in Latino voter preferences.

We do not mean to imply by our findings on SES that Latino voters are not distinct from non-Hispanic whites. What we find here is that their propensity to report voting is indistinguishable from whites once we control for economic and social factors. What the two groups will vote for is quite different. As we shall see below, Latinos and non-Hispanic whites do have a number of differences in terms of partisan skew, orientations toward government, and issue opinions (about which we have had a lot to say). Latinos are likely quite distinct from white voters on several important dimensions, and group identity might play important roles in evaluating the political world, preference formation, and other forms of political action (Santoro and Segura 2011).

For Asian Americans there is a paradox that requires some deeper consideration. Asian Americans turn out poorly not just in raw terms, but also they are underperforming even after considering their social and economic circumstances. This may, in fact, point to an absence of group identification as a resource. Alternatively, it may reflect a disconnect between that identity and any political implications. This question is one of the many unanswered puzzles stemming from the study of minority politics.

APPENDIX: Table 6-A-1 and Table 6-A-2

Statistical Estimations for Figure 6-5

Estimates in Figure 6-5 are changes in predicted probabilities obtained from logit estimations of self-reported vote. Logit—short for logistical regression—is a statistical model based on the logistic function, which produces an S curve confined between zero and one. It is suited for dichotomous dependent variables (variables coded one and zero only). In the first instance, reported in Appendix Table 6-A-1, we estimate differences between minority and non-Hispanic white turnout accounting solely for race and ethnicity. In the second, reported in Appendix Table 6-A-2, we control for income, education, age, contact, religious identity, religious observance, and the interactive identification of Latino Catholics and African American churchgoers. All estimations use the 2008 American National Election Study, weighted.

TABLE 6-A-1 Logit Results: Self-Reported Vote by Racial ID, 2008

Number of obs = 2,100
LR chi2(3) = 17.91
Prob > chi2 = 0.0005
Log likelihood = –1110.7427   Pseudo R2 = 0.0080

Variable	Coefficient	Standard error	Significance	Change in probability
African American	0.00	0.17		0.00
Latino	–0.67	0.17	***	–0.13
Asian American	–0.70	0.31	*	–0.15
Constant	1.32	0.06	***	

Source: American National Election Study 2008.

Note: Statistical significance (two-tailed): * p ≤ .05, ** p ≤ .01, *** p ≤ .001.

TABLE 6-A-2 Logit Results: Self-Reported Vote by Racial ID, Controlling for Socioeconomic Status, 2008

Number of obs = 2,059
LR chi2(13) = 387.24
Prob > chi2 = 0.0000
Log likelihood = –904.73951   Pseudo R2 = 0.1763

Variable	Coefficient	Standard error	Significance	Change in probability
Party contact	0.99	0.14	***	0.14
High income	0.31	0.24		0.04
Low income	–0.24	0.15		–0.03
Income missing	–0.18	0.37		–0.03
Education (5-Cat)	0.74	0.07	***	0.39
Age	0.02	0.00	***	0.19
African American	0.61	0.29	*	0.08
Latino	–0.29	0.30		–0.04
Asian American	–1.27	0.37	***	–0.25
Attend church	0.13	0.04	**	0.07
Black X church	–0.02	0.13		–0.01
Catholic	0.22	0.18		0.03
Latino X Catholic	0.15	0.41		0.02
Constant	–1.25	0.25	***	0.14

Source: American National Election Study 2008.

Note: Statistical significance (two-tailed): * p ≤ .05, ** p ≤ .01, *** p ≤ .001.

Participation beyond Voting and Minority Politics

So far we have discussed political participation largely in terms of a ladder of different kinds of engagement, mostly insofar as electoral politics is concerned. But there is also scope for participation beyond voting and elections, ranging from contacting an official through to the unconventional political behavior of civil disobedience. In this chapter we examine these kinds of behaviors. We begin with the figure below, which shows a different kind of ladder for different kinds of participation from the one seen in Chapter 6.

Figure 7-1 presents a rough scale ranging from conventional political action through actions of protest and civil disobedience to violence and outright terrorism. The kinds of activities we have discussed so far are located to the left side of this scale and are either squarely in or close to conventional politics. Some of these actions would seem quite commonplace. Figure 7-2, for example, displays several ways in which people may take part in politics that go beyond voting but are nevertheless legitimate, appropriate, and even desirable examples of "voice."

When we compare people who contact their elected officials with those going on a march or a demonstration, we see the familiar responsiveness of participation to costliness. It is relatively inexpensive to call or e-mail or even write to an elected official, but it involves a lot more effort to take time to go to a demonstration. With all racial and ethnic groups, we see a drop-off across the two activities. We also see that Anglo participation is generally higher than for minority groups, but that the gap closes when we consider marches. This closing of the gap between minorities and Anglos also occurs when we consider who responded "yes" to the question "In the past 12 months have you attended a meeting about an issue facing your community or schools?" And this pattern of participation seems to run counter to what we might expect in terms of the costliness of participation, since people across all racial and ethnic groups are very active. In terms of participation of this kind, Anglos are not the most participatory group. Furthermore, differences across racial and ethnic groups for these activities seem less pronounced than differences in contacting local officials. What we see, then, is that the gap between Anglo and minority participation seems widest in voting (the previous chapter) and less wide as we move up the ladder of participation, at least as long as we stay at the left-hand

FIGURE 7-1   **Unconventional Political Behavior**

0	1	2	3	4	5
Conventional politics Voting, lobbying, donating	Petitions Demonstrations	Boycott	Unofficial strikes/ rent strikes	Unlawful demonstrations Occupation Violence	Sabotage Terrorism

Sources: Dalton (2002, 61, with modifications); see also Dalton and van Sickle (2005).

FIGURE 7-2   **Nonelectoral Participation**

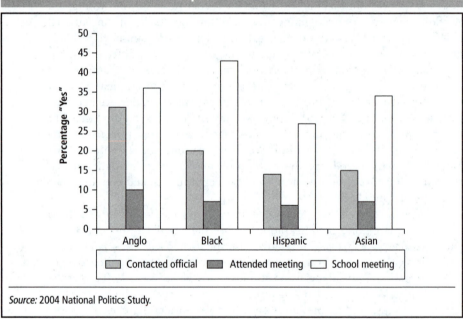

Source: 2004 National Politics Study.

side of the scale of unconventional political participation. Once we begin to move to the right of the scale, however, these kinds of actions are not only more violent, but also they raise serious legal, moral, and ethical questions for the people engaged in them. To be clear, there are major distinctions to be made between the kinds of activities on the left-hand side of Figure 7-1 and the right-hand side of the figure. Our purpose in introducing them is to underline the point that political participation does not begin and end with voting. While we have spent some time looking at the left side of the figure above, what about the kinds of participation as we move to the right side of the figure.

The history of the United States throughout the twentieth century provides many examples of political action ranging the length of the scale when we consider ethnic and racial issues. One of the major examples is, of course, the series of acts and protests, the marches, boycotts, and demonstrations organized by the Civil Rights Movement. Cesar Chavez and the farmworkers movement organized strikes and boycotts. The American Indian Movement (AIM) and the Black Panthers conducted more violent protests still. Other notorious examples of violence that have had racial and ethnic components include the LA riots post–Rodney King, the "Zoot Suit" violence of Anglos against Latinos and the horrendous history of lynchings of African Americans.

But it is important to note that racial and ethnic protest movements were not the only form of more radical protest movements in the United States throughout the twentieth century, nor the only examples of political violence—far from it. The long record of violent political disputes in the United States includes the bombing of the *Los Angeles Times* offices and the death of 21 people in 1910 and the Wall Street bombing of 1920 that killed even more people. Political violence continued into the postwar period through the 1960s' Students for a Democratic Society and the Weathermen up through the Oklahoma City bombing of 1995, which killed 168 people. In the current century we have also seen the bombings of medical facilities that perform abortions and the murder of doctors and staff in these clinics. We have seen repeated assassination attempts made on U.S. politicians. All of these are examples of violent political action that did not involve racial and ethnic minorities.[1] It is important to stress that political violence is not the hallmark of one particular group; violent action has come from both left and right. But for the most part these are (thankfully) exceptional acts. Most of the time for most everyone, political participation takes the form of conventional politics.

One question, of course, is what prompts people to take part in protest action? The answer to this question is complex and has generated a huge literature on the causes of riots and rebellions. For the most part that literature is beyond our purposes here, except to mention a few points that relate to protest and participation.

One assumption shared by many theories of protest is that some grievance or deprivation is needed. On the face of it such a statement might seem so obvious as to not need stating. But if it were the case that a grievance is *all* that is needed before someone starts protesting, then the streets would be full as everyone starts protesting, because we all have grievances. In a sense it turns the question around to ask why it is that minorities are not engaging in *more* acts of unconventional political behavior than has been the case. What is important, then, is one defines the grievance or the deprivation that motivates the protest. Lots of people have complaints, but not all of those complaints are translated into political action. Something other than a grievance has to be present; some other condition must hold. For one thing, the grievance must by unsatisfied (Piven and Cloward 1977). In one especially influential argument, the important aspect to the grievance is not one of absolute but of relative deprivation. That is, the spark to protest is often a comparison made to others: If everyone is doing poorly, then this might not trigger protest, but if some similar people are doing better, then this may well spark protest. If no one has a car or his own house, then this will not generate as much discontent as if a few people have a car or some other possession (Gurr 1971). This is more than simple jealousy on the part of the protestor but one of expectation. To continue with the examples of consumer goods for a moment, someone could own a house or a car because he or she acquired a skill or a trade, while you did not. You might, therefore, see this ownership of these goods as entirely fair and legitimate. But if the reasons for the disparity are not related to effort or merit or some similar legitimate factor, then you may have grounds for complaint.

Of course, there are other reasons why inequality does not lead to more action. Part of this might be that those without material advantages believe they might one day have them. This logic has, for example, been used to explain why the United States has not seen the same kind of class-based politics experienced in Europe. On the other hand, we should not conclude that only material inequality moves people to action. The perception of injustice might well have to do with legal status, social bias, or other characteristics that cause individuals to take action. Gay and lesbian activists, crusaders against antisemitism, and Arab Americans, among others, fight (usually politically, sometimes physically) injustices that are far less material in their origins.

Being unhappy about something is one thing—doing something about it is another, and doing something that involves confrontation rather than foot dragging or passive resistance (Scott 1985; McAdam 1983) is another thing still. A series of other arguments relating to protest emphasizes the importance of resources and skills that, with participation in general as with protest in particular, will allow aggrieved citizens to translate their grievances into action.

There are, then, many overlaps in the kinds of factors that help drive protest and those that help drive participation more generally, although the kinds of resources that assist protesters are not necessarily the same as those that help promote conventional political action. It is unlikely, for example, that the rich will engage in protest against the system. Similarly, it is not the old but the young who are more likely to engage in the kinds of protest and violence we see as we move to the right of the protest scale.[2] The resources that this literature discusses, then, are not so much individual and personal as collective, identity based, and infrastructural. It is important to have capacity in the form of an organization or similar vehicle to help foster and encourage mobilization. While the individually wealthy may not protest, those groups that are rich in organizational resources are likely to do so (McCarthy and Zald 1977). Moreover, having a range of organizations committed to similar goals and strategies helps. There may, for example, be a demonstration effect: as one group engages in protest behavior, others notice and copy this strategy. This spread or diffusion of tactics, which has been the hallmark of the African American Civil Rights Movement and subsequent social movements, is especially likely to happen where there is a large and dense network of social movements and organizations (Minkoff 1997).

Organizations, or at least their members, learn from each other and may be encouraged by successful protests either to engage in protest themselves or to engage in some other action. In addressing the collective action problems associated with group political mobilization, Chong (1991) outlined the importance of success in overcoming reluctance of new participants. Moreover, confrontation may yield more immediate expressive benefits than less aggressive tactics, and it may also pay benefits in recruiting and retaining group members. That said, having an organization solely committed to protest activity is probably not a good idea from the organization's point of view.

Minkoff (1993) studied a range of women's and racial-ethnic groups in order to answer the question: what helps a social movement to survive for a long period of time? She found that over and above liabilities such as smallness (that is, small groups have a harder time surviving),[3] groups that tend to shy away from violence and develop moderate and nonpolitical objectives survive longer. That is, even if protest activity by groups is a successful tactic—and even if it is so successful that the tactic is copied by similar groups—it may not be a long-term one: Groups cannot only engage in organizing and encouraging people to go on protests. If a group organizes a string of street demonstrations at some point, it needs to have a different answer to the question "What are we going to do next?" than "Let's organize a street demonstration—again." If the organization is to survive for a long period of time, the organizers need to do other things as well. These things might be to organize social or charitable events or to be more obviously political and involve running or backing candidates in elections. Again, however, Chong would remind us that these less glamorous, less immediately rewarding tactics are often less enticing to potential activists.

One idea of additional conditions that must hold is that protest comes when there are often few alternative strategies. One strategy is that of exit, or, quite literally, leaving an unpleasant or untenable political situation. For many immigrants to the United States, this is precisely the kind of factor that drove them to move to the United States and, also, means that pressures for change (voice) in their home country are relieved. In Hirschman's vivid phrase, when faced with an unappealing situation, people have a choice between exit, voice, and loyalty (Hirschman 1970). Sometimes where physical exit is impossible and voice would be too dangerous or costly, citizens may simply disengage altogether. One response to repressive regimes, for example, is to become very passive and disengaged in politics. These are habits that, as we noted earlier, many first-generation immigrants may find hard to shake. On the other hand, if exit is not an option but repression is not too severe, then "voice" as a response to an unsatisfactory situation could result in protest.

Arguments relating to political opportunity structure have a similar line of reasoning to Hirschman. These arguments focus not so much on the choice of the individual citizen but on the kinds of institutional environment she or he faces (McCarthy and Zald 1977; McAdam 1983; Meyer 2004).[4] The structure of existing institutions will either permit or restrict the kinds of chances for political action because there is an interaction between existing political structures and the choices made by protestors. Doug McAdam in his pathbreaking study of the relationship between African American social movements and segregationists during the period of the Civil Rights Movement used the term *tactical interaction* to describe this relationship. When a political system is vulnerable to a challenge, the challengers devise protest techniques some of which "offset" their powerlessness (see also Scott 1985). Often, however, the innovations only temporarily benefit challengers, as their opponents themselves respond to neutralize the new tactic and regain the upper hand. Protest and political opportunity, then, are a kind of game between challengers and the powerful, with peaks and lulls in protest activity matching periods of innovation in protest tactics and then the response to that innovation, which leads to a period of relative quiet while another kind of protest is thought up (McAdam 1983).

It is not entirely agreed upon, however, as to which institutions will operate in which ways (see Dalton and van Sickle 2005, Meyer 2004 for a review). Some scholars see protest more likely to take place when the system is fairly open and is relatively permissive of such kinds of things; others see protest as a response to a closed political system in which conventional participation is restricted. Of course, with too much restriction and repression the costs of protests are high, in which case we may see a more complex U-shaped (curvilinear) relationship between protest and repression. Alternatively, following the logic of Kahneman et al. (1982), should repression become so severe that life is intolerable, the comparative downsides for action are so low that the individual may become risk acceptant, willing to act with nothing to lose.

But whatever kinds of activity we are talking about, so long as it requires a number of people to accomplish it (that is, it requires collective, not just individual, action), then there will still be the hurdle of free riding to overcome. In other words, there will still be the problem posed by equation (1) in the previous chapter. It is not at all likely that the benefits of participation that are a consequence of an individual taking action as part of a group will outweigh the cost to that individual of taking that action. In fact for some classes of outcomes ("public goods"), an individual may receive the benefit whether he or she helped bring it about or not. So, for example, whether we join the Sierra Club or not, we all benefit from cleaner air. Similarly, whether we pay money to PBS or not, we can all watch *Sesame Street,* and whether we decide go on the march and brave the abuse or not, we all benefit when civil rights legislation passes. If someone can get the outcome (clean air, PBS, civil rights) without paying the cost of contributing (taking time to take part, making a donation, going on a march), then many individuals will choose not to contribute, even if they want the outcome to happen. In many situations, then, people can choose not to participate and "free ride" on the efforts of others. The problem comes when too many people decide that way. That is, what happens to *Sesame*

Street if no one gives to PBS? What happens to civil rights legislation if everyone decides to avoid the abuse and stay at home watching television? Not surprisingly, both scholars interested in these kinds of mass political participation and the organizers involved in various efforts have given a great deal of thought to ways in which the free-rider problem may be overcome.

One key factor in overcoming the free-rider challenge—at least for the example of collective action represented by the Civil Rights Movement—was that the success in accomplishing goals helped motivate people to keep participating in politics (Chong 1991, 234). People may well have reputations, standing, and a sense of belonging within a community that they wish to protect, all of which helps motivate people to take part and "do the right thing" for the sake of that community. But people also are not entirely irrational; if that participation does not work, then they will sooner or later quit taking part.

Another important line of argument is found in a study of black and Latino empowerment in ten California cities titled *Protest Is Not Enough* (1986). For Browning, Marshall, and Tabb—the scholars who conducted the study—protest behavior is all very well but may not accomplish goals; it may simply end up as an expression of opinion or discontent. What is needed before policy change happens, at least for these scholars, is incorporation into and participation in any ruling coalition. On the other hand, protest can provide tangible evidence of the sense of grievance and the breadth of individuals affected, perhaps engendering greater interest from those not directly involved and greater unanimity of sentiment and commitment from those taking part.

Summarizing the discussion so far, the politics of protest is a little different from more conventional forms of political participation except that it pushes at the boundary of what is acceptable and that the protest can flirt with the possibility of violence. Nevertheless, there are many similarities in terms of the kinds of arguments that apply and the kinds of obstacles to overcome. One way of illustrating some of these arguments is in relation to two important examples of minority politics that seem to be prompted by the closing off of representative politics to minorities—the Civil Rights Movement and the immigration protests of 2006.

THE CIVIL RIGHTS MOVEMENT

From the mid 1950s through to the late 1960s, the Civil Rights Movement transformed American political life. The general history of the movement is both well known and well documented, not least in the documentary *Eyes on the Prize* (see McAdam 1983; Chong 1991; Sitkoff 1993). Here we will only briefly review some major points about the Civil Rights Movement in relation to our discussion of protest politics. The term *Civil Rights Movement* implies a greater degree of homogeneity and unity than existed since "the movement" consisted of a broad coalition of organizations political, social, and religious that engaged in a wide range of activities with the goal of securing political and social equality for African Americans (Rosenstone and Hansen 2003,189). The range of organizations involved included the National Association for the Advancement of Colored People (NAACP), the Southern Christian Leadership Conference (SCLC) and its antecedent the Montgomery Improvement Association, the Congress of Racial Equality (CORE), the Student Nonviolent Coordinating Committee (SNCC), and the Voter Education Project, along with a number of other groups and organizations, notably churches. A range of different tactics went along with this range of groups, and the tactics changed as time progressed. Among the tactics adopted by various organizations and branches was litigation—suits were brought against discriminatory statutes. Civil disobedience also was used, through sit-ins and freedom rides to protest against the segregation of public transport, and boycotts of public transportation and businesses were also used as tactics to fight against segregation. In addition was a series of marches and rallies across the United States in support of civil rights. All of these tactics—and more—put pressure on American political leaders to introduce reforms, which they (eventually) did in 1957 and, notably, in 1964 with the Civil Rights Act and the Voting Rights Act of 1965.

The litigation strategy that led to the *Brown v. Board of Education* (1954) decision was met with increasing resentment by southern governments. In their own acts of civil disobedience, several governments refused to comply with the ruling, and, indeed, throughout the period in open acts of disobedience, many southern politicians persistently refused to obey or implement a series of laws. This resistance was encouraged by the decision in *Brown* II (1955), in which the Supreme Court, rather than order its ruling implemented, instructed segregated jurisdictions to comply "with all deliberate speed," a term understood by southerners as providing a window for that resistance. At least in part as a response to the situation, post–*Brown* the Civil Rights Movement began to adopt tactics of direct action.

As these tactics were put into place, flashpoints came at places and times that are now infamous—the Montgomery Bus Boycott; the desegregation of Little Rock, Arkansas, in 1957; the Freedom Rides on buses throughout the South; the Birmingham Boycott; lunch counter sit-ins; the marches; and the 1963 March on Washington, where Martin Luther King, Jr. gave his "I Have a Dream" speech. These flashpoints and subsequent ones such as the Selma to Montgomery marches were often occasions of violence against the protestors. The costs associated with participating in these activities were huge. Marchers and protestors ran the risk of imprisonment or losing jobs. And, as all too many were made aware, there were far more unpleasant and violent alternatives. While, in retrospect, it is easy to think that one would have obviously done the right thing at the time and joined the marchers or the boycotts, more than a few people must have given very serious thought to whether the costs of joining in the movement were too high. Even if most everyone wanted to do the right thing (and that is, of course, an unrealistic assumption), that isn't enough to get the right thing done.

Given the importance of the Civil Rights Movement in American history, it has received a great deal of attention as history, and as an important example of protest it has received a great deal of attention for what it can teach us about unconventional protest, more generally. We have referred to several of these lessons already and will not repeat them here. One of the major points about the Civil Rights Movement is that it rested on the organizational foundations of a series of organizations. These organizations were critical in helping to coordinate action among the participants (organizing times and dates for marches and publicizing boycotts) but were also important in building a sense of community and a shared identity. Seeing oneself as part of a larger group or community is an important conceptual and perceptual step for people to take. And such groups as the SCLC or the churches were important ways in which that collective identity was built, nurtured, and sustained.

Even more than that, however, one's standing and reputation in these organizations could be, and often was, linked to participation in the various protests. Chong (1991) suggests that black ministers, respected community leaders with more to lose, were initially reluctant to be more directly involved, until they recognized that their reputation as community leaders was imperiled by that reticence. Moreover, one's failure to live up to the participation could also be monitored by these organizations. One of the lessons of the Civil Rights Movement, then, is that it shows how valuable organizations are in helping to overcome the free rider problem even when the costs of participation are extraordinarily high.

IMMIGRATION PROTESTS, 2006

The immigration protests are somewhat different from the U.S. Civil Rights Movement on a number of grounds. First, while the success of the Civil Rights Movement can rightly be seen as a success for people of all colors and ethnicities, it was primarily centered on the claims of one group—African Americans. By contrast, the immigrants' rights rallies—while largely driven by Latino support—were cross-racial and cross-ethnic in the constituency. The protests were also driven by a specific policy concern rather than a set of concerns and grievances: the Civil Rights Movement may have had a narrower demographic constituency, but it had a broader set of goals. Finally, the Civil Rights Movement was built on a series of organizational building blocks that helped it succeed and persist, while the immigrants rights' rallies were built on less well organized foundations and seemed, at times, to be quite spontaneous.

As an example of political protest, then, the mass demonstrations of 2006 were very different from the Civil Rights Movement and so are an interesting example to consider.

In the spring of 2006, a series of rallies took place in many cities across the United States. Beginning with a relatively small demonstration in Philadelphia, a series of copycat demonstrations took place across the United States with perhaps as many as three-quarters of a million demonstrators taking part in a peaceful and orderly March 25 demonstration in LA. Throughout the rest of March and through April, other demonstrations occurred across the country in a range of cities, including Boston, Chicago, Detroit, Dallas, Phoenix, and Seattle. Even smaller cities such as Aurora, Illinois, Garden City, Kansas, Des Moines, and Knoxville saw protests and demonstrations. The scope of the protests peaked on April 10, with protests in roughly 100 cities nationwide, but continued for the rest of the month. May 1 was the Great American Boycott ("El Gran Paro Americano"). While the boycott had uneven success, protests and marches across the country were as large as previous ones, with perhaps as many as 1 million people taking part in LA, about half a million in Chicago, as well as many thousands taking part in other cities nationwide.

The main spark for the protests was controversial and punitive proposals for immigration reform—specifically a December 2005 bill adopted by the House of Representatives that would have made undocumented persons felons under the new law. Many, but by no means all, of those taking part were undocumented. Plainly, immigration reform is an issue of major concern to many.[5] But how is it that this concern was translated into mass participation and protest?

Given what we said about the "irrationality" of participation, these rallies are hard to explain—especially when one considers how large they were and how widespread. After all, the cost (C) of the protests was quite large. For the school kids who took part, perhaps only specialists in education saw ditching school for a day or two as a "cost," but for adults taking an unpaid day off from work, there was a real cost to taking part.

The example of the rallies in 2006 illustrates several points about the role of participation—and participation in the sense of taking part over and above voting (See Box 7-1).

First is the idea that a sense of shared or linked fate united people as part of a mass demonstration or mass mobilization. That is, in terms of equation (2) in chapter 6, there was a strong D component in the way in which people saw the issue and the value of participation: Immigration reform did not just affect "me"—it affected "us." That shift in perception, from me to us, is an important one in generating political participation in these wider forms. What is harder for the immigrant protests over the longer term is building that sense of "us" among a disparate social constituency—Latino, Asian, and even Anglo. That sense of community was much more generally shared by African Americans during the Civil Rights Movement because of the shared experience of segregation, an experience all African Americans shared, and an experience they endured entirely and inescapably as a result of their race.

A second point is that these protests show the importance of mobilization efforts—of being asked to participate—to this kind of participation in particular. A sense of shared fate is not automatic, nor does it happen by itself. People have to create that sense and begin to mobilize others around that identity or idea. These demonstrations point up one of the fundamental points of the work of Verba, Schlozman, and Brady (1995): people participate if they have been asked to. Of course, the question remains: who will do the asking in the first place? At some point, participation—just like a youth sport organization's midseason pizza party—depends on one or two people deciding to make the

The spring of 2006 saw millions of people turn out and demonstrate in support of immigrant rights in cities across the United States in 39 states and 140 cities. Protests began in the morning of May 1 on the East Coast and moved west across the country. The size of the marches varied from 500,000 in Washington, D.C., 30,000–40000 in Atlanta, 200,000 in Phoenix (CNN 2006), with between 500,000 to 1 million in Los Angeles (Pantoja et al. 2008, 499). Perhaps as many as 5 million people in total took to the streets (Barreto et al. 2009; Voss and Bloemraad 2011).

The immediate cause of the marches were protests against a bill in Congress, H.R. 447, better known as the Sensenbrenner bill after its author, Rep. James Sensenbrenner. Among other effects, this bill would make it a felony to be in the United States illegally, triggering a permanent bar from naturalization to U.S. citizenship. In part to demonstrate that many immigrants saw themselves not as aliens but as members of the American fabric, marches often displayed the Stars and Stripes and held signs that read "We Are America" (CNN 2006).

Many observers repeatedly describe these events using the term *unprecedented* (Barreto et al. 2009; Pantoja et al. 2008; Voss and Bloemraad 2011). It is extremely unusual to see so many people mobilized to take part in such a short period of time.

Given what we have said about participation, one obvious question is how did so many people get mobilized to take part? Ordinary people needed to be encouraged to attend these events. This meant not just telling people that there was an important issue at stake and that a protest was needed, but also informing people about the event itself in very specific terms (when and where to show up). Lobby groups and community organizers played a role in mobilizing their members, but a key part of this mobilization was Spanish-language media (Felix et al. 2008).

> Adrian Velasco first learned of House legislation to overhaul immigration policy on Los Angeles's Que Buena 105.5 FM. Over two weeks, the 30-year-old illegal immigrant soaked up details about the planned march against the bill from Hispanic TV and radio. On Saturday, he and three friends headed downtown.
>
> "They told all the Hispanic people to go and support these things," Velasco said. "They explained a lot. They said, 'Here's what we're going to do.'"
>
> One of those doing the most talking was El Piolin, a syndicated morning show radio host who is broadcast in 20 cities. (Flaccus 2006)

It is worth noting two things in particular about these efforts by El Piolin and others. First, the media gave out quite specific hints and suggestions. For example, El Piolin suggested carrying American flags to express the protesters' love of the United States and to wear white to symbolize peaceful intent. He urged parents to bring children as a way to help ensure the marches would be nonviolent, and he also reminded people to bring drinking water and trash bags (Flaccus 2006). These were very specific instructions, indeed. They were especially useful not just in shaping the march to be peaceful and nonviolent but also in simply telling people who may not have had much personal experience in political participation how to participate in a democracy. After all, many immigrants come from regimes that are not democratic and are often hostile to even peaceful protests. In a sense, El Piolin and his colleagues played an educational role—teaching people how to be participants in a democracy.

Second, it is important to underscore that these messages were not just carried by one or two radio stations but across Spanish-language media, television and radio. By itself, the growth of Spanish-language media is a concrete expression of the growing diversity of the United States. In this specific example, it shows the importance of coordinated and repeated messaging as an aid to helping to promote political mobilization.

first step to ask others for their participation. In this instance Spanish-language radio was the source of one of the first steps within a large section of the energized public.

We began by noting the weak organizational underpinnings of the immigrant protests. This is not to say that there was no coordination and planning, nor that existing Latino and immigrant organizations played no role. But the immigrant protests were not the product of concerted long-term planning, and this weakness matters in terms of translating the popular participation into political power. The Civil Rights Movement was built on a series of organizations. While radio as a device is able to communicate goals and intentions and allow groups to coordinate ("We will meet at city hall at 9 o'clock"), it is harder for radio to move beyond that. Radio announcers who were deeply involved in mobilizing the marchers are well positioned to urge listeners to protest but they are less well suited to organizing and maintaining an ongoing, coordinated political effort. In light of the lessons learned from the Civil Rights Movement, the translation of the immigrant protests into something more enduring is less likely even if protest behavior, as some think, becomes a more common form of political activity.

SUMMARY

One of the questions scholars face now is whether the forms of political participation of the twentieth century, in particular, participation as voting, will be as relevant for the current century. While we have dealt with conventional participation and unconventional participation in two separate chapters, the two kinds of participation are connected, and here we will try to reconnect them. In the past, the tradeoff has been between protest and ethnic participation on the one hand and voting in two-party politics on the other (Santoro and Segura 2011). In the coming era, the tradeoffs may be different. For example, web-based participation may give citizens a sense of a more direct connection to politics through online communities and campaign organizations. These kinds of participation are becoming more important, or, at least, they are being given more media coverage, which is not quite the same thing. Of course, in part these kinds of channels have been noticed by candidates all of whom now have extensive web campaign operations with web pages, Facebook accounts, Twitter feeds, podcasts of speeches, and so on. In which case these "new" media are not so much challenges to existing channels of participation as adjuncts to them.

Although one way in which these new media do challenge existing candidates is by taking away a measure of control of the "message." An example of that would be the ill-advised remarks of U.S. senator George Allen (R-VA), who used a slur at a public meeting to an Asian American onlooker who was taping his rally. Senator Allen did not expect his moment of pique to become a popular and highly damaging download on YouTube. No longer can candidates be sure of controlling the spin.

One worry, however, is that minority voters will be left out of these new media. Some scholars talk of a "digital divide" between those with computers and Internet access and those without. How great a consequence this is depends in part on how fully electronic forms of communication will replace more traditional forms of communication. As the evidence from experiments on campaign get out the vote efforts suggest, the "human touch" is a powerful one.

In many ways, discussions of political participation become oversimplified very quickly. While there are many ways of participating in the political process, these different modes of participation tend to correlate with each other quite highly. Academic discussion, therefore, focuses quickly on the shorthand topic of voting, because of that correlation. After all, if they are all related, if one constructs a theoretical model for one mode of participation, it will apply to others—so why not model the most common form of participation—voting? Up to a point that is fair enough: researchers only have so many hours in a day, and winning some insight on participation is far better than having none. Yet simplifying in this way does mean scholarship talks less about the nonvoting forms of participation than, perhaps, it should. This means, in turn, that events such as 2006 come as more of a surprise than they should. And while the different ways of participation do trend together, they do not do so for everyone—some people pick and choose as though from a menu and we do not understand that choice.

Similarly, the decision to participate is seen in highly abstract and highly individualized concerns, and theoretical models of participation are often reduced to a series of correlations of various factors such as education or income. Yet for voters, and for minority voters in particular, context would seem to be especially important in shaping the different barriers to participation either in terms of the specific group under discussion or in the specific kinds of participation. One of the consistent lessons from the study of minority political participation is the importance of the context to the decision to participate. It is a lesson that has implications for the study of participation in general.

One truism about politics is that "all politics is local"; all participation may be local, too, and the study of minority political participation is especially important in helping to understand that point. The presence of local groups promoting and encouraging (or alternatively discouraging) participation can plainly have an effect. How these groups or actors are distributed—whether there are church groups in the community or activists in the city—can help us to understand variations not just in the level of participation but also the kind of participation that takes place. Leighley's work marks a notable exception in outlining the importance of context in shaping the costs and benefits of political participation for minorities (Leighley 2001).

The key addition, in our view, of the minority politics literature is that "all politics are social." That is, patterns of demographic change, social interaction, cultural expression, and ethnocentric organizations and candidacies add an important additional layer of explanation.

In general, then, scholarship on participation can greatly benefit from a better understanding of minority political participation, since minority participation will allow for greater study of these contextual factors. It is not so much that we need to throw out theories by scholars such as Verba, Schlozman, and Brady and begin again, but we should rework them into more general arguments taking account of, and theorizing about, the nature of contextual effects. This will not only help us understand minority participation, but it will also be where studying minority participation will help us understand political participation more broadly. The range and variety of contexts—social, religious, linguistic, and organizational—present in minority and immigrant communities mean that there is great possibility for understanding and developing theories about what kinds of contexts have what kinds of effects on political participation.

Representation: Representatives, Elections, and Electoral Reform[*]

In Chapter 6 we saw that the vote is a symbol of citizenship and belonging: citizens—members of the community—may vote; noncitizens, that is, nonmembers, may not.[1] While gaining a meaningful right to vote was the goal of both the suffragettes and the voting rights element of the Civil Rights Movement, the vote is not actually an end in itself. Rather, the vote is also a means to a more instrumental end: it helps accomplish representation in the policy process.

Women, of course, achieved their goal with the adoption of the Nineteenth Amendment to the Constitution, adopted in 1920, which finally established them as full citizens with the granting of the franchise. The Civil Rights Movement reached that goal with the adoption of the Voting Rights Act of 1965, a landmark piece of legislation intended to ensure that African Americans could both vote and have their vote counted. When the act was renewed in 1975, it was extended to "language" minorities, an effort to explicitly address its provisions to Native Americans and U.S.-born Hispanics living in linguistically isolated communities. In principle, as a consequence of being able to cast a ballot, citizens should be represented, and the Voting Rights Act was a major legal step toward allowing all Americans to exercise the right to vote.

Fair access to the ballot box is only the first step. The right to vote is without consequence if there are few or no candidates interested in the votes of minority citizens. If, for example, the political process is sufficiently dominated by the majority, if parties are nonresponsive, if electoral arrangements make it hard for sufficient numbers of minority votes to be cast for a preferred candidate, access to the voting booth cannot be turned into actual effect on policy outcomes—the things people care about.

Chapter 2 suggested that the rapidly changing demography of the United States, if reflected in who votes, will have a great deal to do with shaping the political future in the next era. If, however, the changing demography is not reflected in changing distributions of electoral power, then the pace of change

[*]Portions of this chapter were adapted from Lublin, David I., and Gary M. Segura. "An Evaluation of the Electoral and Behavioral Impact of Majority-Minority Districts," in *Designing Democratic Government: Making Institutions Work*, edited by Margaret Levi, James Johnson, Jack Knight, and Susan Stokes (New York: Russell Sage Foundation, 2008), pp. 174–184. © 2008 Russell Sage Foundation, 112 East 64th Street, New York, NY 10065. Reprinted with permission.

and the movement of the political system in the direction we anticipate will be significantly slowed.

In Chapter 3 and, in particular, Tables 3-4 and 3-7, we reported that in 2011, African Americans, Asians, and Latinos collectively made up only 73 of 435 (16.8 percent) House members, and four senators (4 percent). And in Table 3-8 a little math makes it clear that in the lead-up to the 2008 election, minorities were only 13.3 percent of lower houses and 12.7 percent of state senates. Yet, in Table 3-4 we show that minorities as a share of the electorate have climbed to 26 percent in some elections.

One thing is clear. The representation of African Americans, Asian Americans, and Latinos in public office dramatically trails their share of the national turned-out electorate and, given turnout and demographic and citizenship distinctions, trails their population share even more dramatically. The lack of minorities in elected office relative to their share of the population, or even relative to their share of the electorate, is not alone sufficient to suggest that minority views are not represented in the policymaking process. The meaningful right to vote for minority citizens can and should make even Anglo elected officials more responsive. And there is good evidence to suggest that, at least today, white Democrats representing substantial minority constituencies are generally responsive to minority voters (Griffin and Newman 2008). But even under these circumstances, the representative must need the minority votes before she or he is likely to be responsive to them. For minority voters to have voice, they must have electoral influence—not necessarily by electing minority elected officials (although that is often the best shortcut to reliable representation) but at least being a pivotal portion of the winning coalition. Under what conditions will minority voters have an electoral impact sufficient to command responsiveness from their elected officials? Or, perhaps more to the point, what are the obstacles to the realization of that impact?

In this chapter, we will make three critical claims central to our view that the demographic change of the U.S. population will shape our collective political future. First, there remain significant obstacles to equitable representation of minority voters. Second, minority representation is important, and its effects are, on balance, strongly positive for the political system as a whole. Finally, the future of that representation is significantly threatened by limitations handed down by the decisions of the federal judiciary. It is hard to understate the importance of the role of the courts and law in shaping minority representation and in determining how provisions of the Voting Rights Act (VRA) are to be implemented. In this chapter we will refer to a series of important court cases that have had major consequences for minority representation.

Before we begin, it is worth noting that an equitable scheme of representation does not specifically require the proportional presence of legislators relative to racial and ethnic group population share. Nonminority representatives can (and have) faithfully represented the interests of minority constituents, while some minority group members elected to office can (and have) worked almost entirely against the preferred policy positions of their respective groups.

But disproportionality is often a good indicator of the extent to which racial and ethnic minorities have been systematically unable to select *first-choice* candidates for public office. And while equity does not necessarily require that the legislature's composition mirror the population's, wild disproportionality or even the total absence of representation of minority communities should at least raise questions about whether the system can be even remotely responsive.

For these reasons we proceed from the simple assumption that systematic underrepresentation of racial and ethnic minorities in public office, relative to their population size, is an indicator of political disadvantage.

THE STRUCTURE AND IMPACT OF MINORITY VOTE DILUTION

As we saw, minority voters are underrepresented proportionally; that is, the share of elected officials who are members of a minority group is smaller than the share of the population who are minority. Historically the underrepresentation was far worse than it is today, and it was the rule rather than the exception that non-Hispanic white males composed nearly the entirety of most elected bodies.

A variety of factors not specifically related to the electoral system can play a role in underrepresentation. Members of some groups might be disadvantaged in resources, making competitive candidacies hard to mount. Minority voters, as we have discussed, turn out less frequently at the ballot box, and some groups have the antecedent obstacle of naturalization to U.S. citizenship before mobilization is even possible. Nevertheless, it is clear that electoral structures have significantly shaped opportunities for minority voices to be heard and minority candidates to be elected. Some of these obstacles remain today.

There are two broad electoral factors explaining this disproportionality of representation—the outright denial of the vote to minorities and vote dilution. The first is simpler to describe, define, and (as we will see) fix. Everyone is familiar with the kinds of laws, literacy tests, and poll tax requirements that denied the vote to American citizens simply because of their race or ethnicity. In the first half of the twentieth century the level of vote denial to African Americans was staggering. Even though they composed significant proportions of the population of southern states, almost no blacks were allowed to vote. Even after a series of voter registration drives and court cases, it was still the case that by 1965 only about 36 percent of African Americans in southern states were registered to vote, compared with 73 percent of Anglos (Engstrom 1994). For long periods in American history, then, the question of minority representation was moot because minority citizens were denied the vote—and hence denied a voice.

African Americans were not alone in being discriminated against. Even after passage of the Indian Citizenship Act of 1924, Native Americans were denied the vote in many states. It was not until 1948 that the laws preventing Native Americans from voting in Maine, Arizona, and New Mexico were overruled by federal courts. Laws prohibiting Asian immigrants from naturalizing to U.S. citizenship (and hence voting) were not repealed until the 1940s and

1950s. In fact it was not until 1944 that Thurgood Marshall, then an NAACP attorney and later a Supreme Court justice, won the case of *Smith v. Allwright*, in which the Supreme Court ruled "whites only" primaries were illegal. The actual practice of discrimination in all these instances often continued well after discriminatory laws were overturned, but the importance of the legal fight to ensure voting rights should not be understated.

Defining Minority Vote Dilution

Even when these legal restrictions on voting were eased, vote dilution meant it was harder for minorities to gain representation. Vote dilution is a less obvious way of denying political power to an out-group than outright denial of vote. It is the result of the interactions of majority voting patterns and local electoral laws that function to exclude minorities or minority-preferred candidates from public office. In all instances, vote dilution results first and foremost from majority—usually, but not always, non-Hispanic whites—bloc voting against minority or minority-preferred candidates. That bloc voting, however, is more or less successful depending on the institutional arrangements in the local jurisdiction. Voting systems and processes vary considerably across the United States, especially at the local and county levels, and vote dilution is more or less possible depending on the specific arrangements.

The American system of elections is inherently geographic; all of our legislative systems tie representatives to some area of territory. Two arrangements that characterize most systems of representation in the United States are a districted system and an at-large system. In the first, each member of a legislature (whether a county board, a school board, a city council, or Congress) represents a geographic district that is only part of the overall jurisdiction. For example, a city council may have nine representatives, each representing a geographic portion of the city that contains approximately one-ninth of the city's population. This system is used in most states for their legislatures and in the election of representatives to Congress (in any state with more than one House member). Election to that office is generally determined by a plurality of the voters in that geographic district. We will refer to this as a single-member-district system, hereafter called "SMD."[2]

In the second system members are elected at-large. What this means is that each member represents the entire jurisdiction. In our example of the city council with nine members, each member represents the entire town on the city council and, in theory, is responsive to a citywide electorate. Elections here are generally plurality—if there are five seats up for election in a given election year, every voter casts five votes for their five favorite candidates, and the top-five vote getters win the five seats. We call this system an at-large-plurality system, hereafter "ALP."

Minority vote dilution can happen in either system. For SMD, it simply involves drawing district boundaries in order to minimize the number of officials elected by that out-group. Since districts require the drawing of boundaries—and this means defining who the voters are in a given district, those in charge of drawing the district boundaries then have a great deal of power to shape the result.

It is important to note that gerrymandering in this way is not unique to race politics, nor even unique to the United States. In Mexico, for example, drawing boundaries in a way that meant rural areas had more seats than their population justified helped the PRI (the Institutional Revolutionary Party) to hold on to power for so long. Britain, in another example, had centuries of representation in Commons for districts—called rotten boroughs—where previously sizable towns had become wholly unpopulated, allowing powerful interests to use the seats to enhance their influence.[3] In the United States redistricting is often used for similar partisan ends as the majority party tries hard to draw district boundaries that keep it in power. Gerrymandering is a worldwide political tactic. Not surprisingly it is also used to help shape minority representation (or the lack thereof) in the United States. Between 1980 and 1990, for example, only one of Georgia's ten congressional districts was majority-black despite the fact that African Americans accounted for 27 percent of the population of Georgia in that period. Plainly, then, minorities could not achieve descriptive representation in these circumstances, even when allowed to vote.

There are several ways of using district boundaries to undercut the representation of specific groups. "Cracking" spreads out the voters among a series of districts in order to keep them as small vote blocs within each seat.

For an illustration, consider "Smallville," an imaginary town in your state with a 25 percent African American population (see Figure 8-1). If Smallville had a five-member city council, meaning each member had about 20 percent of the city's population within the boundaries of his or her district, we would

FIGURE 8-1 **Smallville**

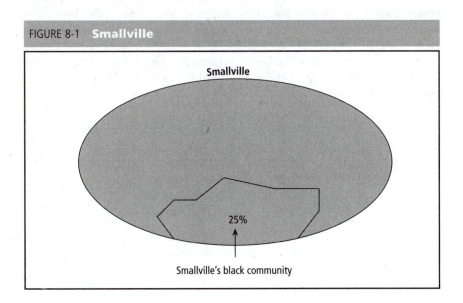

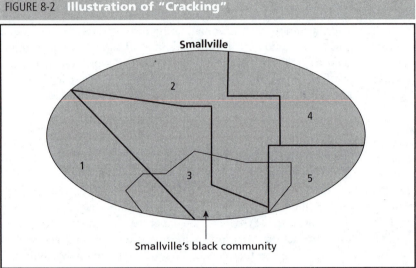

FIGURE 8-2 Illustration of "Cracking"

expect that the city's African American voters would have considerable influence on at least one member, perhaps even electing a member of their community to office. But this need not be so. If the population were "cracked" across the five city council districts, African American voters would be a tiny minority in each and have little effect on the outcomes. What this looks like is illustrated in Figure 8-2.

Fortunately for the black population of Smallville, this sort of districting is very likely to run afoul of the Voting Rights Act and a (successful) legal challenge is likely. Although the legal environment for voting rights challenges has been changing—something we will discuss at length further along—in cases such as this, when there is a definable action (drawing districts) that breaks a community of interest apart, thereby diminishing its electoral impact, the clear provisions of Section 2 of the VRA render these actions a violation of federal law.

If the city had followed the law or, barring that, been forced to by a federal court, the resulting districting scheme would almost certainly result in one city council seat in which the African American population's views are determinative, as illustrated in Figure 8-3.

Another source of vote dilution in districts is "packing," a process that puts as many voters of one type into a single district as possible in order to minimize the number of seats that are won by the targeted group. In this instance, the minority population share is so sizable that its complete exclusion through cracking is either nearly impossible or easily identified and subject to a VRA claim. Packing districts, however, allows the majority to hold the line on the overall number of districts where minorities have real impact on the outcomes,

FIGURE 8-3   **Districts Drawn within VRA Guidelines**

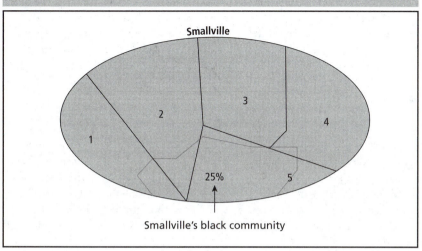

at a number smaller than their population share might have suggested. Unfortunately for the minority voters involved, this is much harder to demonstrate in court.

Return for the moment to Smallville and imagine that its black population share is now 50 percent, instead of 25 percent, as illustrated in Figure 8-4. You will note that we have used the exact same district boundaries, but now something is deeply amiss. The African American population share has climbed to

FIGURE 8-4   **Packing an Enlarged Minority Population**

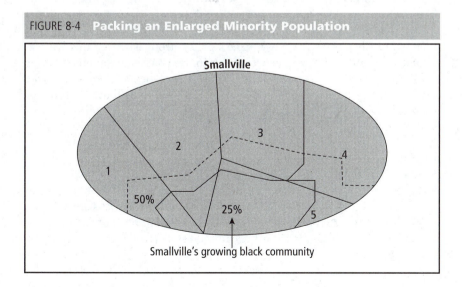

half of the city, yet black voters are shaping outcomes only in that same one district. Black voters remain small minority shares of the electorate in the other districts. Should the city propose this same scheme for districting, in which 100 percent of one district is minority, and in no others are minority voters likely to win the day, it would be a clear illustration of packing. That 50 percent share of the city's population could have been 100 percent of two districts and half of a third, or form clear majorities in three of the five seats. Instead, its electoral strength has effect in only one district's elections.

As a practical matter, it is harder to sustain an accusation of packing. First, the cases are seldom as egregious as the example we present here. And second, this involves a more nuanced and subjective estimation of what constitutes fair representation. In the cracking example, we could easily conclude that a minority composing one-quarter of the jurisdiction's population is unfairly underrepresented with no seats and that 20 percent of the seats (one of five) seems more "fair" in some sense. But when can that minority population make a "fair" claim for an additional seat? At 40 percent, sure, but what about 30 percent?

In truth, since the number of representatives is fixed, the population share of any group (which can vary from 0 to 100) will never exactly match its share of seats in which group members have significant electoral impact. In a five-seat council the only "shares" that can result are values of 0, 20, 40, 60, 80, or 100 percent, but populations can have value such as 23.6 or 58.1 percent. Moreover, disproportionality is not sufficient to make a VRA claim, and the federal courts have reiterated this repeatedly, as has Congress. There must be evidence that the process and outcomes systematically deny a meaningful voice to a group of citizens, and other aspects of the process are key.

In examining real-world cases, we need to make a number of assumptions about those "other aspects" that must be true to make a claim of minority-vote dilution. First, we need to assume that the minority group is a community of interest—that is, that the voters in the racial minority group share political interests. In Chapters 4 and 5, we make a pretty strong case that this is a reasonable assumption. But we need to be able to show that the claim holds at the community level for the provisions of the VRA to be at issue. Second, we assume that majority voters—usually whites—are unwilling to vote for minority candidates, or any candidates preferred by minority voters. This, too, will vary from place to place and across the minority groups in question, and so it requires a jurisdiction level evaluation. Finally, you will note that the black community in Smallville was sufficient in size and geographic concentration for us to successfully draw a district. If this is not the case—as it is never the case for women, for example—then districting cannot be held accountable as the cause of underrepresentation, for no district scheme could alleviate this. As we will explain shortly, these assumptions are critical when we examine vote dilution in the other common system of local representation, at-large-plurality.

Vote dilution in at-large-plurality systems is harder to identify than forms of dilution—especially cracking—in districts, since it relies on a variety of individual behaviors not conveniently written into local law or maps for federal courts to review. To exclude minority influence in local elections in an at-large-plurality environment, bloc-voting preferences on the part of the majority are sufficient to exclude minority voices, provided there are sufficient candidates in the race to meet the majority's preferences and not so many that coordination is a problem. Since all voters get one vote per available seat in ALP systems, a sufficiently committed majority can cast those votes for its preferred candidates and, in effect, elect the entire body without votes from the minority playing any role.

Consider, for example, "Pleasant Town" a medium-sized suburb of a major city with a 30 percent Latino electorate. If the town had a five-person council, three seats would be up for election in one election year and two in the other. If this year Pleasant Town had three seats up, with six candidates running—four white and two Hispanic—the 70 percent white majority could, with only modest overlap in preferences, elect the entire council. Since each voter gets three votes (equal to the number of seats), the majority could distribute those votes across the four white candidates and, even if they did so evenly, there is no way for the 30 percent minority, no matter how unified, to elect a member. Sample results are illustrated in Table 8-1.

The results in Table 8-1 illustrate the outcome of racially polarized bloc voting in an at-large-plurality environment. We assumed an electorate of 20,000 voters broken down into 70 percent non-Hispanic white and 30 percent Latino. We use the most restrictive assumption—that Latino voters were completely supportive of their candidates and wasted no votes and that the number of Latino candidates was not larger than the number of available seats.

TABLE 8-1 Sample Election Results in ALP System with Bloc Voting

Pleasant Town's recent election results			
Candidate	Non-Hispanic white votes	Latino votes	Total vote
Dr. Scott	13,000	3,600	16,600
Mr. English	12,450	1,200	13,650
Ms. Church	12,050	750	12,800
Mrs. Brewer	4,190	450	4,640
Mr. Gutierrez	125	6,000	6,125
Ms. Sanchez	185	6,000	6,185

Note: Assumes 20,000 voters each cast 3 votes with no votes wasted.

Nevertheless, the majority population was able to claim all three seats. Worse, none of those elected owed their victory in any way to the votes of Latinos. If all of the Latino voters in Pleasant Town had not participated, it would not have mattered a bit to the outcome of the election.

Now, the majority could have more evenly divided its votes across the four candidates but, with 42,000 available votes (70 percent of 20,000 x 3 votes each), it would not have mattered. Indeed, the number of white candidates could have been five or six, and still an even division of vote would not have provided a window for a Latino to be elected. Now, in such an evenly divided case, Latino voters *may* have been able to influence which majority-group candidate was elected, but minority-preferred candidates remain excluded.

Of course, this exclusion is driven, first and foremost, by the high level of racial polarization in the white majority's voting choices. As a practical matter, vote dilution in at-large systems depends on the relative population shares of the two groups, the degree of majority racially polarized bloc voting, and the number of majority-group candidates splitting the vote. When racial polarization is relatively weaker and the vote more divided, a larger minority population might find an occasional opportunity for victory. However, when the population share is somewhat smaller and white unity is higher, no amount of group mobilization and effort can change the outcome from certain defeat.

Vote dilution is easier to identify and correct in SMD settings. Moreover, it is more difficult to completely exclude minority voices in an SMD system, since minority groups often form neighborhood or local majorities. It is for this reason that generations of voting rights activists have preferred to fight for minority representation in districted settings.

We would be remiss if we did not mention the important role of the size of a legislature—be it a city council, school board, county board, or state legislative chamber. Other things equal, it is always easier to secure minority representation with a greater number of seats. The reason for this is straightforward: whether in an at-large-plurality system or a districted system, the threshold for election is lower when the number of seats is greater.

Consider our Pleasant Town example. If the council size had been 9 seats instead of 5—meaning that 4 or 5 of the candidates would be elected, rather than 3, Latinos would not have been excluded. Likewise, we could imagine Smallville having an 11-member council. In that environment, African American representation is far more likely to approach proportionality because the relative size of the geographically concentrated population necessary to win a district is smaller. This effect is illustrated in Figure 8-5.

Figure 8-5 shows two additional advantages of larger council sizes. First, the size of the minority population necessary to reach the threshold of representation is smaller. In Smallville, a 5 percent Asian American community can achieve representation when the city is divided into 11 districts (meaning about 9 percent of the city is in each district). Second, when multiple minority groups are seeking representation in elected office, a greater number of seats

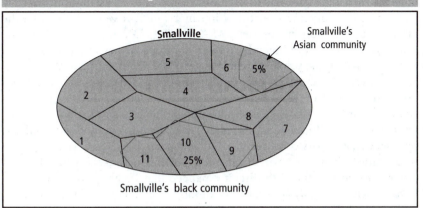

FIGURE 8-5 **Effect of Larger Council Size in Districted Elections**

Smallville

Smallville's Asian community

Smallville's black community

reduces the likelihood of zero-sum competition across groups for limited seats. In short, with more seats, more groups can be represented.

Voting Rights Act and Minority Vote Dilution

When the VRA was originally adopted in 1965, the institutional structures and behaviors understood to inhibit minority voting and representation included poll taxes, white primaries, literacy tests and grandfather clauses, subtle and direct resistance to black voter registration, and outright intimidation and violence. Section 2 of the Voting Rights Act applied to all jurisdictions in the United States and specifically prohibited behaviors designed to thwart legitimate and meaningful electoral participation.

In addition to the general provisions of Section 2, a set of "special" provisions in Section 5 subjected jurisdictions found to have a history of discriminatory electoral behavior—dubbed "covered jurisdictions" by virtue of a coverage formula built on minority turnout and social histories of the jurisdiction—to a provision requiring the preclearance of the voting rights division of the Justice Department before any rules affecting the conduct of elections could be changed. Preclearance meant almost continuous scrutiny for jurisdictions with unsavory histories.

The extension of the VRA to language minorities in 1975 highlighted a different set of barriers—the publication of election materials only in English and the systematic exclusion of Native Americans and Latinos from the voter rolls.

It is less clear that electoral systems themselves were understood to be a source of disenfranchisement at the time of the adoption of the VRA. That notion came to light in a series of court cases in the early 1970s that laid bare the insufficiency of access to the ballot box in ensuring meaningful opportunities to participate.[4] Beginning with *Whitcomb v. Chavis* (1971), an unsuccessful attempt to strike down an Indianapolis multimember at-large voting scheme, the Supreme Court noted at least the possibility that the electoral system itself might be found to have had a disenfranchising effect. That notion was fully realized in the Supreme Court decision in *White v. Regester* (1973) and the Fifth Circuit decision in *Zimmer v. McKeithan* (1973). In *White* the Supreme Court struck down multimember representation schemes in Dallas and San Antonio, challenged by both African American and Latino citizens. While these systems were not inherently unconstitutional per se, when found in combination with a history of social and political exclusion, the use of slating groups—endorsement lists—that systematically excluded blacks and Latinos, a lack of minority elected officials, and the general nonresponsiveness of white officials representing minority constituents, a "totality of circumstances" suggested that the at-large scheme was part of a systematic unequal access to the political system. In *Zimmer,* the Fifth Circuit expanded that "totality" to include other factors, including really large districts, runoff requirements, and the absence of geographic distribution requirements for members of the local legislature. In *Nevett v. Sides* (1978), the Fifth Circuit again expanded "totality" to include evidence of white bloc voting, which was necessary in order to establish the central claim, that minority voters did not have a meaningful chance to elect first-choice candidates.

By the end of the 1970s, the legal regime regarding voting rights appeared settled. At-large systems could be challenged as dilutive if the "totality of circumstances" suggested that a jurisdiction's history, electoral outcomes, and voting behavior of its citizenry could collectively be evaluated as discriminatory in effect. In almost all instances, the preferred method of redress was the conversion of at-large systems into SMD systems, where African Americans and Latinos could use their geographic concentration to exert electoral influence on one or more districts.

That legal regime was turned upside down with the Supreme Court's decision in *Mobile v. Bolden* (1980). The Court, fractious and badly divided, overturned a lower court ruling and upheld the at-large electoral system of Mobile, Alabama, which had been in place since 1911 without ever electing a black to the city commission. The lower courts found a history of discrimination, unresponsive legislators, and questionable practices, to accompany the obviously exclusively white results. But the Supreme Court said that apparently exclusionary results are not sufficient to show a constitutional violation. In order to raise a constitutional challenge to an electoral scheme, the plaintiffs had to show "discriminatory intent," something that could be difficult for plaintiffs facing long-standing electoral arrangements dating from an era with few physical records and, of course, no e-mails or the like to document the social views of those framing the arrangements. In effect, *Mobile v. Bolden* overturned the "totality" criteria and dramatically narrowed the interpretation of Section 2.

In response, the Congress, when extending the VRA in 1982, specifically rewrote Section 2 to overturn the Supreme Court's decision. The language and legislative intent around the rewritten Section 2 restored the "totality of circumstances" criteria and indicated unequivocally that exclusionary and wildly disproportionate results did serve to make a claim of vote dilution even in the absence of evidence of intent. Congress still made it clear that there is no "right" to proportionality in election outcomes, merely that the history of outcomes is a factor that should be considered when evaluating a claim of vote dilution.

Of course, the federal courts had to interpret the rewritten Section 2, something accomplished in the Supreme Court case *Thornburg v. Gingles* (1986). The result was the "*Gingles* standard," a three-pronged test to determine when an electorally excluded group has a legitimate claim, which was essentially the "totality" criteria refined and distilled. For the Supreme Court majority in the *Gingles* case, a persuasive claim required, first, that the group be sizable enough and geographically concentrated enough to be able to secure representation in another system. If the group is so small, or so spread out, that an SMD system serves them no better, then there is no case. Second, the group must be politically cohesive; that is, in political terms, it must be a group with shared political interests and preferences. In the absence of group preferences, it is impossible to make the claim that the "group" is disadvantaged. Finally, there must be evidence of majority racially polarized bloc voting. If the majority faction in the jurisdiction shows a regular willingness to vote for minority-favored candidates, then there is no basis for the claim that the group is somehow excluded.

The *Gingles* standard had an impact far beyond the boundaries of challenges to at-large systems as dilutive, because in *Gingles* the court implicitly also identified when a subpopulation's size and circumstances warranted more conscious attempts to secure representation. Jurisdictions of all sorts, from state legislatures to county commissions, interpreted these changes as effectively directing the creation of districts that provided opportunities for minority voters to elect first-choice candidates wherever circumstances warranted such efforts—circumstances defined in some detail by the *Gingles* standard. In the wake of the 1990 census, legislatures and redistricting commissions had the first opportunity in the wake of the revisions to Section 2 and the decision in *Gingles* to draw district lines. The result was a huge increase in the number of districts where minority voters could determine outcomes, often termed "majority-minority." Not surprisingly, the result was a significant surge in minority office holding, as illustrated in Figure 8-6.

Though majority-minority districts existed prior to 1991, the rewritten Section 2 and its judicial interpretations set into motion the rapid increase in the number of majority-black and majority-Latino districts in city and county councils, state legislatures, and Congress. It had the intended effect, as a far greater share of minority citizens were able to see first-choice candidates elected to public office.

FIGURE 8-6 **Increase in Minority Elected Officials**

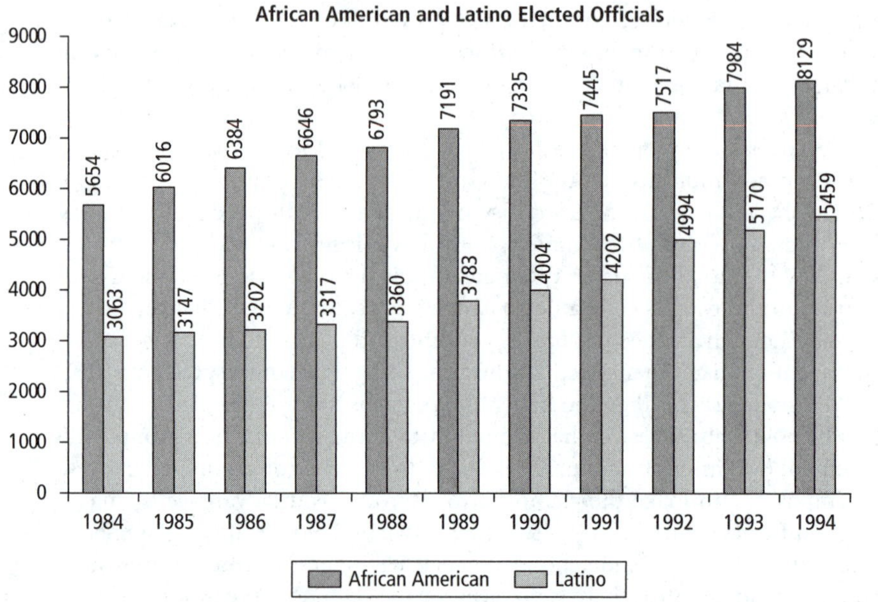

African American and Latino Elected Officials

Year	African American	Latino
1984	5654	3063
1985	6016	3147
1986	6384	3202
1987	6646	3317
1988	6793	3360
1989	7191	3783
1990	7335	4004
1991	7445	4202
1992	7517	4994
1993	7984	5170
1994	8129	5459

Source: U.S. Census Bureau. 2010. *Statistical Abstract of the United States.* www.census.gov/compendia/statab/cats/elections/elected_public_officials—characteristics.html.

Evolving Federal Jurisprudence on Majority-Minority Districts

The rush to create new majority-minority districts, while resulting in a substantially increased presence for African Americans and Latinos in elective office, may have had a number of unintended side effects that illustrate some of the complexities of representation. Some scholars suggest that these districts played at least a small part in the Republicans gaining control of the House of Representatives in 1994 because the newly created majority-minority districts had the effect of depopulating the surrounding districts of minority—largely Democratic—voters, making formerly safe Democratic districts competitive, and competitive districts Republican leaning. While the numerical logic of this claim is difficult to dismiss, there is considerably less evidence that the effect was meaningful in more than a handful of House districts, especially in the context of the ideological tide present in that election and sweeping through white southerners at the time (Lublin 1997).

A second effect was the renewed skepticism of the federal courts. Beginning with *Shaw v. Reno* (1993), and including *Miller v. Johnson* (1995), and *Bush v. Vera* (1996), the Supreme Court took issue with the predominance of race as the principal factor in drawing these majority-minority districts. When legislatures felt compelled to draw these districts, they required some sense of how large the minority population had to be in order for this to happen—was 50 percent + 1 of the population enough or not? An effective minority district is one in which minority voters have a real opportunity to elect a candidate of their choice. Early work suggested that a district may need to be as much as 65 percent minority population for this to occur given lower rates of turnout of minority voters. Subsequent work by David Lublin (1999) suggested a lower figure of 55 percent—but clearly the need is to have a sizable majority of voters within a district to assure descriptive representation.

The difficulty is that in drawing these districts a whole set of competing values and interests have to be balanced. Drawing majority-minority districts meant that the state was considering racial identity in making law. Moreover, as we move up levels of representation, the level of geographic concentration necessary to draw a district easily was harder and harder to find. While a neighborhood of 5,000 minority residents in a town of 25,000 is easy to find and demarcate, drawing a congressional district of 600,000-plus residents meant drawing majority-minority districts that had tortured boundaries, amalgamating minority populations across disparate regions and metropolitan areas.

In *Shaw v. Reno* (1993) the Supreme Court pushed back against the practice, declaring that while race can be *a* factor, it could not be the *primary* criterion used in drawing district boundaries, and that doing so violated the equal protection of white citizens. One district in North Carolina stretched for hundreds of miles and, at points, was no wider than the Interstate highway. In another example, Georgia drew a majority African American district that stretched from Atlanta to the Atlantic and covered over 6,000 square miles. Not surprisingly, this district's particular boundaries challenged the idea that the district represented a community in any meaningful sense and also led to a series of legal challenges that culminated in *Miller v. Johnson* in 1995.[5]

Since the decade of the 1990s, the pace of jurisprudence on this issue has slowed considerably. Several cases, however, have changed the legal landscape in ways not always supportive of minority representation and in ways that suggest future courts may not be as friendly to assisting minority representation as their predecessors. In *Georgia v. Ashcroft* (2003), the Supreme Court controversially allowed Georgia to reduce the minority population share in majority-minority districts, ruling that this did not hurt minority voting interests, since minority voters retained significant influence in the outcomes in the districts at issue. Finally, in *Bartlett v. Strickland* (2009), the Court ruled that the minority group at issue must constitute a numerical majority of a prospective district before the *Gingles* standard implies an affirmative duty to create a majority-minority district or before the jurisdiction is vulnerable to vote dilution litigation. This decision was seen as limiting the frequency with which sizable minority populations would be protected in the districting process, and eliminating the possibility that two minority groups—African Americans and Latinos, for example—could together constitute a community of interest for the purpose of triggering the protections of Section 2.[6]

As Court support for majority-minority districts has waned, a number of questions remain about the value of descriptive representation in a political rather than legal sense. It is all very well drawing districts to ensure minority voters get to choose a candidate and increase the chance of minority candidate winning, but does it matter? That is, do we have reason to believe that the election of minorities, or securing the meaningful impact of minority voters on elections, matters to their quality of representation? And does it matter to the citizens themselves, that is, how they interact with the political system?

The answer to both questions appears to be yes: yes, minorities enjoy better representation as a consequence of changes of the kind discussed above, and yes, it matters to how they interact with the political system.

YARDSTICKS OF EVALUATION: WHEN IS REPRESENTATION "GOOD"?

In 2006, Stephen Cohen, was elected to Congress from Tennessee. In a column in the *Boston Globe*, reporter Jeff Jacoby noted that Cohen, who is Jewish, was aware that his district was predominantly Christian. During the campaign Cohen promised to work hard on issues of concern to Christian voters and if elected would seek membership in the Congressional Christian Caucus. In January 2007 as a first-term member he did apply to the caucus and was rejected from membership because he was not Christian. The caucus leader issued a statement saying, "[Cohen] does not, and cannot, meet the membership criteria, unless he can change . . ."[7]

The disagreement between Cohen and the caucus leader is over the nature of representation: one side believes that representation is about what a person does (sometimes known as "substantive" representation), while the other side believes that in representation who you are matters ("descriptive" representation).

The distinction made between what a person does and who a person is relates to the idea of descriptive representation. According to Hannah Pitkin, descriptive representation can be defined as "the making present of something absent by resemblance or reflection, as in a mirror or in art" (Pitkin 1967, 11). That is, representatives should in some general sense look like the people they represent. It is an idea that is sometimes contrasted with the idea of substantive representation, which is how we might see what Congressman Cohen was aiming for in making the claim "I may not be like voters in my district—but I'll work really hard on their behalf."

There are some obvious issues here when we consider descriptive and substantive representation in general. First, it is not always apparent which kinds of social and political distinctions should be descriptively represented: class, religion, ideology, language, and gender come to mind as possible distinctions we might want to see reflected in the legislature. But there are many other demographic traits that are important in society. For example, we know that age and education are traits that make for social distinction, so should these be represented too, and should we have over-sixty-year-olds and high school dropouts in our legislatures? Occupation is another obvious example and would suggest that the overwhelming number of attorneys in politics is distorting. If we are aiming at complete description, perhaps one possibility is not to have elections but instead to choose people from the population randomly to be our representatives.

Second, pitting the term *substantive representation* against *descriptive representation* is misleading because it implies they are at odds with each other and also that there is nothing substantive about descriptive representation. But neither of these things needs be true. For example, a person who looks like the voters will bring to policymaking the outlook and sensibilities of a shared experience beyond their effort.

Third, to talk about substantive representation also blurs another important distinction over what it is we expect a representative to do. After all, descriptive representation alone may not be enough. It is not as if any candidate is as good as any other—provided he or she is a member of a minority group. If an election is between two minority candidates—for example, both are African American or both are Latinas—voters still have to choose one and descriptive representation alone does not offer guidance because both candidates are descriptively representative. We need other criteria to help us decide.

All of which brings us to the question of racial and ethnic representation (which we left out of the list a moment ago). When it comes to representing racial minorities, are there special concerns or special considerations that we need to address?

Let us turn back to the story that we began with—Congressman Cohen and his attempt to join the Christian caucus. The story, by the way, is *not* true. There is no Congressional Christian Caucus,[8] and Cohen did not seek to join it or start such a caucus. Jacoby made up that account in order to help make a point about the real story. The real story is that Congressman Cohen, who is white, was indeed elected to Congress in Tennessee in 2006. His district, which was previously represented by Harold Ford, is 60 percent black. In January 2007, Congressman Cohen asked to join the Congressional Black Caucus and was rejected. Rep. William Clay, D-MO, of the Congressional Black Caucus was quoted as saying, "Mr. Cohen asked for admission, and he got his answer. He's white and the Caucus is black. It's time to move on. We have racial policies to pursue and we are pursuing them, as Mr. Cohen has learned. It's an unwritten rule. It's understood." The statement from Representative Clay's office said, "Quite simply, Rep. Cohen will have to accept what the rest of the country will have to accept—there has been an unofficial Congressional White Caucus for over 200 years, and now it's our turn to say who can join 'the club.' He does not, and cannot, meet the membership criteria, unless he can change his skin color. Primarily, we are concerned with the needs and concerns of the black population, and we will not allow white America to infringe on those objectives."

So why talk about the Christian caucus if it is not true? Jacoby had his own reasons for doing so in his newspaper column: he thought the Black Caucus was wrong to reject Cohen and, further, that if we thought about the idea of representation in a nonracial context, we would see how wrong that would be. Unless, that is, we think there is something fundamentally different about the representation of race and ethnic issues as opposed to the representation of religious, linguistic, class, or gender differences. But if there is something inherently different about the representation of race that means Cohen cannot speak on "black" issues, then does that mean Clay should not be allowed to speak on "Latino" issues or "Asian" issues or "white" issues (should such things exist)?

The same issue of "who is an appropriate representative?" comes up again in many different ways. For example, many cities and counties have laws requiring that representatives live in the district they represent. In July 2007, the *Los Angeles Times* reported on Supervisor Yvonne Burke. Burke, who is African American, is the county supervisor essentially for heavily African American South Central LA. The newspaper account provided the following interpretation: while Supervisor Burke has a mailing address in the district, she really lives in the upscale region of Brentwood in a 4,000-square-foot residence with a swimming pool and tennis court. The area that Burke is elected to serve has, quite unlike Brentwood, chronic problems of unemployment, crime, homelessness, and ongoing difficulties with the hospital. Even though Supervisor Burke is descriptively representative on racial grounds, her critics within the district argue that she does not share life experiences or life chances with her voters—and these are crucially important attributes to represent. At least part of Supervisor Burke's response to the story was similar to Congressman Cohen's: "Excluding weekends," Burke said, "there is not a day that I'm not here. Not one day,"[9] That is, she does understand the district and the needs of the district because she works hard at it.

There are, then, differences in how a representative—any representative—relates to the district. But for minority voters the problem that persisted until the late twentieth century was that having a district in which a minority candidate had any chance of winning was, to say the least, a rarity. To some extent the question of whether one should have descriptive or substantive representation was moot when there was next-to-no representation.

The Voting Rights Act meant that minority voters could take part in the political process, which meant, in turn, that minority candidates could take a meaningful part in the process. David Lublin (1997) and Pei-te Lien et al. (2007) show

> a substantial relationship between the VRA and the election of non-white officials at the national state and local levels. However, we also observe significant racial differences in the pattern of the relationship. We find greater VRA coverage at the congressional than at the state level. Eighty percent of Latino and 66 percent of Black members of the U.S. House were elected from majority-Latino districts and majority-Black districts, respectively; such is not the case with [Asian Americans and Native Americans].
>
> (Lien et al. 2007, 492–493)

Voters may well see the minority candidate in the ways that the argument of descriptive representation suggests: at last they have "someone like them" in office. The existence of minority candidates, and minority incumbents, may also signal to voters that they really do have a chance of winning and having their votes counted within the system, which should, we expect, have follow-on consequences for how willing those voters are to turn out and vote and how they feel about the system.

THE REPRESENTATIONAL CONSEQUENCES OF RACIAL REDISTRICTING

But before we conclude that we should simply try to draw as many majority-minority districts as circumstances—and the federal courts—will allow, we should talk more about the process of representation. Do majority-minority districts help substantive representation as well as descriptive representation?

There is a long-standing question of what a representative (descriptive or otherwise) is meant to *do* once in office. Too rigid a definition of descriptive representation implies that any minority candidate is as good as any other, which is clearly not true. But in circumstances where there are several minority candidates running, we need some way of sorting out for which to vote; that is, for minority voters as for any other voters, there needs to be a basis for judging one's representative as doing a good or bad job.

At the simplest level, of course, we need to ask whether a minority legislator was, in fact, the first-choice candidate of the minority voters. This is particularly true when there is a significant partisan mismatch. In Chapter 3 we recounted the recent election of several African American and Latino Republicans to Congress or other high offices without winning the votes of their co-ethnics. In those cases it is relatively easy to see the substantial disconnect between the minority legislator—elected with mostly nonminority votes—and the minority population. In other instances, though, it is less clear.

The growth of co-ethnic *co-partisan* representation—usually, but not always, through the creation of majority-minority districts—raises an obvious question regarding the quality of representation provided by those legislators—minority and white—elected. The logic of racial districting, of course, assumes that officeholders chosen by minorities, usually though not exclusively minorities themselves, would better represent the interests of minority voters than white officeholders with a minority of non-white constituents. That is, co-ethnic representation or white representatives who need minority votes produce better descriptive *and* substantive representation. Is this so?

The evidence is generally supportive of both claims. But the imperative to ensure descriptive representation—the election of minority officeholders—really subsumes two smaller and more specific claims: first, that minority representatives are generally "good" at representing their constituents and, second, that they

BOX 8-1   The 2010 Election

The 2010 election was something of a watershed in the election of Republican minorities to the U.S. Congress and to statewide office. Most notably, two Latino governors in New Mexico and Nevada, a new Latino senator from Florida, and six new Latino or African American members of Congress were elected. This development was heralded by GOP leadership as an important indicator of broadening minority support for the GOP. Lamar Smith, writing in the *Washington Post,* summarized his views this way: "The conventional wisdom, however, is wrong. The 2010 election actually paints a very bright picture of the Republican Party's relations with this country's growing Hispanic population" (*Washington Post,* November 27, 2010).

Is this claim fair? In one instance, we would conclude that it was. Marco Rubio's (R-FL) election to the Senate came with significant Latino support, bolstered by the generally Republican tilt of South Florida's Cuban population. Polling data suggest that Rubio won as much as 62 percent of the Latino vote (which, at 16 percent of the estimated Florida electorate, suggests that 6.7 percent of Rubio's 49 percent of the total vote came from Latinos). Importantly, national origin clearly mattered in this contest, as the same poll estimates Rubio received 78 percent of the Cuban vote but only 40 percent of the non-Cuban Latino vote. Nevertheless, any fair evaluation of this election suggests that Rubio was elected with modest to strong Latino support, overall.

This was not the case with the other two statewide winners in 2010. Brian Sandoval's election as governor of Nevada, with 53 percent of the vote, had nothing to do with Latino preferences. The Latino Decisions poll estimate was that only 15 percent of Latino voters selected Sandoval over his Democratic opponent, meaning that Latinos composed less than 2 percent of his 53 percent share of the vote. The story is similar in New Mexico, where Susanna Martinez was elected governor with 54 percent of the overall vote. Polling there suggests that she polled only 38 percent of the Latino vote, meaning that Latinos composed about 14.1 percent of the 54 percent she received, a significant impact, for sure, but far less than a majority. Since her election, Governor Martinez has gone on to propose an Arizona-style anti-immigration law, hardly the legislative priority of New Mexico's Latino population.

For five of the six new House members, their election had little to do with the districts' minority voters. Tim Scott (R-SC) was elected in the First Congressional District of South Carolina, which is 75 percent white. Allen West's (R-FL) Twenty-second Congressional District in Florida is 82.3 percent white. Jaime Herrera Buetler (R-WA) represents the Third District of Washington, in the northern suburbs of Portland, which is only 4.6 percent Hispanic and almost 90 percent white. Raul Labrador (R-ID) was elected to represent the First District in Idaho, which is only 6.8 percent Hispanic but almost 92 percent white. And Bill Flores (R-TX) represents the Seventeenth Congressional District in Texas. While this district is over 15 percent Hispanic, it is the 79 percent white population that dominated the electorate and determined this outcome. For those five newly elected members of the House, it would be very difficult to interpret their election as representing the diversification of views among Latino and African American voters.

The one case for which it is more difficult to tell how minority voters voted is in the election of Francisco Conseco (R-TX), who defeated incumbent representative Ciro Rodriguez for election to the Twenty-third District seat, 49 percent to 44 percent. In that district, which is 55 percent Hispanic and 41 percent white, Latinos play a pivotal electoral role. For Canseco to have succeeded, even under extreme assumptions regarding white preferences, he must have received a quarter of the Latino vote, if not more. Since Hispanic voters alone could have determined the outcome of the election had they been sufficiently united behind a single candidate, we must conclude that shifts in Latino preferences made it possible for Canseco to win.

Of course, whether any of these newly elected officials becomes an authentic representative of their co-ethnic fellow citizens remains an open question. But for most of them, co-ethnic voters were not a part of their electoral coalition and unlikely, given the logic of the electoral connection, to be the focus of much of their officials' activities while they hold office.

are "better" than white representatives. For quality of representation to serve as sole justification for race-based districting, both of these contentions would need to be true.[10]

In terms of the quality of minority representation of minority voters, there is something of a one-sided dispute. Carol Swain (1993) suggested that the quality of representation by African American legislators was uneven and sometimes not as good as representation by white Democrats. "A shared racial or ethnic heritage is not necessary for substantive representation and says little about a politician's actual performance" (Swain 1993, 11). Her research supports the idea of substantive representation of minority interests even by nonminorities. Swain argues that by a variety of measures white Democrats represent blacks as well as black Democrats do; there is a reasonable chance that Congressman Cohen could do a good job of representing black voters in his district. If he does not, then voters can simply vote against him at reelection. More to the point, Swain argues that the creation of majority-minority districts may simply mean that representatives from other districts can ignore the requests and interests of minority voters—because those voters are not in their district.

Swain's findings of responsive white politicians are from an era when evidence of vote dilution could get the district lines redrawn, and her discussion of cases of successful black candidates in the absence of an African American electoral majority understates exactly how rare the occurrence is and omits any fair consideration of cases where minority candidates lose all elections in the face of white racial polarization. Since her book appeared, a series of scholars—McClain (1994), Lublin (1997), Whitby (1998), Canon (1999), Haynie (2001), and Tate (2003)—have all found moderate-to-strong support for the contention that African American elected officials better represent black voters. The scholarly consensus on this issue is clear. Minority elected officials are generally more responsive and better represent minority electorates, *ceteris paribus.*

We should not conclude, however, that whites can never effectively represent minority citizens, or the reverse, for that matter. First, there is considerable evidence that white Democrats are responsive when black voters are present in significant numbers in their districts. Canon (1999) documents substantial effort at outreach, through staff allocation, minority aides, and the location of legislative offices. In terms of voting within the legislature (or roll call voting), the effect of black constituents on white legislators is best demonstrated by the effect of their removal (Overby and Cosgrove 1996; Sharpe and Garand 2001). Using the natural experiment created by redistricting, evidence suggests that white representatives become less responsive to the interests of black constituents when the African American vote share declines, particularly if the decline is sharp. White representatives, then, are not necessarily "bad" representatives of minority voters simply because they are white. Moreover, if white Democrats are sensitive to the needs of large blocs of black voters, and that sensitivity declines when the share of black constituents drops, this implies a potential cost of racial redistricting.

A second cautionary note is that the quality of co-ethnic representation is not the same for everyone—some minority elected officials do a better job than others. Canon (1999), for example, demonstrates that legislative and campaign styles, particularly whether the African American legislator consciously appealed to both blacks and whites in order to be elected, would substantially moderate their floor votes and speeches. It is these representatives who are more likely to be given positions of party leadership, and Canon contends that their legislative effectiveness, in terms of bill sponsorship and passage, is greater. These findings echo Guinier's (1995) earlier concern regarding the authenticity of black representatives who believed they were beholden to either white voters or party leaders for their position. And in a recent effort, Grose (2011) suggests that black representation yields considerably less than meets the eye with respect to changing legislative outcomes.

Finally, Tate (2003) has raised the possibility that African American representation has strayed from black voter preferences by being more liberal than the constituencies that they represent, a concern echoed for both black and Latino representatives in Griffin and Newman's more recent book (2008). Looking at trends in public opinion on welfare, crime, and food stamps, Tate describes an African American public that is considerably more conservative in the mid-1990s than it had been a decade earlier. At the same time, African American legislators remain among the most reliably liberal and likely to vote the party line. This is not to say that the ideological disconnect is greater between black officials and constituents than among whites, nor that black constituents are "unrepresented" in any meaningful way. Rather, Tate's findings remind us not to make assumptions about the policy preferences of the electorate when evaluating minority representation.

There is far less documentation and investigation of the quality of representation among Latino officeholders. Vega (1993), looking at the effectiveness of the Congressional Hispanic Caucus, was unimpressed. Hero and Tolbert (1995) examined representatives' roll call ratings from the Southwest Voter Project—where each is scored regarding his or her voting record on Latino issues—and found only a modest and insignificant effect from the ethnicity of the legislator, without regard to share of the district that was Hispanic. In short, they could find no direct evidence of differences between Latinos and whites in representing Latino constituencies, nor did they identify much effect of Latino constituency share on representative behavior. Kerr and Miller (1997), however, took issue with these conclusions, and in more recent work Leal, Martinez-Ebers, and Meier (2004) find that the share of Latino elected officials on school boards affects the share of teachers and administrators in a school district that are Latino. This result, however, has not been replicated at the state legislative or federal level.

For Asian Americans, there is an almost total absence of information by which to evaluate co-ethnic representation. As such, it is far harder to assess the responsiveness of Asian American legislators at any level of government.

THREE CAVEATS ABOUT MAJORITY-MINORITY DISTRICTS

Before we continue, we should note some caveats or cautions when talking about majority-minority districts and how good they may be at ensuring minority representation. First, even though we are discussing the importance of descriptive representation, it is important to note that having large numbers of minority voters does make representatives pay attention to the concerns of minority voters. Minority voices may be heard even if they are not in the majority within the district or if the representative is Anglo.

In so-called minority-influence districts, the minority population may not be large enough to elect a candidate of its choice but is sometimes able to affect (influence) the election outcome. Some suggest that a population of around 40 percent minority increases the responsiveness of white representatives to minority concerns. Moreover, depending on partisan distributions and the willingness of white Democrats to vote for minority nominees, 40 percent is often sufficient to elect a minority to office, since the group dominates the Democratic primary. The tradeoff is between two 60 percent minority districts with diminished or no influence elsewhere versus three 40 percent minority districts electing responsive representatives and, occasionally, co-ethnics. If either minority electability or white responsiveness results, this arrangement might be preferable—that is, it could result in a greater number of overall pro-minority votes on each legislative issue, and a "substantively" better represented community.

The key to building minority-influence districts is not to have minority voters scattered in tiny, and easily ignored, numbers within each district but for them to compose a substantial vote bloc. Of course, if majority group voters are sufficiently polarized in their electoral preferences, on racial lines, then no percentage less than 50 percent would allow minority voices to be heard. Influence districts rely on the assumption that at least some members of the majority group are willing to vote with the minority voters in the district.

Another concern is that drawing influence districts looks an awful lot like cracking—that is, gerrymandering minorities out of electoral relevance, rather than facilitating their efforts. Some voting rights advocates in the wake of *Georgia v. Ashcroft* (2003) expressed considerable concern that the decision, which would have allowed minority vote share to drop below 50 percent in some districts in pursuit of greater overall influence, opened the door for significant retrogression and the reduction of minority vote shares to levels that would significantly reduce their impact.

A second major caveat regarding our enthusiasm for majority-minority districts, following on from the previous point, is that majority-minority districts create safe districts, that is, ones in which the incumbent generally wins with a very large majority. Safe districts in general are probably bad for the process of representation, and safe seats are a feature of American elections regardless of whether they are majority-minority or not.

U.S. legislative elections are typically not very competitive, driven primarily by the drawing of districts according to partisan preferences. As the Center for Voting and Democracy (CVD) reports: "In each of the four national elections since 1996, more than 98 percent of incumbents have won, and more than 90 percent of all races have been won by non-competitive margins of more than 10 percent."[11] Although these figures are skewed upward because incumbents who are in trouble often do not bother to run for reelection, it is still the case that U.S. elections are remarkably noncompetitive. In fact, in some cases they are literally uncompetitive—CVD reports that of the thirty seats up for grabs in Massachusetts State House races in 2000–2004 (ten in each election), fully half were uncontested. And while the Supreme Court has ruled against trying too hard to draw districts to promote racial representation, the Court has never had a problem with partisan redistricting (see Issacharoff and Karlan forthcoming).

But what is so bad about safe seats? Safe seats have a series of downsides to them so far as representation is concerned. If a representative may be sure of victory then he or she has little incentive to work very hard on behalf of constituents. Incumbents in safe seats may also be more extreme than incumbents in competitive seats, since they reflect the views of core primary voters rather than voters in the electorate as a whole.

Where minority representation in safe seats is concerned, the claim of descriptive representation may not be a complement to substantive representation—it may be a substitute for it. Unresponsive incumbents, who are unresponsive because they are safe, can simply rely on their provision of descriptive representation and not have to work hard to provide substantive representation. In just one example, long-time Democratic representative Matthew Martinez, after being defeated in a primary for reelection, switched parties and filled out the remainder of his term as a Republican, at the very least raising the question of whether he had been working very hard on behalf of his overwhelmingly Democratic Latino-majority district.

Third and finally, we might note a practical problem: the drawing of majority-minority districts is becoming increasingly difficult. Even up through the late twentieth century, the drawing of majority-minority districts was quite easy in most places, given that there was residential segregation and—especially in the East and South—that segregation was between just two racial groups, whites and blacks. If we have just Anglos and African Americans, who live in different communities quite apart from each other, then it can be fairly easy to draw lines around geographic communities and draw the boundaries of districts for Congress and the statehouse. But when we have some level of residential integration, and when the number of groups multiplies, it becomes harder to draw compact districts that allow the representation of a coherent geographical area or region. This is important not simply because it makes the job of cartographers harder, but also because of one of the objections to the redistricting in Georgia was that it violated a sense of community. Americans often claim a sense of identity or belonging to a town or city or region; people from South Texas may have things in common regardless of race or ethnicity that make them different from people in the Bronx, and both of those regions will have an identity distinct again from people in Minnesota. Having a representative from the region or city matters to many voters. Now, in fairness, many racial and ethnic minority groups see themselves as political communities with shared interests. That claim, however, struggles to find a footing in a system of representation that is still, at its core, geographic in nature.

This question of residential patterns and the difficulty of drawing lines also matters in terms of interminority cooperation and competition, and ultimately representation. In 2009 a special election was held for California's Thirty-second Congressional District. The election came down to an election between Judy Chu and Gil Cedillo—an Asian woman and a Latino—in a district that is 63 percent Latino, 22 percent Asian, and 12 percent Anglo. If we were to adopt a fairly crude version of the descriptive representation argument, we could say, "Oh, it is a Latino seat, and so a Latino should represent the district." But saying so would still leave a sizable number of Asian voters without "their" representative; Asian voters, in other words, are both a numerical and ethnic minority within a minority-held seat. It is a hard problem to solve while there is only one seat to win.

THE BEHAVIORAL CONSEQUENCES OF RACIAL REDISTRICTING

While there is a general consensus regarding the representativeness of minority legislators, or at the very least African American legislators, what if any effect majority-minority districts and co-ethnic representation have on the citizens living in them is far less clear. Providing socially and politically marginalized citizens the opportunity to elect a candidate of choice should, one would think, produce changes in their attitudes about—and behavior toward—government. These include changes in a sense of political empowerment and efficacy, level of trust in elected officials, feelings of alienation from the political system, and forms of political participation including, most importantly, voting.

Unfortunately, the study of these behavioral impacts is complicated by several issues. First, and perhaps most obviously, behavioral or attitudinal effects vary across different minority groups. For example, findings with respect to turnout have differed between Latinos and African Americans. The demographic realities of these populations differ considerably. Noncitizenship, for example, undermines Latino political strength but, of course, is not a significant barrier for African Americans, a population with a growing but still small share of immigrants. Latino populations are growing rapidly, whereas black population shares are comparatively stable. Asian population growth often matches Latinos in terms of rate, but their overall population is so small that co-ethnic representation is a far less common occurrence.

Moreover, the circumstances that give rise to minority districting solutions, including residential segregation, political unity, and racially polarized bloc voting by whites against candidates of color, appear to vary significantly from African Americans to Asian Americans to Latinos. For these reasons and others, we should not expect uniform findings across minority groups (Bowler and Segura 2005).

Second, citizens are represented at many levels of government, from school boards and special districts, through city and county councils, up to state legislatures and the U.S. House of Representatives. Descriptive representation—either as a function of a majority-minority jurisdiction or of some other path—may or may not be present at every level. Whatever the effects, they may not be identical at each level of government. For example, voters likely attach more significance to co-ethnic representation in Congress than to the local transportation authority.

Third, a troubling conceptual problem has to do with the nature of representation. A generation ago, Weissberg (1978) illustrated the conceptual difference between collective representation—meaning an entire population and an entire legislature—and dyadic representation—meaning a single legislator and his or her district. The likelihood is high that the "level" of representation will vary across these levels of analysis. In our case the descriptive representation of minority communities also occurs at both the collective and dyadic levels, and each has the potential of influencing the behavior and attitudes of minority citizens. For example, we might expect a sense of empowerment to result from a newfound opportunity to elect co-ethnic representatives. Citizens living in majority-minority districts might have greater feelings of efficacy and institutional trust, higher approval of the representative institution, and so forth. But a significant increase in minority-group legislators may have a positive effect on the views of all members of that group, without regard to whether they specifically live in one of the minority-represented districts. A dramatic increase in Latino seat share in the California legislature, as occurred in the 1990s, may improve the perceptions of government among all Latinos, even those not directly represented by co-ethnic legislators. This likelihood is increased by the reality that a substantial share of the electorate, without regard to race or ethnicity, have no idea which district they live in or who "their" representative is.

Finally, effects will not be constant over time. Guinier (1995) suggested as much when she expressed her concern regarding depressed mobilization after the first or second electoral victory, as a consequence of either electoral complacency or disappointment with the failure of descriptive representation to yield tangible benefits. Although the first election of a co-ethnic representative may spur significant improvement in minority voter participation and assessment of legislative institutions, the effects may diminish over time. Such a spike may cause us to overestimate the empowering effects of co-ethnic legislators. To more accurately assess the effect of co-ethnic representation on behavior, we need to compare minority populations long represented by whites with two groups, those whose co-ethnic representation is novel and those whose co-ethnic representation is well established.

Attitudes toward Government

We first examine the attitudes of citizens toward government, a topic we cover in detail in Chapter 9. While we have discussed the representational impacts of majority-minority districting, there is a companion question of whether respondents *feel* better represented. The election of co-ethnic representatives may raise the legitimacy of the regime and specific institutions in the minds of the citizens.

Gay (2002) examined the question of trust in institutions. Using ANES data, she examined whether co-ethnic representation affected the approval of Congress and the respondent's specific member, among white and black citizens. Her findings are mixed. On the one hand, whites are clearly less supportive of African American representatives, even controlling for party and ideology. On the other, when controlling for other factors, African American respondents did not hold a significantly more positive view of black representatives (though the bivariate relationship appeared to suggest this).[12] However, it is the case that the likelihood of contacting an elected official is affected by the race of the representative for both whites and African Americans. Whites are less likely to contact black officials (compared with white officials), while black citizens are more likely. At the dyadic level, then, Gay's findings offer only tepid support for the claim that black voters feel better served by black elected officials, and she finds no relationship at all between the race of a representative and that respondent's overall view of Congress.

These findings differ considerably from those of Tate (2003). Using the National Black Election Study, she examines several aspects of citizen attitudes toward government as a function of the race of members of Congress. Even controlling for party and other indicators, she finds that race exerts a powerful force on citizen satisfaction. Specifically, African American citizens gave higher overall approval to co-ethnic legislators and saw them as more helpful and in better touch with the constituency. In addition, black voters living in districts represented by African Americans were better informed about politics, demonstrating greater knowledge about House members and candidates. Finally, black representation affected approval of Congress as an institution and overall trust in government, but only in the aggregate. While increasing collective black representation was associated with higher levels of trust, dyadic descriptive representation did not have any effect over and above that driven by the total level of black representation. Curiously, Tate did not find any effect on "empowerment," measured by her as interest in politics, sense of political efficacy, and voting.

All of these pieces examined the effect of descriptive representation on African Americans. Once again, there is less work on Latinos. Pantoja and

Segura (2003a) examined the empowerment thesis among Latinos by mapping survey data from the Tomás Rivera Policy Institute into state legislative and congressional districts in Texas and California. They examine the effect of co-ethnic representation on the sense of alienation from government manifested by citizens—here measured as the belief that government is run in the interest of others and not them—and find that co-ethnic representation reduces alienation among citizens living in those districts as compared with those not co-ethnically represented. However, Pantoja and Segura also find that the relative importance attached to having descriptive representation does not appear to be affected. Latinos with Latino representatives feel no more or less strongly about the usefulness and value of descriptive representation than Latinos without the experience.

In summary, the claim that co-ethnic representation results in empowerment to a community is still uncertain. Although the evidence to date is mixed with regard to the contributions descriptive representation makes to the attitudes and perceptions on racial and ethnic minorities, the impact is clearly not missing altogether. Co-ethnically represented minorities appear better informed, somewhat more approving and trusting of their elected officials, and significantly more likely to contact them. The extent and limits of these effects are not fully clear, nor are the similarities or differences across groups, suggesting the need for considerable additional inquiry.

Impact on Voting

Finally, several scholars have suggested that majority-minority districts mobilize minority electorates, and they find modest support at the mayoral level (Bobo and Gilliam 1990; Lublin and Tate 1992). The basic argument is that majority-minority districts provide minority voters with a chance to elect a candidate of choice to office, in some cases for the first time and in the wake of a history of political exclusion. This newfound sense of electoral empowerment increases group incentives to vote.

The preponderance of early research, however, reported no meaningful change in the turnout rates of minority voters (Brace et al. 1995; Gaddie and Bullock 1995). More ominously, Guinier (1995) and others suggested that low levels of competition in majority-minority districts and disappointment associated with the lack of perceived policy effects from increased descriptive representation serve as dual disincentives to participation. Any gains in turnout, she suggests, are short lived.

Among the key questions in this line of inquiry is whether the eventual outcome—the long-term rates of participation—are higher or lower than participation rates were prior to the creation of the minority district. This question, we would suggest, is of pivotal importance in any effort to evaluate the net effect of these specific aspects of the Voting Rights Act on minority representation. If turnout increases, minority voters are better off in every election. But if having co-ethnic representation lulls voters into complacency, and lowers their turnout, then there are fewer minority voters in all other races—governor's races, Senate elections, ballot initiatives—diminishing the impact of minority voices and interests on up-ballot races—that is, contests for higher office—where the outcome is less certain.

Some scholarship (Barreto, Segura, and Woods 2004) has suggested that Guinier's concerns about the noncompetitive nature of majority-minority districts, and what if any impact this lack of competition will have on the political behavior of those living in the districts, are overblown. As a consequence of partisan gerrymandering, and the nature of racially polarized bloc voting, it is largely the case that living in a noncompetitive electoral environment is the rule, rather than the exception, for all Americans, regardless of race. That is, given districts that protect incumbents, the high rates of residential segregation, and the few instances of non-whites being elected in majority-white electoral districts, we can safely predict *both* the party and the race of the eventual winner of legislative elections in most districts in the United States. It is possible that disappointment with the lack of progress may have a unique effect on the political empowerment of racial and ethnic minorities. But, as a methodological note, the appropriate comparison is between racial and ethnic minorities living in districts they are sure to win and racial and ethnic minorities living in districts they are sure to lose.

There have been several efforts to address the broader question. Gay (2001) found only modest evidence of increased African American turnout, concluding that the likely overall effect of majority-black districts was negligible. By contrast, she did find significant declines in turnout among non-Hispanic whites.

In a second effort, Barreto, Segura, and Woods (2004; see also Barreto 2007) set out to determine whether living in majority-minority districts was mobilizing for Latinos and whether these effects would be better estimated by considering the larger electoral context. Focusing exclusively on legislative elections and using turnout data at the individual level, they estimated the influence of both single and overlapping majority-minority districts on individual level minority voter turnout, comparing the actual turnout of voters over multiple elections. They found a consistently positive effect on Latino turnout; that is, co-ethnic representation at every level had the effect of increasing the likelihood that a Latino voter turned out on Election Day. Having the opportunity to elect a candidate of your choosing appears to be a consistently empowering circumstance. Latinos vote more when in a majority-Latino district, contrary to the expectations of those who expected or feared minority demobilization. Moreover, the larger electoral context was found to play an important role in establishing the incentives or disincentives to vote. If living in one majority-Latino district is good for turnout propensity, living in two or even three is better. Non-Hispanics living in Latino-majority districts, however, have less to cheer about and less to drag them out to the polls on Election Day. Like Gay, Barreto et al. also found that non-Hispanic whites appear to vote less.

Griffin and Keane (2006) found another quirk. Their findings with respect to African Americans are more akin to those of Barreto et al. than to Gay's.

Co-ethnic representation does appear to spur participation among African Americans, but there is a catch. The increase in participation comes only from those black voters who share the ideology and partisanship of the representative, usually Democrats. Conservative black voters—like white voters previously described—are *demobilized* by African American representation.

In a fourth piece, Banducci, Donovan, and Karp (2004) compare the experience in the United States with that of New Zealand, where that country's electoral system has been similarly tweaked to provide greater representational opportunities for the indigenous Maori population. They find that Maori turnout over the long run is enhanced as a consequence of co-ethnic descriptive representation. The significant differences between the New Zealand and U.S. electoral systems, and the implied differences in the resulting incentive structures, make it difficult to generalize these specific findings to the United States. Nevertheless, the central finding—that descriptive representation is mobilizing and empowering—is informative to the debate regarding the U.S. context.

Conflict between Gay's findings on African Americans and Barreto, Segura, and Woods' findings on Latinos, as well as the relatively limited scope of this entire line of research, raises a number of nagging and important questions, suggesting the need for more research. With respect to the specific, conflicting results in the pieces cited, they could be reflective of group differences between African Americans and Latinos or, alternatively, simply reflective of differing ways of going about the research. Only through the examination of similar data on both groups using the same method can we reasonably draw conclusions about the similarity or differences in their experiences. The answers to such research may provide important insights into the larger question of the efficacy of majority-minority districts in securing African American and Latino representation.

Second, it remains unclear whether the relationship between minority voter turnout and minority group share of a district's electorate is an enduring one. While both Gay and Barreto et al. examine majority districts at various stages of their development—that is, some in their initial election, others well established—we suggested earlier that the effects may differ in magnitude and even in direction at different stages in the "life-cycle" of majority-minority districts.

Third, is any mobilization effect a product of electoral opportunity or electoral success? Specifically, credit for increasing voter participation can conceivably be assigned to two phenomena. The actual election of a co-ethnic representative might be the specific force that increases turnout: Asian Americans will be more likely to turn out and vote knowing that the seat will be won by an Asian American candidate. Such electoral success can and has occurred in the absence of majority-minority districts, at least at the state level, and has also occasionally failed to be realized even when the district has a secure majority of minorities. Alternatively, the demographics of the district or jurisdiction—providing for the possibility of electoral success, realized or not—might be sufficient to boost voter participation. The presence of African American or Latino candidates has a mobilizing, and conceivably empowering, effect wholly apart from their chances of winning. Existing studies have often failed to distinguish these effects, but this is certainly a question that deserves more study.

Fourth, does the turnout effect apply only to elections in which the co-ethnic candidate is running or in which the majority-minority jurisdiction is at stake? This question is addressed to some of the externalities that may result from the behavioral effects of majority-minority districts. While we might have strong expectations that turnout will increase for elections within minority districts, it is also of interest whether the empowerment effect will extend to elections when no legislative race is on the ballot. For example, did co-ethnically represented minority citizens turn out at higher rates in the 2003 gubernatorial recall in California, or was their turnout indistinguishable from minority voters represented by Anglos? Are citizens co-ethnically represented at the state or federal House level more likely to participate in local politics? In short, we do not know, but if we are interested in the broader question of empowerment, the potential externalities deserve consideration.

ALTERNATIVES TO MAJORITY-MINORITY DISTRICTS

Given the difficulties—legal, political, and cartographic—associated with districts, interest has turned to experimenting with electoral system reform. There are many alternatives to dividing an area into districts and letting the candidate with the most votes win. These alternatives share a number of common features that are helpful in light of political and judicial circumstances, not the least of which is that no district line drawing is required, avoiding most of the vexing constraints raised in the recent jurisprudence.

You will recall that the principal alternative to SMD (single-member-district) systems used in many jurisdictions is an at-large election. We earlier indicated that at-large elections were very high on the "avoid" list for voting rights activists because, under plurality voting rules, they allow a determined majority to determine all outcomes. Minorities often are completely excluded.

But at-large systems avoid the districting problem and offer some other advantages. Among these other advantages are representatives motivated to solve problems that affect the entire jurisdiction, and thus less particularism and pork barrel. Most importantly for the voting rights question, at-large systems allow minorities who are not residentially concentrated to work together. While the districted system relies on residential segregation of minorities to provide electoral opportunities, an at-large system can allow the pooling of votes from widely separated parts of the jurisdiction. There is some evidence that this has helped women and gays and lesbians (Welch 1979; Segura 1999), for example, groups whose residential concentration is not usually sufficient to rely on districts to solve the representation problem.

But at-large plurality systems are often dangerously dilutive. The trick, then, is to find an at-large system that permits the advantages and limits the opportunities for minority vote dilution. Fortunately, three such systems exist.

The simplest of the three is called "limited voting," and it effectively replicates the at-large structure with one key modification. In an at-large system each voter gets a number of votes equal to the number of seats at stake. Under limited voting the number of votes each citizen gets is less than the total number of seats. For example, if five seats are available, each citizen gets three votes, which makes if difficult to completely exclude minority voices. Under limited voting, even a highly polarized majority electorate does not have sufficient votes to choose all of the winners without considerable coordination and good luck, if at all. Limited voting permits the pooling of votes by minority citizens not segregated in a single neighborhood and avoids the legal pitfalls of district line drawing.

Guinier (1995) advocates a second different version of "at-large" elections called "cumulative voting." Her critique of majority-minority districts is similar, but even more thoroughgoing, than Swain's (1993). One of Guinier's points is that districted elections actually contribute to racial polarization, a view that is consistent with Justice Sandra Day O'Connor's opinion in *Shaw v. Reno* (1993). If representatives have to appeal to only one ethnic group that is dominant within the district, then the representative may stress division between ethnic groups as a campaign strategy: after all, he or she has no need to try to build cross-race coalitions. Cumulative voting, argues Guinier, helps to encourage cross-race coalitions, prevents vote dilution, and helps to encourage candidates to work hard for voters while guaranteeing a minimum of descriptive representation.

We can go back to Pleasant Town, which has three seats up for election, to see how it works. Each voter is again given three votes, just as in an ALP (at-large-plurality) system, but this time a voter can award all three votes to a single candidate, if the voter wishes, or give one vote each to three candidates or some combination (two votes to one, one to another). In this way if minority voters do decide to rally round a candidate, they can give all their votes to that candidate. In such a case that candidate cannot be denied election by the votes of the majority. Looking again at the Pleasant Town results presented in Table 8-1, the Latino minority could have raised the vote share of one of their two candidates to 18,000.

Several points are worth making about this system. First, it is at work in a number of communities across the United States, in part as a response to suits brought under the Voting Rights Act to encourage minority representation. In the Texas panhandle and New Mexico, it is used in school board and city elections to encourage Latino representation. Versions of it are used in Alabama to redress African American underrepresentation and in South Dakota to encourage the representation of Native Americans.[13]

Second, this system works in a manner readily understandable to the voters. In the earliest political science work on the implementation of cumulative voting, the evidence was clear that voters understood how to use the system, and those who benefited (minority citizens) liked the new system, while those who lost their monopoly of power (majority citizens) disliked it (Engstrom and Brischetto 1998; Brischetto and Engstrom 1997).

One downside is that how well the system works does depend in part on the size of the body being elected. Some implementations of cumulative voting often have just two or three seats up for election. Sometimes this is too few to ensure minority representation (the size of the minority has to approach 50 percent to win one of two seats for sure, 30 percent for one of three seats). In this system, as in all others, minority vote dilution is harder as the number of seats in the body increases.

One other downside is that fielding too many candidates could split the vote. Whether splitting the vote is a good thing or a bad thing for minority candidates does depend on who is doing the splitting. What this means is that cumulative voting provides incentives for voters and candidates to follow the advice "Get yourselves organized," to form and maintain political organizations that help to mobilize support for specific candidates. For minority voters it may often be the case that organizing is easier said than done, and so perhaps a system such as cumulative voting might provide higher, rather than lower, barriers to minority representation. But organization does help the voices of all citizens be heard, and if the system provides incentives to organize, then perhaps it will encourage new groups to form.

A final alternative to plurality voting in an at-large system is a form of "preference voting." Each citizen has one vote and uses it to rank candidates in order of preference—first, second, or third, and so on. The votes are tallied to see who has received most first choices. If a candidate has over 50 percent of those votes, then he or she is elected. If no candidate meets that threshold, the candidate with the fewest first preferences is ruled out of the contest; then election officials look to see whom those voters who had voted for that candidate put down as their second choice. These second choices are added to the tallies of the remaining candidates. If a candidate has over 50 percent of the votes, he or she is elected; if not, then the candidate with the fewest votes (those votes now being a mix of first preferences and second preferences transferred from the first candidate who was eliminated) is eliminated and votes for that candidate redistributed to the remaining candidates until a candidate has over 50 percent of the vote. In some ways the system can be said to have similarities to a runoff system, and some people term this an instant runoff system. The version of this used in multimember districts is called the single transferable vote (STV). The idea is the same: Voters are essentially asked, "If you can't have your first choice, who would you like?" and candidates are eliminated from the contest and preferences redistributed until winners are found. For obvious reasons, the demographic majority cannot secure all seats in the first round, and minority voters are not disadvantaged by splitting their vote (as they might be in a cumulative scheme), since the poorer-performing minority candidate would eventually have his or her ballots reallocated, many presumably to the other minority community's preferred candidate.

Preference voting systems tend to be the most faithful representation of the distribution of community preferences, and they help minority communities (racial, political, and so forth) have a voice more consistent with the size of the community. Among the disadvantages, though, are the rather significant complexities associated with how the votes are counted, making the system opaque to voters who have often shown an unwillingness to adopt such policies when they are on a ballot. Preference voting is used in a number of places in the United States (for example, San Francisco and the city of Oakland), but it is neither widespread nor likely to become so in the near future.[14]

Limited voting and cumulative voting have been introduced in the United States in many communities to address inequitable representation at the local level. These systems, and similar ones, all avoid the districting trap and, in a number of ways, redress the problems associated with at-large systems. While these systems are in use, it is unlikely in the near term that widespread adoption of these approaches will emerge as a viable alternative to the majority-minority district strategy for state and federal elections.

BACK TO REPRESENTATION: SOME CONCLUDING THOUGHTS

For much of our history, racial and ethnic minorities have been on the political periphery, all but absent from elective office and, by some measures, badly represented by those whites in whose district they resided. Their exclusion was largely driven by the widespread refusal of whites to vote for candidates of color, even at the expense of party loyalty, a refusal that—though diminished in certain circumstances and in certain areas of the country—remains relatively widespread today. Importantly, we are not referring here to just *any* candidate of color. There are cases when minority candidates are elected with Anglo votes, indeed, cases in which they are elected almost entirely with non-Hispanic white votes. Much harder to find are minority candidates *actually preferred by minority voters* who are still able to attract significant white support.

The creation of majority-minority districts as a consequence of the 1982 amendments to the VRA and subsequent legal interpretation have improved the opportunity for African Americans and language minorities to elect candidates of choice. The number of persons of color serving in elected legislative office, from the school board level through the U.S. House of Representatives, has dramatically increased.

In this effort, we have attempted to assess what that increase has meant for the political representation of African Americans and Latinos, holding aside the smaller Asian American population, who experience far fewer instances of co-ethnic representation and about whom there is almost no research. The findings in the extant work suggest that minority voters are somewhat better represented by minority legislators and that co-ethnic representation has improved levels of approval, contact, in some instances trust, and perhaps even turnout. On the other hand, there is widespread agreement that this increase in minority seats did not help the Democratic Party. The creation of majority-minority districts appears to have undermined the electoral prospects of that party (though the degree of this loss, and its phenomenal impact in terms of seats, remains a matter of debate), with the potential effect of reducing the number of legislators whose votes are consistent with the preferences of a majority of non-white citizens. Moreover, the perceived link between minority voters and their interests, on the one hand, and the Democratic Party, on the other, has been strengthened among white voters, raising the potential for additional electoral costs for Democrats—an observation we made in Chapter 3.

In the coming decade, both political parties and a variety of institutions—including Congress and the federal judiciary—will be forced to engage the broader question of whether and to what degree the Voting Rights Act serves the interests of racial and ethnic minorities and American democracy. The VRA, its amendments, and their interpretation have clearly provided for a significant increase in majority-minority electoral districts that otherwise would not have been created. In turn, majority-minority districts undoubtedly increase the frequency of co-ethnic representation. And co-ethnic representation is usually more authentic and more reliable, and it results in an array of behavioral effects generally perceived to be good for minority influence.

Although majority-minority districts have had notable successes and very positive impacts, they have, however, been associated with a long history of litigation. Moreover, even friendly critics of the districts suggest that there may be some downsides and, perhaps, other, better ways of doing things.

The central question, of course, is who shall speak for minority communities? Is descriptive representation a minimum goal or a sufficient one? Do minority communities want delegates, or are communities better served by trustees? These are not issues confined to minority politics but are questions for democratic politics more broadly. Nevertheless, they are issues that are both relevant to minority politics and raised by studies of minority politics.

Core Orientations to the Political System

Scholars have been interested in the ways in which Americans view and relate to the political system since the earliest work on behavioral politics. Questions relating to how much people trust their government or feel alienated from it have long been of interest. The arguments advanced throughout this book have concerned the strategic place of minorities in the wider political process. Questions of how much minorities trust their government or feel alienated from it will affect whether or not minorities become engaged. If the minority electorate sees utility from engaging the political system to secure better policy outcomes for themselves and their families, then those voters will participate in politics and—given current patterns—heavily tip the scales in a Democratic direction, unless a variety of changes occur in the parties or the groups.

But therein lies the rub—*if* minority citizens see utility in politics, then those other consequences will follow. But if minorities are dissuaded from participation in politics because they believe they cannot affect outcomes or because they believe that electoral outcomes do not really change anything, then minorities may not engage in politics. Should that happen, the shift we suggest is coming could be delayed or derailed altogether. So the shift we see as coming does depend on many factors, one of which is that minorities take part in politics, which in turns seems to require that minorities see the political process as "for them" (too). In examining this chain of "ifs" and "thens," we found that the literature discusses four key concepts that categorize how voters relate to the political system: alienation, efficacy, trust, and sophistication. In this chapter we discuss minority politics in relation to these concepts, which represent important stepping-stones for minority participation. As we will see, minority opinions on these four concepts present something of a puzzle— minority voters are not nearly as disaffected from the political system as they "should" be.

We will show that, contrary to expectations, minority Americans do not appear any more distant or disconnected from their government and politics than are other Americans. In fact, in some instances minority citizens hold views that reflect an electorate more empowered and less disaffected than whites do. However, when we examine their levels of political information, there is at least some reason for concern regarding whether these groups have the information necessary to navigate the waters of American politics.

CORE ORIENTATIONS TO AMERICAN GOVERNMENT AND POLITICS

The topics of alienation, efficacy, trust, and sophistication are such common themes in the literature that we might call them the "greatest hits" of behavioral political science. They are also closely related concepts, and that can sometimes lead to problems distinguishing between them, although scholars typically see them as reflecting different—and important—aspects of how individuals view the political system in which they live. Take trust, for example. For our purposes, *political trust* is the willingness to believe that policymakers and institutions generally do what is right, or at least try to do what is right. The concept is often measured by asking voters whether (and how much) they trust in Congress, the police, or other officials and institutions. Trust in political institutions can clearly be valuable if for no other reason than that governments and government officials will find their jobs easier if people trust them. There is plainly also going to be an overlap between trust and alienation. If you are someone who thinks government is indifferent or hostile to your interests, you very likely do not trust it.

A second concept that is closely related to trust is alienation (Finifter 1970). We define political *alienation* as the belief that government is not for or about you and not working on behalf of your interests. An individual who thinks that the benefits of government are for a few rich people, or people not like him or her, or that government does not care about the problems they are facing, can be understood to be alienated from the system.

A third concept in the greatest hits of political behavior, also closely related to alienation and trust, is *political efficacy*, which is the belief that the political system is responsive to your actions. The concept of efficacy is generally broken down into internal and external efficacy. Internal efficacy is the belief that you have sufficient input and capacity that your actions shape outcomes. Efficacious people believe it matters that they vote, call a legislator, protest, or work in an organization, and they feel qualified to do so. Inefficacious people think none of that will matter to the outcome. External efficacy is the belief that outcomes matter to policies, that is, that elections matter to what government does. If someone believes that decision makers and policymakers do the same thing regardless of voter choices, then this individual lacks external efficacy.

These issues highlight the conceptual overlap that plagues this literature. Citizens who believe their participation has no effect are very likely to be alienated. One often-used survey question asks voters to say whether government is too complicated "for someone like me" to understand. This has been used as a measure of both alienation and efficacy because a survey respondent may be put off by the complexities of politics *and* report that he or she does not have the necessary knowledge to affect it. Finifter (1970) in a well-known article identifies this question as a measure of alienation, whereas Flanigan and Zingale (2005) use the same question to illustrate the stability of efficacy over time. Suffice it to say that clearly distinguishing between the three concepts can be something of a challenge.

Finally, there is the concept of *political sophistication*. This multifaceted term has been used to capture levels of ideological thinking (Converse 1964), levels of political knowledge, and attention to and interest in politics and public affairs. Loosely speaking, politically sophisticated individuals are able to draw connections between issues, hold opinions across issues consistent with their core beliefs about politics and government, are aware of what is happening in the political system, and have a decent grasp of how it all works.

Sophisticated individuals are more likely to be efficacious—if people see no payoff for engaging the political system, there is little incentive for them to gather information and stay informed. Sophistication can also be related to trust and alienation, but the direction of that relationship is not always clear. Informed and sophisticated persons are less likely to feel that the political system is beyond their comprehension, but they may well come to lower their views of the system and its responsiveness.

Ideally, it is better for a democracy when more people are engaged in the political process, interested in public affairs, and familiar enough with institutions and actors to help encourage participation. Of course, should sophistication be motivated by a high degree of alienation—should one's attention be drawn to politics because of high levels of anger or dissatisfaction—then sophistication may not be a good thing but, rather, a symptom of something wrong in politics. Similarly, if institutional barriers and the behavior of others effectively excluded your voice from having any effect in the political system, there would be little incentive to gather information and pay attention to politics. Nevertheless, these would appear to be extreme cases. In general, it is better in a democracy when people know and understand more about their governance.

It is very tempting to assume that trust and efficacy are "good," and that alienation is "bad"; but these kinds of normative claims need to be treated with caution. It is not surprising that those claims might seem to be relevant. After all, what is really at stake in these orientations is the fundamental legitimacy of the political regime. If large numbers of the public feel that government institutions and actors are untrustworthy, that people are powerless to affect change, and that government is either completely disinterested in their interests or, worse, actively working against them, then the legitimacy of the regime is severely undermined. Democracy survives only when very large shares of the population agree that outcomes, even outcomes that they did not prefer, were arrived at through a fair process.

Just as paying attention to politics may not reflect interest in politics but may reflect someone's suspicion that something wrong is going on, then trust, too, need not always be a good thing. If voters are *too* trusting, this invites abuse and nonresponsiveness. Some level of mistrust—or at least some level of skepticism—would seem to be required of a democratic citizenry. Moreover, if government has done you harm, trust would be irrational. If a group or interest has been mistreated by government—if, for example, government institutions had taken property, deprived the group of rights, or otherwise disadvantaged them with respect to others in the society—it is trust that would be ill advised. It is entirely sensible to distrust harmful institutions, to feel alienated when interests are discounted or adversely affected.

Take, for example, the Tuskegee experiments. Between the 1930s and early 1970s, 399 African American men with syphilis were left untreated as part of a long-term clinical study by the U.S. Public Health Service on the effects of the disease. Even after penicillin was found to be an effective treatment, the men remained untreated, infected wives, had children born with congenital syphilis, and died of the disease. Should African Americans familiar with the study trust their government? Would a lack of trust be a sign that they were poorly socialized to the democratic system or, rather, that they were sophisticated, informed, and had good reason to distrust government?

TRUST AND ALIENATION

Generally speaking, over the past fifty years we have seen a gradual decline in levels of trust in government among members of the U.S. public as a whole. In talking about this topic, it is important to make, and keep, a distinction between liking the current leaders in power and trusting in the U.S. government as an organization or institution. We might understandably expect Republicans not to think very highly of Barack Obama, in the same way that Democrats did not think very highly of George W. Bush. That kind of hostility ebbs and flows with the party in power in fairly straightforward ways: Democratic voters like Democratic politicians, and Republican voters like Republican politicians. But that does not necessarily mean that either Democrats or Republicans feel worse about the U.S. government. Flanigan and Zingale (2005) make the distinction between what citizens think about the individuals in government and the institutions of government. It is the latter that is of interest when we want to discuss trust in government. When we look at what people think about the institutions of government, we see a secular decline (that is, a downward trend over time) in the level of trust people have in the U.S. government to do what is right. This trend seems to hold across ideologies and across both African Americans and Anglos.

For those who see trust as a good thing, this decline is seen as a worrying trend. Having trust in government is important to its legitimacy and facilitates government action and popular cooperation. During times of war or economic crisis or other emergencies, a government must make difficult decisions. If ordinary people do not have much trust, the government may find it hard to get citizens to go along when difficult decisions have to be made—even if the decisions may be quite necessary. Tyler (2005), for example, shows that the public's willingness to cooperate with police is related to the level of trust people have in the police, which is, in turn, shaped by how fair they believe the police to be. He also finds that minorities are especially mistrustful of the police—at least in New York City.[1] What people think about government therefore matters to government itself: a lack of trust in government, or a sense of alienation from it, leads to challenges to that government and can make the job of government harder. When people do not particularly care for the institutions of government, they are also likely to seek changes in the form of that government (Avery 2009).

It has not all been downhill for levels of trust. There have been some times in recent years when general levels of public trust in government have increased. In the period after 9/11, opinion poll data showed a dramatic increase in the number of people willing to say that they trusted the government. In fact some scholars argue that, broadly speaking, we should be careful to distinguish between foreign policy and domestic policy: Americans are much readier to trust their government of whatever party when it comes to foreign affairs than to domestic policy (Hetherington 2006).

Yet, despite some upticks, the overall trend in levels of trust in government in the United States has been downward. This trend is especially worrying given that, cross-nationally, at least, economic prosperity is strongly associated with levels of trust: people in richer countries tend to be more trusting of their government than are people in poorer countries. Thus the cross-sectional pattern we see is consistent with an argument suggesting that over time the richer we become, the more we should trust government—but that is not the pattern we see. This means that we may need to look to forces other than economics to explain declines in trust.

Dalton (2005) argues there are two broad groups of explanations. One group ties this dislike to the fact that citizens may know just enough to be unhelpfully critical of politicians; a little learning, in other words, is a dangerous thing. To know Congress is not to love it but, rather, to develop a dislike for the whole business of politics: the more we see, the less we like it, in a case of familiarity breeds contempt. People tend to know very little about courts, compared with Congress, and seem to think more highly of courts. John Hibbing and Elizabeth Theiss-Morse (1995) argue that we think better of courts in part precisely because we simply know and hear less about them.

A second group, to which Dalton belongs, attributes a decline in trust to the general rise of a more educated—and hence more critical—citizenry. As education levels rose throughout the late twentieth century, as more people attended college, people developed a more thoughtful and more informed view of politics. This more informed view may involve some thoughtful criticism because people are less willing to take the comments of political leaders at face value and much more likely to be skeptical and arrive at their own conclusions on political matters. Dalton argues that a key element in all this is the expectations people have of government; when government fails to meet those expectations, people's levels of trust fall (Dalton 2004). In part, people lose trust because politicians and politics fail to perform to expectations. This is not just a matter of repeated scandals—though such events as Vietnam, Watergate, Iran-contra, Monica Lewinsky, and the torture issue in Iraq certainly do not help to encourage citizen trust—but of something more fundamental. Plainly the list of scandals involving U.S. politicians since Watergate has done damage to the standing of politicians, but some scholars point to a more fundamental problem at work: people are dissatisfied with the way in which democracy works as a process.

TRUST AND ALIENATION AMONG MINORITIES

Given how important these core concepts are, minority opinions on them are interesting and relevant. As we noted at the outset, minority participation—and hence the shift in politics—depends on minority citizens feeling politics is worth their while. Minority evaluations of government are also interesting in a conceptual sense. Considering that these core orientations are important, then how voters develop orientations toward government is important. We have mentioned some ways in which citizens may develop political attitudes. What is especially interesting about minority opinions is that they tell us about the key role that experience with government plays in helping to shape attitudes. Often the role of experience with government as a major factor that leads to opinions on trust, alienation, and so on seems to take a backseat to factors such as socialization or education or economic well-being. Yet as we know, all levels of government in the United States, federal, state, and local, have, over the years created and maintained systems of racial exclusion, segregation, Jim Crow, and systematic disadvantage. Minority voters played almost no role in the election of representatives at the state and federal levels across broad sections of the United States, in some cases until the 1990s. Minorities were excluded altogether from naturalization, from meaningful influence on government through vote suppression, linguistic isolation, gerrymandering, and white racial polarization. In the wake of the political history of minorities in American society, and in the presence of ongoing struggles over such issues as language policy, civil and voting rights, poverty, and immigration, it is reasonable to ask how minorities feel about their government and the role that they themselves play.

What is critical in these arguments is how people's expectations about government are formed—at least in part they can be driven by personal experience with government. It is this element that is especially important when we consider minority attitudes toward government. As we suggested above, we might expect minorities to exhibit a great deal of alienation from government and also to have low levels of trust and efficacy because their expectations of how government will behave are grounded in years of experience and mistreatment.

To be sure, everyone can point to some experience with government that has left a poor impression. Many of us, for example, have waited in line for ages at a government agency such as the Department of Motor Vehicles only to be greeted by someone who was clearly having a bad day. Those sorts of things happen in interactions with any organization but somehow seem different

BOX 9-1   Professor Henry Gates and the Police

In July 2009 a Harvard professor, Henry Gates, ran into trouble with a local police officer, and the incident attracted national attention:

> Sgt. James Crowley, who is white, responded to a report of a possible break-in at Gates's house July 16 and ended up arresting the professor on his front porch for "exhibiting loud and tumultuous behavior in a public place." Gates [who is African American] called Crowley a "rogue cop" and characterized him as racist, rude and threatening.
>
> President Obama, who is a friend of Gates's, said the police acted "stupidly" by arresting Gates. He later backed off the remark and invited Gates and Crowley to the White House for beer and a photo-op[1].

His experience was not an isolated one for many minorities, and U.S. history provides reasons for thinking that minority opinions toward government will be distinctive simply because of the history of minority experiences with all branches of government. We have all heard of the phrases *Driving While Black* and *Flying While Arab*. These phrases capture the systematically different treatment of people by the institutions of government based on race and ethnicity. The internment of Japanese Americans during World War II represented a dramatic and traumatic example of "racial profiling," since this indignity largely did not extend to Americans descended from other WWII enemies. Arizona Latinos expect to be stopped and asked for documentation (a case we will discuss in Chapter 11). African American farmers, discriminated against by the Agriculture Department, successfully sued the government for redress, but Congress systematically refuses to fund the settlement. All these examples, like the Gates incident, underline how minorities are likely to have quite different interactions with the political system than Anglos in everyday ways, interactions certain to shape their views.

[1]Milloy, Courtland. 2009. "Professor Gates Should Skip the Blather and Sue." *The Washington Post*, August 5. www.washingtonpost.com/wp-dyn/content/article/2009/08/04/AR2009080402971.html.

when it is the government. We can attribute bad experiences with government to any number of causes, but seldom can we fairly attribute them to our being singled out—the DMV does not hate just me.

If, however, one's experience with government is systematically bad—and, importantly, distinct from what others are experiencing—then a new dynamic has entered the picture. Back to the DMV, if the person behind the counter was being grumpy and unhelpful only with women, or only with Asian Americans, then something altogether different is happening. And if rude treatment or slow service characterizes how someone is treated not only by the DMV but also by the school principal, the registrar of voters, the city councilman, and the local police, the citizen in question is likely to draw conclusions about his or her relationship to government.

If there is one point at which government fails to live up to its more noble promise, it is in its treatment of minorities in everyday interactions. This treatment has been systematic and enduring: the historical experience for many minorities has not been a few "one-off" experiences with an individual government official having a bad day but repeated interactions with a government that treats them differently and, often, harshly. Part of the issue here is that even for minorities who are sympathetic to the government, repeated mistakes and repeated heavy-handedness take their toll.

Take, for example, the period after 9/11. Many Americans who have little or no sympathy with the bombers but might share some sort of link through religion, ethnicity or dress—Muslims, Christians from Middle East nations, and Sikhs—were stopped and investigated by security forces. Even the most patient and sympathetic of these Americans would be understandably frustrated when, time and time again, they were pulled aside for special treatment simply because they wore a turban or carried a Quran.

It is quite straightforward to suppose that uneven treatment should have an effect on the levels of trust, alienation, and efficacy we might observe in minority Americans when we compare them with non-Hispanic whites. Furthermore, the socialization processes among minority youth may mean that these kinds of attitudes—trust, alienation, and efficacy—may be passed on to children. Attitudes toward government and expectations about government are often formed at an early age; during their upbringing, children are socialized into a range of political and social attitudes, many of which concern government itself. In one of the few studies that compare across racial and ethnic groups at this early age and in one of the even fewer that include Native Americans, Kim Fridkin and colleagues surveyed middle school children (Fridkin et al. 2006). They found that minorities in general, and Native Americans in particular, were less likely than Anglos to have basic information about government and hold positive attitudes toward government.

What of some of our other measures of how citizens relate to government? Is there evidence that minorities are, as we expect, more cynical, less efficacious, and less trusting?

Frankly, the evidence in support of the existence of severe minority alienation and low trust and efficacy is, at best, mixed. For starters, examine Table 9-1, which reports levels of trust in the government in Washington. Among non-Hispanic whites, about 43.6 percent of respondents said that the government in Washington can be trusted most of the time or just about always. Compare that figure with the three minority groups in question. For African Americas, only 22 percent are in those two highest categories, but for Asians and Latinos, the numbers are 47 percent and 53.5 percent, respectively. Therefore, while black Americans show significantly less trust than whites in the federal government, Latinos and Asians manifest significantly *more* trust, perhaps owing in part to the large representation of immigrants among these last two groups.

The evidence is again mixed when it comes to the concept of alienation. One aspect of alienation is that government benefits others unfairly. This is often captured in a question asking respondents whether government "run by a few big interests" or government "run for the benefit of all" is closer to their view of what is happening. As we see in Figure 9-1, about 73 percent of whites

TABLE 9-1 Trust in the Federal Government by Race and Ethnicity (in percentages)

Response category	Weighted pooled national sample	Unweighted responses by race and ethnicity			
		White (non-Hispanic)	African American	Hispanic or Latino	Asian American
Just about always	6.4	5.6	3.1	15.8	3.9
Most of the time	37.1	38.0	18.9	37.7	43.1
Only some of the time	47.1	48.8	56.4	37.6	45.7
Never	9.4	7.6	21.7	8.8	7.3
Total N	3,185	908	747	726	492
		Chi-square probability = 0.000			
		F-test probability from ANOVA = 0.0000			

Source: 2004 National Politics Study.

Question wording: How much of the time do you think you can trust the following institutions? Just about always, most of the time, only some of the time, or never? What about . . .

a) . . . the government in Washington?

FIGURE 9-1 Alienation Measure by Race and Ethnicity (in percentages)

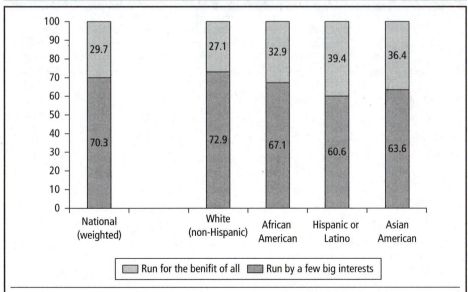

Source: ANES Pre/Post 2008.

Question wording: Would you say the government is pretty much RUN BY A FEW BIG INTERESTS looking out for themselves or that it is run for the BENEFIT OF ALL THE PEOPLE?

hold the cynical view, the highest of any group, while the comparable number is 67 percent of African Americans, 61 percent of Latinos, and 64 percent of Asian Americans. On this measure, whites are appreciably more alienated than non-whites, and this is despite the tremendous advantage in wealth, income, and other measures of social well-being enjoyed by average white Americans.

Similarly, the question of whether government is too complicated to understand—a measure of alienation for some and efficacy for others—also offers less than convincing evidence that minorities are uniquely disaffected from government. Roughly one-third of all groups in Table 9-2 report that politics and government are too complicated most or all of the time. There is no statistically discernible difference by group (bear in mind the Asian American sample is exceedingly small). While we might have reasonably expected lesser-educated groups of citizens, and particularly immigrants socialized in another polity, to find the machinations of government and politics in the United States inaccessible, the distributions look surprisingly similar across the four race and ethnicity groups we report.

Table 9-3 reports findings from a second question that probes the intersection of alienation and efficacy, that is, whether public officials care what "people like me" think. Since the question directly refers to citizen preferences

TABLE 9-2 Frequency with Which Government and Politics Are Too Complicated to Understand, by Race and Ethnicity (in percentages)

Response category	Weighted pooled national sample	Unweighted responses by race and ethnicity			
		White (non-Hispanic)	African American	Hispanic or Latino	Asian American
All the time	10.2	10.8	9.1	10.4	21.1
Most of the time	22.7	23.7	24.6	23.8	10.5
About half the time	26.7	26.2	23.6	32.0	36.8
Some of the time	33.3	32.1	34.4	31.6	31.6
Never	7.1	7.2	8.3	2.2	0.0
Total N	1,137	595	276	231	19
		Chi-square probability = 0.095			
		F-test probability from ANOVA = 0.2974			

Source: American National Election Study 2008.

Question wording: How often do politics and government seem so complicated that you can't really understand what's going on? ALL THE TIME, MOST OF THE TIME, ABOUT HALF THE TIME, SOME OF THE TIME, or NEVER?

TABLE 9-3   Attitudes Regarding Whether Public Officials Care What "People Like Me" Think, by Race and Ethnicity (in percentages)

Response category	Weighted pooled national sample	Unweighted responses by race and ethnicity			
		White (non-Hispanic)	African American	Hispanic or Latino	Asian American
Strongly agree	22.3	22.9	31.0	28.7	18.1
Somewhat agree	29.6	29.6	29.9	28.2	38.2
Somewhat disagree	28.7	28.3	24.0	23.5	32.4
Strongly disagree	19.4	19.2	15.1	19.6	11.3
Total N	2,861	901	742	731	487

Chi-square probability = 0.000

F-test probability from ANOVA = 0.0000

Source: 2004 National Politics Study.

Question wording: I don't think public officials care much about what people like me think.

and government response, this is soundly a measure of internal efficacy, though the emphasis on what officials "care" about has more than a hint of the affective response implicit in the alienation concept.

The data in this table again provide a mixed picture of the orientations toward government among different groups. On the one hand, fully 52.5 percent of non-Hispanic whites somewhat or strongly agree that public officials do not care about their opinions, a high number reflecting surprisingly low efficacy among the country's majority. On the other hand, these data suggest a somewhat greater chasm between minority Americans and their government. Among African Americans, 60.9 percent of respondents fall into these "low efficacy" response categories. For Latinos, the comparable number is 56.9 percent, and for Asians, 56.3 percent. So, while whites are surprisingly disaffected, all three minority groups feel even more distant from policymakers, with African Americans holding the least efficacious views.

Finally, we turn our attention to a simpler measure of efficacy, that is, whether the subject believes she or he has any effect on the political system. In Table 9-4, we report distributions on these questions.[2] This is a less ambiguous measure of efficacy in that we are asking individuals whether or not they can affect government. Among non-Hispanic whites, 33.2 percent fall into the two most efficacious categories. For African Americans, 42 percent fall in these categories, for Latinos it is 45 percent and for Asian Americans it is 37.2 percent.

Oddly, it appears that all racial and ethnic minorities polled feel they have greater influence on what government does than do non-Hispanic whites. How

TABLE 9-4 Individual Estimation of Ability to Shape Government, by Race and Ethnicity (in percentages)

Response category	Weighted pooled national sample	Unweighted responses by race and ethnicity			
		White (non-Hispanic)	African American	Hispanic or Latino	Asian American
Least efficacious (no say or strongly agree) (1)	17.3	17.9	17.0	16.2	11.4
(2)	26.7	28.9	23.9	22.0	20.0
Moderate amount/ neither agree nor disagree (3)	19.7	20.0	17.1	16.7	31.4
(4)	22.9	22.2	22.6	24.8	14.3
Most efficacious (a great deal or strongly disagree) (5)	13.4	11.0	19.4	20.2	22.9
Total N	2,236	1,182	566	431	35

Chi-square probability = 0.000

F-test probability from ANOVA = 0.0020

Source: American National Election Study 2008.

Question wording: TWO EFFICACY QUESTIONS, EACH ASKED TO HALF THE SAMPLE, WERE ASKED. THE QUESTIONS WERE: People like me don't have any say about what the government does. (Do you AGREE STRONGLY, AGREE SOMEWHAT, NEITHER AGREE NOR DISAGREE, DISAGREE SOMEWHAT, or DISAGREE STRONGLY with this statement?) How much can people like you affect what the government does? A GREAT DEAL, A LOT, A MODERATE AMOUNT, A LITTLE, or NOT AT ALL?

can we interpret this last finding? Since whites are advantaged politically, economically, and socially, we might conclude that some or all respondents have a distorted view of the political system; that is, whites may be far too pessimistic about their influence and are systematically underestimating it, while minorities could be far too positive about their ability to shape outcomes (or both things could be going on). We do not want to overinterpret these findings. Some members of every group place themselves in the two most efficacious categories. Moreover, since the question is not asked in a comparative manner, we have no idea what respondents believed was the appropriate amount of influence to have, nor whether they were assessing their own impact vis-à-vis others. In fact, we can be pretty sure that they were not doing the latter, and we might be better served with a straightforward question of which group has more political power. Nevertheless, this finding defies both conventional wisdom and our expectations.

Summary

It is, to say the least, difficult to summarize the data on alienation, trust, and efficacy. A fair assessment is that, when we consider all aspects of trust, cynicism, the perception of distance from government, the opaqueness of government and politics to the average person, and whether an individual feels empowered to shape her or his political work, there does not seem to be a simple or straightforward pattern distinguishing minority (versus white) orientations to the political system.

On the one hand, African Americans are clearly less trusting of the government in Washington than are whites, and in view of the historical record, this is hardly surprising and in line with what we expect to see more generally. Similarly, all three minority groups perceive to a greater degree that government is disinterested in their opinions and input. On the other hand, Latinos and Asians appear to be more trusting of the federal government than whites. All racial and ethnic groups respond more or less the same to whether politics and government are hard to understand. And white citizens express the most cynicism about government responding to "a few big interests." Finally, almost inexplicably, whites are less likely than all minority groups to feel as if they can have an impact on government.

Minority citizens appear to hold orientations to the political system that are neither more nor less empowered and engaged than their white countrymen. Given the examples we set out above, this pattern is puzzling. After all, the examples of poor treatment of minorities by government should, one would think, produce alienation and mistrust. How might we explain this puzzle?

We can offer several potential answers to the puzzle, although there seems to be no settled sense of which of these answers is the "right" one. First, these core orientations reflect a gap between expectations and performance that is a gap between what government promises and how it acts. The effects of poor treatment may be offset by lower expectations: if someone expects to have to wait several hours in line to register a car, then a forty-minute wait at the DMV may not seem so bad. To say the least, government treatment of racial and ethnic minorities has a long history of mistreatment, ranging from slavery, the Chinese Exclusion Acts, and Jim Crow through Operation Wetback and other unsavory moments in our history. Perhaps minorities simply have low expectations of government that are easily satisfied.

Another reason why orientations toward government among minorities may not be as poor as we might have expected is that government can also do positive things for minorities. While some branches of government at some times have displayed hostility to minorities, other branches have been responsive and even helpful, especially as minorities have become politically active. One of the consistent findings in research on this topic is that who is in power can make a difference. That is, descriptive representation can help increase levels of trust in government among minorities (Pantoja and Segura 2003a), a topic we explored in depth in Chapters 3 and 8. The size of this effect is sometimes a matter of debate, but generally speaking the findings to date tend to confirm that the presence of minorities in positions of political power makes minority citizens feel better about the political system, to some degree. The rapid growth in the number of representatives, particularly since 1990, may help underpin minority attitudes toward government. Symbolic politics may have some effects but is not enough in and of itself: when descriptive representation produces substantive policy change of interest to minority communities, then this results in shifts in attitudes. In some ways this is a reassuring set of findings democratic government should be responsive to the policy demands of citizens, and when it is, citizen attitudes respond.

One other answer is to differentiate among different minorities. In particular, the large numbers of immigrants present in the Latino and Asian populations provide a different picture of attitudes toward government. Recall that even though African Americans were less trusting, Latinos and Asians were more trusting than whites. Latinos were the most efficacious, Latinos and Asians the least cynical.

Each of these groups has large immigrant populations, and while there may not be settled answers into minority opinions as a whole, we do have some insight into immigrant attitude. Immigrants appear to have a more favorable view of politics than U.S.-born citizens, even within the same racial and ethnic groups. One of the most persistent findings, at least so far as Latinos are concerned, is that immigrants tend to have a significantly more positive view of government, especially at the national level, than do U.S.-born Latinos. Table 9-5 reports measures of trust in government and alienation broken down between foreign- and native-born Latinos (Michelson 2003a). Michelson finds that U.S.-born Mexican Americans are less trusting and more alienated from their government than foreign-born citizens and residents.

In an important extension, Wenzel's study (2006) of Latino communities in South Texas finds results consistent with Michelson: immigrants tend to have a more positive view of U.S. government than native-born citizens do. Key to Wenzel's study is that the between-group difference is maintained even within a given racial or ethnic demographic. The effects of self-selection and comparison to home country may, perhaps, be reflected elsewhere as well. Some work in the UK setting suggests that this is not simply true for the United States: non-white respondents to surveys often register more trust in political institutions (but not the police) than white respondents in Britain (Fahmy 2005).

The consequence of the positive views held by immigrants is that while, on average, Latinos as a whole seem more trusting of government (Abrajano and Alvarez 2007), the effect is really driven by immigrants. Immigrants see value in both the U.S. political system and the efficacy of political participation within the United States, at least at some stage in their life cycle as residents and citizens of the country (for example, Branton 2007; Michelson 2001, 2003a). Less work has been done on the views of Asian immigrants on this issue, but it is not unreasonable to assume that they, too, hold a high opinion of their chosen

TABLE 9-5   Trust and Alienation Differences between Foreign- and U.S.-Born Latinos (in percentages)

Government officials do what is right	All	U.S.-born	Foreign-born
Just about always	16.1	7.3	25.0
Most of the time	30.5	32.9	28.0
Some of the time	43.3	48.0	38.6
Almost never	10.1	11.8	8.4
N	1,531	771	760
Government is run	All	U.S.-born	Foreign-born
By the few in their interest	37.7	51.6	23.6
For the benefit of all	62.3	48.4	76.4
N	1,471	738	733

Source: Melissa R. Michelson. 2003. "The Corrosive Effect of Acculturation: How Mexican-Americans Lose Political Trust," Table 1, Social Science Quarterly 84(4) (December): 918–933. Reprinted with permission of John Wiley & Sons, Inc.

country, which is potentially affecting what the overall distribution looks like within the group.

More recently, another window into how immigrants view this country opened. In the wake of Congress's attempt to criminalize undocumented status in December 2005, a wave of protest marches occurred across 150 American cities and involving more than 3 million participants. Research into support for these marches suggests that protestors and their supporters displayed greater efficacy and trust in government (Pedraza et al. 2011). Pedraza and his colleagues conclude that support for the protests was, in fact, an expression of faith in the responsiveness of the American political system. If, in fact, the system were nonresponsive, what would be the utility in protesting?

This kind of optimism about the value of the U.S. political system raises two questions: First, where does it come from; that is, why do immigrants have a rosier view of politics than the U.S.-born? And, second, what happens to it once immigrants arrive?

One possibility is that immigrants might be reluctant to state their true opinions. For some immigrants, answering public opinion survey questions might be novel, and the worry could be that the government or immigration authorities would get to hear of any criticism. While this is a concern—trying to get people to say what they really think is a perennial concern for poll-sters—the evidence seems to be that immigrants are giving their real opinion. Different populations of immigrants have been asked in different ways and by different researchers what they think of the political institutions of their new home and, for the most part, like them more than native-born residents do.

A second possibility is a socialization effect. Depending on the age at which people immigrated, their attitudes will not have been shaped by direct experiences with the U.S. government. So their expectations of the U.S. system of government will likely focus on the promise of government, their hopes for their future. In a sense, and speaking very loosely, when we look within racial and ethnic categories, the difference in views toward governments between immigrants and U.S.-born people gives us some idea of how much of an effect experience with government has on people's views and how variation in the socialization process may conceivably affect how people come to view their government.

A third possibility is that some scholars see this pattern as a product of the act of immigration. Immigrants, we must always remember, are a self-selected population. Their presence in the United States is by choice, so we should not be surprised to find that they *like* their choice. It is the sacrifice made to move to countries that helps make immigrants see—and perhaps want to see—the good in their new host country (for example, Maxwell 2009). And perhaps, most importantly, their view of American government and politics will inevitably be driven by how this compares with their view of the politics in their countries of origin (Wals 2011).

The argument of self-selection is not entirely satisfactory. It does not fit very easily, for example, with relatively low levels of political passivity among many immigrants (Ramakrishnan 2005). Nor does it fit very well with the motives for immigration, except for those who are political refugees. After all, immigrants are like people the world over—they tend to have little concern for politics but a great concern for jobs and families. Perhaps a simpler explanation is a fourth possibility. For many immigrants the American political system, despite its flaws, offers an objectively more democratic, a more effective, and a markedly less corrupt political system than that on offer in their country of origin. It is not just the sacrifice of emigration that leads to positive attitudes; it is also the actual benefits of their new home. It is not surprising, then, that immigrants tend to see the U.S. political system in quite positive terms.

While there is still discussion among academics over why it is that immigrants may be more positive about the political system than the U.S.-born, there is greater consensus over what happens to that optimism: it becomes corroded by actual experience of the U.S. system (for example, Branton 2007; Michelson 2001, 2003a). Acculturation and assimilation seem to bring with them disappointment, a process that is sometimes termed "adverse socialization." In many ways, this is not surprising. All the reasons we offered for the expectations that minorities would be less efficacious and trusting essentially recognize that there are racial hierarchies in American society and real disadvantages for those at the bottom. New arrivals may not be familiar with their "place" in that racial hierarchy, nor do they necessarily understand the obstacles this places to social mobility. But with the passage of time and the accumulation of experience, they quickly learn.

Whatever the reason, there is clearly a process of adverse socialization, effectively "teaching" immigrants that the U.S. political systems is not quite as responsive and attentive as they might have hoped.

Minority (and immigrant) relationships to government have been, and are, politically consequential for the United States. Protest over discrimination and the exclusion of minorities from a share in power have been motors that have driven legal and political fights since the United States was founded. In a very direct way, too, minority experience is important to how we understand the topic of trust in government. Declining trust is a worrying problem faced by many governments around the world—not just the American one. The important lesson from minority experience is that it is experience with government that is consequential in shaping attitudes toward government. Social changes in levels of education, recurrent political scandals, prosperity, and levels of public information all shape attitudes toward government. But it can be everyday experiences that help shape attitudes toward government in fundamental ways. The example of Henry Gates and the police officer may well have been a news headline for just a couple of days, but it provides an insight into how people in general—minorities and Anglos alike—form their opinions of government.

This in itself points up yet another instance of how the study of minority politics can help us to understand broader ideas of politics. The change in how immigrants see the political system offers us a window into how people develop the core orientations. In particular, immigrant attitudes seem to underscore the importance of experience in helping to shape attitudes toward government and leading to an amendment or updating of attitudes formed by socialization.

POLITICAL SOPHISTICATION AND MINORITY POLITICS

We have talked extensively about a sense of engagement or disaffection with government; explored the concepts of alienation, efficacy, and trust; and concluded that there is no longer an evidentiary basis to suggest that minority voters are any more put off by the system than their fellow citizens. We have not, as of yet, addressed whether minority voters are sufficiently sophisticated to pursue or defend their interests in the political process. It is to this fundamental question that we now turn.

As we mentioned earlier, sophistication is conceptually vague and has been used to refer to the levels of ideological thinking or constraint across issues (Converse 1964, among many others), the overall understanding of the mechanics and chief actors in the political system (Ferejohn and Kuklinski, 1990), and the level of attention and interest devoted to politics. For the moment, we will set aside the discussion of ideology and constraint. In Chapter 5 we illustrated in some detail the political distinctiveness of minority communities and demonstrated that, on average, these groups consistently hold issue positions to the left of non-Hispanic whites. At the aggregate level, at least, "constraint" appears to be present. At the individual level, there is good evidence (Barreto and Segura 2010) to suggest that ideology as we usually conceive of it, "liberal" and "conservative," is not meaningful to minority voters and does not reflect their distribution of preferences in the way it does for whites.

But information levels and interest in politics deserve some additional attention. The first rule of political self-defense is awareness of what exactly is happening. What you do not know can and will hurt you. So for minority voters to affect the political system in a manner that moves it toward their needs, the first step is to be aware. Table 9-6 reports results from an analysis of two questions regarding political awareness, one reflecting interest in the 2008 election and the second capturing a more generic interest in government and politics.

There is a small but significant difference across racial and ethnic groups regarding their level of attention. African Americans report more attention to politics, government, and the election than do non-Hispanic whites. Asians and Latinos report slightly less. But the differences are tiny—in fact, since both questions range from one (1), meaning low or no interest, to five (5), meaning high interest, what is most remarkable is the clustering of responses for all

TABLE 9-6   Self-Reported Interest in the National Election and Politics and Government, by Race and Ethnicity

Question	White (non-Hispanic)	African American	Hispanic or Latino	Asian American	ANOVA F-Test
A1a. Interest in the election	3.55 (1.45) N = 621	3.80 (1.40) N = 272	3.33 (1.44) N = 218	3.41 (1.04) N = 19	$F = 2.13$ F - prob = .095
A1b. Interest in government and politics	3.47 (1.04) N = 564	3.59 (1.07) N = 300	3.31 (1.07) N = 215	3.00 (.92) N = 16	$F = 2.67$ F - prob = .047

Source: American National Election Study 2008.

Note: Cells contain group means (weighted), with standard deviations in parentheses and cell Ns.

Question wording: A1a. Some people don't pay much attention to political campaigns. How about you? Would you say that you have been VERY MUCH interested (5), SOMEWHAT Interested (3) or NOT MUCH interested (1) in the political campaigns so far this year? (Responses reverse ordered from original.) A1b. How interested are you in information about what's going on in government and politics? EXTREMELY INTERESTED (5), VERY INTERESTED, MODERATELY INTERESTED, SLIGHTLY INTERESTED, or NOT INTERESTED AT ALL (1)? (Responses reverse ordered from original.)

groups on both questions around the same value of 3.5. The only outlier here is Asian interest in politics and government, but even here the differences are half a point on a five-point scale, and of course we again urge caution regarding the very small Asian sample.

Our take on the level of interest in politics is that there is little variation of importance. Minority voters appear about as attentive as white voters and, in some cases, more so. But does this attention yield meaningful information; that is, how much do minority voters actually know about the political system and, in this instance, its actors? Using a four-item battery of factual knowledge questions, we assess the level of information across groups. The results are reported in Table 9-7.

Here the story is not as encouraging as some of the patterns we set out earlier in this chapter. If we examine the distributions and the mean number

TABLE 9-7   Individual Scores on Four-Item Factual Knowledge Battery, by Race and Ethnicity (in percentages)

Number of correct responses	Weighted pooled national sample	Unweighted responses by race and ethnicity			
		White (non-Hispanic)	African American	Hispanic or Latino	Asian American
0	13.8	5.6	21.6	41.8	10.0
1	13.8	11.4	18.4	19.5	11.1
2	23.7	23.9	21.8	18.2	19.5
3	22.8	25.2	24.2	11.9	29.7
4	25.9	33.9	14.0	8.6	29.7
Total N	3,006	837	712	730	478
Mean response	2.05	2.62	1.80	1.21	2.45
(std dev)	1.42	1.23	1.36	1.30	1.35

Chi-square probability = 0.000

F-test probability from ANOVA = 0.0000

Source: 2004 National Politics Study.

Question wording: Now I have a set of questions about a few public figures. In the interest of YOUR time, we were instructed not to take time in the interview to answer any questions about the next series of questions. What job or political office does . . .

a) . . . Dick Cheney NOW hold?

b) . . . Colin Powell NOW hold?

c) . . . William Rehnquist NOW hold?

d) . . . John Edwards NOW hold? (added 9/16/04)

The variable being tabulated is the total number of correct responses to these four questions.

of correct responses, we see plainly that African Americans and Latinos have less knowledge of important political players than whites and Asians do. In fact, each group manages to average between one and two correct answers in identifying the secretary of state, the chief justice, the vice president, and the vice presidential nominee of the out-party, and this is *during* the national election. At first glance, this is sobering news as we assess the ability of minority voters to act strongly on their own behalf in the political system. How can they act if they do not know some basic facts?

We should be cautious about interpreting this finding. For one thing, there is a big distinction to be made between factual knowledge and knowledge in use. For example, lots of African American and Latino citizens may not be able to place the name John Edwards, but this does not mean that they cannot identify John Kerry as the Democratic nominee and vote accordingly. Similarly, a standard question is to ask factual questions about public figures. It is not clear that being able to name John Roberts as the chief justice is as useful as, say, identifying which party wrote anti-immigrant legislation or which party passed the most Civil Rights Movement legislation or which holds issue positions consistent with your own. The data we presented in Chapter 5 suggest that on this critical test, minority voters do just fine—they identify with and vote for parties that—and candidates who—share their issue beliefs, far more often than not.

SUMMARY

We started this chapter by noting that the core orientations of citizens toward government are important in and of themselves. So far as minority voters are concerned, these orientations have the added consequence of encouraging or dampening minority participation and, hence, accelerating or retarding the chance of minorities to reshape the American political system in a manner more favorable to their interests and, in so doing, usher in a period of Democratic dominance. In looking at minority orientations, we examined both the attitudinal bases of political action—trust, alienation, and efficacy—and the cognitive resource basis, political interest and information. Some findings do make a great deal of sense and do emphasize the role of experiences with government in shaping attitudes toward government. Given experiences we would, for example, pretty confidently anticipate finding low levels of trust in government among African Americans. Similarly, the positive attitudes of immigrants are understandable and help to explain some patterns we see among Latino and Asian American communities as a whole. Even so, on the whole it is probably fair to say that our findings were mixed, and more mixed than expected. On the one hand, the results on core orientations were so scattered and occasionally inverted that we feel compelled to conclude that minorities are no more or less disaffected by the political system, or disempowered. Rather, on a number of measures, minority citizens appear similar to whites, exhibit different behaviors by different groups, and even have more favorable orientations than do white citizens. Based on the data we present here, we have no basis for alarm at core orientations among minorities to the political system.

We offered a variety of reasons for why this unexpected finding might be so, not the least of which is the important role of immigration. The evidence suggests that foreign-born Latinos (and likely Asians) hold higher opinions of the American system than do their native-born co-ethnics. The good news there is that minorities are not disempowered. The bad news is that "adverse socialization" appears to occur as generally positive views about the system are displaced by more cynical ones. In short, minorities seem to be taught by experience to distrust the U.S. political system.

Our findings with respect to interest and information were also mixed. Factual information regarding key actors in the political system was poor for both African Americans and Latinos. But their interest in politics was near, or even surpassed, that of whites. It is certainly not a good thing that minority voters lack important knowledge, but considering the close connections between their issue views and voting behavior, we are optimistic regarding their ability to act on behalf of their interests.

On the whole the findings reviewed in this chapter show that minority citizens are not as disaffected from the political system as we might expect. If we were to characterize those findings we might say that they are encouraging—but puzzling. It is encouraging that on the whole citizens see the political system in positive terms. Such positive views set up the basis for minority political engagement. But there are patterns that still need to be explained.

10

chapter

Values and Beliefs: Is There a "Culture War" Across Racial and Ethnic Groups?

A s we have argued throughout this book, "minority politics" is not something separate from or insulated from something called "American politics." Rather, minority politics is part and parcel of the wider politics of the United States. In this wider setting it has become commonplace to talk about the role of values in politics and the rise of "value-based" politics and even culture wars. Since the 1990s, it has been common to hear that, for many voters, values determined vote choice in election after election during that period, especially during 2000 and 2004. What exactly *values* means is less clear. For example, the connection between values and party choice is supposed to be especially clear when we consider abortion and same-sex marriage—the GOP is where this idea of cultural-based or values-based politics seems to play the greatest role. But values can take on other connotations, including social and economic values of equal treatment, self-reliance, and free markets. These topics, too, have played a significant role in contemporary American politics and its debates. Even the signature issues of gay rights and abortion are really part of a larger debate about the place of religion in American life and the degree to which it is a defining characteristic of the nation.

Values are a significant complication in American politics, essentially because they redefine the terms of debate away from economic circumstances and the effects of particular policies (Frank 2004) and can provide convenient cover for those wishing to denigrate or demonize other groups of citizens. Helping the poor, for example, can be reinterpreted as undermining the norm of self-reliance and hard work (Kinder and Sanders 1996). Opposition to immigration can be rephrased as a defense of traditional American values from dilution or destruction at the hands of those who do not subscribe to the same norms (Huntington 2004). Even regional and rural-urban distinctions can be reinterpreted—as they were by 2008 GOP vice presidential candidate Sarah Palin—as a conflict between coastal elites and "real Americans."

The implications of value-based politics for minority politics are potentially profound. Value-based interpretations of minority inequality at best excuse inequality and can, at worst, blame minorities themselves for their economic disadvantage. Values can not only help us distinguish between the "deserving" and "un-deserving" poor but also give some guidance as to whether action is or is not needed. Policy solutions to poverty and inequality may be pushed off the political agenda, or not even gotten to, as a direct consequence of the supposed lack of appropriate values. Citizens, labeled and dismissed as "not sharing" the "right" values, do not require a policy response by government. Refocusing the contestations of politics on dimensions of beliefs and religiosity also has the potential to undermine economically self-interested behavior of minority voters and erode the political distinctiveness we identified in Chapter 5. Values politics can, as Frank argues, undercut economic self-interest. This can be as true for minorities as for Anglos, and it can undercut Democratic support among minorities just as among Anglos, too. If sufficient minority voters are convinced—as we believe a fair number of other Americans have been convinced—to set aside questions of equality and opportunity in favor of debates over whose values reflect "real" Americans, the partisan shift we have predicted in this book so far will almost certainly not come to pass.

In this chapter, we explore the nature of values politics and explicitly examine three kinds of "values." Specifically, we look at religiosity, we look at beliefs regarding the roles of government and the free market in solving social problems, and we look at orientations regarding individuality, self-reliance, and equality of opportunity. We show that the significant attachments of minority communities—and especially African Americans and Latinos—to their religious beliefs serve at once to illustrate the remarkable consistency of their views with stereotypical characteristics of "real" Americans but also create at least the possibility that religious value appeals to black and Latino voters might fall on welcoming ears. Our second finding is that minority citizens have very different expectations of government and significantly lower faith in the market to solve societal problems when compared with non-Hispanic whites. Finally, despite their disadvantaged circumstances, minority citizens, we will show, share, and in some cases exceed, white commitments to self-reliance and individualism in shaping life chances. This last finding is important because it belies the claim that minority citizens' views are responsible for undermining minority socioeconomic progress. Minority disadvantage is not, therefore, a function of having the "wrong" values but a function of social prejudices and intergenerational disadvantage, and it is long overdue for solutions and redress.

NATURE OF VALUES-BASED POLITICS

One of the clearest statements of the GOP's commitment to values-based politics came in Pat Buchanan's speech to the Republican Party convention in 1992. This speech is seen by many as an early and powerful statement of values-based politics and one that set the template for subsequent GOP candidates, most notably George W. Bush but for others, too. Sarah Palin, Mike Huckabee, and

Mitt Romney were all candidates that, in 2008 and afterwards, sought to position themselves as politicians who care about values. A passage in Buchanan's speech illustrates some key elements of this values-based approach to politics:

> George Bush [Sr., president 1989–1993] is a defender of right-to-life, and lifelong champion of the Judeo-Christian values and beliefs upon which this nation was built.
>
> Mr. Clinton, however, has a different agenda.
>
> At its top is unrestricted abortion on demand. When the Irish-Catholic governor of Pennsylvania, Robert Casey, asked to say a few words on behalf of the 25 million unborn children destroyed since *Roe v Wade,* he was told there was no place for him at the podium of Bill Clinton's convention, no room at the inn.
>
> . . . The agenda Clinton & Clinton would impose on America— abortion on demand, a litmus test for the Supreme Court, homosexual rights, discrimination against religious schools, women in combat—that's change, all right. But it is not the kind of change America wants. It is not the kind of change America needs. And it is not the kind of change we can tolerate in a nation that we still call God's country.[1]

> (Pat Buchanan, speech delivered at the 1992 Republican National Convention, Houston, Texas, August 17, 1992)

The ideas and views expressed in this speech are examples of the ideas that inform discussions of "Red" and "Blue" ideological divisions in politics.[2] They are ideas that also inform those of commentators such as Thomas Frank, author of *What's the Matter with Kansas* (2004). Frank argues that it is by appeal to a series of cultural statements that the GOP has built a predominantly white electoral coalition in which some blue-collar voters vote against their own economic self-interest in order to support a cultural agenda. That is, it is common to see voting behavior explained as being driven by concerns over the economy. Some of these concerns might focus on the health of one's own finances or concerns about unemployment and will drive vote choice in straightforward ways: the better-off will support lower taxes and fewer social services being provided by government, while the less-well-off may be less bothered about taxes (especially on the wealthy) and may support expanded social services such as extended unemployment benefits.

Frank, like others, argues that values politics up-ends that relationship. What we see, they argue, are blue-collar workers—whose own economic interests "should" lead them to vote Democrat—voting Republican. Having been convinced that issues such as abortion and school prayer are those on which vote choices should be made, these voters march into the polls and vote against their own economic interests in pursuit of these values. This is how values politics trumps self-interest.

It is quite reasonable to point out that there is nothing wrong with values trumping economic interest. After all, the point about the appeal to the values people hold is to appeal to something that is, at the same time, very significant to the individual and yet leads to concern over events in wider society. Compared with that kind of appeal, one based simply on self-interest sounds narrow—even selfish. No wonder some people do not vote that way. Moreover, values politics operates at the other end of the socioeconomic scale as well. How else can we explain Democratic votes among high-income individuals, unless we can point to principled beliefs that point in the direction of policies that do not serve the individual's economic interests? Values politics, then, operates at both ends of the income distribution and explains votes for both parties that are seemingly in conflict with the voter's economic self-interest.

The debate over the role of values has led to a preoccupation over the past few elections with the division of the United States into Red and Blue, with a few voices arguing that, really, most people in the country today are Purples. Talking about Red and Blue gives us a convenient shorthand way to discuss political division, but it can be a bit misleading. It may only have referred to a period of politics at the beginning of this century and applies only to a few people at the extremes—most ordinary people are more moderate than pundits and partisans would have us believe.

One of the difficulties in talking about values politics comes in defining just what we mean by the term *values politics*. We want to understand how citizens understand politics and the political system, how their views of society—individuals and communities—and their personal beliefs and commitments shape their behavior. Vague statements are all very well when made by a candidate looking for votes, but we would like a little more precision. In particular, we would like more precision over what we mean by *values*. Unfortunately, it can be quite difficult to figure out where values politics stops and regular old issue-based politics begins. Issues and values are related: a voter's values will inform and motivate how he or she stands on a specific issue such as abortion or gay marriage. It seems intuitive to say that the idea of values in politics is broader than opinions on specific issues. The way in which the concept of values politics is used in discussion and analysis, then, refers to something more general than issues—something that underlies them, such as the role of religion in that person's life and worldview. Another set of values might relate to a general sense of the proper role of government (as small as possible versus as big as seems necessary), but the point is that these kinds of predispositions or beliefs are far more general than a specific issue, often helping people to figure out where they stand on a particular issue. Values would also seem to be more enduring than issues. Issues may come and go with each election, but it seems that values are likely to be held for a longer period of time.

Another way in which values differs from simple issue positions is that values are sometimes used as litmus tests for who is like us and who is not, who is a friend and who is definitely not a friend. In more academic terms, the kinds of values someone holds become markers for group affiliation and also for expressive politics—that is, the values held by a voter are an expression of that voter's identity and, also, a way to establish who is in the same group as the voter and who is an opposing group. In many ways values seems to be similar to partisanship and, in fact, values have a strong relationship to partisanship because values help to shape an individual's party loyalty and vote choice. In the Buchanan speech, for example, it is quite clear what kinds of people he sees as allies and what kinds of people he does not see as allies. A certain set of attitudes and opinions thus becomes a marker for "people like us" and "people like them," and elections are a way of counting whether there are more of "us" or "them."

A third way in which values politics seems to be a little different from other kinds of politics is that values politics expands the definition of what we consider "political." There used to be an old definition of politics as "who gets what, when, and how" (Lasswell 1935), but values politics has nothing to do, really, with the distribution or redistribution of benefits and services from government. Rather, this is a politics about right and wrong, good and bad, worthy and unworthy. For sure, these distinctions have huge effects on the distribution of social resources, but that is not the basis on which these issues are debated.

A whole host of issues we are familiar with as part of the political process need not be included as political. For example, one could see questions such as sexual morality, pornography, and procreation as moral choices that are matters of individual conscience and should be left to individuals. As a matter of individual conscience they have no necessary political dimension—there is no inherent need for government to get involved. But government has become involved, in countless ways. Government once prohibited contraception, same-sex sexual activity, marriage between people of difference races, and the publication of pornography. Government action in each instance reflected the imposition of one set of beliefs—values, if you will—on other members of the society. Subsequently, government allowed each of these things.

If adherence to a certain set of values becomes not just a marker of group belonging but also a driver of issue positions and policy choices, then what might once have been a matter of conscience or belief becomes a political question. In fact it becomes more than a political question; it becomes a *partisan* question. The main point, however, is that values introduces into politics an additional set of concerns, issues, and debates that we may not otherwise have. This is not to say that to expand politics in this way is either a good thing or a bad thing—though most readers are likely to have one view or the other—it is just a feature of contemporary American politics.

A fourth property of values politics that distinguishes it from issues is that it can, under some circumstances, present some difficulties for "normal" democratic and electoral politics. Disagreement over values implies disagreement over a set of topics over which there can be no negotiation, no room for compromise: politics becomes a cut-and-dried matter of doing what is right. The trouble is, there is disagreement over what is right (or wrong), and once we get into these kinds of disputes, there may be little room for compromise and negotiation. While, for some, words such as *compromise* and *negotiation* are weasel words, they are important to democratic practice. In democratic societies part of the purpose of politics is to find compromises and establish bargains and negotiations so that life goes on and fighting does not erupt. Values-based politics seems to suggest that there are areas over which no bargains and no compromise are possible. Some things may not be a matter for compromise. The Civil Rights Movement might be one such example where compromise was not possible. But if many disputes are not for negotiation under any circumstances, it is hard to see how democratic politics can continue without disruptions and blockage. Historically, one way out has been to say, "Some matters over which there can be no bargain are matters of individual conscience." If some questions are matters of individual conscience, then there is no real need to talk about compromise or negotiation: individuals will act according to their moral code in their personal life (or not), which means that politics and the government have no role to play. If, however, values are not defined as matters of individual conscience but instead are defined as political questions—ones in which the government should rule or regulate—then this necessarily generates conflict. There is, for example, no easy regulatory middle ground that can accommodate different views on when life begins. Individuals may be able to decide this matter for themselves quite easily, but collections of individuals will disagree, and there is no easy way to see that disagreement ending unless one side "wins."

This last point might help to explain why modern politics is so contentious and the parties so polarized. Values politics helps support a kind of politics that has people choosing sides and then fighting for that side to win out over the other one. Values politics seems to concern a set of opinions and attitudes that form a dividing line in politics between those in group X and those not in group X. Values politics sees politics as combative and highly conflictual with little room for the middle ground. Such a picture is certainly one in keeping with the many discussions of Red and Blue America and the emotions we see and hear on cable TV shows and talk radio. It is also in keeping with the idea that politics is quite polarized. But it is worth bearing in mind that this is in part a consequence of seeing politics as about values. It is also worth bearing in mind that the kinds of analysis that make for good television may not always be good analysis.

We now have some sense of what values politics is and how it may help to shape contemporary U.S. politics. It is a picture of U.S. politics that makes sense and suggests that all the media commentary about Red and Blue is a way of accurately talking about U.S. politics. Despite the popularity of the idea of values politics or cultural politics—especially in cable TV and talk radio commentary—the idea of values politics is not without controversy. There is a sizable and sophisticated literature within political science that disagrees with the view that voters really do make decisions on the basis of cultural concerns or values rather than economics. The idea of values politics is that it is something other than economics that will drive vote choice. That "something other than economics" may be religion or someone's attitudes toward government more broadly, but it is expressly not something such as how well the economy is doing or how someone's personal economic circumstances have changed. It does seem to be the case that, of late, moral issues are more important to vote choice, but these issues have not replaced economic concerns as the major driver of vote choice (Bartels 2006; Ansolabehere et al. 2006; Fiorina and Abrams 2008). There also seems to have been a shift in voting blocs with blue-collar southern whites moving from Democrat to the GOP over the past generation or so. This is a trend that overlaps the Protestantism of many southerners, and so the appearance of moral drivers of vote choice may be overstated, and some scholars argue that there are economic reasons motivating the shift of southerners to the GOP (Shafer and Johnston 2006). It also seems to be the case that the parties have become more polarized, but this may be more at the level of party elites, since it does not seem to be matched by polarization among voters (Baldassarri and Gelman 2008; Fiorina and Abrams 2008); party elites and talk shows may be divided into battling tribes of Red and Blue, but voters may not be nearly so motivated and divided.

For all the sound and fury, then, there may be a lot less going on in terms of value politics than may sometimes be claimed or even wished for.

VALUES POLITICS AND MINORITY POLITICS

What relevance does this discussion of values politics have for minority politics? There are two main ways in which we can see value politics and minority politics as tied together: the way in which race shows up in relation to the discussion of values and the question of whether minorities themselves hold values that are somehow distinct from those of Anglos. We will address each of these points in turn.

Race and racial politics only seems to appear in discussions of values politics in the background. The role of race is generally implicit rather than explicit, but this is very different from saying that race is of no relevance to discussions of value-based politics. Values politics is arguably one way of rallying whites to the GOP, in part by suggesting (either implicitly or explicitly) that racial and ethnic minorities, immigrants, and others do not share core "American" values. The argument is that values-based politics is part of building electoral coalitions that are racially skewed: for the GOP this means, as we have seen elsewhere in this book, a predominantly white electoral coalition, a coalition that may well help win elections in the U.S. South but seems to be out of step with demographics in the rest of the country. Still, there are enough short-term electoral benefits to make it worth the while of GOP candidates and strategists to pursue values politics as a strategy.

Many commentators on the right would deny the interpretation of values-based politics as a kind of code or subtext for race-based politics. They would argue that the appeal of values-based politics is to people of faith of all races and ethnicities and, further, that the specific issues raised as part of values politics have no racial text or subtext. For example, attitudes toward gay rights are associated with religious affiliation, and this is not simply a property of Anglos: Latino Catholics and African American Protestants were important components of the vote coalition that passed the antigay-marriage Proposition 8 in California. On questions of faith, then, the dividing line is not drawn along racial or ethnic lines but along a line separating the devout from the nondevout that is largely blind to color.

Some kinds of questions do seem more clearly bound up with race. For example, Samuel Huntington's book *Who Are We? The Challenges to America's National Identity* (2004) offers the argument that Latin American (and particularly Mexican) migration to the United States represents a threat to the unity and dominance of our cultural virtues, which he identifies as Anglo-Protestant values. Fear of, and adverse reactions to, the nation's growing Hispanic population, then, are neither inappropriate nor a reflection of ethnocentric or racist thoughts but, rather, a response to a cultural threat. The policy implications of this view—with respect to immigration, language policy, education, and countless other issues—are both straightforward and profound.

Similarly, arguments over support for the unemployed, welfare and public assistance (Hancock 2003), and other aspects of the social safety net often implicitly or explicitly descend into an exploration of the values of the recipients, a line of argument that goes all the way back to Glazer and Moynihan (1963). If poor values—rather than a history, legacy, and current reality of poor treatment—are the source of minority disadvantage, then they are not worthy of state intervention, protection, and support. Rather, the locus of responsibility for minority poverty and cultural change is all on the minorities themselves, suggesting a very different type of policy intervention—or indeed no effort at all—to redress inequality. Overall, then, what we see is that while the politics of race and ethnicity are not necessarily front and center in the rhetoric of their proponents, they figure quite prominently in the implications. Values politics is a way in which minority citizens are constructed to be on the wrong side of the "us versus them" line.

RELIGIOSITY AND MINORITY AMERICANS

Throughout this book we try to locate minorities in relation to the opportunities and challenges of American politics as a whole. If it is the case that minorities do differ from the values or cultural politics strand of GOP thought reflected in Pat Buchanan's speech, then we can expect that minority voters will remain loyal to the Democrats. If, by contrast, minority voters share many of the cultural and value commitments that are prominent in the values politics debate, then perhaps the close association of minority voters to Democratic candidates is potentially short lived.

We turn now to look at this question in relation to three sets of values that figure prominently in discussions of this kind: the importance of religion in shaping political views, attitudes regarding the role of government and the free market in improving the lives of Americans, and views regarding individualism, equality, and self-reliance. We focus on these three dimensions because we think that, apart from hot-button issues we hear about so much, these are the core dimensions that can define points of commonality and distinction between whites and non-whites—to the extent that an "us versus them" dividing line can be seen in people's views on religion, the appropriate role of government, and critical aspects of individual responsibility. These three areas reflect some of the disagreements at the core of the debates over values politics.

We turn first to religious belief and religious observance. The role of the black church in shaping political engagement and action is long established (Sitkoff 1978). African American ministers were pivotal in the Civil Rights Movement and played key political roles in many of the historic events. Moreover, the effect of African American churches and their leaders on the views of ordinary citizens is ongoing (Alex-Assensoh and Assensoh 2001; Smith and Harris 2005; McDaniel 2008). It would be reasonable to expect that religion and religious views would matter a great deal to African American citizens.

BOX 10-1   Religion and Younger People

Religiosity seems to be an anchoring factor in both values and values-based politics. The United States has higher rates of religiosity—higher rates of church attendance and of devotion—than most other countries in the Western world. This would seem to offer one reason why religious values figure prominently in the politics of the United States.

There is evidence that the role of religion in America may change a little in the future. Younger Americans are less devout than older Americans, and this seems to be the case across racial groups. A 2010 Pew study finds that:

> Americans ages 18 to 29 are considerably less religious than older Americans. Fewer young adults belong to any particular faith than older people do today. They also are less likely to be affiliated than their parents' and grandparents' generations were when they were young. Fully one-in-four members of the Millennial generation—so called because they were born after 1980 and began to come of age around the year 2000—are unaffiliated with any particular faith.

The report cautions that religion does seem to become more important as people age. Thus differences between young and old may overstate how different the generations will be; lower church attendance among today's 20-somethings does not necessarily imply lower figures when members of that generation are in their 50s—they may in fact look very similar to today's 50-somethings in terms of how often they attend church or pray.

But there are differences in opinion content that would seem to suggest some changes in value politics. Consider this report from Pew (2010):

> In their social and political views, young adults are clearly more accepting than older Americans of homosexuality, more inclined to see evolution as the best explanation of human life and less prone to see Hollywood as threatening their moral values. At the same time, Millennials are no less convinced than their elders that there are absolute standards of right and wrong.[1]

Young people have values—but they are different ones from those of older Americans.

---

[1] Pew Forum on Religion and Public Life. 2010. "Religion among the Millennials." http://pewforum.org/Age/Religion-Among-the-Millennials.aspx (accessed February 4, 2011).

We know a lot less about religion among Latinos and Asian Americans. Latino Catholicism is sometimes considered a source of weak civic engagement (Verba et al. 1995) given the relative hierarchical nature of the Catholic Church, but more recent research (Jones-Correa and Leal 2001) suggests that there is little evidence for this claim. There is some newer exploration of the growing influence of evangelicalism among both Latinos and Asian Americans (Kim 2004; Walsh 2003; Alumkal 2003; Heredia and Wong 2010), but it is fair to say this literature is in its infancy.

We cannot, in this book, explore the full range of distinctions between the role of religion in the politics and views of American minority voters and its role among whites. Such an effort would be another book in itself. We can and should, however, look into the key metrics of religious observance to see if they might provide insight into our key questions—how values debates shape minority politics and whether minority Americans exhibit values that meaningfully differ from whites.

Tables 10-1 and 10-2 display some very simple evidence that speaks to the role of religion in people's lives. Table 10-1 examines the frequency of church attendance reported by Americans of various racial and ethnic identities. The results are consistent with received wisdom about African Americans and Latinos being relatively devout. About 5 percent more Latinos and 10 percent more African Americans than whites report going to church weekly.

The same story emerges with respect to prayer. In Table 10-2, we report frequency of prayer by racial and ethnic category. While only 37 percent of

TABLE 10-1   Frequency of Church Attendance, by Race and Ethnicity (in percentages)

Response category	Weighted pooled national sample	Unweighted responses by race and ethnicity			
		White (non-Hispanic)	African American	Hispanic or Latino	Asian American
More than once a week	3.1	3.0	5.8	3.3	3.3
At least once a week	39.8	41.2	48.2	46.1	42.4
At least once a month	17.0	15.1	18.7	19.4	13.6
A few times a year	28.5	28.8	22.0	25.7	27.9
Never	11.6	11.9	5.3	5.5	12.7
Total N	2,787	808	695	690	330

Chi-square probability = 0.000

F-test probability from ANOVA = 0.0000

Source: 2004 National Politics Study.

Question wording: How often do you attend religious services?

TABLE 10-2   Frequency of Prayer, by Race and Ethnicity (in percentages)

Response category	Weighted pooled national sample	Unweighted responses by race and ethnicity			
		White (non-Hispanic)	African American	Hispanic or Latino	Asian American
Several times a day	31.7	29.9	49.9	29.5	17.1
Once a day	21.0	20.5	21.9	30.4	20.0
A few times a week	18.0	18.1	17.3	20.1	17.1
Once a week or less	16.0	16.6	8.3	13.4	25.7
Never	13.4	14.9	2.7	6.7	20.0
Total N	3,174	1,175	567	434	35

Chi-square probability = 0.000

F-test probability from ANOVA = 0.0000

Source: American National Election Study 2008.

Question wording: People practice religion in different ways. Outside of attending religious services, do you pray several times a day, once a day, a few times a week or less, or never?

Asians and just over 50 percent of non-Hispanic whites report at least daily prayer, the numbers are substantially greater for Latinos (60 percent), and African Americans (72 percent).

In asking how important religion is to people in practice, we can gain some insight by simply asking how often they attend a place of worship. Of course, that is not the end of the importance of religion in people's lives. People rely on their faith for guidance during their everyday lives. Asking people about these other, more personal and more meaningful ways in which religion figures in their lives might give us a better sense of how religious "values" breaks down across different racial and ethnic groups. Table 10-3 illustrates the degree to which people feel that religion is important to them and a source of guidance, a critical component of making religious values politically relevant. The results here are striking as well.

Both African Americans and Latinos are significantly more likely to report a "great deal" of reliance on religion for guidance in life, when compared with whites. While about 31 percent of whites report this level of reliance, the number for Latinos is 38 percent. But neither can hold a candle to African American religiosity. Fully 58 percent of black respondents report a great deal of reliance on religious guidance, while another 21 percent report quite a bit. African American citizens are simply far more likely than other Americans to find guidance in religion. By contrast, if we look at the opposite end of the scale—those to whom religion is not important—only 11 percent of African Americans and 19 percent of Latinos offer this response, compared with 32 percent

TABLE 10-3   Importance of, and Guidance from, Religion in Everyday Life, by Race and Ethnicity (in percentages)

Response category	Weighted pooled national sample	Unweighted responses by race and ethnicity			
		White (non-Hispanic)	African American	Hispanic or Latino	Asian American
Important/great deal of guidance	34.5	30.8	58.0	38.3	19.7
Important/quite a bit of guidance	20.4	20.5	20.7	23.7	16.1
Important/some guidance	16.5	16.7	10.1	19.3	20.2
Not important, don't know	28.8	31.7	11.1	18.7	44.0
Total N	2,304	1,177	567	432	35
	Chi-square probability = 0.000				
	F-test probability from ANOVA = 0.0000				

Source: American National Election Study 2008.

Question wording: Do you consider religion to be an IMPORTANT part of your life, or NOT? If respondent SAYS THAT RELIGION IS IMPORTANT: Would you say your religion provides SOME guidance in your day-to-day living, QUITE A BIT of guidance, or a GREAT DEAL of guidance in your day-to-day life?

of non-Hispanic whites. For Asian Americans, sample size is again a worry on this measure, but to the extent the estimate is reliable, they appear to be the least religious of any of these communities.

What implications might we draw from these three tables? Minority citizens go to church and pray more often than whites and report significantly greater reliance on religion for guidance—in the case of African Americans, the effect is extreme. There is something of a puzzle here. Not just a majority but a supermajority of all minority voters who are on average quite devout vote Democratic, while the (less religious) white population votes majority GOP. Yet the GOP is the party with whom religious observance is most closely associated. There are at least two potential explanations for these outcomes. First, religion may not have as important an effect on political choice among minorities, even though religion would seem to have a strong role in their everyday lives. Second, religion may not mean the same thing among minorities. That is, the way in which the church is organized and conducted may differ both by faith and by congregation. It is possible that some churches may be as much involved in affirming a community as encouraging political engagement. Churches may also help assimilation among immigrant groups. Chen (2006) and Kurien (1998) both identify ways in which religious practice—Christianity and Hinduism—can be Americanized to help immigrants come to terms with

BOX 10-2   Muslims and Democracy

One of the major topics of discussion over the past few years has been the relationship between Islam and democracy. It is a discussion that is complicated by the variety of practices within Islam, notably those between Shia and Sunni, but other differences exist within these branches of Islam, too. One of the discussions concerning the relationship between Islam and democracy has considered the question cross-nationally and assessed whether majority-Muslim nations have populations that are supportive of democracy and whether those populations see democracy in the same terms (for example, Ciftci 2010; Hofmann 2004).

Another discussion, and one relevant to this book, is the one concerned with the attitudes of Muslim minorities within already democratic societies toward the value of democracy itself. It is one that continues to be of major interest to scholars interested in Europe. Unlike the United States, where immigrant populations are very often Christians entering into a relatively devout society, many of Europe's immigrants are often Muslim entering into a relatively secular society (Foner and Alba 2008). One consequence of these trends has been a more active debate considering the roles of immigration and multiculturalism in European society (Meer and Modood 2008).

Sometimes, this debate has led to odd political pairings. For instance, conservatives and feminists may share similar views on the importance of assimilation and integration (but for different reasons). For example, a leading anti-immigration politician in the Netherlands, Pim Fortuyn, was gay, something of a surprise in an ideology generally understood as emanating from the right of the ideological spectrum. Fortuyn rested his opposition to Muslim immigration on his fear that the climate of tolerance gays and lesbians enjoyed in the Netherlands would be significantly eroded if observant Muslims changed the national political and social culture. In another example, this fear has led to policies that seem strange to American eyes, such as France's statutory attack on the wearing of the hijab (or headscarf) and other face coverings in public places.

In the United States the role of immigration is quite different. It is also the case that there are important differences in terms of both the Arab American population and Islam. In the United States many Arab American immigrants are Christian, while perhaps as many as a quarter of American Muslims are African Americans. Mindful of these various complications, the evidence to date suggests that mosques function as other kinds of churches, encouraging a sense of group consciousness as well as helping to promote civic participation, and the American Muslims are willing to engage the democratic process (Jamal 2005; Ayers and Hofstetter 2008; Jalalzai 2009), with possibly some differences between varieties of Islam (Contractor 2010). As, however, some work shows part of the answer depends on how welcoming the parties are to Muslim participation (Barreto and Bozonelos 2009).

their new home—sometimes in ways that are not always political. In her study of Taiwanese Christians, Chen (2006) finds that, among other features, religion helped assimilation to middle-class American family life and in particular parent-child relationships. Sometimes, then, churches may be about things that are different from—and in some ways more important than—politics.

But even if churches engage with politics, they may differ in how explicitly they do so. In one of the few works on this topic, in relation to Latino and

Asian engagement in evangelical Protestant churches, Wong, Rim, and Perez (2008) found very little overt political organization, although congregants may engage in political discussion among themselves.[3] As they point out, churches and religious leaders may have to be wary of being too overtly political—and so alienating congregants. Other churches may be different and may be more tolerant of and receptive to political appeals. But we quickly reach the limit of how much is known about the political context provided by churches among minorities. There is clearly scope for a lot more work that establishes the variety of experiences within churches

Whatever the case, the strong religious identification of Latinos and African Americans lays bare two realities. The first is that on the basis of religiosity, minority citizens look more "American" than white Americans, if we want religious values and identification to be a criterion of the "us versus them" divide. On the basis of religion, we could not conclude that minority values are so different as to be threatening—unless we would wish to claim that there is such a thing as "too" religious for Americans. Second, if religion became more salient to minority voting decisions—or at least those aspects of religious belief currently shaping the views of white Christians—the close association of non-white voters and Democratic candidates could be threatened.

GOVERNMENT VERSUS FREE MARKET SOLUTIONS

We turn now to the second values dimension we find important: the role of government and the market in solving social problems. Here we see a very different pattern. Figures 10-1 and 10-2 report what respondents believe about the growth of government—that is, whether it was justified and helpful. The story from these survey questions is the same: minorities are much less suspicious of government, and more willing to have government intervene to address social problems, than are Anglos.

Figure 10-1 reports respondents' take on why government has grown so large. As you can see, non-Hispanic white voters are more or less evenly divided over the question of whether government stuck its nose into matters where it did not belong, or whether government grew because our nation's problems required it. By contrast, look at the distributions among minority respondents. Huge majorities of every other group overwhelmingly report that the size and complexity of the nation's problems demanded government increase its capacity to address them. Between 72 and 78 percent of Asian Americans, Latinos, and African Americans believe that government grew out of necessity. This represents, we believe, a meaningful and fundamental difference in how Americans of different racial and ethnic backgrounds see the political world.

The results in Figure 10-2 are consistent with those in Figure 10-1. Here the question is whether we want government to do more, or whether the less the better. Again, racial distinctions on this question are profound. Whites, again, are more or less evenly divided. By contrast, almost 69 percent of Asian

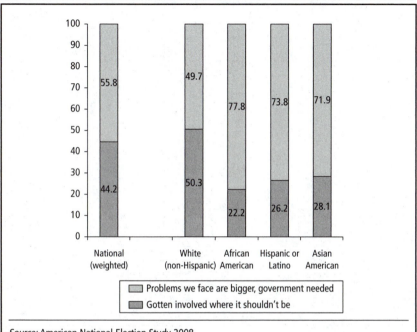

FIGURE 10-1   **Attitudes Regarding Government Growth, by Race and Ethnicity (in percentages)**

Source: American National Election Study 2008.

Question wording: Which of two statements comes closer to your own opinion: ONE, the main reason government has become bigger over the years is because it has gotten involved in things that people should do for themselves; OR TWO, government has become bigger because the problems we face have become bigger.

Americans favor government doing more, and among African Americans and Latinos, the comparable percentages are over 80 percent. You will recall from Chapter 5 that we argued there is a strong policy basis for partisan division between whites and minorities—nowhere is this better illustrated than in this table. Minority voters and white voters have markedly different expectations regarding the vigor and reach of government.

Figure 10-3 reports results from a somewhat different question, one designed to capture conviction in the core ideological belief of free market conservatism—that the market can solve most problems. It is clear that a majority of no group believes this. Even among whites, almost two-thirds of the respondents say that we need a strong government. But that number, again, pales in comparison with the support for government action among minorities. Almost 76 percent of Asian Americans and between 83 percent and 85

FIGURE 10-2 **Views Regarding Government Action to Solve Problems, by Race and Ethnicity (in percentages)**

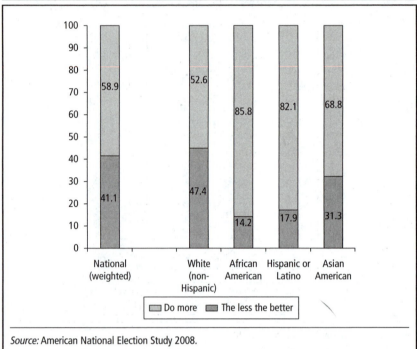

Source: American National Election Study 2008.

Question wording: Which of two statements comes closer to your own opinion: ONE, the less government, the better; OR TWO, there are more things that government should be doing?

percent of African Americans and Latinos place greater trust in government action to solve problems than in the famous hidden-hand of the marketplace. These findings, including the distribution among Anglos, gives lie to the oft-repeated contention that America is a center-right nation. A large percentage of our citizens, of every group, prefer to rely on a capable government than on the market to solve our problems.

What, then, can we say about free market values and minority politics? As we just indicated, the ideological distinctions between racial and ethnic groups regarding government action are significant. Minority citizens prefer a more energetic government, by large and statistically significant margins. On the one hand, such opinions no doubt feed stereotypic assessments of minorities as wanting to rely on government for everything, an erroneous interpretation of these data but one you are likely to hear in the midst of heated rhetoric. On the other hand, these data do suggest, again, that minority ideology and partisan-ship are consistent and rational and that an anticipation of a large movement

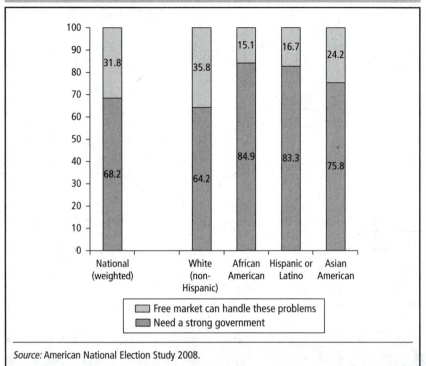

FIGURE 10-3   **Preferences for Free Market versus Government Solutions, by Race and Ethnicity (in percentages)**

Source: American National Election Study 2008.

Question wording: Which of two statements comes closer to your own opinion: ONE, we need a strong government to handle today's complex economic problems; OR TWO, the free market can handle these problems without government being involved.

of minorities into the GOP camp is very likely to be in vain. If, for a moment, we can stereotype GOP ideology as "market good, government bad," it's just crystal clear that supermajorities of minority Americans do not agree.

INDIVIDUALISM, EGALITARIANISM, AND SELF-RELIANCE

If support for an energetic government was related to an absence of belief in individual effort, one of the things that we might expect to see is less tolerance for versions of what we might term "American individualism," the idea that while there may be some inequality, if people work hard enough they will be able to make it. It seems reasonable to suppose that support of government action is related to doubts over what we have loosely termed "self-reliance," that we might expect strong minority objections to the ideas that individuals can make it on their own with hard work, and that inequality is not necessarily a permanent roadblock to people's aspirations.

Stereotyping notwithstanding, however, the belief in an energetic government aggressively addressing social problems is not the same as dependence or a "welfare mentality." As the results we are about to share suggest, belief in an effective government and belief in self-reliance and individual effort can go together quite nicely. Bundling those attitudes that are not supposed to go together merely involves recognition that, for all their efforts, not everyone who works hard reaps the benefits (and, though seldom discussed, not everyone reaping the benefits of success has worked all that hard).

Table 10-4 reports what Americans believe about the relationship between hard work and success. It is pretty clear that Americans of all racial and ethnic groups buy the central claim of this "meritocratic" value. Among African Americans, 77.5 percent agree or strongly agree with this claim, and that is the lowest number among the four groups. For non-Hispanic whites and Asian Americans, the comparable numbers are 82 and 82.5 percent, respectively, and for Latinos, support for this abstract commitment to hard work is a shockingly high 92.5 percent. On this most basic measure of individualism, there are few to no meaningful differences between whites, Asians, and African Americans, and Latinos exhibit even greater commitment to this "American value."

Table 10-5 focuses our attention specifically on minorities. This table reflects the distribution of beliefs on the question of whether minority

---

TABLE 10-4 Attitudes Regarding Whether Hard Work Leads to Success, by Race and Ethnicity (in percentages)

Response category	Weighted pooled national sample	Unweighted responses by race and ethnicity			
		White (non-Hispanic)	African American	Hispanic or Latino	Asian American
Strongly agree	52.0	49.1	47.4	75.8	50.3
Somewhat agree	31.1	32.9	30.1	16.7	32.2
Somewhat disagree	11.2	12.6	12.6	4.4	12.9
Strongly disagree	5.7	5.5	10.0	3.1	4.6
Total N	3,218	913	754	753	497
Mean response	1.71	1.76	1.78	1.36	1.74
Standard deviation	0.88	0.88	0.97	0.72	0.88

Chi-square probability = 0.000

F-test probability from ANOVA = 0.0000

Source: 2004 National Politics Study.

Question wording: America is a land of opportunity in which you only need to work hard to succeed.

TABLE 10-5   Attitudes on Minority Self-Reliance, by Race and Ethnicity (in percentages)

Response category	Weighted pooled national sample	White (non-Hispanic)	African American	Hispanic or Latino	Asian American
		Unweighted responses by race and ethnicity			
Strongly agree	30.2	27.8	32.4	44.0	23.9
Somewhat agree	33.4	34.0	27.8	28.9	34.9
Somewhat disagree	21.9	23.6	21.0	15.1	24.3
Strongly disagree	14.5	14.6	18.7	12.1	16.8
Total N	3,177	903	747	737	493
Mean response	2.21	2.25	2.17	1.95	2.37
Standard deviation	1.03	1.01	1.08	1.03	1.02

Chi-square probability = 0.000

F-test probability from ANOVA = 0.0000

Source: 2004 National Politics Study.

Question wording: If racial and ethnic minorities don't do well in life they have no one to blame but themselves. Do you . . .

Americans are ultimately responsible for their own circumstances, a somewhat controversial claim and one often associated with racial hostility, given the long history of white privilege (Katznelson 2005) and minority disadvantage in American society. Not surprisingly, almost 62 percent of white survey respondents agree that minorities have no one but themselves to blame for their life outcomes. How strongly do minorities disagree with them?

It turns out that many, even most, minority group members surveyed agree. About 60 percent of African Americans and Asian Americans agree that minorities are the masters of their own fate. The comparable number among Latinos is over 70 percent. A fair interpretation of these figures is that even when we focus specifically on minorities and their circumstances in life, minorities believe every bit as much in self-reliance as whites do, and perhaps even more so. These findings are in no way consistent with the notion that minorities do not share American values; nor are they consistent with a stereotype of dependence.

Inequality exists in American society—inequality of opportunity and inequality of outcome. While minority respondents appear committed to the notion of self-reliance, how do they feel about this inequality? Are they troubled by it?

Table 10-6 reports attitudes toward the core principle of equal opportunity. The question was phrased in a reverse manner—suggesting that unequal

TABLE 10-6   Attitudes Regarding Whether Inequality of Opportunity is a Problem, by Race and Ethnicity (in percentages)

Response category	Weighted pooled national sample	Unweighted responses by race and ethnicity			
		White (non-Hispanic)	African American	Hispanic or Latino	Asian American
Strongly agree	14.1	12.5	18.3	22.4	18.2
Somewhat agree	30.9	32.1	26.1	32.4	39.6
Somewhat disagree	26.2	27.6	18.9	21.6	21.9
Strongly disagree	28.8	27.8	36.8	23.6	20.3
Total N	3,174	903	737	732	488
Mean response	2.70	2.75	2.70	2.47	2.52
Standard deviation	1.03	1.01	1.15	1.07	1.01
		Chi-square probability = 0.000			
		F-test probability from ANOVA = 0.0000			

Source: 2004 National Politics Study.

Question wording: It is not really that big of a problem if some people have more of a chance in life than others.

opportunity is *not* a problem. Almost 45 percent of non-Hispanic whites agree that unequal opportunity is no big deal. More surprisingly, the number for African Americans is essentially the same, and both Latinos (approximately 55 percent) and Asian Americans (about 58 percent) are even more tolerant of inequality.

It is somewhat surprising and disheartening to find so many Americans willing to accept unequal *opportunity.* Keep in mind that we are not talking about equal *outcomes,* since an individualist society with free market institutions cannot (and, some would certainly argue, should not) force equal outcomes of circumstances. But equal *opportunity* is a core principle of American society—and many Americans see no problem if our society fails to live up to that standard.

Nevertheless, we would describe views across groups on this as consensual. All four groups had distributions that are nearly even. That Latinos and Asian Americans are somewhat more accepting of inequality is likely a reflection of the large number of immigrants in those two communities and the relative inequality in their countries of origin. But the tolerance for inequality among whites and blacks, at 45 percent, is also quite high.

Finally, in Table 10-7, we turn our attention to whether Americans feel that inequality and discrimination are problems that hurt society. The results on this question are somewhat inconsistent with some previous patterns, particularly for Latinos. Many minority Americans perceive unequal treatment in our society and think it is harmful. This question produces some of the largest

	Weighted pooled national sample	Unweighted responses by race and ethnicity			
Response category		White (non-Hispanic)	African American	Hispanic or Latino	Asian American
Strongly agree	29.1	24.9	58.2	41.2	24.2
Somewhat agree	35.8	36.6	27.2	33.9	21.2
Neither agree nor disagree	17.3	18.1	7.0	13.8	33.3
Somewhat disagree	12.6	14.0	4.9	8.9	21.2
Strongly disagree	5.2	6.4	2.7	2.3	0.0
Total N	2,036	1,078	514	384	33
Mean response	2.29	2.41	1.71	1.95	2.60
Standard deviation	1.16	1.17	1.01	1.04	1.01

TABLE 10-7   Attitudes Regarding Whether Inequality or Discrimination is Hurting America, by Race and Ethnicity (in percentages)

Chi-square probability = 0.000

F-test probability from ANOVA = 0.0000

Source: American National Election Study 2008.

Question wording: If people were treated more equally in this country we would have many fewer problems. (Do you AGREE STRONGLY, AGREE SOMEWHAT, NEITHER AGREE NOR DISAGREE, DISAGREE SOMEWHAT, or DISAGREE STRONGLY with this statement?)

between-group differences we have observed. Among Asian Americans, the percentage agreeing that unequal treatment is hurting America is only 45 percent (though the sample size is very small), and among non-Hispanic whites, that number is 61.5 percent, a fair majority. By contrast, about 75 percent of Latinos and 85 percent of African Americans agree with this statement.

Taken together, there is a general image that emerges from Tables 10-4 through 10-7. Minority Americans are categorically not supporters of radical redistribution; nor do they eschew a belief in the importance self-reliance. While there are between-group differences that are important, a more accurate take is that minority Americans believe in individual effort and hard work and have somewhat lower expectations of equal opportunity than we might have expected, yet they recognize that unequal treatment is hurting some Americans.

DISCUSSION: WHAT TO MAKE OF VALUES POLITICS AND MINORITY POLITICS?

The discussion of minority values allows us not only to make some observations about minority politics but also to draw some important conclusions about the role of values in American politics more broadly. Minority values contain a combination of views that—according to many cable and talk radio commentators—are not supposed to go together. Minorities are both religiously devout and welcoming of government, they believe in their own self-reliance but think government needs to do more, and they are (surprisingly) tolerant of inequality and think that hard work will lead to success. Minorities also believe that the free market will not solve our problems and that unequal treatment is hurting America. These combinations of opinions are not really supposed to exist side by side, yet they do for millions of Americans.

This means two things—both of which have consequences for the general discussion over values in American politics as well as our discussion of minority politics.

First, it is plain that there are limits to values politics. There are few things more important to people than personal faith. Faith will color how people act and think in deep and abiding ways. Faith is a fundamental building block of how people see the world. No wonder, then, that a strand of thought within the GOP has sought to express a call to faith. Minority voters are deeply devout—more devout than Anglos—but have not responded to that Republican call.

Second, and following on from that point, it is clear that "values politics" does not come in the same rigid and fixed combinations that we may think. While commentators and candidates on both left and right argue that certain values *have* to go together, this is simply not how tens of millions of voters see things. Minority voters are both devout *and* supportive of government *and* supportive of the idea of the benefits of individual hard work. This point reminds us of the purpose of speeches such as Buchanan's or related analyses on cable or radio. For candidates the division into Red and Blue on the basis of values politics is a rhetorical device aimed at building electoral coalitions. It provides a simple narrative for what the issues of the day are (or should be). But that is very different from it being a correct read of the American public and, particularly, minority communities. As we have seen, dividing the United States into Red and Blue on the basis of "values" is an overly simple narrative that hides a great deal of complexity and hides the fact that millions of people have combinations of attitudes that straddle what are supposed to be dividing lines. This is not so much a case of a set of opinions being "Purple," in the sense of being moderate on all issues, but of opinions being made up of stripes of Red and Blue.

What of our central claim—that minorities are likely to become the lynchpin of Democratic majorities in the coming era? There is little in their values to suggest otherwise. Yes, minority voters are faithful and believe in self-reliance. But this faith and individualism is coupled with an even stronger endorsement of an active and energetic government solving social problems, and a concern—their own industry notwithstanding—that persistent inequality hurts America. Minority voters are neither economic radicals nor closet free-marketeers. What that means is that a political strategy built on painting them as the former or recruiting them on the belief that they are the latter seems unlikely to succeed.

Immigration and Its Discontents

*E*pluribus unum ("one out of many") is one of the few Latin phrases that people come across these days—at least if people spend some time looking at the coins in their change.[1] The phrase touches on a persistent theme in U.S. politics—the building of one nation from people of different national origins and backgrounds. Immigration and immigrants, and the politics surrounding both, have always been part of U.S. political history. These days they are an especially important part of minority politics in the United States.

Both Latinos and Asian Americans can be understood as "immigrant-derived" populations in that a huge portion of both populations is within two generations of the immigration experience and nearly all are within three generations of immigration. Asian Americans, and in particular Chinese and Japanese Americans, have been present in the United States since the middle of the nineteenth century. Asian American communities have long been a part of West Coast immigration patterns and were, for example, a major part of the workforce that built the railroads. Asian immigration, including that from places other than China and Japan, became an even more important part of U.S. population growth in the latter half of the twentieth century. Some of these trends were a consequence of U.S. foreign policy experiences in Southeast Asia. Similarly, significant Latino populations passed into U.S. jurisdiction with the Treaty of Guadalupe, in 1848, which concluded the Mexican-American War, and again at the conclusion of the Spanish-American War fifty years later. Nevertheless, large-scale Latin American migration began in earnest in the 1960s and accelerated appreciably in the 1980s and 1990s.

African Americans and their politics have, until recently, not been connected to the issues of immigration. However, growing immigration from Africa, as well as Afro-Caribbean immigration from French-, English-, and Spanish-speaking nations of the Caribbean region has begun to link black politics with the issue of immigration within the black community as well as between African Americans and newer immigrant groups.

Immigration, over time, enlarges the electorate and introduces new desires and needs to the mix of issues considered by the political system. One of those issues is the question of immigration itself. Immigration shapes who is enfranchised, just as did the Civil Rights Movement and, before that, expanding the franchise to include women. Reactions to immigrants and immigration reshape the politics of the existing American electorate with concerns over wages, jobs, cultural dissimilarity, assimilation, and education. Reactions to immigrants and immigration almost certainly shape their view of the political system into which they are incorporating and can have long-term partisan effects. One way in which we see this is that immigration is an issue with the rare ability to divide parties internally.

In this chapter we focus our attention on the role of immigration and immigrants in the future of American politics. We cannot, in this short space, address the myriad policy issues and social, political, and economic effects of immigration, nor even the oft-debated questions of why immigrants come or if America is better for them. Each of these topics requires book-length treatment. Rather, we want to examine the particular aspect of immigration that speaks to our thesis—how immigrants are incorporated into the American political system.

We begin by revisiting the historic role of immigration as politically divisive and racialized. The rough politics surrounding immigration and immigrants today is hardly new in our historical experience. A repeated element in this political history is the perception that immigrants are sufficiently "different" from other Americans that they can never be fully incorporated. This, in turn, suggests we look at what it means to be an American (and therefore who can belong). Are there racial and ethnic differences that reflect what newcomers themselves think it means to be American? Finally, we examine the path from immigration to political participation and suggest that the full incorporation of immigrants into American society is a contested process and one that is very likely to leave lasting partisan sentiments among new Americans and to reinforce the patterns we have observed elsewhere in this book.

PLACING IMMIGRATION IN CONTEXT

Immigration and immigrants represent an interesting moment of cultural conflict and dissonance for American society. All Americans, save for Native Americans, have an immigration experience in their family history, though, clearly, the circumstances of black "migration" to the United States were coercive and not directly comparable. For white Americans there is an immigrant past that, rather than being a source of shame or merely remembrance, is romanticized and celebrated as a political or religious search for liberty or a family determined to find greater opportunity. U.S. history is full of emotional symbols of those experiences—examples include the *Mayflower,* oxcarts and wagons, Ellis Island, the Oregon Trail, and the Statue of Liberty.

Such romance, however, has usually not been extended by early arrivers to those who come later. The nineteenth century saw bitter resentment of the Irish and other Catholic immigrants. It also saw distaste for Jewish immigration and, in the late twentieth century, cultural fear of Asians and Latinos, which characterize our current debates. The rhetoric aimed at newcomers generally reflects beliefs in their cultural inferiority, belief that their core cultural characteristics were (or are) too "different" to be assimilated into American life, and an oft-repeated accusation that these new arrivals are refusing to adapt to American cultural life. Indeed, we can go all the way back to the period preceding the founding of the Republic and find the expression of anti-immigrant rhetoric, couched in cultural fear and racial terminology, from even among our most sage founding fathers who feared German immigration.

> [W]hy should the Palatine Boors be suffered to swarm into our Settlements, and by herding together establish their Language and Manners to the Exclusion of ours? Why should Pennsylvania, founded by the English, become a colony of *Aliens,* who will shortly be so numerous as to Germanize us instead of our Anglifying them, and will never adopt our Language or Customs, any more than they can acquire our Complexion.
>
> (Benjamin Franklin, 1751, "*Observations Concerning the Increase of Mankind, Peopling of Countries, etc.*")

Versions of Benjamin Franklin's fears—and his expression of them—can be found throughout U.S. history. Who expresses the fears may change, and whom they are fearful of may change, but the basic rhetoric is the same. The quote from Franklin is notable for both its stridency and its familiarity. Immigrants were "Aliens," their behavior described in animalistic terms such as "herding" and "swarm," and their differences described in both cultural terms (for instance, "Language" and "Customs") and racial ones (for example, "Complexion"). It is also worth noting that the perceptions of cultural difference were perceived to be threatening to the existing cultural mode in this society and permanent, as Franklin describes his fear that the Germans would Germanize Americans because of their refusal to fit in.

Franklin's claims represent a motif that is repeated often in U.S. history. A significant spasm of anti-immigrant sentiment occurred in the middle of the nineteenth century with the emergence of the virulently anti-immigrant and anti-Catholic Know-Nothing Party.

Anti-immigrant sentiment was also critical to the emergence of the Progressive movement for government "reform" in the early twentieth century and even played a role in the founding of the American Political Science Association (Fraga et al. 2006). The movement to "reform" cities, replacing partisan mayors with nonpartisan local elections and city managers, was an attempt to thwart the influence of immigrants who had successfully gained voice in urban political machines.

Immigration as the source of contentious politics in the United States is not a new phenomenon. Neither is the racialization of the immigration debate. For much of our history, the United States prohibited naturalization of persons who were "non-white," and, indeed, the legal history of the United States is replete with cases of persons of various groups—Jews, Arabs, Turks, South Asians, and Mexicans—suing the federal government

TABLE 11-1   Foreign-Born Population by Region of Origin, 2000 and 2008

	2008 Population	2000 Population	Percentage, 2008	Percentage, 2000
Mexico	11,451,299	9,163,463	30.1	29.4
South and East Asia	9,079,578	7,195,764	23.9	23.1
Caribbean	3,439,422	2,954,820	9.0	9.5
Central America	2,749,071	2,029,383	7.2	6.5
South America	2,555,720	1,920,007	6.7	6.2
Middle East	1,344,782	1,137,898	3.5	3.7
All others	7,406,230	6,732,146	19.5	21.6
Total	38,016,102	31,133,481	100.0	100.0

Source: Statistical Portrait of the Foreign-Born Population in the United States, 2008," Table 3. Foreign-Born, by Region of Birth: 2000 and 2008. http://pewhispanic.org/files/factsheets/foreignborn2008/Table%203.pdf.

Note: Middle East consists of Afghanistan, Algeria, Egypt, Iran, Iraq, Israel/Palestine, Jordan, Kuwait, Lebanon, Morocco, Saudi Arabia, Sudan, Syria, Turkey, and Yemen.

for the designation of "white" so as to permit naturalization (Haney López 1997). The exclusion of East Asians was accomplished in the latter part of the nineteenth century with the Quota Acts and Chinese Exclusion Acts, and as a practical matter the disadvantageous treatment of Asians in the U.S. system continued until the 1960s.

Table 11-1 reports the region of origin for America's foreign-born population. Around 44 percent come from Mexico, Central America, and South America. Another 9 percent come from the Caribbean, and over 40 percent of that number comes from the Dominican Republic and Cuba. In 2008, Latinos accounted for just shy of half of all immigrants. East and South Asia accounted for another 24 percent, and the non-Spanish-speaking Caribbean, overwhelmingly English- and Creole-speaking Afro-Caribbean persons, accounted for another 4.5 percent (half of the 9 percent figure reported). The Middle East contributed another 3.5 percent and the remaining 20 percent encompass the rest of the world, including Europe, Canada, Australia, New Zealand, and Africa (exclusive of "Middle East" countries). America's immigrant population is, in short, overwhelmingly non-white.

Figure 11-1 places this very non-white distribution in context by comparing it to an earlier era in American history. The figure illustrates the significant change in the racial distribution of immigrants to the United States since the reopening of significant immigration in the mid-1960s. Whereas, historically, Canadians and Europeans constituted a significant share of immigrants, today Asians and Latin Americans are now a huge majority. We also have among the

FIGURE 11-1   **Immigrants by Place of Origin, 1960–2008**

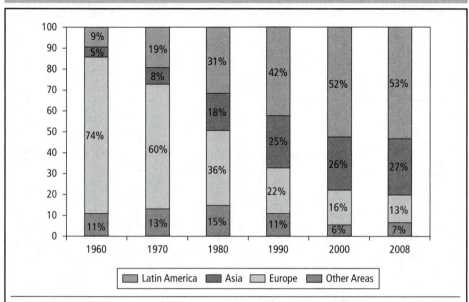

Sources: William L. Kandel, *The U.S. Foreign-Born Population: Trends and Selected Characteristics* (Washington, D.C.: Congressional Research Service, 7-5700, www.crs.gov R41592, 2011); U.S. Census Bureau, "Profile of the Foreign-Born Population in the United States: 2000, 2001," 11; and CRS presentation of 2008 American Community Survey data.

highest percentages of immigrants speaking one language (Spanish, 45 percent) and from one country (Mexico, 33 percent) in our history. The racial diversification of immigration to the United States, coupled with the size and cultural force of Mexican and other Spanish-speaking persons, is fundamental in the activation of both racial threat and cultural fear so often reflected in the rhetoric.

Immigration has also a newfound salience in contemporary politics that was absent for most of the past century. Widespread familiarity with the immigration experience, once such a large part of our national life, declined dramatically after the closing of Ellis Island in the early 1920s. For much of the rest of the twentieth century the raw number of immigrants, and immigrants as a share of the overall U.S. population, declined precipitously. Since 1970, however, immigration has increased to the point where the raw number of immigrants is at a historic high while immigrants as a percentage of our population are rapidly approaching the historically high levels found pre-1920. These trends are reflected in Figure 11-2.

A quick examination of Figure 11-2 suggests that an America with few immigrants is a historical rarity; that is, the low salience of immigration in the

FIGURE 11-2   **Total U.S. Population and Size and Share of U.S. Foreign-Born Population, 1850–2008**

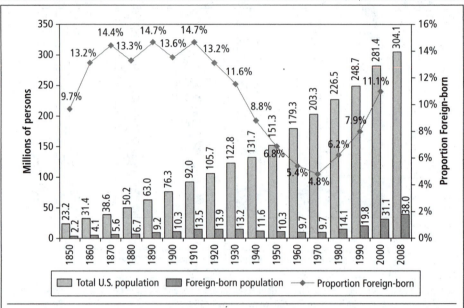

Sources: William L. Kandel, *The U.S. Foreign-Born Population: Trends and Selected Characteristics* (Washington, D.C.: Congressional Research Service, 7-5700, www.crs.gov R41592, 2011); U.S. Department of Commerce, Bureau of the Census, *1949 Historical Statistics of the United States, 1789–1945*, Series B 182-194 (1850–1890); 1960 Statistical Abstract, Population Section, Table 29 (1900–1950); 2000 Statistical Abstract, Population Section, Table 46 (1960–1990); 2003 Statistical Abstract, Population Section, Table 48 (2000); and *American Factfinder*, 2008 ACS data (2008).

middle of the twentieth century should be understood as the exception rather than the norm. Nevertheless, an America with few immigrants was the norm for most decision makers in American society during their formative years.

The geographic distribution of immigrants is also widespread. In 2010 there were six states with over 1.7 million foreign-born persons and thirty-seven states with more than 100,000 immigrants. This dispersion represents a fairly swift change. In 1990 only four states had populations over 1 million and only twenty-three states had more than 100,000. In 1990 fewer than 20 million immigrants resided in the United States. In 2010 the number was around 40 million. The earlier concentration of immigrants in few states and the atypically low level of immigration in the middle of the twentieth century created an environment in which many Americans older than thirty-five or so, and most Americans in nonborder and noncoastal states, had little direct experience with immigration and its social effects. That is no longer the case today. Table 11-2 reports the top ten states in terms of immigrant population.

TABLE 11-2   Top 10 States: Immigrant Populations, 2009

State	Raw population	% population
California	9,946,758	26.9
New York	4,178,170	21.4
Texas	3,985,239	16.1
Florida	3,484,141	18.8
New Jersey	1,759,467	20.2
Illinois	1,740,763	13.5
Massachusetts	943,335	14.3
Arizona	925,376	14.0
Georgia	920,381	9.4
Washington	810,637	12.2

Source: Data taken from the Migration Policy Institute; 2009 estimates are based on the U.S. Census Bureau's American Community Surveys.

Latino immigration dispersion is the biggest driver of the overall distribution of immigrants by state. For example, the top states reported in Table 11-2 are also the top states for Latino immigrants. Asian immigrants are distributed somewhat differently, as we illustrate in Table 11-3. While several of the top states overlap, Asian immigrants are also concentrated in states such as Michigan and Virginia while not as prevalent in, for instance, Arizona.

TABLE 11-3   Top 10 States: Foreign-Born Asian Population, 2009

State	Raw population (in 1,000s)	State's share of national Asian immigrant population
California	3,489	32.8
New York	1,102	10.3
Texas	702	6.6
New Jersey	548	5.1
Illinois	449	4.2
Florida	347	3.3
Virginia	334	3.1
Washington	316	3.0
Michigan	279	2.6
Massachusetts	260	2.4

Source: U.S. Census Bureau, American Community Survey, 2009.

As a political issue, immigration is complex. For example, not everyone on the left supports high levels of immigration or favors immigrant rights. While liberals certainly have an ideological commitment to sympathize with poor workers trying to better themselves, organized labor has historically been concerned by the downward pressure immigrants may place on wages. As the supply of labor increased, and as the willingness of immigrants to tolerate seemingly intolerable work conditions grew, immigration was seen as an obstacle to economic mobility and improved conditions for workers. There are also voices on the left that see immigration as posing problems for natural resource management and sustainability, as illustrated in a controversial anti-immigrant stance taken by the Sierra Club in the 1990s. Even when we consider attitudes by race, other complexities emerge. African Americans, for example, have been much more ambivalent about the value of immigration than have many other groups.

On the other hand, immigrant—particularly Latino—movement into organized labor has, to a significant degree, reversed the historical pattern among organized labor. As the fastest-growing segment of the labor movement, immigrant Latinos represent new opportunities to organize.

For the very same historical reasons that labor opposed high levels of immigration, many business owners (notably in agriculture and services) were historically more supportive of immigration, occasionally favoring amnesties and work permit programs that allow them to keep the costs of production low. Immigration, in large measure, made the Industrial Revolution possible. Today, immigrants make up a huge portion of the agricultural, food-processing, hospitality, and construction workforces.

While capital historically favored higher immigration levels (immigrants provide inexpensive labor), the right has also come to be divided over the issue. On the right, the division has largely been driven by cultural fears and the racial composition of the immigrant population. There are also voices on both left and right whose views on immigration are driven by a genuine commitment to the idea of the rule of law. The objection is, ostensibly, not to immigration or immigrants but to illegal/undocumented immigrants of all origins because they violate the law.

In short, the politics of immigration inculcates racial sentiments, ethnocentric cultural fears, divided economic interests, and between-group competition. These elements make the issue uniquely hard for the political process to address, as party leaders face a host of conflicting demands from party constituencies, and always with an eye on what sort of politics the immigrant might engage in once he or she is a full member of our society.

IMMIGRATION AND CULTURAL POLITICS

In large measure immigration and its attendant issues of legal status, naturalization, assimilation, and language policy are largely missing from the black experience, at least until very recently. By contrast, they have profound effects on the political incorporation and political experiences of both Latinos and Asian Americans (Ramakrishnan 2005). Immigrants begin their presence in American society as noncitizens, which complicates their claim to inclusion in the American polity and on societal resources—even after naturalization. For example, racial hostility toward Latinos and Asians can be couched in anti-immigrant language. Immigration can be cast as a law and order issue not an expressly racial one. If immigrants are cast as lawbreakers and somehow alien to the home society, they may, therefore, not be entitled to its protections. There are countless examples of this approach, most notably the anti-immigrant and English-only laws (Schmidt 2000) and ballot propositions that have proliferated across the states. Proposition 187 in California, which prohibited the provision of state services—including education and health care—to undocumented aliens, also allowed state workers to withhold services to applicants *suspected* of being undocumented. While the basis of such suspicion was left unclear in the legislation, Latino activists logically concluded that apparent ethnic identity would be the most likely candidate (Sierra et al. 2000). This pattern was replicated, most recently, in the adoption of SB 1070 in Arizona, a law that was also ostensibly directed at undocumented immigration. In Arizona today, just as in California in the mid-1990s, these policies are widely perceived by Latino citizens as a racialized attack.

The recency of most Asian American and Latino immigration raises questions of whether these populations represent threats to American national identity (Huntington 2004). Immigrants, the argument goes, neither speak the language nor wish to learn, and they do not subscribe to political, social, and even religious norms that are deeply constitutive of the national culture and have contributed to the national success. As such, their presence and rapid increase threaten to undermine national consensus and commitment to these norms and, by extension, the economic, military, and social achievements that followed upon them.

Such a charge is more difficult to raise against African Americans, whose presence in the cultural fabric dates back to before the founding and who cannot be described as newcomers. This is not to say that no such charges are ever leveled at African Americans. For example, Kinder and Sanders (1996) have recounted how anti-black bias may masquerade as a defense of "American values," including individualism and self-reliance, that, they suggest, some whites believe African Americans do not share, a claim we addressed directly in Chapter 10. Nevertheless, immigrant populations are uniquely vulnerable to suspicions that they constitute an inassimilable "other." In his book *Who Are We? The Challenges to America's National Identity* (2004), Samuel Huntington sees immigration, and in particular Latino immigration, as a threat to traditional American cultural values. He sees American culture and U.S. political traditions as defined by Protestantism and the English language. Latin American immigrants, he contends, do not share American cultural values and have resisted assimilation. They compare unfavorably to past waves of immigration in their steadfast refusal to adapt to the Anglo-Protestant culture.

BOX 11-1   Arizona SB 1070

In the spring of 2010, Arizona governor Jan Brewer signed into law SB 1070, a state-level attempt to regulate immigration by making undocumented status a crime under Arizona law and empowering the police to stop and detain anyone they "suspected" of being undocumented. Immigrants were required by the law to carry their documents with them at all times and to produce them on demand.

The law was greeted by Latino advocates and their allies with tremendous outcry. Latino voters in Arizona overwhelmingly opposed the law, across all generations, as we report in Figure 11-3. There were national efforts at boycotting Arizona and its businesses, moving the Major League Baseball All-Star Game, and lawsuits from private advocacy groups such as the Mexican American Legal Defense and Education Fund and from the Department of Justice. Parts of the law were enjoined from enforcement by the federal courts.

Why the outcry? Since there is good evidence that undocumented aliens compete for jobs with and affect the wages primarily of other Latinos (Borjas 1990; Hanson 2002), we could imagine that the law would enjoy greater support. But Latino voters in Arizona, like those in California after Proposition 187 passed, believed that the law would be used to harass them. In fact, 72 percent of those voters felt certain that racial and ethnic identity would be the basis of police "suspicion," and 85 percent felt it likely that U.S. citizens and legal residents would be caught up in that enforcement. Figures 11-4 and 11-5 illustrate that point.

Finally, when asked if the law had an implicitly racial component, Latino voters offered a resounding yes. As illustrated in Figure 11-6, an overwhelming majority of 76 percent of Latino registered voters felt that the law would never have been adopted if most immigrants were Europeans.

It is important to remember that the figures we report here are taken from a survey of registered voters conducted the weekend after the bill was signed into law. Voters are citizens

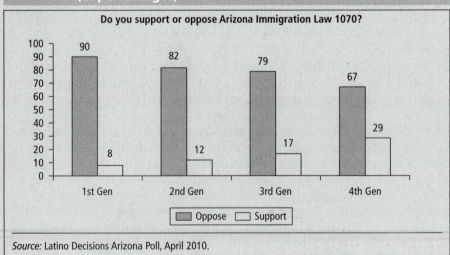

FIGURE 11-3   **Latino Citizen Opinion on SB 1070, by Generation (in percentages)**

Source: Latino Decisions Arizona Poll, April 2010.

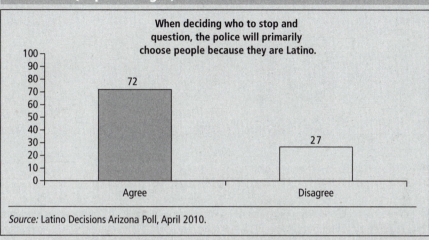

FIGURE 11-4 **Will SB 1070 Be Enforced through Racial Profiling? (in percentages)**

When deciding who to stop and question, the police will primarily choose people because they are Latino.

Agree: 72
Disagree: 27

Source: Latino Decisions Arizona Poll, April 2010.

secure in their constitutional rights. The law did not target them. Yet they felt threatened by its presence, believed citizens would be affected, thought race was both the motive and the method of enforcement, and held the Republicans responsible. When asked which party was responsible for the law, 59 percent said that Republicans were responsible but only 2 percent

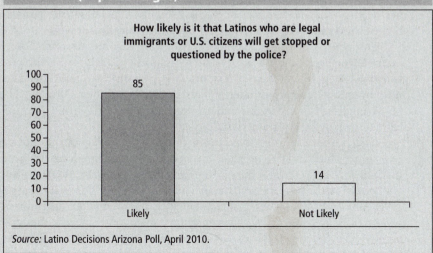

FIGURE 11-5 **Will SB 1070 Affect Citizens and Legal Immigrants? (in percentages)**

How likely is it that Latinos who are legal immigrants or U.S. citizens will get stopped or questioned by the police?

Likely: 85
Not Likely: 14

Source: Latino Decisions Arizona Poll, April 2010.

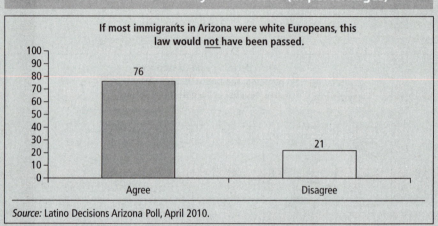

FIGURE 11-6   **Was SB 1070 Racially Motivated? (in percentages)**

If most immigrants in Arizona were white Europeans, this law would not have been passed.

Source: Latino Decisions Arizona Poll, April 2010.

held Democrats responsible. Almost one-third of all respondents held "both parties" responsible, suggesting Latino patience with Democratic inaction on immigration was running low. It is difficult to imagine that the passage of SB 1070, its provisions, and the Latino electorate's reaction will not have a significant effect on partisanship and the two-party vote in the coming era.

Nowhere is this argument regarding immigrant cultural threat more clearly played out than in the language debates. Huntington's argument today represents a fairly widely held belief regarding immigration, and the response has been significant backlash in language politics, including the passage of English-only laws and the abolition of bilingual education programs.

The politics of cultural conflict can quickly become personal. Take, for example, Joe Vento, the owner of Geno's Steaks in Philadelphia. "Vento posted two small signs in October 2005 at his shop in a diverse South Philadelphia neighborhood, telling customers, "This is America: When Ordering please Speak English."[2] Similarly, a Flushing, New York, geriatric facility banned its Haitian employees from speaking Creole.[3]

Evidence for claims such as Huntington's—that immigrants do not share American values and are resisting incorporation into American culture and tradition—is largely, or in some cases entirely, missing (Segura 2005). A substantial body of research in political science and sociology (see Portes and Rumbaut 1996; Alba and Nee 2003; Ramakrishnan 2005; and Wong 2006) examined the process of assimilation and social integration among contemporary immigrants, both on its own terms and with specific reference to political action. While each

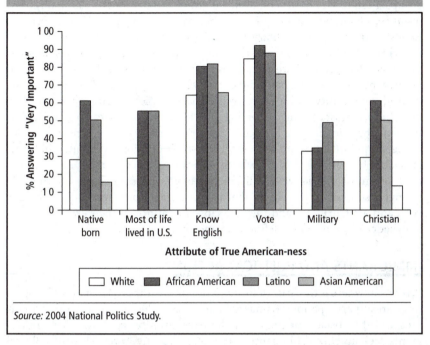

FIGURE 11-7 **Belief in Defining Characteristics of Being "Truly American," by Race and Ethnicity, 2004**

Source: 2004 National Politics Study.

offers a unique and important take on the immigrant experience in this era, collectively they portray a process of incorporation that is far more complex than the false dichotomy of straight-line assimilation on the one hand or long-maintained separatism, as Huntington feared, on the other. Rather, the immigrant experience needs to be understood as one that varies considerably across generations, racial groups, and national origin groups, in part as a consequence of the unique national histories of donor countries, in part due to the patterns and constancy of immigrant flow into the United States, and, importantly, in large part driven by the social, economic, and political conditions faced upon arrival (Fraga and Segura 2006).

But like Huntington, Americans can and do hold beliefs about what constitutes "true" American identity. We look, again, to the data to evaluate what Americans think being an American is all about. In 2004 the National Politics Study asked Americans from all social backgrounds the degree to which each of the following was part of their definition of what a true American is: being born in the United States; living most of your life here; knowing how to speak English; voting; serving in the military; and being a Christian. The results are presented in Figure 11-7.

Support for each of those characteristics varied considerably, but voting and knowing English were attributes that attracted the most support across groups. Results vary quite a bit between groups, sometimes in telling ways. For instance, a far greater share of Latinos believe that being native born, speaking English, serving in the military, and being Christian are key components of American identity than do non-Hispanic whites, despite the obvious observation that a far greater share of Latinos were not born in the United States, did not live most of their life here, and do not know English well. This immigrant-derived community had a more restrictive definition of *American-ness* than did whites, almost certainly reflecting their belief that in the eyes of their countrymen, they do not yet meet the definition. Yet, Asian Americans do not appear to hold these more narrow views—their opinions were often indistinguishable from those held by whites. African Americans, most interestingly, held the most restrictive definition of *American-ness* overall, offering the strongest support to the claims that true Americans are born here, live here, vote, and are Christian, and they are close to Latinos in their enthusiasm for knowledge of English as a defining characteristic.

IMMIGRANTS AND POLITICAL ACTION

Perhaps nowhere is the issue of immigration more important than with respect to political participation (Ramakrishnan 2005). The ineligibility of non-citizens and the obstacle presented by the naturalization process to legal immigrants seeking citizenship contribute to significantly lower levels of political mobilization. Even among those who have successfully naturalized, new citizens have generally been found to turn out to vote far less often than other Americans (DeSipio 1996), further undercutting the political impact of Asian American and Latino political preferences.

Low rates of political participation among immigrants can be attributed, at least in part, to their resource disadvantages, particularly with respect to socioeconomic resources and political information. Newcomers often find themselves near the bottom of the economic ladder, and the absence of income, time, and most importantly education handicap them in any effort to gather and act on useful political information. In an alternative view, Tam Cho (1999) has argued that what is at issue is really the political socialization of new citizens. Socioeconomic resources, while critical, are brought to bear with only the appropriate norms of political participation. Foreign-born persons, particularly those whose formal education took place outside of the United States, may not have accumulated sufficient political information, nor acquired the social expectations, necessary to turn resources into action.

Some more recent work (Pantoja et al. 2001; Barreto et al. 2005a and 2005b) has found unusually high turnout among the newly naturalized, particularly Mexican Americans, in the wake of ethnically targeted ballot initiatives in California and elsewhere. In some instances, newly naturalized Latino voters voted at rates exceeding those of both native-born Latinos and groups with historically high rates of turnout, particularly middle-class non-Hispanic whites. It is not yet clear if this phenomenon represents a permanent shift or can be generalized beyond locales where Latino immigrants perceive themselves to have been targeted.

Complicating this analysis is the observation, for which there is a growing body of evidence, that the determinants of political behavior are not the same for these immigrant populations as they are for other Americans, African Americans included. For example, Alvarez and Garcia Bedolla (2003) find that models of partisanship vary significantly across groups. Hajnal and Lee (2011) go further and suggest that existing models of partisanship do not work well in understanding the relationship between Asian and Latino immigrants and the two major parties. Beyond partisanship, both Lien (1994) and Leighley and Vedlitz (1999) are persuasive that models of political participation vary as well. Santoro and Segura (2011) suggest that even types of political participation will vary substantially across generation, with voting probability increasing in a nearly linear fashion across generations, whereas the probability of more group-based action—after initially increasing between the foreign born and the first-generation U.S. born—actually declines among third- and fourth-generation Latinos.

It is indisputably the case that immigration and national origin have meaningful political effects among both Asian Americans and Latinos, in terms of political attitudes, participation, enfranchisement, and policy challenges. Moreover, the very issue of immigration serves as an important context that frames the entire political environment of both groups.

BLACK IMMIGRATION

These social realities are not accounted for—and logically should not have been—in the study of African Americans, at least until very recently (Rogers 2001). The extension of findings regarding African American politics to other minority groups, we suggest, is severely constrained by this key distinction.

One curious development has been the emergence of a black immigrant population. This population is very new, small, and very segmented. It includes persons of African origin who have immigrated to the United States, as well as Afro-Caribbean populations from English-, French-, and Spanish-speaking island nations.

Although far smaller than the Asian and Latino immigrant population, black migration to the United States represents a new wrinkle in the politics of immigration and adds a new complication to our understanding of black identity and its meaning. Early evidence suggests that relations between black immigrants and African Americans are at the very least complicated and to some degree occasionally distant and conflictual (Rogers 2006).

Figures 11-8 and 11-9 illustrate the growth of black immigrants as a phenomenon in U.S. society. African immigration is small compared with Latin and Asian immigration, but it is growing. In the late 1980s only about 25,000 African immigrants entered the United States annually, a number that climbed to almost 60,000 by the early 2000s. As with other immigrants before them,

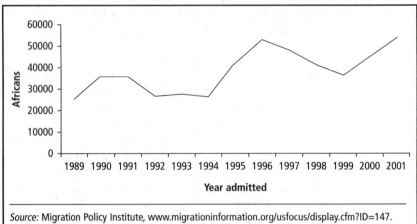

FIGURE 11-8 **African Immigration to the U.S. by Year, 1989–2001**

Source: Migration Policy Institute, www.migrationinformation.org/usfocus/display.cfm?ID=147.

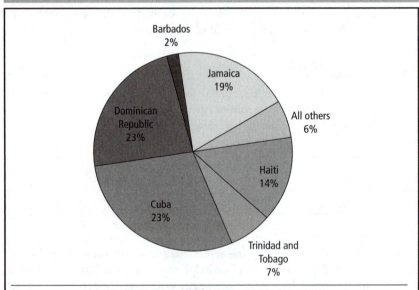

FIGURE 11-9 **Caribbean-Born Population in the U.S. by Country of Origin, 2000**

Sources: U.S. Census Bureau. Census 2000 and Julia Gelatt and David Dixon. 2006. "Detailed Characteristics of the Caribbean-Born in the United States." Migration Policy Institute, www .migrationinformation.org/usfocus/display.cfm?ID=408.

Note: Other Caribbean countries includes those reporting their birthplace as Dominica, St. Lucia, St. Kitts-Nevis, Montserrat, Aruba, the Netherlands Antilles, the Cayman Islands, the British Virgin Islands, Guadeloupe, Turks and Caicos Islands, Martinique, Anguilla, the West Indies, and St. Barthelemy.

TABLE 11-4 Metropolitan Areas with Largest African-Born Population

Metropolitan area	African-born population	African % of total	African % of foreign-born	Share of U.S. African population
New York, NY	99,126	1.06	3.16	11.25
Washington, DC-MD-VA-WV	93,271	1.89	11.21	10.58
Los Angeles-Long Beach, CA	43,024	0.45	1.25	4.88
Atlanta, GA	36,645	0.89	8.7	4.16
Minneapolis-St. Paul, MN-WI	30,388	1.02	14.4	3.45
Boston, MA-NH	29,475	0.87	5.80	3.34
Houston, TX	26,266	0.63	3.07	2.98
Chicago, IL	23,355	0.28	1.64	2.65
Dallas, TX	20,975	0.60	3.55	2.38
Philadelphia, PA-NJ	20,391	0.40	5.71	2.31

Sources: 2000 census and Migration Policy Institute, www.migrationinformation.org/usfocus/display.cfm?ID=147.

their settlement patterns are clustered. The 2000 census estimated a total population near 880,000, and today that number is well above 1 million. But they are present in relatively high concentrations in a few major cities, reported in Table 11-4. In Minneapolis, African immigrants have reached as much as 15 percent of the black population.

Afro-Caribbean immigrants are a much larger group, approaching 3 million in the 2000 census and around 3.5 million as of today. But Figure 11-9, which shows the country of origin, also illustrates the remarkable diversity in this group. Over 40 percent of all Caribbean American immigrants are from the Spanish-speaking nations of Cuba and the Dominican Republic, meaning their black identity—to the extent that they embrace one—overlaps with a Latino identity as well. Jamaica, Haiti, and Trinidad and Tobago make up the lion's share of the rest.

THE PROCESS OF POLITICAL INCORPORATION

Since this book is about U.S. politics, and particularly the increasingly critical role citizens of color play in shaping its electoral future, our interest in immigration is focused most directly on political incorporation; that is, to reshape American politics, immigrants and their communities must come to regard the United States as their long-term home and U.S. politics as the place in which the decisions most key in shaping their lives and opportunities are made. How precisely does this happen? More to the point, can we identify conditions in which the process happens faster or slower, with greater or lesser success?

The process of incorporation is shaped by social, economic, and political factors. These include both institutional components—laws, structural political arrangements, and the like—as well as attitudinal components— that is, how Americans feel about immigrants, and vice versa. While they vary, institutional barriers to immigrant incorporation have been erected from time to time in several nations, including this one. These may include statutory bars to naturalization, as existed in the United States with respect to non-whites for most of the nineteenth century and to Asians for the first half of the twentieth century; multiple-generation bars to naturalization or acquired birthright, as was the case in Germany; or even "reform" efforts that thwart the accumulation of political power by newly enfranchised segments of a society under the guise of fighting corruption (Fraga et al. 2010). Even when these barriers are removed or absent, there is considerable variation in the trajectories of inclusion. And the barriers themselves almost certainly reflect the interests and views of at least some of the social and political forces at work within the receiving community—institutional impediments to immigrant incorporation arise from the behavioral and attitudinal responses that immigrants and their offspring face from the long-standing population. Although we have suggested that anti-immigrant fear and resentment are a long-standing feature of our politics and reflective of the ironic strain of xenophobia in an immigrant nation (Hofstadter 1964), the levels or intensity of that fear and resentment have varied considerably across groups and circumstances over time.

We contend that the behavioral and attitudinal factors regarding immigration will have substantial impact on where and how immigrants take their place in the American polity (Fraga et al. 2010), notwithstanding their institutional impact. Even in the complete absence of structural barriers, hostility from the receiving community (Pedraza 2010) can slow or altogether thwart progress of the individual or community from the status of "outsider" to one of "member." It is to these obstacles that we turn our attention here.

In order to understand how attitudes shape the speed and outcome of immigrant incorporation, we want to draw attention to four specific distinctions that help us to understand the process and its components. These include, first, the question of agency, or the ability to act to determine outcomes. That is, who in the relationship between immigrants and American society has the most power to shape that relationship? The second key distinction is that political incorporation happens in the social, economic, and political realms all at once with inevitable connections among and between them. A third key element is the wide variation in outcomes across individuals, communities, and cohorts (Pedraza 2010). Since the process of incorporation will occur at a different pace and with differing levels of success in different social environments, how does one know when the immigrant community has been "incorporated" fully? Is incorporation a process or an outcome?

"Agency": Who Has the Ability to Shape Outcomes?

An obvious but often overlooked observation we start with is that the process of incorporation presupposes the agency of both the immigrant population and the receiving population (Fraga and Segura 2006); both immigrants and their descendants, on the one hand, and individual members of the receiving society, on the other, play a role in shaping the process of incorporation (Pedraza 2010). Ideologically driven arguments from the left or the right frequently focus on only one to the exclusion of others. For example, the persistent exclusion of an immigrant or community from the political system is often conceptualized by advocates on the right as resulting from the personal or cultural failings of the immigrants themselves, what Hero (1992) refers to as "deficiency" claims. By contrast, observing that same exclusion, the left sees only the nefarious motives and actions of the receiving polity. Clearly both are at issue.

Immigrant participation in politics, how they see themselves as members of the society, and whether they act on their own behalf (to any effect) certainly reflect the impact of decisions made by the immigrants themselves, as well as community leaders and advocates. Choices by immigrants to avoid organized labor, to focus inward toward co-ethnics for social and economic connections, or to eschew the political process altogether will clearly slow political incorporation and the socioeconomic benefits that inhere. By contrast, entrepreneurial activities, social bonds across group boundaries, the self-recognition of the group as *part* of the "American" society, and perception of where and how political action might yield results are likely to have important returns to individual and group quality of life and well-being. The latter choices are clearly more "incorporative."

Huntington (2004) and others argue that immigrants have made poor choices. In our view, however, they are wrong to conclude that those who are excluded have made these choices for themselves.[4] In fact, immigrants often have little choice to begin with over matters that shape their relations with the rest of society. As Pedraza (2010) argues, immigrants make choices in a climate that either encourages or discourages "good" decisions. Key outcomes, such as socioeconomic mobility and the accumulation of skills, are invariably at the mercy of those who hold greater power in society: the receiving community. The decision to seek advanced education and/or training assumes the existence of quality educational institutions and meaningful access. Whether skills or education translates into economic progress also depends on the absence of discriminatory economic behavior.

Similarly, the development of an American identity among immigrant populations—a willingness to see themselves as part of our social fabric—is also limited by popular beliefs of what constitutes "American-ness" and whether these immigrants meet those standards (Smith 1997); the data we presented regarding attributes of true Americans speak a bit to this problem.

Whether immigrant political action leads to political success also depends on the willingness and desire of more established players in the political process to coalesce with these new voters. In short, the "outcomes" on each element of incorporation depend, at least in part, on decisions being made by *both* the immigrants themselves and the receiving members of the society in which they hope to claim membership.

The flaw of assuming that immigrants have a free hand to make choices is that immigrants are the weaker party. It is U.S. citizens who retain the most power in shaping outcomes and in shaping the circumstances, incentives, and choices of immigrants. One subtle illustration of this problem is the question of whether Latino immigrants and their descendants should be understood (and conceive of themselves) as a white ethnic group or a distinct racial community. Skerry (1997) suggests that political leaders for their own purposes might choose the latter, even if such a decision increases the chance of permanent social marginalization for the group in question. There is good reason to suspect that strength of in-group identification is more of a resource than an impediment (Dawson 1994), but it is surely the case that a self-conception as a permanently marginalized out-group may have real and negative consequences for social mobility.

But Skerry's argument presupposes that Latinos as a group somehow entirely control how they are viewed in society. It is as if Latino leaders could wake up one Tuesday, announce that Latinos are "white," and Latino status as a racial minority would disappear. We find this outcome very unlikely. It is the white majority that gets to define the "us" (Bonilla-Silva 2001, 2006; Smith 1997), views historically enacted into public policy (Haney López 1997). Given all we know about how race and identity are understood in society (Omi and Winant 1994; Haney López 1997), Latino opportunity for self-definition is limited. In short, whether Latinos are perceived as white will involve a great many choices, but few of those actually belong to the Latinos themselves.

A second example, directly relevant to political incorporation, comes from Huntington's (2004) examination of Latin American immigration. In recounting his view that Mexican immigrants do not and maybe cannot assimilate, he compares their circumstances to those of Puerto Ricans and Native Americans, whose distinctiveness he describes as "*in* but not fully *of* the American republic," which is "reflected in the arrangements negotiated with them" (Huntington 2004, 45–46, emphasis in the original). This analysis is completely ahistorical (Segura 2005). Neither the existence of native reservations nor the legal status of the Commonwealth of Puerto Rico really reflects any agency to speak of on behalf of the Native Americans and Puerto Ricans themselves. Rather, they live in political and social circumstances created by the American polity. Within those constraints, those communities and their members make decisions, as surely Latin American and Asian immigrants do, but the constraints are imposed, severe, and (at least in the near term) intractable.

Distinguishing among Political, Cultural, and Economic Factors

The issues surrounding immigration and immigrant experience are further complicated by ways in which different issues and problems are simultaneously shaped by politics, the economy, and the cultural and social practices in society. For example, educational opportunities, regarding beliefs about the boundaries of American identity, and even patterns of personal and residential segregation (Charles 2003) all have political aspects as well as economic and social ones (Johnson et al. 2003).

Think first about economic well-being, income, jobs, and the like. The ability of immigrants to shape their own future is driven by many factors, including their education and skill acquisition, the drain of financial resources represented by remittances to their home countries (especially to nonfamily recipients), and the important and growing influence of organized labor. As we indicated in our discussion of agency, economic decisions of whites have an important role as well, including employer preferences. Economic discrimination has an impact, as do various facets of labor market regulation and even the availability of opportunity for education, opportunities we have suggested are driven by decisions made largely by nonimmigrants.

Turning to social and cultural concerns, decisions regarding social connectedness and social capital, residential and social segregation, and transnational ties will all shape the emotional investment of immigrants in U.S. politics and the resources available for action. Immigrants who reach out, cross ethnic lines for community action, and limit transnational ties (Segura 2007) are likely to engage the U.S. system. By contrast, in-group isolation and residential self-segregation (Charles 2003), weak language accrual, and longing for a return to home country do not bode well for effective engagement.

On the part of the American majority, narrow definitions of *Americanness*, the racialization of arriving populations, and policies demanding (rather than facilitating) assimilation will affect both the attitudes of immigrants and their resources, and severely limit the ability of immigrants to imagine themselves as part of the broader American community. Perhaps no issue better reflects the two-sided nature of this process than the question of English-language acquisition and the policies addressed to this question. Bean and Tienda (1987) and Alba and Nee (1997) have long demonstrated that Latino immigrants have an English-acquisition pace on par with that of previous waves of immigrants. Recent data collection reiterates this finding, and data from the Latino National Survey illustrate not just language-acquisition progress but also the pace of assimilation and acculturation on multiple additional dimensions (Fraga et al. 2010). This pace, however, is regularly misperceived by native-born Americans whose observations are colored by the continuous flow of new arrivals that causes them to misperceive that long-term residents had not acquired the language (Jiménez 2005). Huntington (2004) repeats this misperception as an accusation regarding the unwillingness of Latin immigrants to acculturate.

These misperceptions give rise to English-only laws, either legislative enactments or ballot initiatives mandating the conduct of public business only in the English language. These laws are never accompanied by funding for English-language instruction to facilitate the insisted-on transition. Huntington also speaks nostalgically of "Americanization" efforts at the turn of the last century, without acknowledging that no such effort exists today. Since there is no sincere effort to help immigrants learn English, these laws are better understood as an expression of frustration (or worse) rather than a considered public enactment in pursuit of a rational state interest, and they may be perceived by an immigrant community as a form of resistance or exclusion.

Debate, then, over the English skills of immigrants illustrates the two-party nature of the process of immigrant incorporation. It also clearly illustrates the importance of politics and policy, even in this predominantly social process. Opportunities (and incentives) for social assimilation are shaped by electoral and policy decisions, just as assimilation shapes the future opportunities for immigrants to participate (Johnson et al. 2003).

Finally, we do need to consider politics. And in this regard there are considerable challenges that immigrants must choose to confront and negotiate. Immigrants themselves face a political socialization challenge. They must learn a political system that is likely to be very different from the one they left and contain institutional arrangements, coalitions, associations of beliefs with partisan attachments, and even deeply held norms to which they are unaccustomed.

Several important aspects of the U.S. system that they will not know are how racial and class hierarchies influence U.S. politics, the place of Latin American and Asian immigrants in those preexisting hierarchies, and how those hierarchies map to the partisan political world. Immigrants do not come to the United States with a clear or even nascent understanding of minority politics and the politics of race, and that understanding is a necessary step to engaging the parties and political establishment to pursue their interests.

An important contextual variation will shape the behavioral choices of immigrants with respect to political engagement. Are immigrants entering in a milieu with developed co-ethnic politics? Immigrants entering the U.S. political system are more likely to be engaged and far more likely to see themselves as part of the process when co-ethnic political organization and representation exist (Pantoja and Segura 2003b; Lublin and Segura 2008).[5] Ethnic political organizations can play a crucial role in the naturalization process, in English-language and civics skill acquisition, and, most importantly, in voter registration and mobilization (Ramakrishnan 2004, 2005; Lien 1994; Tam Cho 1999). Among Latinos, the naturalization efforts in the late 1980s and early 1990s of the National Association of Latino Elected Officials (NALEO) played an important role in the widespread Latino mobilization through California and beyond in the wake of the Immigration Reform and Control Act (IRCA)

(Pantoja et al. 2001). Similarly, Southwest Voter has worked for two generations to get eligible Latinos registered and turned out to vote.

Likewise, successful political engagement, including the election of Latinos to public office, appears to have a positive effect on Latino mobilization (the evidence for Asians is less clear). As we indicated in Chapter 8, co-ethnic representation has been associated with higher levels of trust and efficacy (Pantoja and Segura 2003b) as well as turnout (Pantoja et al. 2001; Barreto et al. 2004). Co-ethnicity reduces the cultural (and occasionally linguistic) barriers between the elected officials and their immigrant constituents and leads to immigrants seeing politics as the path to success, using community identification as a political resource, and assessing the overall trustworthiness of the system and their role in it.

As with the other dimensions, the receiving community, especially non-Hispanic whites, will play an important role in determining the pace and shape of the incorporative process. Incorporation will occur more quickly and fully when it is in the interest of an existing political force to do so. For example, if one of the political parties sees an opportunity for enlargement and electoral advantage in the full-scale inclusion of the immigrant community in its coalition, the party can substantially reduce the costs of incorporation and provide resources to facilitate the process. Such was a common story at the turn of the last century. By contrast, incorporation is delayed or resisted when existing forces see short-term political advantage in using this exclusion as the basis for mobilizing existing coalition partners. That is, if the interests of the new groups are inconsistent with those of the existing coalition partners, a party may have little choice but to exclude the new aspirants and work to disadvantage them in the political system (Hero 1992). In short, not all votes are equally attractive across parties, political circumstances, immigrant groups, and time.

A Variety of Outcomes

Some time ago many sociologist abandoned "straight-line" notions of social assimilation as the universally applicable model. There are some exceptions, of course, but the straight-line conceptualization suffered from three related problems. First, there was an inherent assumption that movement along a path from immigrant to "American" was unidirectional and not subject to setbacks or occasional reversals (Gans 1992; Barkan 1995). Second, the straight-line model implied a sameness of experiences and reactions across immigrants and immigrant communities. Finally, the straight-line model offered an expectation that movement on multiple dimensions—that socioeconomic, political, and social assimilation—was simultaneous. Older arguments about assimilation seemed to assume that assimilation was the same for everyone, proceeding at the same pace and in the same way. As it turns out, these assumptions often turned out to be untrue.

In rejecting these simplifying assumptions, some of the sociological literature has identified the assimilative process as "segmented," uneven in tempo and direction (Zsembik and Llanes 1996), varying considerably across dimensions of life, and varying greatly by communities and individuals (Portes and Rumbaut 1996; Portes and Zhou 1993; Rumbaut 1997; Zhou 1997). The process of incorporation into the political structure is likely to be the same; even movement toward a more successful participation, in the long run, might first be evident in an emergent ethnic pattern of identity and mobilization. Rather than a concurrent decline in ethnic attachments and increase in political participation, the reality might be far more complex and involve tradeoffs across *types* of political engagement, which, themselves, are better suited to different political environments and circumstances (Santoro and Segura 2011).

For example, the process of political adaptation and incorporation across generations may exhibit different patterns for different types of participation. Specifically, while enthusiasm among Mexican Americans for voting—and self-reported vote—increases almost linearly across the first four generations in the United States, ethnic political activity does not decline in a similar way. Rather, ethnic political activity increases across the first two generations and only then begins to decline as ethnic attachments wane (Santoro and Segura 2011). The implications of this finding are twofold. First, ethnic attachments as a politically relevant factor are learned; new arrivals do not come to the U.S. polity with any intuitive understanding of the structures of minority politics, racial beliefs, and structural inequality. Rather, ethnicity as a political cue is learned, and ethnic forms of political expression increase, not decrease, across early generations. Second, assimilative or incorporative processes do not have only a positive effect on political power. In cases where the ethnic politics model of engagement has been more successful in securing political outcomes for the group in question—and there are long-standing findings regarding ethnic organizations and grassroots strategies of power seeking (Ambrecht and Pachon 1974; Browning et al. 1984)—the movement from ethnic political action to plain old voting within a broader political coalition might reflect the incorporative process but is not clearly an immediate gain for the group in question.

The treatment of immigrant communities varies as well. For example, there appear to be distinct effects on white opinions toward immigrants based on their proximity to Asians versus Latinos. For whites, living closer to Asians raises their opinion of immigrants and fosters more liberal policy views, whereas proximity to Latinos makes whites more conservative on the same policies. By contrast, African Americans' views of immigrants gets more negative when they are more proximate to Asians, exactly the opposite of the effect among whites (Hajnal et al. 2009). This finding clearly illustrates that views vary, they vary across groups, and they vary across targets.

The overall process of political incorporation has, in our view, a clear and sustained "path" from exclusion to inclusion. That notwithstanding, we think it is fair to say that any straight-line or classic model of incorporation would face the same critiques and inconsistencies as the similar approach to assimilation. We are better served to expect that the path to political incorporation is neither straight nor free of obstacles and setbacks, and the pace at which immigrants and/or immigrant communities find themselves fully functioning in the political system—or at least functioning at the same level as other Americans—will vary considerably.

When is Incorporation Complete?

When might we say that an immigrant or immigrant community has been politically incorporated? The very question involves an outcome focus that somewhat misses the complexity of a process that is uneven across individuals and communities, as we just illustrated. Moreover, this conceptualization of incorporation as an outcome—one either is or is not "incorporated"—more or less presupposes that native-born Americans are, themselves, fully incorporated. Under this conceptualization, immigrants and their communities are incorporated when they are just like all other Americans.

We take issue with this view. Circumstances of marginality, exclusion, the barriers to participation, and hostility by the majority are characteristics of at least parts of other groups in American society, including racial and ethnic minorities born into the United States, as well as gays and lesbians, women, the poor, and others. This is not to say that neither individuals within those groups nor any parts of those communities are politically incorporated. Rather, we suggest that along with the unevenness of outcomes within groups, we are better served to conceive of incorporation as a continuum and a process instead of a (false) dichotomy between assimilated and nonassimilated.

For our purposes, an immigrant or an immigrant community is more "incorporated" into the American polity, by which we mean the process has advanced sufficiently, when three conditions are met. First, the individual or a significant share of the community must feel that the American polity is the one to which they belong and that politics is an effective vehicle for achieving life goals. A deeply held sense of alienation, or the belief that politics is disconnected from life outcomes, is evidence both that incorporation has not occurred and that it may not occur anytime soon.

Second, the immigrant or the community must have sufficient educational, social, and economic resources to pursue their preferences through political action. This is not to say that their resource base must be as large or as slack as those of native-born Americans, only that there are *some* resources available for dedication to politics. Groups and individuals with greater resources devoted to securing their interests could be understood as more incorporated than those with less, other things being equal.

Finally, immigrant incorporation at the individual or community level has progressed further when attitudes of born (primarily white) citizens are not uniformly hostile to political engagement on the part of the immigrant; that is, at least some reasonable share of Americans views the incorporation of immigrants as legitimate and their association as political coalition partners as desirable. By contrast, delegitimization of immigrant participation, or uniform refusal to engage in coalitional or cooperative politics with them by a broad cross section of political actors, signals an incomplete incorporative process and much further to go.

SUMMARY

The take-away lesson from this chapter is that the process of political incorporation is, in the last analysis, political. Incorporation is a contested process,
involving competing interests making sometimes-contradictory claims on
resources and the attention of legislators, with varying results.

If we proceed from the normative assumption that the incorporation of
immigrants is "good," that new members of this or any society "should" be
brought into the political system, we have already missed a great part of the
politics. Not every individual member or collective political force in this (or
any) society sees the political incorporation of immigrants as a normative
good, or even as neutral. Objections can run the gamut from economic threat
to cultural fear to old- and new-style racism, complete with unsubstantiated
empirical claims and more bread-and-butter allocation decisions. As de la
Garza and his colleagues illustrated years ago (1996), the fear of immigrants
can often be based on empirical understandings that not only are wrong but
also are, in fact, an inversion of the actual relationships. In their instance, the
subject was "American" values, and the data suggested that those values were
held more tightly and in higher regard by the immigrants themselves than by
the white Americans among whom they were living. Empirical evidence notwithstanding, the expression of cultural threat lives on.

Of course, if there are forces opposed to incorporation, surely there are
individuals and groups, apart from the immigrants themselves, who would
benefit from the process. This too is more likely than not to be political, though
the role of immediate economic benefit, lower labor costs, and even socioreli-
gious affinity should not be underestimated. Here, again, the connections
between political and ostensibly nonpolitical incentives are apparent.

Our hope in this chapter was to illustrate the complexity associated with the
simple question of how immigrants and their descendants become, in a meaningful political sense, American. We have suggested here four claims: that the actions
that matter are not just those of immigrants but also (perhaps more so) those of
the American people; that incorporation involves economic, social, and political
factors and that these processes overlap considerably; that there is and will always
be a variation of outcomes; and that the end-point, the conclusion of this process,
is not easy to define or recognize, inviting a comparative assessment of immigrant
and native political circumstances, rather than an absolute "pronouncement."

Thinking more broadly, the politics of immigration will have a great deal to
say about how new Americans, overwhelmingly Asian and Latino, will view the
political system and the actors in it. Hostile reactions to immigration will inevitably shape views of the newly naturalized—indeed, may shape how many people actually do naturalize—and appear likely also to shape the propensity of new
Americans to participate in politics. While anti-immigrant politics might have
immediate political benefit by appealing to the long-standing dislike of immigrants in the American tradition, the long run looks to be less advantageous.
Rather, a swell of new Americans will enter the system skeptical of its benefits,
with mixed enthusiasm for participation, and with a significant partisan skew.

12

Intergroup Conflict and Cooperation[*]

A central argument in this book has been that minority citizens are positioned to shape the future of American partisan and electoral politics. Minority political preferences will provide the driving force in the balance of power between the parties. One possibility is that growing minority electorates, firmly connected to Democratic identification and vote, will yield long-term electoral gains for a Democratic Party that will rely ever more heavily on the minority vote. On the other hand, minority political diversification, coupled with persistent white preference for the GOP, could spell a long and lonely exile from power for Democrats.

These two options frame minority politics in terms of their relationship to whites. And in many ways this is how minority politics has long been cast. Throughout the nineteenth and much of the twentieth century, the frame was one of African American challenge to white racism, restriction, and reaction. The changing demographics of the United States mean that the simple frame is no longer the only way of seeing minority politics. In this chapter we consider one aspect of that change: America's growing diversity means that political relations no longer concern just two groups (blacks and whites) but are now multiracial. In this multiracial political context the questions of intergroup relations and intergroup coalitions become much more complex. This chapter considers intergroup relations in more detail. We begin by outlining the importance of building coalitions in politics.

COALITION BUILDING

The need to build coalitions is a fundamental part of politics. It is especially easy to see when it comes to political parties. All parties in a system such as the one in the United States are actually coalitions of political forces, where individual constituency groups see sufficient common purpose or governing beliefs that they can unite behind a set of candidates. All coalitions are subject to occasional strain when interests diverge, and the coalitions underpinning

---

*Portions of this chapter were adapted from Segura, Gary M., and Helena Alves Rodrigues. 2006. "Comparative Ethnic Politics in the United States: Beyond Black and White." *Annual Review of Political Science,* 9:375–395.

the Republican and Democratic Parties are no exception. Party success depends on the ability of the party's governing elites to maintain common purpose and enthusiasm among the constituency groups, and the emergence of a competitive or conflictual relationship between two constituency groups can be deeply problematic for the continued success of the coalition.

Modern-day coverage of elections stresses how political parties build coalitions in terms of their need to piece together blocs of voters in order to win. A party may aim to piece together a coalition across states (the "southern strategy") or across demographic groups ("soccer moms" and "NASCAR dads") or across opinion groups (Evangelicals and gun owners) or across racial and ethnic groups or some combination of demographic and opinion groups. The idea is to build together a group of supporters (a coalition) that is large enough to win an election or a vote in a legislature. In the past, U.S. political parties have used such terms as *Rainbow Coalition* or *Big Tent* to describe the resulting coalition. Social and ethnic divisions have often been the basis of coalitional politics in electoral terms throughout U.S. history. In the nineteenth century there were disputes between native-born Americans and recent immigrants that often involved political disagreements between White Anglo-Saxon Protestants (WASPs) and Catholics. In more modern times the divisions might refer to building a coalition of "the black vote" and/or "the Jewish vote" or other phrases familiar from television coverage. Take, for example, this discussion of some of Hillary Clinton's wins in the primary election in May 2008 from CNN in terms of demographic building blocks.[1]

> Clinton's largest margins, as expected, were registered among voters at the lower end of the socioeconomic ladder. Among white voters without a college degree, Clinton defeated Obama by 50 points. Among white voters making less than $30,000 a year, Clinton's margin of victory was more than 60 points.
>
> Older voters and white women—part of Clinton's core constituency—also rallied strongly to her beleaguered campaign.[2]

Whatever the identity of the group—black, white, blue collar, Evangelical, Southern, union, women, or any other kind of identifiable sociodemographic or opinion bloc—and whatever the kind of election or political contest at stake, the underlying idea is the same: there is a need to make friends in order to win.

Coalitional arrangements can be of two different kinds depending on how long lasting they are. There might be more or less permanent relations between groups. These are often seen inside political parties or social movements that build ties across different blocs. There are also more temporary arrangements. These temporary coalitions might be built to help win on a single piece of legislation or candidate, and once the election or the vote is over, there is no more need for the coalition and it disappears. Perhaps the coalition was intended to be long lasting but disagreements among the members meant it fell apart. We might think of these kinds of temporary agreements, or at least the ones that are intended to be temporary, more as alliances than coalitions, but the idea is the same: majorities are built, not given.

While the idea of building electoral coalitions is familiar to anyone who has seen even a little TV coverage at election time, we do want to emphasize that coalition building does not apply to just U.S. national elections and no other kind of political setting. The process of building a coalition is a fundamental part of any political process, whether it is in a city, a school board, or a social organization. For example, within a city we may still talk of racial and ethnic coalitions, but the categorizations may become finer grained. In an earlier era, in Chicago and other major cities, we used to end up talking about the Polish vote or the Irish vote rather than the "white" vote. Similarly if we are talking about an Asian American or Latino coalition, there may well be a need to build bridges across different national origins (the Vietnamese and the Cambodian vote, say). Whatever the group, the basic process is the same: at some point all political actors face the need to build a coalition in order to win. There is no necessary reason why racial and ethnic minorities will always and everywhere be in an opinion or voting minority. In fact, the whole idea of coalition building is that it allows opinion minorities to become opinion majorities. Coalition building is particularly important for groups that are in an opinion minority and look set to be so for a long time. For example, the work of Aoki and Nakanishi (2001) can be read as arguing that because Asian Americans are a minority even among other minorities, they have to pursue coalition building either across different national origins or between Asian Americans and other groups.

We can see these coalitions at work in city politics, where the blocs that form in national elections may not always apply. Los Angeles is a much-studied example of city politics at work. It is studied in part because it is a big city but also because it is an example of a city that shows different ethnic coalitions rising and falling. Many U.S. localities historically saw politics that involved two groups (in the South the pair being African American and Anglo; in the Southwest, Hispanic and Anglo; and in pockets of the Northwest and the Bay Area it is Asian American and Anglo), but Los Angeles represents a city that is black, brown, and white with substantial Asian American communities. New York and Chicago also show multiethnic politics and, increasingly, cities in the South will see that happen as Latino immigration changes the racial and ethnic balance of that region. Because LA has been at the forefront of general demographic trends, however, different combinations of racial coalitions may develop. Raphael Sonenshein's (1986, 1989) longtime study of coalitional politics in the city shows how coalitions have formed and failed.

For many years the city was run by mayors whose base coalition was of African Americans (predominantly located in South Central, a favorite location for movies) and a heavily Jewish area in the city's Westside. This black–liberal white coalition underpinned the election of the city's first African American mayor—Tom Bradley—and lasted until the mid-1990s, when Richard Riordan, a Republican, defeated the old Bradley coalition by knitting together moderates, the city's business community, and San Fernando Valley Republicans.

The success of Riordan's center-right coalition was short lived in the face of resurgent Democratic and minority communities. But the Bradley coalition was not re-created in the manner it had ruled the city. In two consecutive elections, in 2001 and 2005, that coalition became unsettled and eventually a new winner emerged—Antonio Villaraigosa—a Latino in a city whose East Side had long been predominantly Latino and whose Latino population had increased dramatically, largely as a result of immigration.

In the 2001 election, an Anglo candidate, James Hahn, won the election with an odd constituency—the vestiges of the old coalition of blacks and some liberal whites, in temporary alliance with the conservative white Republicans, who preferred Hahn to the alternative: a liberal Latino. Villaraigosa lost in the general election that year after having placed first in the primary, and his emerging coalition of Latino and white liberal voters was not enough to unseat the temporary coalition of liberal African Americans and conservative whites. By 2005, however, the situation had changed. Hahn had taken the steps of firing a popular black police chief (Bernard Parks), splitting African Americans away from the coalition that elected him. In the 2005 primary, these splits allowed Villaraigosa to win the primary, move on to the general election, and win that election with a multiethnic coalition that echoed the original Bradley coalition with a new group at the top—Latinos.

The example of Los Angeles shows that coalitions can be surprisingly fragile. Even long-term coalitions can fall apart. Coalitions of convenience, such as African Americans and white Republicans, are even less likely to endure. When coalitions fracture, there is a chance for other coalitions to take their place—a point we return to in the conclusion of this chapter.

MINORITY VOTERS AND THE DEMOCRATIC COALITION

Minority racial and ethnic groups in the United States can, to a greater or lesser extent, be understood as members of the Democratic coalition. This coalition is a more or less "permanent" (as opposed to temporary or single-issue) coalition that also includes many environmental groups, trade unions, gays and lesbians, ideological liberals, and others. To the extent that minority groups share goals, preferences, and choice of candidates, they are a powerful resource for Democratic electability. Should, however, two or more of these groups come to regard the others as "rivals," competitors, or even political opponents, the rosy electoral future potentially foretold by a growing minority population would be considerably less promising.

What is the nature of intergroup relations in America? What is the future? Are Latinos and African Americans likely to emerge as two players on the same political team, or will their relationship prove more complex? Are Asian Americans likely to be partners or opponents in rainbow coalition efforts? These questions are central to this chapter and to the claims of the entire book.

RACIAL CONFLICT AND POLITICAL EFFECTS

There is a sizable amount of research on racial conflict in the United States, in political science and sociology, and that literature is growing. Much of it, of course, focuses on conflict between various racial and ethnic minority groups and the white majority. Beginning with Myrdal, V. O. Key, and others, scholars have recounted how whites and non-whites, largely African Americans, have engaged in protracted legal, legislative, and social movement battles to reshape the distribution of power and resources, and the effect this battle has had on politics. Much of this work—Carmines and Stimson (1989), and Grofman et al. (1992), for example—has helped us to understand the racially structured partisan and electoral world in which we find ourselves.

More recent pieces have examined the role of racial context—the demography and geography of race and ethnicity—in shaping attitudes toward target groups (Oliver and Wong 2003) including minority attitudes about race (Gay 2004), orientations toward the political system in general, captured through partisan realignment (Valentino and Sears 2005), as well as attitudes toward specific policy issues perceived to more directly affect minority populations (Branton and Jones 2005; Tolbert and Hero 1996; Feldman and Huddy 2005; Frymer 2005; Soss et al. 2003). A central concept in this literature is the issue of threat (Marcus and MacKuen 1993). It remains an open question whether social and geographic proximity is more likely to be understood as threatening and provoke hostile policy stances by the majority, or, instead, whether proximity will ameliorate stereotypes through positive social interaction and lead not to hostility but to more supportive policy stands. An even more complex possibility is that racial context interacts with racial views to polarize opinion on the policy issue; that is, proximity to other ethnic groups makes some people more supportive of that group but makes others more hostile (Soss et al. 2003).

A second area of focus has examined emerging conflict between whites and Latinos, an issue that has become more pressing and salient as the number of Latinos has increased so rapidly. In some states, ballot initiatives have become focal points of conflict between Anglos and Latinos, many of whom may be immigrants. Ballot initiatives, which have raised questions of social services for immigrants, English-language instruction in schools and official documents and affirmative action, have been perceived as targeting Latinos and immigrants and have appeared in California, Colorado, Arizona, Washington, and elsewhere (Tolbert and Hero 1996). Whatever the policy consequence of these proposals, one political consequence has been to make Latinos substantially more likely to turn out to vote and to lean more toward the Democrats (Segura et al. 1996). Moreover, the creation of a hostile political context or environment has been found to mobilize Latinos, resulting both in increased turnout (Pantoja et al. 2001) and increased political sophistication (Pantoja and Segura 2003b).

The idea of racial conflict and animus between whites and non-whites is well-trodden ground in political science. By contrast, and likely owing to the relatively recent emergence of Latinos and other racial groups in sizable numbers alongside African Americans, much less attention has been directed toward interminority competition and cooperation. We know comparatively little about what Latinos, African Americans, Asian Americans, and others feel toward each other, nor do we have a clear theory for developing expectations regarding when and under what circumstances intergroup relations are likely to be competitive and/or conflictual,[3] on the one hand, or cooperative, on the other. It is to this question that we devote the remainder of this chapter.

AFRICAN AMERICAN AND LATINO RELATIONS

It is broadly and commonly accepted that Latinos and African Americans are likely, even inevitable, coalition partners in American politics. Observers across the political spectrum speak of black-brown coalitions as the natural and expected course of evolution in minority group politics. This may, in fact, turn out to be the case. Latinos and African Americans share a number of politically relevant common characteristics. These include education and income levels significantly below the national averages with all of the attendant correlates, such as lower homeownership rates, higher-than-average unemployment rates, higher likelihood of being victimized by both violent and nonviolent crime, and often significant residential segregation in inner cities or inner-ring suburbs. Occasionally, in fact, African Americans and Latinos are living in shared or adjacent neighborhoods in the same economic circumstances. In addition, as we recounted in Chapter 7, both groups face historically high obstacles to election to public office, not the least of which is racial hostility among non-Latino whites.

Beyond shared objective conditions, (non-Cuban) Latinos and African Americans are more Democratic in partisanship than non-minority Americans are, as we described in Chapter 4. Recounting those findings, non-Cuban Latino voters are stable Democrats at rates exceeding 60 percent (DeSipio and de la Garza 2002), and Democratic identification seems to be positively associated with length of time in the United States, as well as age-related increases in partisan strength (Cain et al. 1991). Latino Democratic partisanship favors the formation of biracial coalitions with African Americans because, of all the partisan social groups in the United States, African Americans are the most loyal to the Democratic Party (Rosenstone et al. 1984, 169–170), a result that is consistent across gender, region, and a variety of demographic categories (Tate 1993). One plausible expectation is that these are the ingredients for a black-brown coalition that will form in opposition to entrenched Anglo interests.

But a contrary view would suggest that there are any number of factors—political, social, and economic—that may well serve to undermine this commonality between Hispanics and African Americans. Existing studies of black-brown coalitions see both competition and cooperation as possible outcomes and, of the two, competition is often estimated to be the more likely outcome. De la Garza (1997) points to a series of factors that may hinder the formation of black-brown alliances, let alone coalitions. African Americans may well resent Latino access to affirmative action programs and be concerned about the consequences of immigration for access to jobs and social services. Other scholars talk about these clashes over policy in quite direct ways because there can be direct competition over access to political power: reapportionment and redistricting might lead to the taking away of black seats in order to provide majority-minority districts for Latinos (for example, McClain 1998). Competition for economic resources and the attention of political parties and actors may well pit the interests of each group against the other. It is ironic in the extreme that commonality of circumstances and competition for scarce resources come hand-in-hand; that is, it is in part because such groups as African Americans and Latinos are similarly situated that they compete in the same sectors of the workforce and over finite resources.

CAUSES OF COOPERATION AND COMPETITION

There are a variety of anecdotal accounts of cooperation across racial and ethnic groups. For example, one news story documented the formation of an alliance between local League of United Latin American Citizens (LULAC) and NAACP chapters in, of all places, Spokane, Washington (Graman 2004). It is clear that there are occasions where leaders or members of the two groups cooperate. It is less clear how common this is.

When we think about how a group finds itself "competing" or "cooperating" with another, we really need to consider the views of both groups in the relationship—how everyday black, Latino, and Asian Americans view one another personally and politically. After all, how ordinary people view each other may shape the strategic choices of their leaders, community elites, and elected officials, and these elites respond to the opinions of their community, even as they often exert considerable effect in shaping those views (Zaller 1991). Coalitions and political cooperation function under elite direction, but community acquiescence is important, too. For example, if Asian American and Latino elites agreed to back a single candidate for office in a city or county, without the agreement of the voters who actually had to cast the ballots, that agreement would not end with an actual coalition. Mass attitudes can facilitate or constrain the coalitional decisions of their leaders but are also shaped by the rhetoric and influence of those leaders.

What circumstances have contributed to successful coalitions? There is a small literature examining whether and when black-brown coalitions have emerged. In what is perhaps the first scholarly attempt to discuss the formation of these coalitions, Charles Henry (1980) described how both groups "suffer" similar social inequalities, such as median household incomes, unemployment, and college competition rates. These similar inequalities should naturally lead to the formation of political alliances, Henry argued, but he finds that Latinos have little interest in forming an alliance with African Americans (Ambrecht and Pachon 1974).

Studies of political context and the creation of interethnic coalitions have generally focused on whether the demographic or institutional circumstances were most likely to result in cooperative or competitive behavior. For example, some municipal-level case studies have focused on elections and candidates and detailed the success or failure of biracial coalitions (Henry 1980; Falcon 1988; Sonenshein 1989). Others have identified the factors predicting the formation of black-brown coalitions (Browning et al. 1986; Meier and Stewart 1991).

According to Sonenshein (1989), visionary group leaders, especially those who supervise strong community organizations, are essential for developing and sustaining multiracial political coalitions. Further, the most effective coalitions are those that begin building in communities with strong political organizations already in place. Kaufmann, like Sonenshein, also argues that the prospects for future coalitions between African Americans and Latinos rest in part on the role that Latino leadership and political organizations play, in this case by promoting strong pan-ethnic identities (Kaufmann 2003).

In a more recent discussion of the coalition prospects between African Americans and Latinos, Vaca (2004) argues that few formal or even informal coalitions exist between Latinos and African Americans because these two disenfranchised groups should not be presumed political allies. Using case studies from New York, Los Angeles, Miami, Washington, D.C., Houston, and Compton, California, Vaca describes how language barriers, competition over affirmative action, and the overlooked contributions of Latinos during the American Civil Rights Movement have prevented the formation of coalitions. African Americans, Vaca defends, view Latinos and their growing numbers as a threat to their social, economic, and political benefits. Further, Latinos, he suggests, do not view African Americans and their experiences with empathy (we will reexamine this claim momentarily). Such contrasting perceptions of each other inevitably lead to strained relations.

Other work offers a similar perspective. Despite similar histories of inequality and racism, African Americans and Latinos have forged only tenuous partnerships. If anything, a focus on racial and ethnic issues can undermine the strength of the coalition. For example, Hochschild and Rogers (2000, 6–7) argue that when a multiracial coalition focuses on issues of racial and ethnic equality, it is likely to fragment into competitive factions. Further, the benefits of biracial coalitions are sometimes unattainable as a consequence of past political disagreement, individual attitudes about the other group, and fear the other minority group might gain the upper political hand (Tedin and Murray 1994). Racial minorities are less likely to respond to calls for coalition building, Guinier and Torres (1999) argue, if their leaders do not speak first to them about matters that relate to their racial experiences. Only then would it be possible to get racial minorities to expand their concerns and embrace issues that interest all groups (Guinier and Torres 1999).

Meier et al. (2004) argue that some issues might be more open to interethnic coalition building than others. They draw the important distinction between zero-sum situations, such as those involving employment and electoral success, and public goods that are not so clearly zero-sum, such as favorable policy. They argue that competition emerges when the focus is on the former, since no form of sharing or logrolling can accommodate two groups with claims on specific resources, be they school board seats or principals' jobs. By contrast, cooperation is more likely when political efforts are focused on policy. Policy outcomes can conceivably be favorable to both groups and, occasionally, lend themselves to logrolling practices in a way that employment and electoral competition do not.

One other contributing factor to cooperation is group size. Cooperation and biracial coalitions are most likely to emerge when the two groups face equal circumstances in terms of status and class and are also of similar size (Giles and Evans 1985). If the two groups are unbalanced in size or relative political power, the racial or ethnic group with the most representation in city and county government may fare better than the other racial or ethnic groups, with respect to public service jobs and other government benefits. Thus the better-positioned group might reasonably be less than eager about forming a coalition (Deutsch 1985; see also Browning et al. 1986; Sonenshein 1986; Warren et al. 1986; Butler and Murray 1991; Meier and Stewart 1991). In fact, those group members might choose to attempt a coalition with whites and may themselves be attractive to whites as a coalition partner. Such an environment will produce far more interminority competition than cooperation.

The checklist of factors that contribute to or provide the conditions for intergroup cooperation (group size, attitude of leaders, attitude of ordinary people, the nature of the issue at stake) suggests that cooperation might be a bit hard to find. Evidence of competition, not surprisingly, is significant. For instance, Latinos have been found to make less progress in terms of socioeconomic well-being and political power in cities with black majorities or pluralities (McClain and Karnig 1990). Further, African American and Latino municipal employment outcomes covary negatively with Anglo municipal employment, suggesting even more competition for these jobs (McClain 1993).

Competition extends to other areas as well, including political representation and the drawing of electoral districts (classic zero-sum issues). For example, while election results from 118 large, multiracial school districts indicate that as the black population increases, political representation of Latinos increases, the reverse is not true. When the population of Latinos grows, blacks do not gain but in fact lose political representation (Meier and Stewart 1991). With respect to the drawing of district lines, the lack of cooperation might intensify because of redistricting, particularly in states such as New York and Texas, where black and Latino leaders have debated the vote dilution of Latinos and the drawing of new majority-black districts (Tate 1993).

How Asian Americans fit into this structure is even less clear. The foundation of cross-group coalitions—presumed to be socioeconomic circumstances for Latinos and African Americans—is largely missing for substantial subgroups within the Asian American population (Lien 2002). Asian Americans have, at least in the aggregate, achieved a level of economic mobility and educational attainment far in excess of both of the other two groups, though we must be careful not to make too much of this claim, since there is wide variation across nationality groups. The potential for commonality to help promote coalitions, then, is less effective as a resource for the formation of coalitions between Asian Americans and other minority groups.

Beyond merely the absence of socioeconomic similarity, at least with respect to African Americans, there is a well-documented and troubled history of intergroup relations (Kim 2003). Kim has documented the sometimes violent conflict between African Americans and Asian Americans, particularly Koreans. Focusing on a specific historical event, the "Flatbush Boycott" of Korean-owned markets in New York City, she offers a theory of between-group minority conflict that assesses the blame in the direction of white Americans, whose imposition of the racialized social hierarchy creates conditions conducive to intergroup conflict. Kim and Lee (2001) offer a framework for understanding conditions under which conflict or cooperation is likely to emerge, and they suggest that Latino and Asian proximity in the racial hierarchy serves to mitigate Latino-Asian conflict and to enhance Latino-Asian cooperation, in comparison with Asian-black relations. Lien (2002, 55) similarly chronicles how white beliefs about Asians differ significantly from those about other minorities, evaluating them more positively and thereby implicitly creating a competitive relationship between Asian Americans and other non-white groups. Scholars of Asian American politics frequently refer to this as the "model minority" problem, and its effects on cross-group coalition formation are conceivably devastating.

MASS ATTITUDES AND INTERGROUP COOPERATION

No matter the political wisdom, coalitions may require a level of popular support before they are realized in action. An important constraint on coalition building, especially electoral coalition building, faced by leaders and elected officials is the underlying sentiment of their group members. Is there sufficient attitudinal support for coalition building across American minority groups? How much in common do members of group X see and feel when they are asked about group Y? And how much does this matter?

In one of the first studies, Jackson et al. (1994) explicitly asked about different coalitional strategies and found that African Americans were generally favorable toward Latinos and Asian Americans. Similarly, Kaufmann (2003) looks at the public opinion of Latinos toward African Americans. She finds that having a shared sense of identity among Latinos, having a sense of shared fate, helps to promote a sense of affinity with African Americans. But she also found distinct differences of opinion among national subgroups of the Latino community—those from Caribbean countries seeing more commonality than

Latinos of Mexican origin. Generally, Latinos hold attitudes toward African Americans that are cooler, and sometimes much cooler, than vice versa (McClain et al. 2007). In contrast, Gay (2006) finds that in locales where Latinos are economically advantaged vis-à-vis African Americans, black citizens are more likely to hold negative stereotypes of Latinos, oppose extension of policy benefits to Latinos, and perceive greater competition.

But reporting these studies in very general terms can lead us to overlook some important nuances. For example, while African Americans may well feel closer to Latinos than the other way around, it is not the case that this necessarily reflects Latino antipathy toward blacks, as opposed to others in American society. Rodrigues and Segura (2007) report that Latinos feel they have as much in common with both groups—that is, not very much. Their findings are reported in Table 12-1.

Table 12-1 uses data from the *Washington Post*/Kaiser study of Latinos in 1999 and charts mean responses to the question "How much do <<respondent's group>> have in common with <<one of the other two groups>>?" Respondents could offer a response from "a lot in common" (3) to "nothing at

TABLE 12-1   Mean Perceptions of Commonality between African Americans, Latinos, and Non-Hispanic Whites

Respondent's ethnicity ↓	Respondent's views toward			
	Latinos	African Americans	Non-Hispanic whites	Between target difference of means
Latino		1.186 (0.988) n = 1,943	1.205 (0.975) n = 1,943	t = −0.796 t-prob. = 0.426
African American	2.108 (0.864) n = 269		1.714 (0.844) n = 269	t = −6.715 t-prob. = 0.000
White	2.096 (0.752) n = 1,690	2.094 (0.756) n = 1,690		t = 0.12 t-prob. = 0.905
Between group ANOVAs F-test	F = 0.03 F-sign. = 0.860	F = 963.39 F-sign. = 0.000	F = 70.68 F-sign. = 0.000	

Sources: Washington Post/Kaiser/Kennedy School, 1999 National Survey of Latino Attitudes, and Rodrigues and Segura (2007).

Note: Variable ranges from zero (0) to three (3), with three indicating "a lot in common."

all in common" (0). The race or ethnicity of the survey respondents is coded in the left-hand column. Across the top are the groups about which they are expressing views regarding commonality. So each row represents the mean responses of the type of respondents in the left-hand column toward each group identified across the top. No group evaluated closeness to themselves. The final column tests whether differences between the two evaluations are statistically significant.

These results are remarkable in several ways. First, non-Hispanic whites appear not to differentiate between Latinos and African Americans and in both instances feel they have quite a bit in common with both groups—around 2 on a scale from 0 to 3. The reader is cautioned that this is likely to be, at least in part, due to social desirability bias; that is, the respondent is telling the survey interviewer what he or she thinks the socially acceptable answer is.

Second, as we just suggested, Latinos also do not differentiate, but report significantly less "in common" with the other two groups. But African Americans do, in fact, differentiate between Latinos and whites. Although the overall level of commonality is higher, they feel they have significantly more in common with Latinos than with non-Hispanic whites. Sadly, that data set (like many others) did not interview sufficient numbers of Asian Americans for a valid comparison.

The results on this issue of commonality are not encouraging. While African Americans appear to recognize those things they have in common with Latinos, the reverse appears less true. In the Latino National Survey (LNS), however, the reluctance of Latinos with respect to African Americans has diminished. In more recent data (2006), when comparing perceived commonality—politically, socially, and economically—between themselves and both whites and African Americans, Latino respondents to the LNS are far more likely to see commonality with African Americans than they do with whites. In fact, while 26 percent of respondents reported more commonality with whites, 36.2 percent saw more in common with African Americans, and 37.8 percent reported feeling the same toward each group. Again, we should not make too much of one finding, but this does suggest some grounds for thinking that there may be grass roots support—or at least the absence of grass roots hostility—to some attempts at black-brown coalition building.

All that said, it may be that persistent racial sentiments, biases, and stereotypes held by one group about another are a significant impediment to political cooperation. This argument can be unpacked into two simpler claims that we can examine. One claim is that some minority groups hold biased or otherwise ungenerous views of another and that, second, such views apply to political decision making, particularly over the choice of which candidate to support.

Tables 12-2 and 12-3 present evidence regarding the first contention. One way to compare what racial and ethnic minority groups think of one another would be to examine direct or indirect measures of racial sentiment. One approach to this is the "stereotype" measure, a long-standing if somewhat blunt instrument to evaluate how a survey respondent characterizes another group on seven-point scales of intelligence—intelligent versus unintelligent—and industry—hardworking versus lazy. Social desirability can influence survey responses (a survey respondent does not wish to appear to be racist to an interviewer by saying too many negative things about group Y). We can get around this problem by comparing someone's placement of their own group vis-à-vis that person's placement of the target group. If we take a 7-point scale and ask someone to say how intelligent someone is, where "very" is scored a one (1) and unintelligent is a seven (7), someone may be reluctant to score a group (Latinos, say) all the way at a seven. But if someone places Latinos as a three (3) on the scale, we can still observe beliefs when we compare that three with the two (2) she gave her own group, because this suggests that the survey respondent believes her own social group is more intelligent.

The data are from the 2008 ANES preelection study. Again, we caution that the very small sample size of Asian Americans undercuts the confidence with which we can interpret those results. Results for non-Hispanic whites, African Americans, and Latinos, however, are based on reasonable sample sizes. Again, we read the rows as reporting the share of each group (on the left) toward a target group (across the top).

Table 12-2 presents the results with respect to intelligent/unintelligent characterizations. Views of non-Hispanic whites conform to previous findings. While white views of Asians are generous—with 27.5 percent perceiving Asians as more intelligent compared with 22 percent seeing Asians as less intelligent—views of African Americans and Latinos reflect long-held stereotypes. Almost 45 percent of whites see African Americans as less intelligent than whites, and 51 percent hold the same view of Latinos, while only a scant few see either group as more intelligent.

For African Americans, results with respect to Latinos are the most striking. About 42.5 percent of African Americans view Latinos as less intelligent, a number that is only about 24 percent in their views of whites and Asians. Asians, again, are stereotyped positively, with 28 percent of African Americans perceiving Asian Americans as more intelligent than blacks. Latinos are even more positive about the intelligence of whites and Asians, with 30.3 percent of Latinos perceiving whites as smarter, while 41.8 percent perceive Asian Americans as smarter. Alas, their views of African Americans are very similar to how African Americans view them. Almost 43 percent of Latinos see African Americans as less intelligent than Latinos on average. Finally, Asian American numbers reflect some of the most extreme views, though these should be taken with the aforementioned caution regarding sample size. While 49 percent of Asian respondents saw whites as less intelligent, 79.6 percent saw African Americans as less intelligent than Asians, and 85.4 percent felt the same about Latinos.

Stereotypical views regarding intelligence are prevalent in all respondents, and with the exception of Asian Americans, who are stereotyped as "more intelligent," these views hold other racial minority groups as intellectually inferior to their own. Table 12-3 turns our attention to the question of industriousness—that is, whether the respondent considers the group more or less hardworking

TABLE 12-2 Comparative Stereotypical Characterization of Racial and Ethnic Groups as "Intelligent" or "Unintelligent" by Respondent's Racial and Ethnic Identification, 2008

	Direction of difference in group stereotype scores	Non-Hispanic whites	African Americans	Hispanics or Latinos	Asian Americans
% of whites scoring target as . . .	more intelligent		3.3	5.5	27.5
	same		51.8	43.5	50.4
	less intelligent		44.9	51.0	22.1
% of African Americans scoring target as . . .	more intelligent	17.8		9.8	28.0
	same	58.1		47.7	47.8
	less intelligent	24.1		42.5	24.2
% of Latinos scoring target as . . .	more intelligent	30.3	8.5		41.8
	same	50.7	48.6		39.6
	less intelligent	19.0	42.9		18.6
% of Asians scoring target as . . .	more intelligent	3.2	1.2	1.2	
	same	47.8	19.2	13.4	
	less intelligent	49.0	79.6	85.4	

Source: ANES 2008 preelection study.

Note: Cell entries represent weighted percentages of positive, negative, and zero differences between respondent's assessment of the stereotypic characteristics of the target group and respondent's own. Cells may not add to 100 percent owing to rounding. Number of respondents vary owing to missing data: non-Hispanic whites from 1,138 to 1,145, for African Americans 544–553, for Latinos 417–423, and for Asian Americans 34–35.

than the respondent's own group. The results here are no more promising for intergroup cooperation than were those of the previous table.

For white respondents, African Americans are singled out on this dimension. Asians are perceived as harder working (by almost 40 percent of whites) rather than lazy, and Latinos also have more respondents rating them as harder working (30.3 percent) compared with lazier (27.2 percent), but for African Americans, almost half of all white respondents believe the group to be less hardworking—that is, closer to "lazy" on the seven-point scale—than whites. Latino perceptions of African Americans are worse, with 66 percent scoring blacks as lazier than Latinos, though over half of all Latinos think the same of non-Hispanic whites. And almost 88 percent of our very small Asian sample believes African Americans are less hardworking than their own group.

TABLE 12-3 Comparative Stereotypical Characterization of Racial and Ethnic Groups as "Hardworking" or "Lazy" by Respondent's Racial and Ethnic Identification, 2008

	Direction of difference in group stereotype scores	Target group			
		Non-Hispanic whites	African Americans	Hispanics or Latinos	Asian Americans
% of whites scoring target as . . .	more hardworking		8.9	30.3	39.2
	same		41.8	42.5	43.1
	less hardworking		49.3	27.2	17.7
% of African Americans scoring target as . . .	more hardworking	23.2		31.5	33.0
	same	47.6		48.9	45.4
	less hardworking	29.2		19.6	21.5
% of Latinos scoring target as . . .	more hardworking	14.6	7.4		20.5
	same	33.8	26.6		41.4
	less hardworking	51.6	66.0		38.1
% of Asians scoring target as . . .	more hardworking	2.6	1.2	5.9	
	same	34.8	11.1	21.3	
	less hardworking	62.6	87.7	72.9	

Source: ANES 2008 preelection study.

Note: Cell entries represent weighted percentages of positive, negative, and zero differences between respondents assessment of the stereotypic characteristics of the target group and respondents own. Cells may not add to 100 percent owing to rounding. Number of responents vary owing to missing data: non-Hispanic whites from 1,133 to 1,141, for African Americans 544–553, for Latinos 418–421, and for Asian Americans 34–35.

Asian respondents do not appear to hold a very high opinion of Latinos either, with approximately 73 percent seeing Latinos as less hardworking than they are. But African Americans hold a fairly positive view of Latinos, with the share seeing them as more industrious (31.5 percent) exceeding the share that sees them as lazier (19.6 percent). African American views of Latinos contrast sharply with Latino views of African Americans on this dimension.

The opinions on stereotypes provide only a limited view into the racial sentiments of minority citizens. Other measures, for instance, the racial resentment index and some psychological tests, are available only in large datasets with respect to African Americans. So it is hard—impossible really, with existing data—to compare across groups (as both targets and subjects) on these measures. The stereotype measure has the virtue of being available for all groups, and though responses are influenced by social desirability, the patterns in the results presented here suggest that citizens are shockingly willing to evaluate other groups as less industrious and intelligent than they and do so largely to the disadvantage of African Americans and Latinos, and these views are not confined to the white majority.

What of the second claim? That these negative stereotypes and ungenerous views are politically relevant? It would be tempting to conclude that these stereotypical beliefs among racial minorities toward one another are a substantial obstacle to coalition building (McClain 2006; McClain et al. 2006, 2007). These opinions would seem to inhibit electoral coalition building and constrain leaders and elites when they seek to build such coalitions. After all, it defies our conventional expectations to suggest that mass populaces with low opinions of each other are likely to rally behind a single candidate, viewpoint, or policy effort. We see these stereotypes as factors that work against—but do not rule out—coalitions. After all, some of the low regard that groups may have for each other may be offset by shared partisanship, underpinned by genuinely shared and left-of-center preferences on many issue dimensions, uniting Latinos, African Americans, and increasingly Asian Americans in partisan and issue coalitions. Still, stereotypes of other groups do not help coalitions, and one way in which they may harm coalitions is that they mean that—even if a coalition is built—it may not be long lasting or very successful.

Fortunately for advocates of minority coalitions, there is far less evidence of this last contention; while minority sentiments toward one another are what they are, in most cases they have not been sufficient to overcome the natural issue basis and partisan basis of their alliance. The best case in point, of course, is the election of Barack Obama.

A number of media observers and Democratic operatives questioned whether Latinos—who overwhelmingly supported Hillary Clinton in the 2008 Democratic Primaries—would ultimately vote for a black candidate. In the end, however, Latinos did vote for Obama. As we illustrated in several different ways in earlier chapters, Latinos, African Americans, and Asian Americans have often come together to vote for candidates of one ethnic group or another. Racial polarization between minorities appears to be confined to the very rare instances when two candidates of different minority groups are facing off against one another, and even then there is no certainty that racial divisions will develop.

With respect to the 2008 election, the results are already clear. Supermajorities of both Asian Americans and Latinos voted for Obama. In addition, research into voting decisions of Latinos suggests that racial sentiments played almost no role. Even in determining which Latinos voted for Obama and which did not, the racial sentiments of the individuals played no role (Segura and Valenzuela 2010). Figure 12-1 illustrates a comparison between the effect of racial resentment on white and Latino vote choice after controlling for other common factors; that is, if people acted on their views on race, what we should see is that as someone becomes more resentful, the chances of voting for an

FIGURE 12-1   **Estimated Effect of Racial Resentment on White and Latino 2008 Obama Vote, Controlling for Other Predictors**

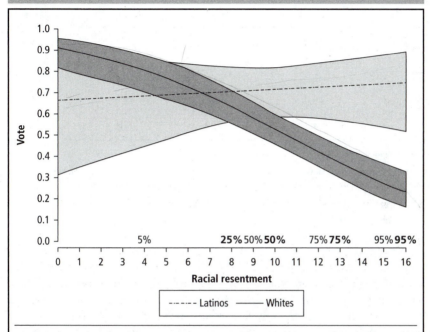

Source: Figure and analysis from Segura, Gary M. and Ali A. Valenzuela. 2010. "Hope, Tropes, and Dopes: Hispanic and White Racial Animus in the 2008 Election." *Presidential Studies Quarterly* 40 (3): 497–514. Reprinted with permission of John Wiley & Sons, Inc.

Note: Figures along the X-axis illustrate the distribution of non-Hispanic white and Latino voters on the racial resentment measure. Figures in bold represent non-Hispanic white voters; figures in italics represent Latino voters. Non-Hispanic white voters have a somewhat broader distribution, shifted toward the higher end of the scale compared with Latinos. For the 5th and 25th percentiles (bold and italic), the figure is the same for both groups.

African American presidential candidate should drop. This does seem to be the case for white voters but not for Latinos. While Latinos may hold unflattering views of African Americans, they did not appear to affect their support for Obama.

Of course, if we want to know if minorities think there is a sufficient basis for cooperation, one obvious approach might be to ask them. Do minority respondents themselves see sufficient commonality for intergroup cooperation, or do they perceive the groups and their problems as too different to be the subject of coalition. Responses to just such a suggestion are presented in Table 12-4, this time with a large and reliable sample of Asian Americans.

Significant majorities of all groups either disagree or strongly disagree with the contention that the groups are too different to be political allies.

TABLE 12-4 Evaluations Regarding the Bases for Intergroup Cooperation, by Racial and Ethnic Identity

Response category	Non-Hispanic whites	African Americans	Latinos	Asian Americans
Strongly agree	5.7	12.6	16.5	10.8
Agree	16.7	16.1	21.3	28.4
Disagree	28.3	22.5	23.3	30.3
Strongly disagree	49.4	48.8	38.9	30.5
N	863	729	722	482

Source: 2004 National Politics Study.

Note: Cell entries are percentages of each group offering valid responses to the prompt: "The problems of Blacks, Hispanics, and Asian Americans are too different for them to be political allies or partners."

Ironically, or perhaps reflecting the partisan world as they perceive it, white respondents were most optimistic about prospects of interminority alliances. Over 77 percent of white respondents disagreed with the statement. But almost 61 percent of Asian Americans, over 62 percent of Latinos, and over 71 percent of African Americans similarly disagreed that the groups are too different to coalesce politically.[4] These results are hardly unanimous but suggest substantial, widespread belief that interminority cooperation and alliance for political ends are possible.

This is not to say that opinions regarding commonality or stereotype are not a problem for cross-minority coalitions. Race is a powerful and pernicious force in society, and we cannot confidently predict that racial sentiments will not someday undermine the Democratic coalition and comity among its minority constituency groups. To date, however, party and issue preferences have trumped whatever racial sentiments are lurking beneath. Intergroup coalitions have been formed despite intergroup suspicion and low regard at the grass roots level.

ASSESSING THE LEVEL OF COOPERATION

Just how much cooperation exists between minority groups in political practice is hard to know, since it depends in part on where one looks. Much of the evidence is based on attitudinal data of the sort we just presented. The kinds of attitudes we see suggest that evidence of "black-brown" coalitions can be hard to find. In one of the most complete studies of black-brown coalitions to date, Rene Rocha (2007) examines black-brown coalitions on more than 1,300 local school boards. As we mentioned elsewhere, while local school boards may not sound as exciting as disputes over the presidency, they are important examples of real-life politics at work in ways that affect families every day. Moreover, local politics is where we can see the variation and nuance in intergroup relations that are often missed when focusing at the national level. One of Rocha's findings is that rather than creating interminority alliances, the presence and growth of Latino populations often seem to promote black-white alliances. Looked at from the point of view of the usual framing of minority politics as the politics of a minority working against Anglo resistance, this is a surprising, and possibly even very surprising, result. However, if African Americans and Anglos share attitudes toward Latino immigrants, then this result is explicable as an expression of common interests between blacks and whites. Again, however, the coalition that is formed is somewhat surprising in terms of minority politics because it is a coalition *with* Anglos rather than against them.

Similarly, in his study of election results for Congress and state legislatures, Casellas (2009) shows that there seems to be a reluctance to form coalitions across racial and ethnic lines. He concludes that African Americans and Latinos are largely voting for their own co-ethnics: such cooperation as exists between African American and Latino legislators at the legislative level does not seem to trickle down to voters. In a very simple and very clever study, Hero and Preuhs (2009) look at legislative scorecards. Prominent interest and advocacy groups rate members of Congress each year on the basis of an identified set of votes important to the interests of the group. These interest groups might be the chamber of commerce or the AFL-CIO, or ratings can be made by racial and ethnic groups such as the Mexican American Legal Defense and Education Fund (MALDEF) and the NAACP. Members of each group select the bills that are important to them and decide whether they support or oppose the measure. If a member of Congress or state legislator votes for a bill that the group wants, then the legislator is seen as friendly to the group. The more bills liked by the group that the legislator supports, the more favorable the legislator is judged to be toward the group.

Hero and Preuhs look at these scorecards given by racial and ethnic interest groups and pay particular attention to *which* issues are scored. What measures are scored tells us a lot about whether the different groups are not just seeing the same policies in the same way (that is, do all interest groups score a "YES" vote the same way) but also whether the groups pay attention to the same bills in the first place. Another element of their work was to examine testimony by groups before Congress: if the different groups testified on the same issues, then the groups would have similar policy concerns to each other; if they testified on different issues, the groups would have different policy concerns from each other. The work of Hero and Preuhs on testimony and group scorecards indicates only a modest overlap in policy concerns between African Americans and Latinos. They conclude—echoing Casellas—that there is tacit noncooperation between Latinos and African Americans—something far short of both outright conflict on the one hand and lockstep cooperation on the other. So far, then, we probably should be referring to black-brown *alliances* rather than black-brown coalitions.

Why is it that relationships between the two groups seem to be so tepid, or even fragile? One answer we have seen already: it is not clear that grass roots attitudes to each other are either warm or reciprocated. But other factors, too, would seem to apply, factors that would hold lessons for intergroup relations in future years. Another reason for fragility is that power is to be shared and this causes friction. This idea underlies more formal political science treatments of coalitions: if power is to be shared, then politicians (or whoever is building the coalition) will want to share it with as few people as possible. The ideal coalition is not an overwhelming majority but one that is just big enough to win power—because then the coalition that wins shares power among fewer people than would be the case in an overwhelming landslide. But the problem remains that power—the power to propose policies, the power to pursue policies—and, of course, who it is who gets to exercise that power can become a source of disagreement among coalition partners.

The work of Reuel Rogers (2004) underscores the point that commonality of race alone is not enough to produce a coalition. In terms of black-brown coalitions, what this means is that commonality of being a member of an ethnic minority is not sufficient to produce a coalition—we are assuming quite a lot when we think that black-brown coalitions should form in the first place, and those assumptions may not hold. The work of Rogers on coalitions between Caribbean- and American-born blacks in New York City politics is important because he provides one of the few studies of coalition building *within* a racial community and at the elite level.

Despite a number of commonalities over and above race, including common experiences, interests, and partisanship, Rogers's study shows that tensions exist along these lines of national origin. He pays particular attention to the way in which elites compete for power and positions and concludes that this kind of competition was critical in helping prevent a coalition happening. He notes that in Hartford, Connecticut, electoral institutions, at large districts, make it easier for the same two groups to arrive at a cooperative outcome and there is far less friction between Caribbean- and American-born black leaders in that city. Frictions over the division of political power may occur within a community and they may also occur between communities in attempts to build "black-brown" coalitions.[5]

Another reason is, as Jackson et al. (1994) noted, coalitions may be unsettled by demographic changes. In the specific case they examined, the changes were generational. Different generations seem to have different opinions toward other groups. Attitudes toward Latinos among African Americans, for example, were warmer among older African Americans, while the younger generation was more hesitant. These kinds of generational differences too are noted in Gilliam (1996), who found younger African Americans more dubious about the value of the Bradley (black-white) coalition in LA than were older voters. Jackson et al. argued that this draws attention to the "entropy" of coalitions—a coalition may form, but as new generations and new players enter the political system, they must either be incorporated into the coalition or decide to form new ones. In terms of intergroup alliances, then, demographic change may well result in changing relative size of populations. Over the past twenty years or so, for example, immigration has helped to drive marked increases in Asian and Latino populations, so much so that African Americans are no longer the largest minority group. In any coalition bargaining over how many votes—how much clout—one group brings to the table relative to another will be an issue. If those votes change over time, then obviously there will be pressure to change old deals and old arrangements, possibly unsettling the coalition.

FUTURE PROSPECTS FOR COOPERATION OR CONFLICT

Politics is often about noble sentiments—but not always. Often politics is about interests. America's minority groups will cooperate when, at the mass or elite level, they perceive that it is in their interest to cooperate—and not otherwise. We see significant evidence that there are sufficient points of commonality between the groups and their political positions that coalition, if carefully orchestrated, is clearly possible. We also see, however, sufficient evidence of affective indifference or distance, a general lack of affinity—particularly on the part of Latinos and Asian Americans toward African Americans—that this coalition is neither inevitable nor, in some cases, even likely. These outcomes, of course, are endogenous to more than individual attitudes and elite strategies, but will be the product of the interaction of both within each group and between these groups, and are clearly going to be affected by the policy actions and political strategies of Anglos in the system, with interests of their own.

The role of political elites in shaping the preferences and attitudes of the mass public is, by now, well known if not well understood (Page and Shapiro 1992; Stimson 1990; Ginsberg 1986; Kuklinski and Segura 1995; Zaller 1991). On the other hand, political coalitions, of necessity, will need to operate at the mass level in order to have impact on electoral and policy outcomes. Leaders need followers, and candidates need voters; antipathy, or at least indifference, among the people can severely undermine efforts at coordination agreed to at the elite level.

Economic circumstances and attitudes are most often identified as the foundation of minority coalitions. Tedin and Murray (1994), for example, have found that individual level concern over economic conditions, such as poverty and unemployment, is associated with support for biracial coalition activities among both African Americans and Latinos, though to different degrees. These expectations have their limits, however. While the most vulnerable in each group, for instance those with less material wealth and political resources, may, by virtue of greater shared circumstances, be more supportive of biracial cooperation, this may not be the case if competition over scarce jobs and resources comes to characterize a particular environment. In that instance, poorer and less-educated respondents are *less* likely to favor coalitional strategies (Jackson et al. 1994). Issues such as competition for resources and status, stereotypes, and cultural differences have already been found to influence the perceptions and behaviors of these two groups (Robinson 2002). These same forces may even trigger hostile rhetoric and outright economic discrimination at the elite level. At the opposite end of the aforementioned socioeconomic (SES) scale, middle- and upper-class Latinos and African Americans have historically used their newfound resources to augment both power and opportunity for themselves and their respective group (Landry 1987; Jennings 1992; Dawson 1994), but this opportunity need not facilitate biracial cooperation. In fact, the coalitional efforts are likely undermined if an influential leader of any group advances only the interests of one group to the exclusion of others (Betancur and Gills 2000).

Attitudes, on the one hand, and political actions on the other are, however, quite distinct, and the mere presence of supportive attitudes—which we have suggested may not be in place—is not alone sufficient to ensure cooperative action. We may find circumstances where general attitudinal agreement between the two groups does not result in similar actions. For example, Latino and African American voters might agree on a wide variety of issues, yet still choose to support different candidates at any level of government.

Political circumstances will vary widely across the United States and over time. The cases of New York and Los Angeles illustrate how context matters (Bowler and Segura 2005) in shaping the individual and collective political decisions of minority voters and their elites as reported in Box 12-1. Scholars seeking to explore the mechanics of black-brown or other transracial coalitions will, therefore, have to address whether emerging cooperation is the product of genuinely shared values and preferences or instead the result of circumstances and structured choices. Similarly, when points of conflict emerge, we will need to differentiate whether the source of that conflict is really in divergent values and preferences or, rather, the product of more tactical or strategic considerations by community leaders.

There are several additional points that may be made concerning what we know about intergroup relationships. First, there are a number of areas of coalition building about which we know very little. We know very little about some specific interrelationships that are very important in some states and cities. For example, we know very little about the relationship between Native Americans and Latinos in New Mexico or the relationship between Haitian Americans and Cuban Americans in Florida. As the diversity of the United States grows, we will come across more of these kinds of interactions across different groups. More importantly, we know very little about how political elites either see the process of coalition building or actually engage in that process: Reuel Rogers's (2006) work is a rarity in scholarship on coalition building.[6]

Second, and returning to the continuum of conflict and cooperation, there remains some uncertainty about where things actually lie on that continuum. That is, just how competitive and how cooperative are relations between the different groups? The answer in the literature to date is something of a squishy

BOX 12-1   Coalitions at the City Level

The 2001 New York City and Los Angeles mayoral elections are a good example of how attitudes and actions are occasionally disconnected, and whether black-brown coalitions can or will emerge. In New York in 2001, Latino and African American voters united to support Bronx Borough president Fernando Ferrer in the Democratic primary. His loss to Mark Green, in what was perceived to be a racially polarized campaign, prompted majorities of both groups to abandon the Democratic nominee and ensure the election of Michael Bloomberg in the general election. By contrast, in the Los Angeles election of 2001, which we have described at length, African American and Latino voters backed rival candidates, each of whom made it to the general election in the nonpartisan system. In the end, a white Democrat was elected on the strength of African American and Republican support, over a Latino candidate with a primarily Latino and liberal base. Attempts to "deracialize" the election by the Latino candidate were, in the end, spectacularly unsuccessful (Wright Austin 2004).

Yet, just four years later, black-brown rivalry in Los Angeles was significantly muted, if not in fact replaced with cooperation, as African American voters disenchanted with that same white Democrat, former mayor James Hahn, chose instead to coalesce with his rival and helped to elect Antonio Villaraigosa on the second try. In this second election, racial distinctions did not serve to effectively separate Latino and African American voters. We have no reason to believe that policy preferences or attitudes varied widely across the settings. Presumably, in both locations and across time, African American and Latino voters prefer candidates of their own ethnicity rather than from the other group, or at the very least, candidates with significant loyalty to their own community. Rather, the manner in which choices were structured—available candidates and the nature of the local electoral system—resulted in different actions in the two cities. On the other hand, it is likely that voters from both groups in Los Angeles shared many policy preferences but did not agree on who best could actualize those preferences.

A second distinction between the cases is that of the strategic conditions faced by minority voters. African Americans and Latinos are both sizable communities in New York, whereas in Los Angeles, Latinos are on the verge of becoming an outright majority in a city whose black population—and black political influence—is perceived to be shrinking. While both minority groups in New York felt their interests would jointly be served with a Ferrer mayoralty, in Los Angeles, the outcome of the 2001 election was perceived as zero-sum. In short, the prospects for political coalition will be inexorably tied to the relative size of two groups, their joint local political history, the perception of rivalry or cooperation with respect to resources, and the available candidates.

one: relations seem not just to be at some midpoint between the two extremes but also to shift from time to time and place to place. Intergroup relations— whether they are more properly called alliances or coalitions—are built on shifting sand. The question of whether there is commonality or competition between groups is in part "real"; that is, there are only so many budget dollars available to spend and only so many elected offices to fill. At heart, then, coalition politics between minority groups remains dominated by the questions that often dominate politics—"who gets what, when, and how?"

But the degree of conflict and consensus also reflects how the actors see things. A recurring theme in this literature is that the ideology of participants, and in particular the idea of a shared fate, can help promote cooperation across groups. Since ideologies are constructed this implies that group leaders are not simply constrained by popular attitudes but can go some way toward shaping them. That is, it may be the case that grass roots opinions in two groups might be such as to limit cooperation—there may even be hostility between the groups. Nevertheless, there are some reasons for thinking that it is possible, in principle at least, for group leaders to try to persuade the grass roots of the benefits of cooperation.

Third, while we have suggested that alliances or coalitions may be quite fragile, this is not necessarily a bad thing. In fact, having a pattern in which alliances rise and fall can be seen as a good thing so far as theories of democracy are concerned, because it means that not everyone is in a permanent (opinion) minority. So, going back to the findings of Rocha (2007) for a moment, one, pessimistic, interpretation of his findings is that coalitions are a way for groups to gang up on each other. But that need not be the case. What we can see is that by building alliances across groups, all groups can get a turn at exercising power: assuming they are able to build an alliance and hold it together.

One way this may work is illustrated in Liu's study (2006) of New Orleans and Memphis city politics. In those cities, whites became an important source of votes in building a winning multiracial coalition when the black vote was split. The situation in those two cities was somewhat unusual in the sense that they are majority-black cities. When Anglo voters are in the majority and they are split, then the same would hold true for minority voters: when there are two blocs of equal size opposed to each other, a smaller group can become "king maker." Of course, as we detailed in Chapter 8, the history of racially polarized bloc voting suggests that some whites try to fix their splits before the ballot box plays a role. Nevertheless, diversity of preferences within groups empowers those able to build political bridges across them.

The general lesson to be drawn from these accounts is that splits within the ruling coalition allow outsiders a chance at power. What this means is that having fragile coalitions in general can be quite a good outcome. In a Madisonian sense, having one group permanently in a majority and a second group permanently in the minority can lead to problems. What we would like is for shifting coalitions and rotation in office. Coalitional politics allow that to happen, and splits in coalitions allow change to take place. It also means that politics in a multiethnic society may be a lot more fluid than politics in places where there are just two groups.

13

"We Have Seen the Future, and the Future Is Ours"

In this book we have tried to show how minority politics—and answers to the questions of minority political participation—can be understood using standard explanations of political behavior. In some ways, in fact, in many ways, minority politics can be understood using standard explanations that are available in political science. What we have also shown, however, is that sometimes those standard explanations of politics fall short when it comes to understanding minority political participation.

The consequence of this falling short is not that political science is useless—after all, it can explain many aspects of minority politics—but that the study of minority politics is important in helping us develop better theories and explanations in politics. In other words the study of minority politics forms part of the study of politics, and it can be an important part in helping to develop explanations of political participation and behavior. We have also shown places where our knowledge on some key questions and on many key groups is, quite simply, lacking. There is a lot of research still to be done on minority politics, and it is clearly work that is worth doing.

Throughout the book we have argued that in the coming century minority politics will be central to American politics, and it will be so in a way that has not been seen before. That may sound like an odd way to phrase things. After all, race has always been central to American politics. In the past much of America's history, and America's politics, has concerned the fight of excluded groups to become included. The fights against slavery, against discrimination, and in support of civil rights were all fights that preoccupied American politics and defined American political history. But now it seems that minority politics is set to enter a new era, an era in which any political parties or candidates seeking to win office will have to court the votes of at least some minorities or consign themselves to long-term competitive disadvantage. Even today it is the case for an ever-increasing number of states and cities that candidates and parties can win only with support from multiple racial and ethnic groups. It seems that in the coming century, then, minority voters will play an increasingly decisive role in electoral politics.

Some commentators are not so sanguine about how that change will unfold:

I believe that white racial anxiety, not immigration, will be the most significant and potentially dangerous socio-demographic trend of the coming decade. The combination of changing demographics and symbolic political victories on the part of nonwhites will inspire in whites a greater racial consciousness, a growing sense of beleaguerment and louder calls to end affirmative action or to be included in it.

(Greg Rodriguez, "Affirmative Action's Time Is Up,"
Los Angeles Times, August 2, 2010)

White response to minority political empowerment might be a growing sense of "linked fate" among Anglos, which could turn into "white backlash," which will make the process of inclusion a fraught one. Indeed, at least one potential narrative to explain the emergence of the "tea party" movement and the incredible amount of anger directed at the Obama administration and the man himself is a story of white backlash, of the incredible psychic shock that the election of a black man to the presidency visited on those whose image of America does not match its demography. There is good polling evidence to suggest just such a linkage (Parker 2010).

Significant movement of more whites into the GOP could well forestall the changes we envision, but our sense of it is that the anger is coming largely from voters already identifying with GOP candidates. That is, those most likely to engage in backlash are those who have resisted the changes so mightily already. While this may represent a hardening of partisan preferences, it is less clear that it signifies change in anyone's preferences.

Then again, one of the accomplishments of the Obama presidency is in showing that the world did not end with the election of a black president. Zoltan Hajnal (2001) has found this pattern at the local level: white voters may be fearful of black candidates, but after there has been an African American elected, that fear ebbs and the realization sets in that government did more or less what it usually does in more or less the same way. In other words, small "d" democratic politics endure and, as a consequence, the questions we have raised in this book also endure.

We have focused our attention in this book on the underlying dynamics of American politics and society that we believe will portend an era of Democratic dominance. Minority voters are more plentiful than before, and this demographic change will move only in one direction for the foreseeable future. Minority voters hold clear opinions on matters of public concern, and they are almost uniformly to the left of white voters, privileging Democratic politics. The issue basis of minority partisan identification significantly constrains the latitude the GOP has in trying to broaden its coalition. More importantly, the historical choices that led to the construction of the nearly all-white party that the GOP is today have real effects on what strategic decisions that party is free to make in the future. Having lost popular support on the New Deal, Social Security, Medicare, and the basic social safety net, the GOP opted to improve its competitive position by moving the segregationist wing of the Democratic Party into its column, breaking the solid Democratic South, and keeping the GOP in the national hunt for 40 years. But that bargain constrains its ability to soften its racial rhetoric or moderate its positions, both of which are important to attracting minority votes.

The degree to which minorities can shape the future of American politics, however, can be constrained by low rates of participation, by obstacles to political representation, and by between-group contestations. Lacking resources, minorities have to struggle to move voters into the booth, into organizations, and into other forms of activity, though ethnic and pan-ethnic identity has emerged as an important alternative. The empowerment of minority voters has also been accompanied by the growth of elected officials, overcoming decades of minority vote dilution, but that growth may also be tenuous as an increasingly conservative and skeptical federal judiciary narrows the range of options under the Voting Rights Act for securing meaningful minority inclusion. And the presence of multiple minority groups within the Democratic coalition, groups with unique histories and interests coupled with important similarities, raises the importance of coalition formation, popular stereotypes, and elite leadership as critical factors that will shape the influence of minority Americans.

The evidence suggests, however, that core orientations and values are not an obstacle—on many dimensions, minorities look an awful lot like other Americans and, occasionally, exhibit more quintessentially American characteristics than whites. Some of those "American" views, ironically, have their origin in the immigration experience, and the specter of adverse socialization raises concerns that in the process of immigrant incorporation, leaders must find ways to retain that engagement.

Those questions—over who is an American, who participates and under what conditions; over the roles of issues and "values"; over who votes and who does not and who they succeed in electing—must be asked in relation to the changing electorate of the United States. We took a stab at answering those questions here. Ultimately, the answers will determine who wins political power in the coming century, how they win, and what they are likely to do with it. In short, minority politics in America is becoming just politics. At last.

References

Abrajano, Marisa, and R. Michael Alvarez. 2008. "Why Are Latinos More Politically Trusting Than Other Americans?" Presented at the Annual Meeting of the Western Political Science Association, San Diego, CA.

———. 2007. "Why Are Latinos More Politically Trusting Than Other Americans?" Social Science Research Network, July 20. http://ssrn.com/abstract=1017861 (accessed March 2, 2011).

Alba, Richard D., and Victor Nee. 2003. *Remaking the American Mainstream: Assimilation and Contemporary Immigration*. Cambridge, MA: Harvard University Press.

———. 1997. "Rethinking Assimilation Theory for a New Era of Immigration." *International Migration Review* 31(4): 826–874.

Alex-Assensoh, Yvette, and A. B. Assensoh. 2001. "Inner-City Contexts, Church Attendance, and African-American Political Participation." *The Journal of Politics* 63(3): 886–901.

Alumkal, Antony W. 2003. *Asian American Evangelical Churches: Race, Ethnicity, and Assimilation in the Second Generation*. New York: LFB Scholarly Publishing LLC.

Alvarez, R. Michael, and Lisa Garcia Bedolla. 2003. "The Foundations of Latino Voter Partisanship: Evidence from the 2000 Election." *The Journal of Politics* 65(1): 31–49.

Ambrecht, Biliana C. S., and Harry P. Pachon. 1974. "Ethnic Political Mobilization in a Mexican American Community: An Exploratory Study of East Los Angeles, 1965–1972." *Western Political Quarterly* 27(3): 500–519.

American Community Survey, U.S. Census Bureau. 2008. "American Community Survey." www.census.gov/acs/www (accessed April 25, 2010).

American National Election Studies. 2005. "Party Identification 7-Point Scale 1952-2004." November 27. www.electionstudies.org/nesguide/toptable/tab2a_1.htm (accessed May 7, 2010).

Ansolabehere, Stephen, and Charles Stewart III. 2009. "Amazing Race." *Boston Review*, January/February. http://bostonreview.net/BR34.1/ansolabehere_stewart.php (accessed September 9, 2010).

Ansolabehere, Stephen, Jonathan Rodden, and James M. Snyder Jr. 2006. "Purple America." *Journal of Economic Perspectives* 20(2): 97–118.

Aoki, Andrew L., and Don T. Nakanishi. 2001. "Asian Pacific Americans and the New Minority Politics." *PS: Political Science and Politics* 34(3): 605–610.

Aquino, Corazon. http://thinkexist.com/quotation/freedom_of_expression-in_particular-free-dom_of/153966.html.

Armour, Stephanie. 2007. "English-only Workplaces Spark Lawsuits." *USA Today*, May 7. www.usatoday.com/money/workplace/2007-05-06-english-only-usat_N.htm (accessed August 26, 2010).

Avery, James M. 2009. "Political Mistrust among African Americans and Support for the Political System." *Political Research Quarterly* 62(1): 132–145.

Ayers, John W., and C. Richard Hofstetter. 2008. "American Muslim Political Participation following 9/11: Religious Belief, Political Resources, Social Structures, and Political Awareness." *Politics and Religion* 1: 3–26.

Baldassarri, Delia, and Andrew Gelman. 2008. "Partisans without Constraint: Political Polarization and Trends in American Public Opinion." *The American Journal of Sociology* 114(2): 408–446.

Banducci, Susan A., Todd Donovan, and Jeffrey A. Karp. 2004. "Minority Representation, Enpowerment and Participation." *The Journal of Politics* 66(2): 534–556.

Barkan, Elliott R. 1995. "Race, Religion, and Nationality in American Society." *Journal of American Ethnic History* 14: 38–75.

Barreto, Matt. 2010. *Ethnic Cues: The Role of Shared Ethnicity in Latino Political Participation*. Ann Arbor: University of Michigan Press.

————. 2007. "Sí Se Puede! Latino Candidates and the Mobilization of Latino Voters." *American Political Science Review* 101(3): 425–441.

Barreto, Matt A., and Dino N. Bozonelos. 2009. "Democrat, Republican, or None of the Above? The Role of Religiosity in Muslim American Party Identification." *Politics and Religion* 2: 200–229.

Barreto, Matt A., Sylvia Manzano, Ricardo Ramirez, and Kathy Rim. 2009. "Mobilization, Participation, and Solidaridad: Latino Participation in the 2006 Immigration Protest Rallies." *Urban Affairs Review*, March 9, 2009.

Barreto, Matt A., Gary M. Segura, and Nathan D. Woods. 2004. "The Mobilizing Effect of Majority-Minority Districts on Latino Turnout." *American Political Science Review* 98(1): 65–75.

Barreto, Matt A., Ricardo Ramirez, and Nathan D. Woods. 2005a. "Are Naturalized Voters Driving the California Latino Electorate? Measuring the Effects of IRCA Citizens on Latino Voting." *Social Science Quarterly* 86(4): 729–811.

Barreto, Matt A., Mario Villarreal, and Nathan D. Woods. 2005b. "Metropolitan Latino Political Behavior: Turnout and Candidate Preference in Los Angeles." *Journal of Urban Affairs* 27(1): 71–91.

Bartels, Larry M. 2006. "What's the Matter with 'What's the Matter with Kansas?'" *Quarterly Journal of Political Science* 1(2): 201–226.

Baumer, Donald C., and Howard J. Gold. 1995. "Party Images and the American Electorate." *American Politics Quarterly* 23(1): 33.

Baumgartner, Frank R., and Bryan D. Jones. 1996. *Agendas and Instability in American Politics.* Chicago: University of Chicago Press.

Bean, Frank D., and Marta Tienda. 1987. *The Hispanic Population of the United States.* New York: Russell Sage.

Berelson, Bernard R., Paul F. Lazarsfeld, and William N. McPhee. 1954. *Voting: A Study of Opinion Formation in a Presidential Campaign.* Chicago: University of Chicago Press.

Betancur, John J., and Douglas C. Gills, eds. 2000. *The Collaborative City: Opportunities and Struggles for Blacks and Latinos in U.S. Cities.* New York: Garland Publishing.

Bobo, Lawrence, and James R. Kluegel. 1993. "Opposition to Race-Targeting: Self-Interest, Stratification Ideology, or Racial Attitudes?" *American Sociological Review* 58(4): 443–464.

Bobo, Lawrence D., Michael Dawson, and Devon Johnson. 2001. "Enduring Two-ness: Through the Eyes of Black America." *Public Perspectives* 12(3): 13–16.

Bobo, Lawrence, and Franklin D. Gilliam. 1990. "Race, Sociopolitical Participation, and Black Empowerment." *The American Political Science Review* 84(2): 377–393.

Bonilla-Silva, Eduardo. 2006. *Racism without Racists: Color-Blind Racism and the Persistence of Racial Inequality in the United States.* New York: Rowman and Littlefield.

————. 2003. "Racial Attitudes or Racial Ideology? An Alternative Paradigm for Examining Actors' Racial Views." *Journal of Political Ideologies* 8(1): 63–82.

————. 2001. *White Supremacy and Racism in the Post Civil-Rights Era.* Boulder, CO: Lynne Reinner.

Borjas, George J. 1990. *Friends or Strangers: The Impact of Immigrants on the U.S. Economy.* New York: Basic Books.

Bowler, Shaun, and Gary M. Segura. 2005. "Social, Political and Institutional Context and the Representation of Minority Americans." In *Diversity in Democracy: Minority Representation in the United States,* edited by Gary M. Segura and Shaun Bowler. Charlottesville: University of Virginia Press.

Bowler, Shaun, Stephen P. Nicholson, and Gary M. Segura. 2006. "Earthquakes and Aftershocks: Race, Direct Democracy, and Partisan Change." *American Journal of Political Science* 50(1): 146–159.

Brace, Kimball, Lisa Handley, Richard G. Niemi, and Harold W. Stanley. 1995. "Minority Turnout and the Creation of Majority-Minority Districts." *American Politics Quarterly* 23(2): 190–203.

Branton, Regina. 2007. "Latino Attitudes toward Various Areas of Public Policy: The Importance of Acculturation." *Political Research Quarterly* 60(2): 293–303.

Branton, Regina P., and Bradford S. Jones. 2005. "Reexamining Racial Attitudes: The Conditional Relationship between Diversity and Socioeconomic Environment." *American Journal of Political Science* 49(2): 359–372.

Brischetto, Robert R., and Richard L. Engstrom. 1997. "Cumulative Voting and Latino Representation: Exit Surveys in Fifteen Texas Communities." *Social Science Quarterly* 78: 973–991.

Brockington, David, Todd Donovan, Shaun Bowler, and Robert Brischetto. 1998. "Minority Representation under Cumulative and Limited Voting." *The Journal of Politics* 60(4): 1108–1125.

Brown v. Board of Education. 1954. 347 U.S. 483.

Brown v. Board of Education (II). 1955. 349 U.S. 294.

Browning, Rufus P., Dale R. Marshall, and David H. Tabb. 1986. *Protest Is Not Enough: The Struggle of Blacks and Hispanics for Equality in Urban Politics*. Berkeley: University of California Press.

Butler, Katherine I., and Richard W. Murray. 1991. "Minority Vote Dilution Suits and the Problem of Two Minority Groups: Can a 'Rainbow Coalition' Claim the Protection of the Voting Rights Act?" *Pacific Law Journal* 21: 623–676.

Cain, Bruce E., D. Roderick Kiewiet, and Carole J. Uhlaner. 1991. "The Acquisition of Partisanship by Latinos and Asian Americans." *American Journal of Political Science* 35(2): 390–422.

California Secretary of State. 2003. "Special Election—Proposition 53." http://vote2003.sos.ca.gov/propositions/2-3-2-arguments.html (accessed April 23, 2010).

Campbell, Angus, and Robert L. Kahn. 1952. *The People Elect a President*. Ann Arbor, MI: University of Michigan Press.

Campbell, Angus, Philip E. Converse, Warren E. Miller, and Donald E. Stokes. 1960. *The American Voter*. New York: John Wiley and Sons.

Canon, David T. 1999. *Race, Redistricting, and Representation: The Unintended Consequences of Black Majority Districts*. Chicago: University of Chicago Press.

Canon, David T., Matthew M. Schousen, and Patrick J. Sellers. 1996. "The Supply Side of Congressional Redistricting: Race and Strategic Politicians, 1972–1992." *The Journal of Politics* 58(3): 846–862.

Carmines, Edward G., and James A. Stimson. 1989. *Issue Evolution*. Princeton, NJ: Princeton University Press.

Casellas, Jason. 2009. "Coalitions in the House? The Election of Minorities to State Legislatures and Congress." *Political Research Quarterly* 62(1): 120-131.

CensusScope. "CensusScope: Census 2000 Data, Charts, Maps, and Rankings." www.censusscope .org (accessed May 9, 2010).

———. "CensusScope—Demographic Maps: African-American Population." www.censusscope .org/us/map_nhblack.html (accessed May 9, 2010).

———. "CensusScope—Demographic Maps: Hispanic Population." www.censusscope.org/us/ map_hispanicpop.html (accessed May 9, 2010).

———. "CensusScope—Multiracial Population Statistics." www.censusscope.org/us/s31/chart_ multi.html (accessed April 23, 2010).

Centers for Disease Control and Prevention. 2009. "FASTSTATS—Life Expectancy." May 15. www .cdc.gov/nchs/fastats/lifexpec.htm (accessed April 23, 2010).

Charles, Camille Zubrinsky. 2003. "The Dynamics of Racial Residential Segregation." *Annual Review of Sociology* 29: 167–207.

Chen, Carolyn. 2006. "From Filial to Religious Piety: Evangelical Christianity Reconstructing Taiwanese Immigrant Families in the United States." *International Migration Review* 40: 573–602.

Chong, Dennis. 1991. *Collective Action and the Civil Rights Movement.* Chicago: University of Chicago Press.

Chong, Dennis, and Dukhong Kim. 2006. "The Experiences and Effects of Economic Status among Racial and Ethnic Minorities." *American Political Science Review* 100(3): 335–351.

Ciftci, Sabri. 2010. "Modernization, Islam, or Social Capital: What Explains Attitudes toward Democracy in the Muslim World?" *Comparative Political Studies* 43(11): 1442–1470.

Clark, William A. V., and Mark Fossett. 2008. "Understanding the Social Context of the Schelling Segregation Model." *Proceedings of the National Academy of Sciences of the United States of America* 105(11): 4109–4114.

CNN. 2008. "Local and National Election Results—Election Center 2008—Elections & Politics from CNN.com." www.cnn.com/ELECTION/2008/results/individual/#mapHCO/H/03 (accessed May 6, 2010).

———. 2006. "CNN.com—Elections 2006." www.cnn.com/ELECTION/2006//pages/results/states/CO/H/03/index.html (accessed May 6, 2010).

———. 2006. "Rallies across U.S. Call for Illegal Immigrant Rights. Hundreds of Thousands Join 'National Day of Action' in Towns, Cities, Monday, April 10, 2006." Posted: 10:08 p.m. EDT (02:08 GMT). www.cnn.com/2006/POLITICS/04/10/immigration/index.html.

———. 2004. "CNN.com Election 2004." www.cnn.com/ELECTION/2004//pages/results/states/CO/index.html (accessed May 6, 2010).

Cohen, Cathy. 1999. *The Boundaries of Blackness: AIDS and the Breakdown of Black Politics.* Chicago: University of Chicago Press.

Congressional Quarterly. 2009. "111th Congress: Minorities." www.cq.com/members/factfilereport.do?report=mff-minorities (accessed July 8, 2009).

Contractor, Cyrus Ali. 2010. "The Dearborn Effect: A Comparison of the Political Dispositions of Shi'a and Sunni Muslims in the United States." *Politics and Religion* 4: 154–167.

Converse, Philip E. 1964. "The Nature of Belief Systems in Mass Publics." In *Ideology and Discontent,* edited by David E. Apter (206–261). London: The Free Press of Glencoe.

Cook, Chris. 2009. "The Schelling Segregation Demo Home Page." January 26. http://www2.econ.iastate.edu/tesfatsi/demos/schelling/schellhp.htm (accessed April 24, 2010).

Cutler, David M., Edward L. Glaeser, and Jacob L. Vigdor. 1999. "The Rise and Decline of the American Ghetto." *The Journal of Political Economy* 107(3): 455–506.

Dalton, Russell J. 2005. *Citizen Politics: Public Opinion and Political Parties in Advanced Industrial Democracies.* 4th ed. Washington, DC: Congressional Quarterly Press.

———. 2004. *Democratic Challenges, Democratic Choices: The Erosion in Political Support in Advanced Industrial Democracies.* Oxford: Oxford University Press.

———. 2002. *Citizen Politics: Public Opinion and Political Parties in Advanced Industrial Democracies.* 3rd ed. New York: Chatham House.

Dalton, Russell J., and Alix van Sickle. 2005. "The Resource, Structural, and Cultural Bases of Protest." Center for the Study of Democracy, UC Irvine. Working paper 05-11.

Dawson, Michael C. 1994. *Behind the Mule: Race and Class in African-American Politics.* Princeton, NJ: Princeton University Press.

De la Garza, Rodolfo O. 1997. "Latino Politics: A Futuristic View." In *Latinos and the Political System,* edited by F. Chris Garcia. Notre Dame, IN: Notre Dame University Press.

De la Garza, Rodolfo O., Angelo Falcon, and F. Chris Garcia. 1996. "Will the Real Americans Please Stand Up: Anglo and Mexican-American Support of Core American Political Values." *American Journal of Political Science* 40(2): 335–351.

DeSipio, Louis. 1996. *Counting on the Latino Vote: Latinos as a New Electorate.* Charlottesville: University Press of Virginia.

DeSipio, Louis, and Rodolfo O. de la Garza. 2002. "Forever Seen as New: Latino Participation in American Elections." In *Latinos: Remaking America,* edited by Marcelo M. Suárez-Orozco and Mariela M. Páez. Berkeley: University of California Press.

Downs, Anthony. 1957. *An Economic Theory of Democracy.* New York: Harper and Brothers.

Engstrom, Richard. 1994. "The Voting Rights Act: Disenfranchisement, Dilution, and Alternative Election Systems." *PS: Political Science and Politics* 27(4): 685–688.

Engstrom, Richard L., and Charles J. Barrilleaux. 1991. "Native Americans and Cumulative Voting: The Sisseton-Wahpeton Sioux." *Social Science Quarterly* 72(2): 388–393.

Engstrom, Richard L., and Robert R. Brischetto. 1998. "Is Cumulative Voting Too Complex? Evidence from Exit Polls." *Stetson Law Review* 27: 813–833.

Epstein, David, and Sharyn O'Halloran. 1999a. "Measuring the Electoral and Policy Impact of Majority-Minority Voting Districts." *American Journal of Political Science* 43(2): 367–395.

———. 1999b. "A Social Science Approach to Race, Redistricting, and Representation." *The American Political Science Review* 93(1): 187–191.

Espiritu, Yen Le. 1992. *Asian American Panethnicity: Bridging Institutions and Identities.* Philadelphia: Temple University Press.

Fahmy, Eldin. 2005. "Ethnicity, Citizens and Political Participation in Britain." Office of the Prime Minister, ESRC/ODPM Postgraduate Research Programme. Working paper 14.

FairVote. 2005. "Dubious Democracy 2005." http://archive.fairvote.org/?page=543 (accessed July 31, 2010).

Falcon, Angelo. 1988. "Black and Latino Politics in New York City." In *Latinos in the Political System,* edited by F. Chris Garcia. Notre Dame, IN: University of Notre Dame Press.

Fauntroy, Michael. 2006. *Republicans and the Black Vote.* Boulder, Colo.: Lynne Rienner Publishers.

Feldman, Stanley, and Leonie Huddy. 2005. "Racial Resentment and White Opposition to Race-Conscious Programs: Principles or Prejudice?" *American Journal of Political Science* 49(1): 168–183.

Félix, Adrián, Carmen González, and Ricardo Ramírez. 2008. "2008 Political Protest, Ethnic Media, and Latino Naturalization." *American Behavioral Scientist* 52 (December): 618–634.

Ferejohn, John A., and James H. Kuklinski, eds. 1990. *Information and the Democratic Process.* Urbana, IL: University of Illinois Press.

Finifter, Ada W. 1970. "Dimensions of Political Alienation." *The American Political Science Review* 64(2): 389–410.

Fiorina, Morris P., and Samuel J. Abrams. 2008. "Political Polarization in the American Public." *Annual Review of Political Science* 11(1): 563–588.

Flaccus, Gillian. 2006. "Spanish-Language Media Credited on Pro-immigrant Rallies, Radio, TV Hosts Pushed for Large, Peaceful Protests." Associated Press, March 29, 2006. www.boston .com/news/nation/articles/2006/03/29/spanish_language_media_credited_on_pro_immi grant_rallies/?rss_id=Boston+Globe+—+National+News.

Flanigan, William H., and Nancy H. Zingale. 2005. *Political Behavior of the American Electorate.* 11th ed. Washington, DC: Congressional Quarterly Press.

Foner, Nancy, and Richard Alba. 2008. "Immigrant Religion in the U.S. and Western Europe: Bridge or Barrier to Inclusion?" *International Migration Review* 42(2): 360–392.

Fraga, Luis R., and Gary M. Segura. 2006. "Culture Clash? Contesting Notions of American Identity and the Effects of Latin American Immigration." *Perspectives on Politics* 4(2): 279–287.

Fraga, Luis R., John A. Garcia, Rodney Hero, Michael Jones-Correa, Valerie Martinez-Ebers, and Gary M. Segura. 2010. *Latino Lives in America: Making It Home.* Philadelphia: Temple University Press.

———. 2006. "Su Casa Es Nuestra Casa: Latino Politics Research and the Development of American Political Science." *American Political Science Review* 100(4): 515–522.

Frank, Thomas. 2004. *What's the Matter with Kansas?: How Conservatives Won the Heart of America.* New York: Owl Books.

Fridkin, Kim L., Patrick J. Kenney, and Jack Crittenden. 2006. "On the Margins of Democratic Life: The Impact of Race and Ethnicity on the Political Engagement of Young People." *American Politics Research* 34(5): 605–626.

Fryer, Roland G. 2007. "Guess Who's Been Coming to Dinner? Trends in Interracial Marriage over the 20th Century." *The Journal of Economic Perspectives* 21(2): 71–90.

———. 2006. "'Acting White': The Social Price Paid by the Best and Brightest Minority Students." *Education Next* 6(1): 53–59.

Fryer, Roland G., Jacob K. Goeree, and Charles A. Holt 2005. "Experience-Based Discrimination: Classroom Games." *Journal of Economic Education* 36(2): 160–170.

Frymer, Paul. 2005. "Racism Revised: Courts, Labor Law, and the Institutional Construction of Racial Animus." *American Political Science Review* 99(3): 373–387.

———. 1999. *Uneasy Alliances.* Princeton, NJ: Princeton University Press.

Gaddie, Ronald K., and Charles S. Bullock. 1995. "Voter Turnout and Candidate Participation Effects of Affirmative Action Districting." Paper presented at the Citadel Symposium on Southern Politics, Charleston, SC.

Gans, Herbert J. 1992. "Comment: Ethnic Invention and Acculturation." *Journal of American Ethnic History* 12: 42–52.

Gans, Joshua. 2009. "Schelling's Segregation Model: Core Economics." March 17. http://economics .com.au/?p=2952 (accessed May 12, 2010).

Garcia, John A. 1982. "Ethnicity and Chicanos: Explorations into the Measurement of Ethnic Identification, Identity and Consciousness." *Hispanic Journal of Behavioral Sciences* 4(3): 295–314.

García, Sonia R., Valerie Martinez-Ebers, Irasema Coronado, Sharon A. Navarro, and Patricia A. Jaramillo. 2008. *Políticas: Latina Public Officials in Texas.* Austin, TX: University of Texas Press.

Gay, Claudine. 2006. "Seeing Difference: The Effects of Economic Disparity on Black Attitudes toward Latinos." *American Journal of Political Science* 50(4): 982–997.

———. 2004. "Putting Race in Context: Identifying the Environmental Determinants of Black Racial Attitudes." *American Political Science Review* 98(4): 547–562.

———. 2002. "Spirals of Trust? The Effect of Descriptive Representation on the Relationship between Citizens and Their Government." *American Journal of Political Science* 46(4): 717–732.

———. 2001. "The Effect of Black Congressional Representation on Political Participation." *American Political Science Review* 95(3): 589–602.

Geron, Kim, and James Lai. 2002. "Beyond Symbolic Representation: A Comparison of the Electoral Pathways and Policy Priorities of Asian American and Latino Elected Officials." *Asian Law Journal* 9: 41–81.

Giles, Michael W., and Arthur S. Evans. 1985. "External Threat, Perceived Threat, and Group Identity." *Social Science Quarterly* 66: 50–66.

Gilliam, Frank. 1996. "Exploring Minority Empowerment: Symbolic Politics, Governing Conditions and Traces of Political Style in Los Angeles." *American Journal of Political Science* 40(2): 56–81.

Ginsberg, Benjamin. 1986. *The Captive Public: How Mass Opinion Promotes State Power.* New York: Basic Books.

Glazer, Nathan, and Daniel P. Moynihan. 1963. *Beyond the Melting Pot: The Negros, Puerto Ricans, Jews, Italians and Irish of New York City.* Cambridge, MA: M.I.T. Press.

Gomez, Brad T., and J. Matthew Wilson. 2008. "Political Sophistication and Attributions of Blame in the Wake of Hurricane Katrina." *Publius* 38(4): 633–650.

Gordon, Stacy B., and Gary M. Segura. 1997. "Cross-National Variation in the Political Sophistication of Individuals: Capability or Choice?" *The Journal of Politics* 59(1): 126–147.

Graman, Kevin. 2004. "Hispanic Organization Plans Coalition with NAACP." *The Spokesman-Review,* March 11.

Green, Donald P. "Donald Green's Homepage." http://vote.research.yale.edu//?q=taxonomy/term/23 (accessed May 17, 2010).

Green, Donald Philip, and Bradley Palmquist. 1994. "How Stable Is Party Identification?" *Political Behavior* 16(4): 437–466.

———. 1990. "Of Artifacts and Partisan Instability." *American Journal of Political Science* 34(3): 872–902.

Green, Donald, Bradley Palmquist, and Eric Schickler. 2002. *Partisan Hearts and Minds: Political Parties and the Social Identity of Voters.* New Haven, CT: Yale University Press.

Griffin, John D., and Michael Keane. 2006. "Descriptive Representation and the Composition of African-American Turnout." *American Journal of Political Science* 50(4): 998–1012.

Grofman, Bernard. 1995. "Shaw v. Reno and the Future of Voting Rights." *PS: Political Science and Politics* 28(1): 27–36.

Griffin, John D., and Brian Newman. 2008. *Minority Report: Evaluating Political Equality in America.* Chicago: University of Chicago Press.

Grofman, Bernard, Lisa Handley, and Richard G. Niemi. 1992. *Minority Representation and the Quest for Voting Equality.* New York: Cambridge University Press.

Grose, Christian R. 2011. *Congress in Black and White: Race and Representation in Washington and at Home.* New York: Cambridge University Press.

Grossman, James R. 1991. *Land of Hope: Chicago, Black Southerners, and the Great Migration.* Chicago: University of Chicago Press.

Guinier, Lani. 1995. *The Tyranny of the Majority: Fundamental Fairness in Representative Democracy.* New York: Free Press.

Guinier, Lani, and Gerald Torres. 1999. "Critical Race Theory Revisited." The second of three Nathan I. Huggins Lectures. Harvard University, Cambridge, MA, April 20.

Gurr, Ted Robert. 1971. *Why Men Rebel.* Princeton, NJ: Princeton University Press.

Hajnal, Zoltan. 2001. "White Residents, Black Incumbents, and a Declining Racial Divide." *American Political Science Review* 95(3): 603–617.

Hajnal, Zoltan, and Taeku Lee. 2011. *Why Americans Don't Join the Party: Race, Immigration, and the Failure (of Political Parties) to Engage the Electorate.* Princeton, NJ: Princeton University Press.

Hajnal, Zoltan, Marisa Abrajano, and Nicholas Warner. 2009. "Immigration and the Political Transformation of White America: How Local Immigrant Context Shapes White Policy Views and Partisanship." Paper presented at the American Political Science Association Convention, Toronto, ON.

Hancock, Ange-Marie. 2003. "Contemporary Welfare Reform and the Public Identity of the 'Welfare Queen.'" *Race, Gender and Class* 10(1): 31–59.

Haney López, Ian F. 2004. *Racism on Trial: The Chicano Fight for Justice.* Cambridge: Belknap Press.

———. 1997. *White by Law: The Legal Construction of Race.* New York: New York University Press.

Harris, Fredrick C. 1994. "Something Within: Religion as a Mobilizer of African-American Political Activism." *The Journal of Politics* 56(1): 42–68.

Harris, Fredrick C., Valeria Sinclair-Chapman, and Brian D. McKenzie. 2005. "Macrodynamics of Black Political Participation in the Post-Civil Rights Era." *The Journal of Politics* 67(4): 1143–1163.

Haynie, Kerry L. 2001. *African-American Legislators in the American States.* New York: Columbia University Press.

Henry, Charles P. 1980. "Black-Chicano Coalitions: Possibilities and Problems." *Western Journal of Black Studies* 4: 202–232.

Heredia, Luisa, and Janelle Wong. 2010. "Holy Alliances: Religious Organizations and the Immigrant Rights Movement in the Obama Era." Typescript.

Hero, Rodney E. 1992. *Latinos and the U.S. Political System: Two-Tiered Pluralism.* Philadelphia: Temple University Press.

Hero, Rodney, and Robert Preuhs. 2009. "Beyond (the Scope of) Conflict: Black and Latino Advocacy Group Relations in the Congressional and Legal Arenas." *Perspectives on Politics* 7(3): 501–517.

Hero, Rodney E., and Caroline J. Tolbert. 1995. "Latinos and Substantive Representation in the U.S. House of Representatives: Direct, Indirect, or Nonexistent?" *American Journal of Political Science* 39(3): 640–652.

Hetherington, Marc J. 2006. *Why Trust Matters: Declining Political Trust and the Demise of American Liberalism.* Princeton, NJ: Princeton University Press.

Hetherington, Marc, and Suzanne Globetti. 2002. "Political Trust and Racial Policy Preferences." *American Journal of Political Science* 46(2): 253–276.

Hibbing, John R., and Elizabeth Theiss-Morse. 1995. *Congress as Public Enemy: Public Attitudes toward American Political Institutions.* New York: Cambridge University Press.

Highton, Benjamin. 2004. "White Voters and African American Candidates for Congress." *Political Behavior* 26(1): 1–25.

Hirschman, Albert O. 1970. *Exit, Voice, and Loyalty: Responses to Decline in Firms, Organizations, and States.* Cambridge, MA: Harvard University Press.

Hochschild, Jennifer, and Reuel Rogers. 2000. "Race Relations in a Diversifying Nation." In *New Directions: African Americans in a Diversifying Nation*, edited by James Jackson. Washington, DC: National Planning Association.

Hofmann, Steven Ryan. 2004. "Islam and Democracy Micro-Level Indications of Compatibility." *Comparative Political Studies* 37(6): 652–676.

Hofstadter, Richard. 1964. "The Paranoid Style in American Politics." *Harper's Magazine*, November.

http://theamericano.com/2010/12/06/reviews-americanos-annual-hispanic-forum (accessed March 1, 2011).

http://twitter.com/GingrichEspanol.

Huntington, Samuel P. 2004. *Who Are We: The Challenges to America's National Identity.* New York: Simon and Schuster.

Hurlbert, Jeanne S. 1989. "The Southern Region: A Test of the Hypothesis of Cultural Distinctiveness." *The Sociological Quarterly* 30(2): 245–266.

Inglehart, Ronald, Miguel Basáñez, Jaime Díez-Medrano, Loek Halman, and Ruud Luijkx. 2004. *Human Beliefs and Values.* Mexico City: Siglo XXI Editores.

Issacharoff, Samuel, and Pamela S. Karlan Forthcoming. "Where to Draw the Line? Vieth v. Jubelirer, Cox v. Larios, and Judicial Review of Political Gerrymanders." *University of Pennsylvania Law Review.* Available at SSRN: http://ssrn.com/abstract=568903.

Jackson, Bryan O., Elizabeth R. Gerber, and Bruce E. Cain. 1994. "Coalitional Prospects in a Multi-Racial Society: African-American Attitudes toward Other Minority Groups." *Political Research Quarterly* 47(2): 277–294.

Jacoby, Jeff. 2007. "Segregation on Capitol Hill." *The Boston Globe*, January 31. www.boston.com/news/globe/editorial_opinion/oped/articles/2007/01/31/segregation_on_capitol_hill (accessed July 27, 2010).

Jalalzai, Farida. 2009. "The Politics of Muslims in America." *Politics and Religion* 2: 163–199.

Jamal, Amaney. 2005. "The Political Participation and Engagement of Muslim Americans: Mosque Involvement and Group Consciousness." *American Politics Research* 33(4): 521–544.

Jenkins, Kirsta, Molly Andolina, Scott Keeter, and Cliff Zukin. "Exploring the Multidimensional Nature of Political Participation." Midwest Political Science Association. Chicago, IL, April 3–6, 2003.

Jennings, James, ed. 1992. *Race, Politics, and Economic Development.* New York: Verso.

Jiménez, Tomas R. 2005. "Replenished Identity." *Dissertation Abstracts International, The Humanities and Social Sciences* 66(1): 353-A–354-A.

Johnson, Martin, Robert M. Stein, and Robert Wrinkle. 2003. "Language Choice, Residential Stability, and Voting among Latino Americans." *Social Science Quarterly* 84(2): 412–424.

Joint Center for Political and Economic Studies. 2008. "Black Elected Officials Roster." www.joint center.org/index.php/current_research_and_policy_activities/political_participation/black_ elected_officials_roster_introduction_and_overview (accessed May 7, 2010).

Jones-Correa, Michael. 1998. *Between Two Nations.* Ithaca, NY: Cornell University Press.

Jones-Correa, Michael A., and David L. Leal. 2001. "Political Participation: Does Religion Matter?" *Political Research Quarterly* 54(4): 751–770.

———. 1996. "Becoming 'Hispanic': Secondary Panethnic Identification among Latin American-Origin Populations in the United States." *Hispanic Journal of Behavioral Sciences* 18 (2): 214–254.

Junn, Jane, and Natalie Masuoka. 2008a. "Asian American Identity: Shared Racial Status and Political Context." *Perspectives on Politics* 6(4): 729–740.

———. 2008b. "Identities in Context: Racial Group Consciousness and Political Participation among Asian American and Latino Young Adults." *Applied Developmental Science* 12(2): 93–101.

Kahneman, Daniel, Paul Slovic, and Amos Tversky. 1982. *Judgment under Uncertainty: Heuristics and Biases.* New York: Cambridge University Press.

Katznelson, Ira. 2005. *When Affirmative Action Was White: An Untold History of Racial Inequality in Twentieth Century America.* New York: W.W. Norton.

Kaufmann, Karen M. 2003. "Cracks in the Rainbow: Group Commonality as a Basis for Latino and African-American Political Coalitions." *Political Research Quarterly* 56(2): 199–210.

Kerr, Brinck, and Will Miller. 1997. "Latino Representation, It's Direct and Indirect." *American Journal of Political Science* 41(3): 1066–1071.

Kim, Claire Jean. 2003. *Bitter Fruit: The Politics of Black-Korean Conflict in New York City* 2nd edition. New Haven, CT: Yale University Press.

———. 2000. *Bitter Fruit: The Politics of Black-Korean Conflict in New York City.* New Haven, CT: Yale University Press.

Kim, Claire Jean, and Taeku Lee. 2001. "Interracial Politics: Asian Americans and Other Communities of Color." *PS: Political Science and Politics* 34(3): 631–637.

Kim, Rebecca Y. 2004. "Second-Generation Korean American Evangelicals: Ethnic, Multiethnic, or White Campus Ministries?" *Sociology of Religion* 65(1): 19–34.

Kinder, Donald R., and Lynn M. Sanders. 1996. *Divided by Color: Racial Politics and Democratic Ideals.* Chicago: University of Chicago Press.

Kinder, Donald R., and Nicholas Winter. 2001. "Exploring the Racial Divide: Blacks, Whites, and Opinion on National Policy." *American Journal of Political Science* 45(2): 439–456.

Kingdon, John W. 1984. *Agendas, Alternatives, and Public Policies.* New York: Longman.

Kuklinski, James H., and Gary M. Segura. 1995. "Endogeneity, Exogeneity, Time, and Space in Political Representation." *Legislative Studies Quarterly* 20(1): 3–22.

Kurien, Prema. 1998. "Becoming American by Becoming Hindu: Indian Americans Take Their Place at the Multicultural Table." In *Gatherings in Diaspora: Religious Communities and the*

New Immigration, edited by R. S. Warner and J. G. Wittner (37–70). Philadelphia: Temple University Press.

Lai, James, and Kim Geron. 2006. "When Asian Americans Run: The Suburban and Urban Dimensions of Asian American Candidates in California Local Politics." *California Politics and Policy* 10: 62–88.

Lai, James S., Wendy K. Tam Cho, Thomas P. Kim, and Okiyoshi Takeda. 2001. "Asian Pacific-American Campaigns, Elections, and Elected Officials." *PS: Political Science and Politics* 34(3): 611–617.

Landa, Janet. 1995. *Trust, Ethnicity, and Identity: Beyond the New Institutional Economics of Ethnic Trading Networks, Contract Law, and Gift-Exchange.* Ann Arbor University of Michigan Press.

Landry, Bart. 1987. *The New Black Middle Class.* Berkeley: University of California Press.

Lasswell, Harold D. 1935. *Politics: Who Gets What, When and How.* New York: Peter Smith Publisher.

Lax, Jeffrey R., and Justin H. Phillips. 2009. "Gay Rights in the States: Public Opinion and Policy Responsiveness." *American Political Science Review* 103(3): 367–386.

Leal, David L., Matt A. Barreto, Jongho Lee, and Rodolfo O. de la Garza. 2005. "The Latino Vote in the 2004 Election." *PS: Political Science and Politics* 38(1): 41–49.

Leal, David L., Valerie Martinez-Ebers, and Kenneth J. Meier. 2004. "The Politics of Latino Education: The Biases of at-Large Elections." *The Journal of Politics* 66(4): 1224–1244.

Leighley, Jan. 2001. Strength in Numbers? The Political Mobilization of Racial and Ethnic Minorities. Princeton, NJ: Princeton University Press.

Leighley, Jan E., and Arnold Vedlitz. 1999. "Race, Ethnicity, and Political Participation: Competing Models and Contrasting Explanations." *The Journal of Politics* 61 (4): 1092–1114.

Lentz, Bob. 2007. "Pa. Shop Owner Backs English-only Policy." *USA Today,* December 15. www .usatoday.com/news/nation/2007-12-14-2553169185_x.htm (accessed August 26, 2010).

Leonard, Jack, and Matt Lait. 2007. "Supervisor's Residence Outside District Raises Legal Questions." *The Los Angeles Times,* July 27. http://articles.latimes.com/2007/jul/27/local/ me-burke27 (accessed July 31, 2010).

Lewis, Leo. 2009. "Google Earth Maps out Discrimination against Burakumin Caste in Japan." *London Times,* May 22. www.timesonline.co.uk/tol/news/world/asia/article6337499.ece (accessed April 30, 2010).

Lien, Pei-te. 2004a. "Asian Americans and Voting Participation: Comparing Racial and Ethnic Differences in Recent U.S. Elections." *International Migration Review* 38(2): 493–517.

———. 2004b. *The Politics of Asian Americans: Diversity and Community.* New York: Routledge.

———. 2002. "Public Resistance to Electing Asian-Americans in Southern California." *Journal of Asian-American Studies* 5(1): 51–72.

———. 2001. "Pilot National Asian American Political Survey (PNAAPS), 2000–2001." www.icpsr .umich.edu/icpsrweb/ICPSR/studies/03832 (accessed May 20, 2010).

———. 1994. "Ethnicity and Political Participation: A Comparison between Asian and Mexican Americans." *Political Behavior* 16(2): 237–264.

Lien, Pei-te, Christian Collet, Janelle Wong, and S. Karthick Ramakrishnan. 2001. "Asian Pacific-American Public Opinion and Political Participation." *PS: Political Science and Politics* 34(3): 625–630.

Lien, Pei-te, Dianne M. Pinderhughes, Carol Hardy-Fanta, and Christine M. Sierra. 2007. "The Voting Rights Act and the Election of Nonwhite Officials." *PS: Political Science and Politics* 40(3): 489–494.

Liu, Baodong. 2006. "Whites as a Minority and the New Biracial Coalition in New Orleans and Memphis." *PS: Political Science and Politics* 39(1): 69–76.

Lopez, Mark Hugo. "Dissecting the 2008 Electorate: Most Diverse in U.S. History." April 30, 2009. http://pewresearch.org/pubs/1209/racial-ethnic-voters-presidential-election (accessed April 25, 2010).

Lublin, David. 1999. "Racial Redistricting and African-American Representation: A Critique of 'Do Majority-Minority Districts Maximize Substantive Black Representation in Congress?'" *American Political Science Review* 93(1): 183–186.

———. 1997. *The Paradox of Representation.* Princeton: Princeton, NJ University Press.

Lublin, David I., and Gary M. Segura. "An Evaluation of the Electoral and Behavioral Impacts of Majority-Minority Districts." In *Designing Democratic Government*, edited by Margaret Levi, Jack Knight, James Johnson, and Susan Stokes. (New York: Russell Sage Foundation 2008), pp. 174–184.

Lublin, David I., and Katherine Tate. 1992. "Black Office Seeking and Voter Turnout in Mayoral Elections." Presented at the Annual Meeting of the American Political Science Association, Chicago IL.

Manning, Alan, and Sanchari Roy. 2007. "Culture Clash or Culture Club? The Identity and Attitudes of Immigrants in Britain." April. http://cep.lse.ac.uk/pubs/download/dp0790.pdf (accessed March 2, 2011).

Manza, Jeff, and Christopher Uggen. 2006. *Locked Out: Felon Disenfranchisement and American Democracy.* New York: Oxford University Press.

Marcus, George E., and Michael B. MacKuen. 1993. "Anxiety, Enthusiasm, and the Vote: The Emotional Underpinnings of Learning and Involvement during Presidential Campaigns." *American Political Science Review* 87(3): 672–685.

Marks, Carole. 1989. *Farewell—We're Good and Gone: The Great Black Migration.* Bloomington: Indiana University Press.

Martin, Roland S. 2008. "Commentary: Democrats Need More Than Working-Class Whites." May 8. www.cnn.com/2008/POLITICS/05/08/roland.martin/index.html (accessed August 1, 2010).

———. 2007. "Commentary: Black-Brown Coalitions Are Tough to Sustain." October 3. www.cnn.com/2007/US/10/03/roland.martin/index.html (accessed August 3, 2010).

Masuoka, Natalie. 2008. "Defining the Group: Latino Identity and Political Participation." *American Politics Research* 36(1): 33–61.

———. 2006. "Together They Become One: Examining the Predictors of Panethnic Group Consciousness among Asian Americans and Latinos." *Social Science Quarterly* 87(5): 993–1011.

Maxwell, Rahsaan. 2010. "Trust in Government among British Muslims: The Importance of Migration Status." *Political Behavior* 32(1): 89–109.

———. 2008. "Muslims, South Asians and the British Mainstream." *West European Politics* 29(4): 736–756.

McAdam, Doug. 1983. "Tactical Innovation and the Pace of Insurgency." *American Sociological Review* 48(6): 735–754.

McCarthy, John, and Mayer Zald. 1977. "Resource Mobilization and Social Movements: A Partial Theory." *American Journal of Sociology* 82(6): 1212–1241.

McClain, Paula D. 2006. "Racial Intergroup Relations in a Set of Cities: A Twenty-Year Perspective." (Presidential Address). *The Journal of Politics* 68(4): 757–770.

———. 1994. "Book Review: Black Faces, Black Interests." *The Journal of Politics* 56(4): 1145–1148.

———. 1993. "The Changing Dynamics of Urban Politics: Black and Hispanic Municipal Employment—Is There Competition?" *The Journal of Politics* 55(2): 399–414.

McClain, Paula D., and Albert K. Karnig. 1990. "Black and Hispanic Socioeconomic and Political Competition." *American Political Science Review* 84(2): 535–545.

McClain, Paula D., et al. 2007. "Black Americans and Latino Immigrants in a Southern City: Friendly Neighbors or Economic Competitors?" *The Du Bois Review: Social Science Research on Race* 4(1): 97–117.

McClain, Paula D., Jessica D. Johnson Carew, Eugene Walton Jr., and Candis S. Watts. 2009. "Group Membership, Group Identity, and Group Consciousness: Measures of Racial Identity in American Politics?" *Annual Review of Political Science* 12: 471–485.

McClain, Paula D., et al. 2006. "Racial Distancing in a Southern City: Latino Immigrants' Views of Black Americans." *The Journal of Politics* 68(3): 571–584.

McDaniel, Eric L. 2008. *Politics in the Pews: The Political Mobilization of Black Churches.* Ann Arbor: University of Michigan Press.

McDaniel, Eric L., and Christopher G. Ellison. 2008. "God's Party? Race, Religion, and Partisanship over Time." *Political Research Quarterly* 61(2): 180–191.

McKenzie, Brian D. 2004. "Religious Social Networks, Indirect Mobilization, and African-American Political Participation." *Political Research Quarterly* 57(4): 621–632.

Meer, Nasar, and Tariq Modood. 2008. "The Multicultural State We're In: Muslims, 'Multiculture' and the 'Civic Re-balancing' of British Multiculturalism." *Political Studies* 57: 473–497.

Meier, Kenneth J., and Joseph Stewart, Jr. 1991. "Cooperation and Conflict in Multiracial School Districts." *The Journal of Politics* 53(4): 1123–1133.

Meier, Kenneth J., Paula D McClain, Jerry L. Polinard, and Robert D. Wrinkle. 2004. "Divided or Together? Conflict and Cooperation between African-Americans and Latinos." *Political Research Quarterly* 57(3): 399–410.

Mendelberg, Tali. 2001. *The Race Card: Campaign Strategy, Implicit Messages, and the Norm of Equality.* Princeton, NJ: Princeton University Press.

Meyer, David S. 2004. "Protest and Political Opportunities." *Annual Review of Sociology* 30: 125–145.

Michelson, Melissa R. 2006. "Mobilizing the Latino Youth Vote: Some Experimental Results." *Social Science Quarterly* 87(5): 1188–1206.

———. 2003a. "The Corrosive Effect of Acculturation: How Mexican Americans Lose Political Trust." *Social Science Quarterly* 84(4): 918–933.

———. 2003b. "Governance and Minority Representation: Political Trust among Chicago Latinos." *Journal of Urban Affairs* 23(3–4): 323–334.

———. 2001. "Political Trust among Chicago Latinos." *Journal of Urban Affairs* 23: 323–34.

Michelson, Melissa R., Lisa Garcia-Bedolla, and Donald Phillip Green. 2008. "New Experiments in Minority Voter Mobilization." http://class.csueastbay.edu/faculty/mmichelson/CVI%202008 .pdf (accessed May 17, 2010).

Milliken v. Bradley. 1974. 418 U.S. 717.

Milloy, Courtland. 2009. "Professor Gates Should Skip the Blather and Sue." *The Washington Post,* August 5. www.washingtonpost.com/wp-dyn/content/article/2009/08/04/AR2009080402971.html (accessed September 5, 2010).

Minkoff, Debra C. 1997. "The Sequencing of Social Movements." *American Sociological Review* 62(5): 779–99.

———. 1993. "The Organization of Survival: Women's and Racial-Ethnic Voluntarist and Activist Organizations, 1955–1985." *Social Forces* 71(4): 887–908.

Nicholson, Stephen P., and Gary M. Segura. 2005. "Issue Agendas and the Politics of Latino Partisan Identification." In *Diversity in Democracy,* edited by Gary M. Segura and Shaun Bowler (51–71). Charlottesville: University of Virginia Press.

Noah, Timothy. 2008. "What We Didn't Overcome on Election Day." November 10. www.slate .com/id/2204251/sidebar/2204308 (accessed May 6, 2010).

Ogawa, Brian K. 1998. *Color of Justice: Culturally Sensitive Treatment of Minority Crime Victims.* Boston: Allyn and Bacon.

Ogbu, John U. 2008. *Minority Status, Oppositional Culture and Schooling*. New York: Routledge.

Oliver, J. Eric, and Janelle Wong. 2003. "Intergroup Prejudice in Multiethnic Settings." *American Journal of Political Science* 47(4): 567–582.

Olson, Mancur. 1965. *The Logic of Collective Action: Public Goods and the Theory of Groups*. Cambridge, MA: Harvard University Press.

Omi, Michael, and Howard Winant. 1994. *Racial Formation in the United States: From the 1960s to the 1990s*. 2nd ed. New York: Routledge.

———. 1986. *Racial Formation in the United States: From the 1960s to the 1990s*. London: Routledge and Kegan Paul.

Overby, L. Marvin, and Kenneth M. Cosgrove. 1996. "Unintended Consequences? Racial Redistricting and the Representation of Minority Interests." *The Journal of Politics* 58(2): 540–550.

Padilla, Felix M. 1985. *Latino Ethnic Consciousness: The Case of Mexican Americans and Puerto Ricans in Chicago*. Notre Dame, IN: University of Notre Dame Press.

Page, Benjamin, and Robert Y. Shapiro. 1992. *The Rational Public: Fifty Years of Trends in Americans' Policy Preferences*. Chicago: University of Chicago Press.

Pantoja, Adrian D., Cecilia Menjívar, and Lisa Magaña. 2008. "The Spring Marches of 2006: Latinos, Immigration, and Political Mobilization in the 21st Century." *American Behavioral Scientist* 52 (December 2008): 499–506.

Pantoja, Adrian D., and Gary M. Segura. 2003a. "Does Ethnicity Matter? Descriptive Representation in the Statehouse and Political Alienation among Latinos." *Social Science Quarterly* 84(2): 441–460.

———. 2003b. "Fear and Loathing in California: Contextual Threat and Political Sophistication among Latino Voters." *Political Behavior* 25(3): 265–286.

Pantoja, Adrian D., Ricardo Ramirez, and Gary M. Segura. 2001. "Citizens by Choice, Voters by Necessity: Patterns in Political Mobilization by Naturalized Latinos." *Political Research Quarterly* 54(4): 729–750.

Paral, Rob, Madura Wijewardena, Michael Norkewicz, and Christina Diaz. 2008. "The New American Electorate: The Growing Political Power of Immigrants and Their Children." Immigration Policy Center. October 23. www.immigrationforum.org/images/uploads/NewCitizenVotersWEBversion.pdf (accessed May 6, 2010).

Parker, Christopher. 2010. "2010 Multi-state Survey on Race & Politics." http://depts.washington.edu/uwiser/racepolitics.html (accessed March 7, 2011).

Pedraza, Francisco I. 2010. "The Two-Way Street of Immigrant Political Incorporation." Ph.D. diss., University of Washington.

Pedraza, Francisco I., Shaun Bowler, and Gary M. Segura. 2011. "The Efficacy and Alienation of Juan Q. Public: The Immigration Marches and Orientations toward American Political Institutions." In *Rallying for Immigrant Rights*, edited by Irene Bloemraad and Kim Voss. Berkeley: University of California Press.

Peffley, Mark, and Jon Hurwitz. 2007. "Persuasion and Resistance: Race and the Death Penalty in America." *American Journal of Political Science* 51(4): 996–1012.

Pew Forum on Religion & Public Life. 2010. "Religion among the Millennials." http://pewforum.org/Age/Religion-Among-the-Millennials.aspx (accessed February 4, 2011).

———. 2008. "U.S. Religious Landscape Survey." http://religions.pewforum.org/pdf/report religious-landscape-study-full.pdf (accessed April 25, 2010).

Pew Research Center. 2009. "Dissecting the 2008 Electorate: Most Diverse in U.S. History." April 30. http://pewresearch.org/pubs/1209/racial-ethnic-voters-presidential-election (accessed April 25, 2010).

Pinderhughes, Dianne. 1987. *Race and Ethnicity in Chicago Politics: A Reexamination of Pluralist Theory*. Urbana: University of Illinois Press.

Pitkin, Hannah. 1967. *The Concept of Representation*. Berkeley: University of California Press.

Piven, Frances Fox, and Richard Cloward. 1977. *Poor People's Movements: Why They Succeed, How They Fail.* New York: Vintage.

Portes, Alejandro, and Rubén G. Rumbaut. 1996. *Immigrant America: A Portrait.* 2nd ed. Berkeley: University of California Press.

Portes, Alejandro, and Min Zhou. 1993. "The New Second Generation." *Annuals of the American Academy of Political and Social Sciences* 530: 74–96.

Putnam, Robert. 2000. *Bowling Alone: The Collapse and Revival of American Community.* New York: Simon and Schuster.

Ramakrishnan, S. Karthick. 2005. *Democracy in Immigrant America.* Stanford, CA: Stanford University Press.

———. 2004. "Second-Generation Immigrants? The 2.5 Generation in the United States." *Social Science Quarterly* 85(2): 380–399.

Ramakrishnan, S. Karthick, and Thomas J. Espenshade. 2001. "Immigrant Incorporation and Political Participation in the United States." *International Migration Review* 35(3): 870–909.

Ramirez, Ricardo. 2005. "Giving Voice to Latino Voters: A Field Experiment on the Effectiveness of a National Nonpartisan Mobilization Effort." The Science of Voter Mobilization. Special Editors Donald P. Green and Alan S. Gerber. *The Annals of the American Academy of Political and Social Science.* 601: 66–84.

Reese, Laura A., and Ronald E. Brown. 1995. "The Effects of Religious Messages on Racial Identity and System Blame among African Americans." *The Journal of Politics* 571): 24–43.

Robinson, Chauncy. 2002. "Can African Americans and Hispanics Form a Coalition in Atlanta?" *Mundo Hispanico.* June 6.

Rocha, Rene. 2007. "Black-Brown Coalitions in Local School Board Elections." *Political Research Quarterly* 60(2): 315–327.

Rodrigues, Helena A., and Gary M. Segura. 2007. "A Place at the Lunch Counter: Latinos, African-Americans, and the Dynamics of American Race Politics." In *Latino Politics: Identity, Mobilization, and Representation,* edited by Kenneth Meier, Rodolfo Espino, and David Leal. Charlottesville: University of Virginia Press.

Rodrigues, Helena A., and Gary M. Segura. 2006. "Comparative Ethnic Politics in the United States: Beyond Black and White." In *Annual Review of Political Science,* 9: 375–395.

Rogers, Reuel R. 2006. *Afro-Caribbean Immigrants and the Politics of Incorporation: Ethnicity, Exception, or Exit.* New York: Cambridge University Press.

———. 2001. "'Black Like Who?' Afro-Caribbean Immigrants, African Americans, and the Politics of Group Identity." In *Islands in the City: West Indian Migration to New York,* edited by Nancy Foner. Berkeley: University of California Press.

Rosenfeld, Steven. 2007. "Turning Back the Clock on Voting Rights." *Social Policy* 38(1): 52–66.

Rosenstone, Steven J., and John Mark Hansen. 2003. *Mobilization, Participation and Democracy in America.* New York: Longman Classics.

Rosenstone, Steven, Roy L. Behr, and Edward H. Lazarus. 1984. *Third Parties in America.* Princeton, NJ: Princeton University Press.

Ross, Lori, Rachel Epstein, Corrie Goldfinger, Leah Steele, Scott Anderson, and Carol Strike. 2008. "Lesbian and Queer Mothers Navigating the Adoption System: The Impacts on Mental Health." *Health Sociology Review* 17(3): 254–266.

Rumbaut, Rubén G. 1997. "Assimilation and Its Discontents." *International Migration Review* 31: 923–960.

Ryan, Scott D., Sue Pearlmutter, and Victor Groza. 2004. "Coming Out of the Closet: Opening Agencies to Gay and Lesbian Adoptive Parents." *Social Work* 49(1): 85–95.

Sanchez, Gabriel R. 2006. "The Role of Group Consciousness in Political Participation among Latinos in the United States." *American Politics Research* 34: 427–450.

Santoro, Wayne A., and Gary Segura. 2011 "Generational Status and Mexican American Political-Participation: The Benefits and Limitations of Assimilation." *Political Research Quarterly*, 64(1): 172–184.

Schelling, Thomas C. 1978. *Micromotives and Macrobehavior*. New York: W.W. Norton.

Schmidt, Ronald, Sr. 2000. *Language Policy and Identity Politics in the United States*. Philadelphia: Temple University Press.

Scott, James C. 1985. *Weapons of the Weak: Everyday Forms of Peasant Resistance*. New Haven, CT: Yale University Press.

Segura, Gary M. 2007. "Transnational Linkages, Generational Change, and Latino Political Engagement." Presented at the Annual Meeting of the Midwest Political Science Association, Chicago, IL.

———. 2005. Review of *Who Are We? The Challenges to America's National Identity*, by Samuel P. Huntington. *Perspectives on Politics* 3(3): 640–642.

———. 1999. "Institutions Matter: Local Electoral Laws, Gay and Lesbian Representation, and Coalition Building across Minority Communities." In *Gays and Lesbians in the Democratic Process*, edited by Ellen Riggle and Barry Tadlock (220–241). New York: Columbia University Press.

Segura, Gary M., and Luis R. Fraga. 2008. "Race and the Recall: Racial and Ethnic Polarization in the California Recall Election." *American Journal of Political Science* 52 (2): 421–435.

Segura, Gary M., and Ali A. Valenzuela. 2010. "Hope, Tropes, and Dopes: Hispanic and White Racial Animus in the 2008 Election." *Presidential Studies Quarterly* 40(3): 497–514.

Segura, Gary M., Dennis Falcon, and Harry Pachon. 1996. "Dynamics of Latino Partisanship in California: Immigration, Issue Salience, and Their Implications." *Harvard Journal of Hispanic Politics* 10: 62–80.

Segura, Gary M., Stephen P. Nicholson, and Adrian D. Pantoja. 2006. "Explaining the Latino Vote: Issue Voting among Latinos in the 2000 Presidential Election." *Political Research Quarterly* 59 (2): 259–271.

Shafer, Byron E. and Richard Johnston. 2006. *The End of Southern Exceptionalism*. Cambridge, MA: Harvard University Press.

Sharpe, Christine LeVeaux, and James C. Garand. 2001. "Race, Roll-Calls, and Redistricting: The Impact of Race-Based Districting on Congressional Roll-Call." *Political Research Quarterly* 54(1): 31–51.

Shavers, Vickie L., Charles F. Lynch, and Leon F. Burmeister. 2001. "Factors That Influence African-Americans' Willingness to Participate in Medical Research Studies." *Cancer* 91(S1): 233–236.

Sierra, Christine Marie, Teresa Carrillo, Louis DeSipio, and Michael Jones-Correa. 2000. "Latino Immigration and Citizenship." *PS: Political Science and Politics* 33(3): 535–540.

Silverleib, Alan. 2008. "Analysis: Clinton Crushes Obama across the Board." May 13. http://edition.cnn.com/2008/POLITICS/05/13/west.virginia.analysis/index.html (accessed August 1, 2010).

Singh, Raj. 2002. "Schelling's Segregation Model." November 25. http://web.mit.edu/rajsingh/www/lab/alife/schelling.html (accessed April 24, 2010).

Sitkoff, Harvard. 1993. *The Struggle for Black Equality, 1954–1992*. New York: Hill and Wang.

———. 1978. *A New Deal for Blacks: The Emergence of Civil Rights as a National Issue: The Depression Decade*. New York: Oxford University Press USA.

Skerry, Peter. 1997. "The Assimilation Dilemma." *Freedom Review* 28(3): 23–36.

Smith, Drew R., and Fredrick C. Harris, eds. 2005. *Black Churches and Local Politics: Clergy Influence, Organizational Partnerships, and Civic Empowerment.* Lanham, MD: Rowman and Littlefield.

Smith, Lamar. 2010. "The GOP's Other Election Day Victory." *The Washington Post,* November 27. www.washingtonpost.com/wp-dyn/content/article/2010/11/19/AR2010111905213.html (accessed March 2, 2011).

Smith, Rogers M. 1997. *Civic Ideals: Conflicting Visions of Citizenship in U.S. History.* New Haven, CT: Yale University Press.

Sonenshein, Raphael J. 1990. "Can Black Candidates Win Statewide Elections?" *Political Science Quarterly* 105(2): 219–241.

———. 1989. "The Dynamics of Biracial Coalitions: Crossover Politics in Los Angeles." *Western Political Quarterly* 42(2): 333–353.

———. 1986. "Biracial Coalition Politics in Los Angeles." *PS: Political Science and Politics* 19 (3): 582–590.

Sonenshein, Raphael J., and Mark H. Drayse. 2006. "Urban Electoral Coalitions in an Age of Immigration: Time and Place in the 2001 and 2005 Los Angeles Mayoral Primaries." *Political Geography* 25(5): 570–595.

Soss, Joe, Laura Langbein, and Alan R. Metelko. 2003. "Why Do White Americans Support the Death Penalty?" *The Journal of Politics* 65(2): 397–421.

Staton, Jeffrey K., Robert A. Jackson, and Damarys Canache. 2007. "Dual Nationality among Latinos: What Are the Implications for Political Connectedness?" *The Journal of Politics* 69: 470–482.

Stimson, James A. 1990. *Public Opinion in America: Moods, Cycles, and Swings.* Boulder, CO: Westview Press.

Stokes, Atiya Kai. 2003. "Latino Group Consciousness and Political Participation." *American Politics Research* 31(4): 361–378.

Swain, Carol M. 1993. *Black Faces, Black Interests: The Representation of African Americans in Congress.* Cambridge, MA: Harvard University Press.

Swann v. Charlotte-Mecklenburg Board of Education. 1971. 402 U.S. 1.

Tam, Wendy K. 1995. "Asians—A Monolithic Voting Bloc?" *Political Behavior* 17(2): 223–249.

Tam Cho, Wendy K. 2003. "Contagion Effects and Ethnic Contribution Networks." *American Journal of Political Science* 47(2): 368–387.

———. 1999. "Naturalization, Socialization, Participation: Immigrants and (Non)Voting." *The Journal of Politics* 61(4): 1140–1155.

Tate, Katherine. 2003. *Black Faces in the Mirror: African Americans and Their Representatives in the U.S. Congress.* Princeton, NJ: Princeton University Press.

———. 1993. *From Protest to Politics.* New York: Russell Sage Foundation.

Tedin, Kent L., and Richard W. Murray. 1994. "Support for Biracial Political Coalitions among Blacks and Hispanics." *Social Science Quarterly* 75: 772–789.

Terkildsen, Nayda. 1993. "When White Voters Evaluate Black Candidates: The Processing Implications of Candidate Skin Color, Prejudice, and Self-Monitoring." *American Journal of Political Science* 37(4): 1032–1053.

Thernstrom, Abigail. 2009. *Voting Rights—and Wrongs: The Elusive Quest for Racially Fair Elections.* Washington, DC: AEI Press.

Thornburg v. Gingles. 1986. 478 U.S. 30.

Tolbert, Caroline J., and Rodney E. Hero. 1996. "Race/Ethnicity and Direct Democracy: An Analysis of California's Illegal Immigration Initiative." *The Journal of Politics* 58(3): 806–818.

Tyler, Tom R. 2005. "Policing in Black and White: Ethnic Group Differences in Trust and Confidence in the Police." *Police Quarterly* 8(3): 322–342.

U.S. Census Bureau. 2009. "United States—Poverty—American FactFinder." October 27. http://factfinder .census.gov/servlet/ACSSAFFPeople?_submenuId=people_9&_sse=on (accessed May 9, 2010).

———. 2008. "American FactFinder." http://factfinder.census.gov/home/saff/main.html?_lang=en (accessed April 30, 2010).

———. 2008. "Population Projections—2008 National Population Projections." www.census.gov/ population/www/projections/summarytables.html (accessed April 25, 2010).

———. 2004. "Projected Population of the United States, by Race and Hispanic Origin: 2000 to 2050." March 18. www.census.gov/population/www/projections/usinterimproj/natprojtab01a .pdf (accessed April 25, 2010).

———. 2002–2007. "American Community Survey." http://factfinder.census.gov/home/saff/main .html?_lang=en (accessed July 7, 2009).

———. 2002. "The Asian Population: 2000." www.census.gov/prod/2002pubs/c2kbr01-16.pdf (accessed May 6, 2010).

———. 2002. "United States—Race and Hispanic Origin: 1790 to 1990." September 13. www .census.gov/population/www/documentation/twps0056/tab01.pdf (accessed April 25, 2010).

———. 2001. "Overview of Race and Hispanic Origin." www.census.gov/prod/2001pubs/ cenbr01-1.pdf (accessed March 7, 2010).

———. 1999. "Nativity of the Population and Place of Birth of the Native Population: 1850 to 1990." March 9. www.census.gov/population/www/documentation/twps0029/twps0029.html (accessed May 5, 2010).

Uhlaner, Carole J. 1989. "Rational Turnout: The Neglected Role of Groups." *American Journal of Political Science* 33(2): 390–422.

Uhlaner, Carole J., Bruce E. Cain, and D. Roderick Kiewiet. 1989. "Political Participation of Ethnic Minorities in the 1980s." *Political Behavior* 113: 195–231.

Vaca, Nicolas C. 2004. *The Presumed Alliance: The Unspoken Conflict between Latinos and Blacks and What It Means for America.* New York: HarperCollins.

Valentino, Nicholas A., and David O. Sears. 2005. "Old Times There Are Not Forgotten: Race and Partisan Realignment in the Contemporary South." *American Journal of Political Science* 49(3): 672–688.

Valentino, Nicholas A., Vincent L. Hutchings, and Ismail K. White. 2002. "Cues That Matter: How Political Ads Prime Racial Attitudes during Campaigns." *American Political Science Review* 96(1): 75–90.

Vega, Arturo. 1993. "Congressional Informal Groups as Representative Responsiveness." *American Review of Politics* 14(3): 355–373.

Verba, Sidney, Kay Lehman Schlozman, and Henry Brady. 1995. *Voice and Equality: Civic Voluntarism in American Politics.* Cambridge, MA: Harvard University Press.

Voss, Kim, and Irene Bloemraad, eds. 2011. *Rallying for Immigrant Rights: The Fight for Inclusion in 21st Century America.* Berkeley: University of California Press.

Waldinger, Roger. 2007. "Between Here and There: How Attached Are Latino Immigrants to Their Native Country?" October 25. www.ime.gob.mx/ime2/2007/native_country.pdf (accessed March 2, 2011).

Wals, Sergio C. 2011. "Does What Happens in Los Mochis Stay in Los Mochis? Explaining Postmigration Political Behavior." *Political Research Quarterly.*

Walsh, Arlene Sanchez. 2003. *Latino Pentecostal Identity: Evangelical Faith, Self and Society.* New York: Columbia University Press.

Walton, Hanes. 1972a. *Black Political Parties: An Historical and Political Analysis.* New York: Free Press.

————. 1972b. *Black Politics: A Theoretical and Structural Analysis.* Philadelphia: Lippincott.

Warren, Christopher L., John F. Stack, Jr., and John G. Corbett. 1986. "Minority Mobilization in an International City: Rivalry and Conflict in Miami." *PS: Political Science and Politics* 19(3): 626–635.

Watson, Elwood. 1998. "Guess What Came to American Politics? Contemporary Black Conservatism." *Journal of Black Studies* 29(1): 73–92.

Weiss, Nancy. 1983. *Farewell to the Party of Lincoln.* Princeton, NJ: Princeton University Press.

Weissberg, Robert. 1978. "Collective vs. Dyadic Representation in Congress." *The American Political Science Review* 72(2): 535–547.

Welch, Susan, and Albert K. Karnig. 1979. "Correlates of Female Office-Holding in City Politics." *The Journal of Politics* 41(2): 478–491.

Wenzel, James P. 2006. "Acculturation Effects on Trust in National and Local Government among Mexican Americans." *Social Science Quarterly* 87(5): 1073–1087.

Whitby, Kenny J. 1998. *The Color of Representation: Congressional Behavior and Black Interests.* Ann Arbor: University of Michigan Press.

White, Ismail. 2007. "When Race Matters and When It Doesn't: Racial Group Differences in Response to Racial Cues." *American Political Science Review* 101(2): 339–354.

White, Stephen, Neil Nevitte, André Blais, Elisabeth Gidengil, and Patrick Fournier. 2008. "The Political Resocialization of Immigrants: Resistance or Lifelong Learning?" *Political Research Quarterly* 61(2): 268–281.

Wilson, William J. 1980. *The Declining Significance of Race: Blacks and Changing American Institutions.* Chicago: University of Chicago Press.

Winter, Nicholas J. G. 2006. "Beyond Welfare: Framing and the Racialization of White Opinion on Social Security." *American Journal of Political Science* 50(2): 400–420.

Wolfinger, Raymond E., and Steven J. Rosenstone. 1980. *Who Votes?* New Haven, CT: Yale University Press.

Wong, Janelle S. 2006. *Democracy's Promise: Immigrants and American Civic Institutions.* Ann Arbor: University of Michigan Press.

————. 2005. "Mobilizing Asian American Voters: A Field Experiment." The Science of Voter Mobilization. Special editors Donald P. Green and Alan S. Gerber. *The Annals of the American Academy of Political and Social Science* 601: 102–114.

————. 2004. "Getting Out the Vote among Asian Pacific Americans: The Effects of Phone Canvassing." *AAPI Nexus: Asian Americans and Pacific Islanders Policy, Practice, and Community* 2: 49–66.

————. 2000. "The Effects of Age and Political Exposure on the Development of Party Identification among Asian American and Latino Immigrants in the United States." *Political Behavior* 22(4): 341–371.

Wong, Janelle S., Kathy Rim, and Haven Perez. 2008. "Asian and Latino Protestant Churches and Conservative Politics in the United States." In *Civic Hopes and Political Realities,* edited by S. Karthick Ramakrishnan and Irene Bloemraad (271–299). New York: Russell Sage Foundation.

Wright Austin, Sharon D., and Richard T. Middleton IV. "The Limitations of the Deracialization Concept in the 2001 Los Angeles Mayoral Election." *Political Research Quarterly* 57(2): 283–293.

YouTube. 2009. "The Logic of Life: Racial segregation." March 6. www.youtube.com/watch?v=JjfihtGefxk (accessed May 12, 2010).

————. 2007. "Pat Buchanan Culture War Speech Part 2." September 17. www.youtube.com/watch?v=pICypNXHKbg&NR=1 (accessed August 23, 2010).

Zaller, John. 1991. *The Nature and Origins of Mass Opinion.* New York: Cambridge University Press.

Zhou, Min. 1997. "Segmented Assimilation." *International Migration Review* 31: 975–1008.

Zsembik, Barbara A., and Daniel Llanes. 1996. "Generational Differences in Educational Attainment among Mexican Americans." *Social Science Quarterly* 77(2): 363–374.

CHAPTER 1

1. The GOP has a second problem as well in the age distribution. Exit polls suggest that a whopping 66 percent of voters under thirty voted Democrat. The only age group that voted majority Republican in 2008 was that over sixty-five, and there only modestly so at 53 percent.

2. Public Policy Polling released result on February 15, 2011, showing 51 percent of likely GOP primary voters believed that Barack Obama was not born in the United States. http://publicpolicypolling.blogspot.com/2011/02/romney-and-birthers.html (accessed February 27, 2011).

CHAPTER 2

1. *In-group* refers to a social identity group with whom the subject identifies. For example, those who think of themselves as "Latino" would see other Latinos or Hispanics as their "in-group." By contrast, an "out-group" is any social identity whose boundaries exclude the subject on the same criterion. For example, for those identifying as "Latino" or "Hispanic," non-Hispanic whites and African Americans may be understood as "out-groups."

2. U.S. Census Bureau, 2010, "Overview of Race and Hispanic Origins: 2010: 2010 Census Briefs," March 2011, www.census.gov/prod/2001pubs/cenbr01–1.pdf (accessed March 7, 2010).

3. U.S. Census Bureau, 2010, "Overview of Race and Hispanic Origins: 2010" March 2011, www.census.gov/prod/cen2010/briefs/c2010br-02.pdf (accessed June 1, 2011).

4. For example, Roland G. Fryer, "'Acting White': The Social Price Paid by the Best and Brightest Minority Students," *Education Next* 6, no. 1 (2006): 53–59. Fryer's argument is not without criticism—and supporters—see, for instance, John U. Ogbu, *Minority Status, Oppositional Culture and Schooling* (New York: Routledge, 2008). Ogbu is one of the scholars who originally identified the issue.

5. The answer, by the way, is that proportionally more children live in poverty by official definitions—approximately 8 million children, or 3 percent of the children under age eleven, while just over 3 million, or 1.2 percent of those sixty-five years and above, live in poverty. Neither of these groups seems to be where poverty hits hardest. Almost 7 percent, or nearly 19 million people in the age group eighteen to sixty-four, live in poverty according to the census figures (U.S. Census Bureau 2009).

6. David M. Cutler et al., "The Rise and Decline of the American Ghetto," *The Journal of Political Economy* 107, no. 3 (1999): 455–506. The website CensusScope, from which our maps are taken, has an excellent section on residential segregation: www.censusscope.org/index.html.

7. Roland G. Fryer et al., "Experience-Based Discrimination: Classroom Games," *Journal of Economic Education* 36, no. 2 (2005): 160–170.

8. For example, Cook 2009 (http://www2.econ.iastate.edu/tesfatsi/demos/schelling/schellhp.htm), Singh 2002 (http://web.mit.edu/rajsingh/www/lab/alife/schelling.html), or as a YouTube video (Gans 2009, see http://economics.com.au/?p=2952). For academic work on this see, for example, William A. V. Clark and Mark Fossett, "Understanding the Social Context of the Schelling Segregation Model," *Proceedings of the National Academy of Sciences of the United States of America* 105, no. 11 (2008): 4109–4114.

9. For an account including maps of the city's spatial segregation of population see Raphael J. Sonenshein and Mark H. Drayse, "Urban Electoral Coalitions in an Age of Immigration: Time and Place in the 2001 and 2005 Los Angeles Mayoral Primaries," *Political Geography* 25, no. 5 (2006): 570–595.

10. Roland G. Fryer, "Guess Who's Been Coming to Dinner? Trends in Interracial Marriage over the 20th Century," *The Journal of Economic Perspectives* 21, no. 2 (2007): 71–90.

11. In a later chapter we take up the question of faith and how important it is to different demographic groups.

12. *Swann v. Charlotte-Mecklenburg Board of Education*, 1971, 402 U.S. 1.

13. *Milliken v. Bradley*, 1974, 418 U.S. 717.

14. Maybe this means that race and ethnic politics have to adopt a term from the comparative literature, "consociational" element.

CHAPTER 3

1. We are not including in this list John Ensign of Nevada. Senator Ensign disclosed a Filipino great-grandparent, but it is fair to say that he does not identify as "Asian American" and that this lineage was not only not a facet of his public persona but, rather, was effectively entirely unknown among the electorate at the time of his election. Senator Ensign resigned from the Senate as this volume went to production.

2. Exit polls have difficulty making accurate assessments of subpopulation distributions and are better suited to national, aggregate predictions. Nevertheless, comparison of exit poll data from two consecutive presidential elections is illustrative of the consistency in the patterns we observe.

3. Leal et al. (2005) have widely disputed this number as artificially low. Exit polls routinely over-represent minority voters living among whites and under-represent minorities living in predominantly Hispanic neighborhoods, thereby providing a conservative, middle class skew to the sub-samples and an overestimation of GOP vote share. This effect is more visible among Latinos, whose votes are distributed more evenly, than among African Americans, whose votes are so overwhelmingly skewed Democratic.

4. Some observers (Frank 2004) even go so far as to argue that this pattern of poor whites voting for the GOP on the basis of cultural issues goes against their economic interests.

5. President Bill Clinton was in a three-party race for both of his elections. If we limited our analysis to voters who voted for one of the two parties, his white vote share would be higher, but this would be artificial. It is exceedingly doubtful that Ross Perot supporters, in his absence, would have voted in any significant numbers for the Democratic Party and, in 2000, they did not.

6. Frankly, we are not quite sure what to make of the South Carolina numbers, which show meaningful improvement among whites for Obama compared with Kerry. The size of the military and retired military population in South Carolina, and the particular role that military service and Vietnam played in the 2004 campaign, may have caused a significant undervote among whites for Kerry, rather than an overvote for Obama. Still, this is an outlier worthy of note.

7. The 112th Congress has fifty-three senators caucusing with the Democrats. Two were elected as independents but caucus with the Democrats. One, Joe Lieberman of Connecticut, was elected as an Independent *against* the official Democratic nominee, who had displaced Lieberman from the party's slate in the primary. He is excluded from this discussion.

8. Mark Udall (D-CO) and Sheldon Whitehouse (D-RI), whom we do not count in this number, had an estimated share of the non-Hispanic white vote that was approximately 50 percent, or a tie.

9. All vote share estimates are from exit polls, usually the pooled media estimates and, in one instance, the *Los Angeles Times*.

10. Beyond the five in office or recently so, we can add Obama (IL 2004–2008), Moseley-Braun (IL 1993–1999), Dennis Chavez (NM 1935–1962), Joseph Montoya (NM 1964–1977), and Spark Matsunaga (HI, 1977–1990).

11. This is the last legislative session for which data for all racial and ethnic groups is currently available at the time of publication.

12. By *lower chamber,* we refer to the state assembly or house of representatives, the most populous branch of the state legislature. The state of Nebraska has a single, nonpartisan chamber and is therefore excluded from this analysis.

13. In Tennessee and Oklahoma, the state senates were actually tied in 2008 16–16 and 24–24, respectively. Evenly distributing the minority members would have broken the ties in the GOP's favor.

CHAPTER 4

1. See, for example, this discussion of "house effects" or why some survey firms come to different results: http://fivethirtyeight.blogs.nytimes.com/2010/11/06/when-house-effects-become-bias.

2. A faithless elector is a member of the Electoral College who defects from voting for her or his pledged candidate. Nothing in the Constitution requires individuals elected to the Electoral College to vote as they said they would, though about half of the states have acted on this to require faithful electors.

3. Even this was not sufficient to assure minority voters a voice. Several states had "whites-only" primaries, under the claim that primary elections were party matters, not state matters, and therefore could be regulated as the party saw fit. White primaries were struck down as unconstitutional in *Smith v. Allwright* in 1944, though the practical effect of this decision was delayed by the continuation of other Jim Crow limitations.

4. National survey samples are often drawn randomly. For every 1,000 Americans, roughly 120 live in California and roughly 4 live in North and South Dakota combined. We would expect a public opinion survey based on a random sample of Americans would have lots of respondents living in California and not many from the Dakotas just by chance alone. Of course, real surveys try to find a representation of the overall population in a social, not just geographical, sense (and so seek a balance of men and women, minorities and Anglos, blue collar and white collar, and so on), but the basic point is the same.

5. American Community Survey, Bureau of the Census.

6. See also the Voting and Registration Supplement to the Current Population Survey, Bureau of the Census.

7. We should note that exit poll estimates for subpopulations are not as reliable as traditional survey data in estimating subgroup preferences. Since exit polls cannot be conducted at every polling station, the probability of selection—especially for groups who are geographically concentrated rather than evenly distributed in the population—is uneven, meaning the estimate is derived from a potentially nonrepresentative segment of the population. This problem varies in intensity depending on the method for conducting the exit poll. For a fuller discussion of these issues, see Leal et al. (2005).

8. This projection is actually for a GOP performance that is slightly better than its victory in 2010.

CHAPTER 5

1. In many of these studies, the N for Asian Americans is very small. In all survey work the size of the sample is important in shaping how much confidence we can place in the results. For many purposes this is a "nonissue": it is fairly easy to acquire a sample of "Americans" and gain a reliable sense of American opinion on, say, foreign policy. But it is much harder to find samples of opinions (that is, numbers of respondents) that are representative of, say, Asian American, Latino, or Native American opinion. Small sample sizes in opinion surveys are a warning of a need for caution in interpreting the results. This problem bedevils work on minority politics in part because while there are hundreds of public opinion surveys, we have very few minority respondents in many of these surveys.

CHAPTER 6

1. This is not to say that there are no points of idiosyncratic variation, or even some ideological disconnect between minority voters and their representatives (Griffin and Newman 2008; Tate 1993; Gay 2004), just that issue agreement is the rule rather than the exception.
2. There are a small number of jurisdictions that permit noncitizen residents to vote for some local offices, for example, in school board elections, but these are rare.
3. This expression is known as the calculus of voting and is a well-known, and well-researched, area in political science.
4. Others question whether all groups are necessarily good for democratic values more broadly. The Aryan Brotherhood and criminal gangs such as the Crips and the Bloods are examples of social groups, but they are not necessarily beneficial ones.
5. For interesting work on "get out the vote" see the website http://research.yale.edu/gotv/?q=taxonomy/term/23.
6. The postcards in the original 1924 Chicago study were mostly printed in English, but some were printed in Italian, Polish, and Czech, recognizing the linguistic diversity of Chicago among Anglo voters at the time.
7. The correlation coefficient, r, is a measure of correlation between two variables that ranges between -1 and 1. The closer its value is to 1, the stronger the positive statistical relationship between the measures. Likewise, the closer to -1 the stronger the inverse relationship. As r approaches zero, this indicates that the variables are less associated with one another. All correlations are calculated from the 2008 American National Election Study and weighted.
8. The question of money in campaigns and campaign finance reform is a complex one. For a list of links on the topic see www.ncsl.org/programs/legismgt/about/links.htm.
9. Alex-Assensoh and Assensoh's own results do not show church attendance as predicting political engagement—but it does predict voting (2001, Table 1, 893).
10. Regression estimates the associations between a dependent variable and several predictors at the same time, with each estimated effect calculated holding the effect of all other predictors constant.
11. Although this is consistent with the idea that Asian Americans have weaker loyalties to political parties.
12. One issue is that data on Asian Americans are relatively sparse. To some extent these findings do depend quite heavily on experience on the West Coast and in Hawaii. Over time the Asian American experience is broadening significantly.

CHAPTER 7

1. Possibly the most dramatic example of violence of the past generation—that of September 11—differs from the examples we have listed here. Our examples refer to domestic violence, that is, acts of violence and protest made by Americans against either other Americans or the U.S. government.
2. It is also men who are more likely to engage in those acts than women.
3. Of course, a counterpoint to Minkoff's view is Olson's (1965): smaller groups had an easier time overcoming the free rider problem that debilitates collective action, through easier monitoring and in-group cohesion.
4. Hirschman is an economist, and the political opportunity structure arguments stem from sociologists. It is not surprising, then, that one perspective looks at the question from the point of view of the individual, the other from the point of view of the social setting.
5. There is considerable overlap between being a member of a minority group and immigrant status, but the overlap is not complete. For example, Irish Americans and Irish nationals are concerned about immigrants' rights issues, while African Americans and Native Americans are often less concerned about the rights of recent immigrants than the rights of people already in the United States.

CHAPTER 8

1. In a very few jurisdictions, noncitizens are afforded the vote in school board or local government elections.
2. Some versions of this system allow the plurality vote getter to achieve election, while others require 50 percent for election and, failing that outcome on Election Day, hold run-offs.
3. Britain reformed the rotten boroughs in the Reform Act of 1832.
4. For a detailed history of the legal issues raised for representation schemes by the Voting Rights Act, see Grofman et al. (1992).
5. Critics of this process often refer to it as "racial gerrymandering," as a series of districts that strung together pockets of minority voters created some very oddly shaped districts. (For pictures of them see Grofman 1995).
6. One additional case, *Northwest Austin Municipal Utility District v. Holder* (2009), had the potential to overturn the entire VRA with respect to the criteria in Section 5 triggering coverage. The Court, however, decided the case on extremely narrow grounds, allowing the jurisdiction in question to exit Section 5 coverage without speaking to the broader questions. This may permit other jurisdictions to exit the Section 5 preclearance regime.
7. Jeff Jacoby, "Segregation on Capitol Hill," *Boston Globe,* January 31, 2007, www.boston.com/news/globe/editorial_opinion/oped/articles/2007/01/31/segregation_on_capitol_hill.
8. There is, however, a Congressional *Prayer* Caucus, which is Christian.
9. See Jack Leonard and Matt Lait, "Burke Has Residence Far Removed from Her Constituency," *Los Angeles Times,* July 27, 2007, www.latimes.com/news/local/la-me-burke27ju127,0,6837597.story?coll=la-home-center.
10. Though, of course, there are other justifications for race-conscious districting, including the inherent value of having members of all sizable social groups present in legislative office, which may be compelling.
11. See www.fairvote.org/reports/?page=543.
12. It is worth noting that the coefficients are in the right direction and, based on the reported standard errors, would appear to approach significance.

13. The system was used in Illinois for much of the twentieth century and is often used on corporate boards.
14. Two groups, the Center for Voting and Democracy (www.fairvote.org) and the Electoral Reform Society (www.electoral-reform.org.uk), have extensive websites that explain and document the many different kinds of electoral systems and how they work.

CHAPTER 9

1. A similar process may unfold when we look at the willingness of African Americans to take part in medical research studies. Knowledge of the Tuskegee study resulted in less trust in the medical research and less willingness to participate in medical research (Shavers et al. 2001).
2. Oddly, this was asked in two ways in the 2008 American National Election Study. One version asked "how much" people like you can affect government, within responses such as "a great deal, a lot, a moderate amount, a little, or not at all." The second version was in an agree-disagree format, again with five response options from "strongly agree" to "strongly disagree." For the sake of simplicity, these two versions are merged in Table 9-5, though they do not look appreciably different separately.

CHAPTER 10

1. The speech can be found on YouTube, and this passage, and the connecting section, is located at www.youtube.com/watch?v=pICypNXHKbg&NR=1.
2. There are several web surveys that help to show you where you stand in this Red/Blue spectrum, for example, http://typology.people-press.org. For American press purposes, *Red* connotes conservative or Republican identities, whereas *Blue* indicates liberal or Democratic identity, all as a result of the accident of how those states were identified on national election maps in 2000. Consistent with other behaviors (such as units of measurement), this sets the United States apart from all other countries, where *red* generally connotes labor or even socialist politics, while *blue* is often associated with economic elites, for example "blue bloods."
3. It seems to be the case that the proportion of Christians among Asian immigrants to the United States is higher than the proportion in their countries of origin (Foner and Alba 2008).

CHAPTER 11

1. Or are fans of Benfica.
2. Bob Lentz, "Pa. Shop Owner Backs English-Only Policy," *USA Today*, December 15, 2007, www.usatoday.com/news/nation/2007–12–14–2553169185_x.htm.
3. Stephanie Armour, "English-Only Workplaces Spark Lawsuits," *USA Today*, May 6, 2007, www.usatoday.com/money/workplace/2007–05–06-english-only-usat_N.htm.
4. For a description of the modern-day Joads, see "Migrant Farm Workers; Field of Tears," *The Economist*, December 16, 2010, www.economist.com/node/17722932?story_id=17722932.
5. See Lublin and Segura (2008) for a fuller explanation of the behavioral and attitudinal effects of co-ethnic representation.

CHAPTER 12

1. See also the comments of Roland Martin on the CNN website, May 8, 2008, which lists many different kinds of demographic and regional constituencies at play in the 2008 Democratic primary fight between Hilary Clinton and Barack Obama. "Commentary: Democrats Need More Than Working-Class Whites," www.cnn.com/2008/POLITICS/05/08/roland.martin/index.html.

2. Silverleib, "Analysis: Clinton Crushes Obama across the Board," May 13, 2008, http://edition.cnn.com/2008/POLITICS/05/13/west.virginia.analysis/index.html.

3. We do not want to imply that competition between groups is equivalent to "conflict." While competition signals different interests pursuing scarce resources, it need not indicate antipathy, nor forestall friendly relations on other dimensions, including simultaneous cooperation in other political venues.

4. And this likely underestimates belief in the possibility that minorities can cooperate, since survey researchers have documented an "acquiescence" bias, that is, the tendency of respondents to "agree" with the question, so as not to appear disagreeable.

5. See, for example, the Roland Martin commentary on CNN, October 3, 2007, referring to examples in Dallas and Houston, "Commentary: Black-Brown Coalitions Are Tough to Sustain," www.cnn.com/2007/US/10/03/roland.martin/index.html.

6. For a similar—and similarly rare—study of Asian American political engagement, see Lai and Geron (2006) and Geron and Lai (2002).

Boxes, figures, and tables are indicated by *b*, *f*, and *t* following page numbers. Note pages start with the letter *N*. Alphabetization is letter-by-letter (e.g., "Protestant churches" precedes "Protest movements").